THE ACCESS HANDBOOK

20 SENTENCE RHETORIC 275

21 FOCUSING ON STANDARD ENGLISH 280
21a Nonstandard Verbs 280
21b Nonstandard Pronouns 286
21c Double Negative 287
21d Double Comparative/Superlative 288
21e Standard *a/an* 288

PART THREE EDITING FOR PUNCTUATION AND MECHANICS 291

22 COMPLETE SENTENCES AND FRAGMENTS 294
22a Exclamation/Question 294
22b Sentence Fragment 295
22c Comma Splice 296
22d Fused Sentence 297

23 LINKING PUNCTUATION 298
23a Comma for Coordinator 298
23b Comma for Subordinator? 299
23c Comma for *who/which/that?* 302
23d Semicolon with *however* 304
23e No Comma for Noun Clause 306

24 INTERNAL COMMAS 308
24a Commas for Modifiers 308
24b Commas for Series 312
24c With Dates/Addresses 314
24d With Coordinate Adjectives 314
24e Repetition/Contrast 315
24f Parenthetic Commas 316

25 UNNEEDED COMMAS 318

26 SPECIAL MARKS 320
26a Using Colons 320
26b Using Dashes 321
26c Using Parentheses 322
26d Slashes 323

27 MARKING QUOTATIONS 324
27a Direct/Indirect 325
27b End Marks 328
27c Insertion/Omission 329
27d Words Set Off 330
27e Titles and Names 332

28 SPELLING WORK 334
28a Spelling Demons 334
28b Spelling Rules 341
28c Variant Spellings 343

29 MANUSCRIPT MECHANICS 346
29a Using Capitals 346
29b Using Hyphens 349
29c Apostrophe for Possessives 352
29d Apostrophe for Contractions 356
29e Using Numbers 357
29f Using Abbreviations 359
29g Using Italics 360

PART FOUR WRITING ENGLISH AS A SECOND LANGUAGE 363

30 ENGLISH AS A SECOND CULTURE 365
30a Learning a Second Culture 366
30b From Narrative to Opinion 367
30c Key Ideas Up Front 368
30d Joining the Dialogue 371

31 ENGLISH AS A SECOND LANGUAGE 373
31a Nouns and Number 374
31b Nouns and Articles 376
31c Verbs and Time 380
31d Verbs and Helping Verbs 384
31e Idiomatic Verbs/Prepositions 387
31f Checking Sentence Structure 394

PART FIVE WRITING THE RESEARCH PAPER 397

32 STARTING YOUR RESEARCH PROJECT 399
32a Defining the Research Paper 399
32b Avoiding Plagiarism 401
32c Defining Your Topic 403

33 SEARCHING FOR SOURCES 408
33a First Search on the Computer 408
33b Newspapers and Periodicals 412
33c Searching the Indexes 418
33d Searching for Books 421
33e Using Nonprint Sources 425
33f Fact-Checking in Reference Books 426
33g Starting Your Source List 430

34 USING YOUR SOURCES 432
34a Focusing Your Search 432
34b Taking Notes 434
34c Organizing Your Notes 436
34d Organizing Your Paper 437

35 DRAFTING AND REVISING 443
35a Feeding Notes into Your Draft 443
35b Writing a Strong First Draft 446
35c Revising Your Draft 447

36 DOCUMENTING YOUR SOURCES 454
36a Following a Documentation Style 454
36b Documenting Your Sources—MLA Style 456
36c Documenting Your Sources—APA Style 487
36d Documentation Styles: CBE, AIP, Chicago 514

PART SIX SPECIAL HELPS FOR WRITERS 515

37 GLOSSARY OF USAGE 517

38 EFFECTIVE BUSINESS COMMUNICATIONS 525
38a Current Business Formats 526
38b Applying for Jobs 530
38c Writing Your Résumé 532

THE ACCESS HANDBOOK

Dolores laGuardia
University of San Francisco

Hans P. Guth
Santa Clara University

Allyn and Bacon

Boston ▪ London ▪ Toronto ▪ Sydney ▪ Tokyo ▪ Singapore

Vice President: Eben W. Ludlow
Editorial Assistant: Grace Trudo
Executive Marketing Manager: Lisa Kimball
Text Design/Composition: Denise Hoffman
Composition Buyer: Linda Cox
Manufacturing Buyer: Suzanne Lareau
Cover Administrator: Linda Knowles
Cover Designer: Suzanne Harbison

A Pearson Education Company
160 Gould Street
Needham Heights, MA 02494

Internet: www.abacon.com

Between the time website information is gathered and then published, it is not unusual for some sites to have closed. Also, the transcription of URLs can result in unintended typographical errors. The publisher would appreciate being notified of any problems with URLs so that they may be corrected in subsequent editions.

Library of Congress Cataloging-in-Publication Data

LaGuardia, Dolores.
The access handbook / Dolores laGuardia, Hans P. Guth.
p. cm.
Includes index.
ISBN 0-205-28620-8 (alk. paper)
1. English language—Textbooks for foreign speakers. 2. English language—Rhetoric—Handbooks, manuals, etc. 3. Report writing—Handbooks, manuals, etc. I. Guth, Hans Paul. II. Title.

PE1128.L29 1999
808'.042—dc21

99-051328

Text credits appear on page 553, which constitutes a continuation of the copyright page.

Printed in the United States of America

10 9 8 7 6 5 4 3 2 1 WEB 04 03 02 01 00 99

The Promise of *The Access Handbook*

All handbooks are not alike. The following goals have guided us in writing this book:

1. *The Access Handbook* does more to help students discover their untapped potential.
2. *The Access Handbook* does more to motivate student writers, helping them overcome negative attitudes or expectations.
3. *The Access Handbook* does more to teach students what they need to know, filling in gaps in previous preparation.
4. *The Access Handbook* does more to make grammar intelligible and useful for today's students.
5. *The Access Handbook* goes beyond error correction to stress positive habit building.
6. *The Access Handbook* defines standards of educated English widely observed in today's society and validated by the practice of the best writers.
7. *The Access Handbook* respects the intelligence of both adult and young adult learners.
8. *The Access Handbook* is for students who will have to be expert users of both print media and electronic media.
9. *The Access Handbook* treats mastering a second language as a formidable educational experience and accomplishment.
10. *The Access Handbook* treats learning English as a second language as part of learning a second culture, with new ways of thinking and writing.

BRIEF CONTENTS

PART ONE
YOUR WRITING GUIDE 1

1 HOW WRITERS WRITE 3

2 WRITING YOUR PARAGRAPHS 49

3 MOBILIZING YOUR RESOURCES 66

4 WRITING/THINKING STRATEGIES 98

6 RESPONDING TO LITERATURE 132

PART TWO
EDITING FOR WORDS AND SENTENCES 151

6 WORKING WITH WORDS 153

7 UNDERSTANDING SENTENCES 182

8 COMBINED SENTENCES 197

9 CORRECTING FRAGMENTS 209

10 WATCHING VERBS 217

11 CHECKING AGREEMENT 224

12 PRONOUN REFERENCE 233

13 PRONOUN CASE 238

14 CHECKING MODIFIERS 242

15 PARALLEL STRUCTURE 248

16 SHIFTS 252

17 CONFUSED SENTENCES 256

18 SENTENCE CHOICES 262

19 SENTENCE STYLE 270

20 SENTENCE RHETORIC 275

21 FOCUSING ON STANDARD ENGLISH 280

PART THREE
EDITING FOR PUNCTUATION AND MECHANICS 291

22 COMPLETE SENTENCES AND FRAGMENTS 294

23 LINKING PUNCTUATION 298

24 INTERNAL COMMAS 308

25 UNNEEDED COMMAS 318

26 SPECIAL MARKS 320

27 MARKING QUOTATIONS 324

28 SPELLING WORK 334

29 MANUSCRIPT MECHANICS 346

PART FOUR
WRITING ENGLISH AS A SECOND LANGUAGE 363

30 ENGLISH AS A SECOND CULTURE 365

31 ENGLISH AS A SECOND LANGUAGE 373

PART FIVE
WRITING THE RESEARCH PAPER 397

32 STARTING YOUR RESEARCH PROJECT 399

33 SEARCHING FOR SOURCES 408

34 USING YOUR SOURCES 432

35 DRAFTING AND REVISING 443

36 DOCUMENTING YOUR SOURCES 454

PART SIX
SPECIAL HELPS FOR WRITERS 515

37 GLOSSARY OF USAGE 517

38 EFFECTIVE BUSINESS COMMUNICATIONS 525

CONTENTS

Preface: To the Instructor xxv

To the Student: How to Use This Book xxxi

About the Authors xxxiii

Orientation: To the Student xxxv

PART ONE
YOUR WRITING GUIDE 1

1 HOW WRITERS WRITE 3

1a Discovering Your Purpose 5
1b Targeting Your Audience 9
1c Working Up Material 12
1c.1 Using Your Resources 12
1c.2 Note-Taking 13
1d Using Prewriting Techniques 14
1d.1 Brainstorming 14
1d.2 Clustering 16
1d.3 Discovery Frames 17
1e Structuring Your Paper 18
1e.1 Using Informal Outlines 19
1e.2 Pushing Toward a Thesis 20
1e.3 From Outline to Draft 21
1f Revising and Rethinking 26
1f.1 Learning from Feedback 27
1f.2 Serving as Peer Reviewer 28
1g Writing/Rewriting Guidelines 30
1g.1 Effective Title 30
1g.2 Pointed Introduction 30
1g.3 Strong Thesis 31
1g.4 Careful Generalizations 32
1g.5 Streamlined Organization 32
1g.6 Strong Supporting Detail 33
1g.7 Effective Transitions 34
1g.8 Responsible Language 35
1g.9 Lively Style 36
1g.10 Strong Conclusion 36

1h Tracking a Sample Paper 36
1i Final Editing 43
1j Sharing and Publishing 48

2 WRITING YOUR PARAGRAPHS 49

2a Focusing Your Paragraph 50
2b Developing Your Paragraph 53
2b.1 Lining Up Examples 53
2b.2 Using a Key Example 54
2b.3 Downshifting 55
2b.4 Assembling Statistics 55
2b.5 Feeding In Quotations 56
2c Transitions as Thought Links 57
2d Revising Your Paragraphs 60
2d.1 Unfocused Paragraphs 60
2d.2 Choppy Paragraphs 61
2d.3 Missing Paragraph Breaks 62

3 MOBILIZING YOUR RESOURCES 66

3a Writing from Experience 66
3a.1 The Connecting Thread 66
3a.2 From Journal to Draft 67
3a.3 Feedback and Revision 69
3a.4 The Personal Connection 71
3b Drawing on Your Reading 74
3b.1 Reading the Clues 74
3b.2 Focused Reading 77
3b.3 From Reading to Writing 78
3b.4 Processing Quotations 80
3c Cyberspace, Internet, e-mail 88
3c.1 Searching the Net 89
3c.2 Evaluating Electronic Sources 90
3c.3 Sample Research Results 91
3c.4 Changing Communication Styles 93
3d Drawing on Interviews 94

4 WRITING/THINKING STRATEGIES 98

4a Tracing a Comparison 100
4b Writing to Classify 106
4c Tracing Cause and Effect 111
4d Weighing Alternatives 114
4d.1 Weighing the Options 114
4d.2 Balancing Pro and Con 115
4e Structuring an Argument 121
4e.1 Styles of Argument 121
4e.2 Arguing from Principle 122
4e.3 Recognizing Logical Fallacies 124
4f Tracing a Process 129

5 RESPONDING TO LITERATURE 132

5a Reading Imaginative Literature 132
5a.1 The Dimensions of Fiction 132
5a.2 The Language of Poetry 134
5a.3 The Workings of Drama 138
5b Writing about Literature 142
5b.1 Live Introduction 142
5b.2 Programmatic Thesis 143
5b.3 Meaningful Plan 143
5b.4 Strong Follow-Through 144
5b.5 Personal Connection 144

PART TWO EDITING FOR WORDS AND SENTENCES 151

6 WORKING WITH WORDS 153

6a Choosing the Right Word 153
6a.1 Tracking New Words 153
6a.2 Distinguishing Synonyms 154
6a.3 Recognizing Connotations 155
6a.4 Inaccurate Words 157

6b Formal/Informal English 158
6b.1 Editing Informal English 160
6b.2 Restricting Slang 161
6b.3 Avoiding Hyperformality 161
6b.4 Recognizing Jargon 162
6b.5 Resisting Euphemisms 164
6c Reducing Wordiness 165
6c.1 Reducing Padding 166
6c.2 Editing for Redundancy 166
6d Sexist and Offensive Language 167
6d.1 Racial and Other Slurs 167
6d.2 Sexist Language 168
6d.3 Nonsexist Pronouns 169
6e Clichés and Buzzwords 170
6f Effective Word Choice 172
6f.1 Blurry and Exact 172
6f.2 Abstract and Concrete 172
6f.3 Mixed/Effective Metaphor 174
6g Using the Dictionary 176
6g.1 Range of Meanings 177
6g.2 Synonyms and Antonyms 178
6g.3 Usage Labels 178
6g.4 Word History 178
6g.5 Latin and Greek Roots 180
6g.6 Encyclopedic Information 181

7 UNDERSTANDING SENTENCES 182

7a Basic Sentence Parts 183
7a.1 Recognizing Nouns 184
7a.2 Recognizing Verbs 185
7b Basic Sentence Patterns 189
7c Filling In Modifiers 192
7c.1 Using Adjectives 192
7c.2 Using Adverbs 193
7c.3 Using Prepositional Phrases 193
7c.4 Using Noun Modifiers 194
7c.5 Using Verbals as Modifiers 194

8 COMBINED SENTENCES 197

8a Avoiding Comma Splices 197
8b Using Coordination 198
8b.1 Effective Coordination 200
8b.2 Weak Coordination 200
8c Using Subordination 200
8c.1 Effective Subordination 202
8c.2 Missing Subordination 202
8c.3 Excessive Subordination 202
8c.4 Upside-Down Subordination 203
8d Using Connecting Adverbs 204
8e Using Relative Pronouns 205
8f Using Noun Clauses 206

9 CORRECTING FRAGMENTS 209

9a Diagnosing Fragments 209
9b Modifiers as Fragments 210
9b.1 Adverbs and Phrases 210
9b.2 Added Adjectives 211
9b.3 Appositives 211
9b.4 Thought Links 211
9c Verbals as Fragments 212
9d Subordinators and Fragments 213
9d.1 *If/when* 213
9d.2 *Whereas* 213
9e *Who/which* and Fragments 213
9f Acceptable Fragments 214

10 WATCHING VERBS 217

10a *-s* for Third Person Singular 217
10b *-d/-ed* for Past Tense 218
10c Verbs with *have* and *be* 219
10d Irregular Verbs 220
10e Problem Verbs *(lie/sit)* 222

11 CHECKING AGREEMENT 224

11a Blind Agreement 225

11b Combined Subject 226

11c Postponed Subject 227

11d Logical Agreement 228

11e Singular or Plural? 228

11e.1 Words in *-ics* 228

11e.2 Indefinite Pronouns 229

11e.3 Sums or Totals 229

11e.4 Irregular Plurals 230

11e.5 *Who, which,* and *that* 230

11e.6 Loose Agreement (*these kind/one of those*) 231

12 PRONOUN REFERENCE 233

12a Ambiguous Reference 233

12b Informal Pronouns 234

12b.1 Orphaned *they/it* 234

12b.2 Informal *you* 234

12c *This* and *which* 234

12d Agreement of Pronouns 235

12e Sexist Pronouns 235

12e.1 Gender-Balanced Pronouns 235

12e.2 Singular *everybody/someone* 236

12e.3 Representative Person 237

13 PRONOUN CASE 238

13a Double Subject/Object 238

13b Object of Preposition 239

13c Subject Form after *be* 239

13d Pronoun after *as/than* 240

14 CHECKING MODIFIERS 242

14a Adverb Form 242

14a.1 Adverbs without *-ly* 243

14a.2 Adverb with Modifier 243

14a.3 Adjective with Linking Verb 244

14b Dangling Modifier 245
14c Misplaced Modifier 246
14c.1 Misplaced Phrase 246
14c.2 Misplaced Adverb 247

15 PARALLEL STRUCTURE 248
15a Faulty Parallelism 248
15b Parallel Series 249
15c Paired Connectives 249
15d Phrase and Clause 250

16 SHIFTS 252
16a Shifts in Tense 252
16a.1 Past to Present 252
16a.2 Recent/Distant Past 253
16a.3 Real/Remote Possibility 253
16a.4 Indirect Quotation 254
16b Shifts in Reference 254

17 CONFUSED SENTENCES 256
17a Skipping and Duplication 256
17b Mismatched Predicate 257
17c *Is when/was when* 258
17d Mixed Sentence 258
17d.1 *Because/because of* 259
17d.2 *Because . . . does not mean* 259
17e Incomplete Structure 259
17e.1 Incomplete Verb 260
17e.2 Missing Preposition 260
17e.3 Shortcut Comparison 260
17e.4 Mismatched Comparison 261

18 SENTENCE CHOICES 262
18a Active/Passive 262
18a.1 Weak Passive 262
18a.2 Evasive Passive 263
18a.3 Shifts to Passive 263

18b Weak/Strong Predicate 265
18b.1 Colorless *be* 265
18b.2 *-ation/-otion* Nouns 266
18b.3 Padding and Tags 266
18c Strong/Weak Repetition 268
18c.1 Intentional Repetition 268
18c.2 Awkward Repetition 269

19 SENTENCE STYLE 270
19a Short/Long 270
19a.1 Choppy Sentences 271
19a.2 Sentence Overloads 271
19b Emphatic/Unemphatic 272
19c Normal/Varied 273

20 SENTENCE RHETORIC 275

21 FOCUSING ON STANDARD ENGLISH 280
21a Nonstandard Verbs 280
21a.1 Forms of *be* 281
21a.2 Missing *-s* Ending 282
21a.3 Nonstandard Past 284
21a.4 Verb with *have/be* 284
21a.5 Missing *be* 285
21b Nonstandard Pronouns 286
21b.1 *-self* Pronouns 286
21b.2 *them* as Pointer 287
21b.3 Repeated Pronoun 287
21c Double Negative 287
21d Double Comparative/ Superlative 288
21e Standard *a/an* 288

PART THREE EDITING FOR PUNCTUATION AND MECHANICS 291

22 COMPLETE SENTENCES AND FRAGMENTS 294

22a Exclamation/Question 294
22b Sentence Fragment 295
22c Comma Splice 296
22d Fused Sentence 297

23 LINKING PUNCTUATION 298

23a Comma for Coordinator 298
23b Comma for Subordinator? 299
23b.1 No Comma for *if/when* 300
23b.2 Comma for *although/whereas* 300
23c Comma for *who/which/that?* 302
23c.1 Restrictive *who/that* 302
23c.2 Nonrestrictive *who/which* 303
23d Semicolon with *however* 304
23e No Comma for Noun Clause 306

24 INTERNAL COMMAS 308

24a Commas for Modifiers 308
24a.1 Essential/Nonessential 309
24a.2 Introductory Modifiers 310
24a.3 Transitional Tags 310
24b Commas for Series 312
24c With Dates/Addresses 314
24d With Coordinate Adjectives 314
24e Repetition/Contrast 315
24f Parenthetic Commas 316

25 UNNEEDED COMMAS 318

26 SPECIAL MARKS 320

26a Using Colons 320

26b Using Dashes 321

26b.1 Dramatic Dash 321

26b.2 Interrupting Dashes 321

26b.3 Connecting Dash 322

26c Using Parentheses 322

26d Slashes 323

27 MARKING QUOTATIONS 324

27a Direct/Indirect 325

27a.1 Identifying Quotations 326

27a.2 Single Quotation Marks 327

27a.3 Block Quotations 327

27b End Marks 328

27c Insertion/Omission 329

27d Words Set Off 330

27e Titles and Names 332

27e.1 Titles of Publications 332

27e.2 Art and Entertainment 332

27e.3 Ships and Aircraft 333

28 SPELLING WORK 334

28a Spelling Demons 334

28a.1 Memory Aids 334

28a.2 Confusing Soundalikes 335

28a.3 Silent Letters 337

28a.4 Odd Pairs 338

28a.5 Special Problems *(it's/its)* 340

28b Spelling Rules 341

28b.1 *ie/cei* 341

28b.2 Doubled Final Letter 341

28b.3 Omitted Final Letter 342

28b.4 *y/ie* 343

28c Variant Spellings 343

29 MANUSCRIPT MECHANICS 346

29a Using Capitals 346
29a.1 Party Labels 348
29a.2 Names of Regions 348
29a.3 Capitalizing Titles 348
29a.4 Titles of Your Papers 348

29b Using Hyphens 349
29b.1 Prefix and Hyphen 351
29b.2 Group Modifiers 351
29b.3 Dividing Words 351

29c Apostrophe for Possessives 352
29c.1 Plural Possessives 353
29c.2 Time and Value 354
29c.3 Indefinite Pronouns 354
29c.4 Groups of Words 354
29c.5 Plurals of Symbols 355

29d Apostrophe for Contractions 356

29e Using Numbers 357

29f Using Abbreviations 359
29f.1 Widely Used Initials 359
29f.2 Titles and Degrees 359
29f.3 Time and Number 359
29f.4 Addresses and Locations 360
29f.5 Measurements 360

29g Using Italics 360
29g.1 Italics for Emphasis 360
29g.2 Words as Words 361
29g.3 Titles of Publications 361
29g.4 Creative Works 361
29g.5 Crafts and Vessels 362

PART FOUR WRITING ENGLISH AS A SECOND LANGUAGE 363

30 ENGLISH AS A SECOND CULTURE 365

30a Learning a Second Culture 366
30b From Narrative to Opinion 367
30c Key Ideas Up Front 368
30d Joining the Dialogue 371

31 ENGLISH AS A SECOND LANGUAGE 373

31a Nouns and Number 374

31b Nouns and Articles 376

31b.1 Definite or Indefinite 377

31b.2 Missing Article 377

31b.3 Unneeded Article 378

31b.4 Idiomatic Articles 379

31c Verbs and Time 380

31c.1 *-s* for Third Person Singular 382

31c.2 *-d/-ed* for Past and after *have* 383

31c.3 Plain Form with *do* 384

31d Verbs and Helping Verbs 384

31d.1 Plain Form after *can/will* 385

31d.2 Passive Verb with *-d/-ed* 386

31d.3 Progressive Verb with *-ing* 386

31e Idiomatic Verbs/Prepositions 387

31e.1 Idiomatic Verbs 388

31e.2 Idiomatic Prepositions 388

31e.3 Idiomatic Verbals 390

31f Checking Sentence Structure 394

31f.1 Verb First 394

31f.2 Subjectless Verb 395

31f.3 Duplicated Subject 395

PART FIVE WRITING THE RESEARCH PAPER 397

32 STARTING YOUR RESEARCH PROJECT 399

32a Defining the Research Paper 399

32b Avoiding Plagiarism 401

32c Defining Your Topic 403

32c.1 The Short Investigative Paper 404

32c.2 The Full-Length Research Paper 405

32c.3 Topics across the Curriculum 406

33 SEARCHING FOR SOURCES 408

33a First Search on the Computer 408
33a.1 Going to Websites 409
33a.2 Discovering Online Sources 409
33a.3 Using Search Engines 410
33b Newspapers and Periodicals 412
33c Searching the Indexes 418
33d Searching for Books 421
33d.1 Secondary and Primary Sources 422
33d.2 Indexes and Catalogs 422
33d.3 Bibliographies and Reviews 424
33e Using Nonprint Sources 425
33f Fact-Checking in Reference Books 426
33g Starting Your Source List 430

34 USING YOUR SOURCES 432

34a Focusing Your Search 432
34b Taking Notes 434
34c Organizing Your Notes 436
34d Organizing Your Paper 437
34d.1 Your Working Outline 438
34d.2 Your Trial Thesis 439
34d.3 Your Formal Outline 440

35 DRAFTING AND REVISING 443

35a Feeding Notes into Your Draft 443
35b Writing a Strong First Draft 446
35c Revising Your Draft 447
35c.1 Responding to Peer Reviews 447
35c.2 Responding to Instructor Feedback 448

36 DOCUMENTING YOUR SOURCES 454

36a Following a Documentation Style 454
36b Documenting Your Sources—MLA Style 456
36b.1 Parenthetic Documentation (MLA) 457
36b.2 Works Cited (MLA) 460
36b.3 Preparing Final Manuscript (MLA) 472
36b.4 Sample Research Paper (MLA) 473

36c Documenting Your Sources—-APA Style 487
36c.1 Parenthetic Citation (APA) 487
36c.2 References (APA) 489
36c.3 Preparing Final Manuscript (APA) 499
36c.4 Sample Research Paper (APA) 500
36d Documentation Styles: CBE, AIP, Chicago 514

PART SIX
SPECIAL HELPS FOR WRITERS 515

37 GLOSSARY OF USAGE 517

38 EFFECTIVE BUSINESS COMMUNICATIONS 525
38a Current Business Formats 526
38a.1 Return Address 526
38a.2 Inside Address and Greeting 527
38a.3 Conclusion and Notations 528
38a.4 Businesslike Style 529
38b Applying for Jobs 530
38c Writing Your Résumé 532

Index 535

Preface: To the Instructor

Why do we call this book *The Access Handbook?*

If writing courses serve a gateway function, we need textbooks that facilitate access. For students with widely varying preparation, we provide access to the world of writing and public discourse. As writing teachers, we aim at broadening access to college education. We aim at providing improved access to the world of meaningful work. For students who bring negative expectations to their English classrooms, we provide access to work with language and writing that makes English classes motivating and rewarding.

Goals of *The Access Handbook*

In writing this book, we have kept in mind the following concerns widely shared by today's writing teachers:

CHANGING STUDENT POPULATIONS As teachers in today's classrooms, we relate to changing student populations. We deal with students from richly diverse backgrounds—with widely varying exposure to standard English, academic discourse, and mainstream culture. We need to engage the native intelligence of these students, to capture and hold their attention. We need to do more to help them master the language skills and writing abilities that will enable them to use language well for their own purposes. We need to find ways of creating a sense of community and common purpose with which students from widely varying backgrounds can identify.

NEEDED: A TEACHING TEXT As teachers today, we do not assume that someone else has taught basic concepts. For today's students, we need books that are both reference books and at the same time effective teaching tools. We have to meet the needs of the learner. We have to establish one key term at a time, explain key concepts in plain English, and build systematically on what has gone before. We have to establish priorities and provide essential terminology to keep our traditional preoccupation with labeling and taxonomy from defeating our students. We need to do more than in the past to help students *understand and use* the information our handbooks provide.

BUILDING IN POSITIVE MOTIVATION As a profession, we have moved from excessive error correction to harnessing positive appreciation of language. We need to build the confidence and competence of the learner if we are to overcome the negative expectations that induce writer's block and English anxiety in our students. We need to recognize and nurture our students' potential, focusing more often on how things are done right. We need to balance positive models or positive inspiration with hands-on guidelines for dealing with common problems faced by less experienced writers.

VALIDATING STUDENT WRITING Students need to believe that they can learn to use language resourcefully, purposefully, and effectively. We need to show that we value our students' intelligence, their gift for language, their wit, and their idealism. In working with student writing in this book, we encourage teachers to see the continuity between good student writing and professional writing. We do not recognize a rigid dichotomy between professional writing and the writing of beginners.

TEACHING SECOND-LANGUAGE AND SECOND-DIALECT STUDENTS Learning a second language, let alone using it effectively in writing, are formidable accomplishments. Bilingual and bidialectal students deserve exceptionally meaningful instruction and habit-building language work. Writing teachers are developing knowledgeable, supportive, and empathetic strategies for helping students face the challenges of learning a second language and a second culture. We need to emulate successful second-language teachers by moving beyond undigested taxonomy and error counts to act as mentor, language coach, and accomplice of the ESL student and bidialectal student.

AN INTERACTIVE COURSE Many writing courses today are moving toward the interaction of a workshop format. Students come to think of their writing as work in progress—moving through intermeshing stages of exploration, gathering, shaping, rethinking and revising, and final editing. The materials in this book facilitate the give-and-take of instructor feedback and peer review. We encourage the collaboration of group projects. We encourage informal sharing, e-mail distribution, class publications, and publication in zines and school magazines.

Teaching Strategies in *The Access Handbook*

Writing teachers have done considerable rethinking of pedagogy—of *how* to reach our shared goals in the light of the best in current theory and classroom practice. Teaching strategies like the following have shaped the organization of *The Access Handbook*:

FROM PREWRITING TO WRITING As writing teachers today, we focus on *what it takes* to generate meaningful student writing. We pay more attention than in the past to what sets purposeful writing in motion.

We try to make our student writers more audience-conscious. Drawing on the whole range of conventional and electronic sources, we teach productive ways to generate input for a paper. We stress *pushing toward* a thesis rather than *starting with* a thesis. We encourage the use of scratch outlines and working outlines. During the revision cycle, we emphasize treating instructor feedback and peer reviews of early drafts as opportunities for genuine rethinking and rewriting.

FROM EXPERIENCE TO EXPOSITION Much strong writing is rooted in personal experience and observation. Many writing teachers, frustrated by the clichés of unmotivated student writing, have discovered that student writing gains in force and conviction when students move beyond secondhand ideas to facing up honestly to lived experience. Finding the connecting thread or focusing on a key issue in their personal history teaches our student writers a basic lesson in structuring an array of data. Today many successful writing courses lead students from an honest accounting of personal experience to exploring issues personally meaningful to them in the public arena.

FROM READING TO WRITING As teachers of research-based writing, we today are moving more naturally from the informal research that goes into most writing to the more structured research of investigative papers or formal documented research papers. We instruct students early in the informal use of sources—encouraging them to work into their text the revealing quotations, the testimony of authorities and insiders, and the authoritative data that help support key points. We encourage them to draw on their reading, their viewing, their talking with others, and their browsing of the net.

FROM THINKING TO ARGUMENT From the beginning, *The Access Handbook* stresses the thinking that goes into writing. The computer has shortened the distance between thinking and writing. Student writers can see a paper take shape as they sift and lay out their material. Going beyond the conventional modes, we teach the weighing of alternatives or arguing from principle as dynamic writing/thinking strategies that serve the writer's purpose. We need to establish a closer connection between the teaching of argument and actual student writing than the separate logic-and-fallacies chapters in conventional texts.

FROM WORDS TO SENTENCES The basic common denominator of effective writers is their command of words. Starting language work by focusing on words—their range and reach and overtones—gives us a chance to highlight the resources rather than the pitfalls of language. Going on to the more technical and demanding study of sentences, we can then hope to balance our emphasis on expanding the student's sentence resources with hands-on instruction in editing for familiar sentence problems.

FROM PRIVATE TO PUBLIC LANGUAGE Composition teachers today provide a better bridge from the private language of the neighborhood or immigrant family to the public standard English of school and office. Bilingual and bidialectal students need to see that our teaching is rooted in shared experience with language learning and language teaching—focused on building up the students' linguistic repertory and on helping them navigate between one set of cultural expectations and another.

Supporting Material for *The Access Handbook*

We have worked to provide an exceptionally student-focused, teaching-oriented set of supporting materials for *The Access Handbook*.

THE INTERACTIVE EDITION OF THE ACCESS HANDBOOK The Interactive Edition of *The Access Handbook* combines the complete textbook with the latest in multimedia, taking your students beyond the traditional learning experience.

- The Interactive Edition CD-ROM contains the complete handbook as well as hundreds of contextually placed media links.
- Video and audio clips, interactive exercises, and links to websites are directly related to key concepts in *The Access Handbook*.
- The links expand chapter content, involve students in the subject at hand, and help them remember what they have learned.

THE ACCESS TUTOR More than a routine workbook, *The Access Tutor* provides the added explanations, the reinforcement of essential concepts, and the habit-building activities needed by students with limited preparation.

- *The Access Tutor* employs a distinctive teaching pattern of CAPSULE RULE—PROBLEM SPOTTER—BACKUP EXPLANATION—EXAMPLE BANK—and REVISION PRACTICE.
- *The Access Tutor* is a consumable teaching resource with tear-out sheets for peer review, prewriting, quick-check quizzes, and review tests.
- *The Access Tutor* is ideally suited for use in writing centers or by writing tutors; it provides explanations accessible to ESL students.
- *The Access Tutor* is accompanied by an *Answer Key* for instructors.

THE ACCESS MANUAL *The Access Manual* provides background, backup, and hands-on advice for both the new and the experienced instructor.

- The opening essay, "**Teaching Writing,**" introduces new faculty to essential professional background and allows experienced faculty to compare notes on shared assumptions and current issues.
- An annotated professional **bibliography** of composition studies, prepared by Jeanne Gunner of Santa Clara University, gives a state-of-the-art overview of the discipline.
- The **Help** sections provide hands-on explanations and advice, helping teachers anticipate issues, deal with recurrent needs, and provide added explanation for key points. Together, these sections provide a mini-course in survival skills for today's composition teacher, including suggestions for motivating student writers, demystifying grammar, and dealing with ESL needs and issues.
- The manual provides "at-your-fingertips" suggested answers and sample responses for the **Your Turn** activities in the text.
- The **Class Use** sections provide backup activities for use in class.

THE COMPANION WEBSITE FOR *THE ACCESS HANDBOOK* The Companion Website for *The Access Handbook* **www.abacon.com/laguardia** employs the power of the Internet to extend the concepts of the handbook.

- Interactive Online Study Guide questions provide immediate feedback to students.
- Weblinks are keyed to specific sections in the handbook.
- Message boards and chat rooms enable instructors and students to communicate with others using the handbook.
- Syllabus Manager provides instructors with online syllabus creation and classroom management.

DIAGNOSTIC TEST BANK/TEST BANK FOR HANDBOOKS, 2000

- Two 50-item diagnostic tests assess student readiness in grammar and usage.
- The reference key identifies the relevant text section of each test-item topic.
- The test bank is available in printed or computerized formats (Windows or IBM).

Acknowledgments

This book has grown out of our teaching in many classrooms, our interacting with students from a rich diversity of backgrounds, and our networking with the many teachers dedicated to the common cause. Our main source of inspiration has been the students we have taught—and talked with and argued with in and out of the classroom. Their native intelligence, gift for language, quick wit, and youthful idealism provide the antidote to cynicism in high places.

We owe a special debt of gratitude to the many students who have given us permission to use their papers as inspiration and encouragement to others. Among the students who have given us permission to reprint or adapt their writing for use in this book and other teaching materials, we wish to thank especially Hilda Bedolla-Verduzco, Alicia Bueschen, Matt Giudice, Nicole Hancock, Marianne Hocson, Luis Lorenzana, Chris Navarro, Sarah Piskun, Merritt Quisumbing, Matthew Roomel, and Meghan Shumm.

We have learned much by working with dedicated teachers in most of the 50 states and across the seas. We owe a large debt to the professional organizations and the forums they provide. The CCCC has long championed the revival of the discipline of rhetoric, the revitalizing of language instruction through renewing the ties between the classroom and the best in language scholarship and linguistics, and the recognition of written communication as the core subject in the student's education for tomorrow's world. The regional conferences dedicated to the teaching of English in the two-year colleges have done much to build the bridge between the most challenging in current theory and the best classroom practice. We treasure our involvement in the Young Rhetoricians Conference in Monterey, California, whose roster of speakers and workshop participants and Rhetoricians-of-the-Year reads like a *Who's Who* of the scholars and teachers that have provided leadership for undervalued writing faculties in their quest for recognition and improved professional status.

Finally, we would like to thank those individuals who reviewed an early version of this text for Allyn and Bacon: Steve Abbott, Columbus State Community College; Nancy C. DeJoy, Millikin University; Paula Gillespie, Marquette University; and Cynthia Haynes, the University of Texas at Dallas.

Dolores laGuardia
Hans P. Guth

To the Student: How to Use This Book

Take time to familiarize yourself with the resources this book gives you to help you become a better and more confident writer.

1 This book provides **writing instruction** focused on what has worked for other writers. It offers you advice and practical help as you meet new challenges and try out new techniques.

- Do not study the *guidelines* in this book as set formulas. Study them as procedures that can serve you well and that you can learn to adapt for your own purposes.
- Study the *sample outlines* and *model papers* especially. What was the writer trying to do? How successful was the writer?

2 The **writing options** in this book ask you to take on a range of tasks encountered by writers. The assignments give you a chance to practice and learn from kinds of writing serving different purposes and aimed at different audiences. Suggested topics move from exploring your personal experience through making the most of your reading to laying out information or ideas, helping your readers think through a current issue, or guiding your readers' choices.

- Give real thought to your *choice of topics*. Try to relate possible topics to special strengths in your background or education. Try to find a personal connection.
- Participate in *class discussion* of possible topics to help you explore the opportunities and challenges they might present. Learn from the questions and reactions of your classmates and your instructor.

3 *The Access Handbook* aims at **complete coverage** of questions you may encounter in writing, revising, and final editing. The book is organized to help you search for help with editing issues often queried by editors and teachers.

- Familiarize yourself with the *numbering system* or numerical key. A guide number like **12** directs you to a general category like Pronoun Reference. A guide number like **12e** leads you to a subsection giving guidelines for avoiding Sexist Pronouns. Complete guide numbers appear in the *Contents* and in a chart in the *inside front cover*.
- Instructors may use guide numbers in reading your papers, or they may use *editing symbols* like **agr** for subject-verb agreement or **ref** for pronoun reference. The *inside back cover* of this book gives an alphabetic listing of common editing symbols with guide numbers.

- Familiarize yourself with how this book can *help with trouble spots* that may have caused problems for you in the past. For instance, have you been asked to avoid clichés? Can you find an entry in the index that will direct you to the right section in the book?

4 *The Access Handbook* is designed to make grammar more usable and accessible, updating terminology where needed to bring it closer to plain English and show its usefulness for the writer.

- Take time to read the overview section on *Understanding Sentences* (Section 7).
- Consult the **index** when looking for material dealing with grammatical terms. For instance, if you look for *coordinating conjunctions,* the index will direct you to the shorter modernized *coordinators.*

5 This book works with **English as a Second Language** from the perspective of teachers who themselves are second-language users of English or who have worked extensively with second-language learners.

- If you are writing English as a second or third language, familiarize yourself with the ESL sections of the book (Sections **30** and **31**). See how they can help you target trouble spots in your writing.
- Take to heart what these sections say to encourage exposure and immersion. Remember the advice on language learning as habit building. Go over needed ESL materials again and again—and again.

About the Authors

Dolores laGuardia teaches at the University of San Francisco, where she developed a humanities sequence titled "American Voices: Ourselves and Each Other," with courses focused on African Americans, Asian Americans, Latinos, Native Americans, religious minorities, and alternative lifestyles. She has served as the writing specialist for a large federal grant designed to improve writing instruction at the two-year college level and has done curriculum work for Bay Area institutions. She has TESOL certification and extensive background in working with second-language students. She has a reputation for squaring the circle as a tough grader who receives outstanding student evaluations, and she has a dedicated following among current and former students. She has conducted workshops on computer education at the prestigious Troitsk Institute outside Moscow. She is co-author with Hans P. Guth of *American Voices: Culture and Community* (Fourth Edition, 2000), *American Visions: Multicultural Literature for Writers* (1995), and *Issues across the Curriculum* (1997).

Hans P. Guth has won a number of excellence-in-teaching awards and has worked with writing faculty in most of the 50 states. He has published pioneering widely used composition texts and influential professional books. A speaker at many national and regional meetings, he served from 1984 to 1994 as co-director and program chair of the annual Young Rhetoricians' Conference in Monterey, whose roster of speakers and participants reads like a *Who's Who* of teacher-scholars active in the writing movement. He has organized or taught in workshops at universities including Stanford, the University of Illinois, Oxford University, and the University of Heidelberg. Dr. Guth has been a leader in the movement to revitalize the teaching of English in American schools and colleges by language instruction grounded in modern language scholarship and by upgrading the status of writing programs and writing faculty. With Gabriele Rico, he is co-author of *Discovering Literature* (Compact Edition, 2000).

Orientation: To the Student

The written word is our most powerful medium of communication. Every day, millions share data and ideas through their writing. They communicate via e-mail, interoffice memos, reports, newsletters, and circulars. They draft proposals, sales presentations, and petitions. In articles, editorials, and letters to the editor, writers discuss the issues. They argue about student loans, marital leave, workfare, or immigration. Ghost writers write speeches. Job seekers and customers write letters of application, letters of inquiry, and letters of complaint. People read books—sometimes 700 or 800 pages long, in small print. They consult encyclopedias online—finding what they need among tens of thousands of words.

What questions do you have as you start a writing class? Here are questions that students in writing courses often ask:

"WHY A WRITING CLASS?" Why is a writing requirement part of a core curriculum or of general education?

- *Writing is the medium of much of your college work.* You will use it to record, compare, and share information. Students and faculty use it to communicate the results of scholarship and research. Writing is a large part of what students, professors, and researchers do.
- *Writing is the central medium of interaction and collaboration in the workplace.* Much of the world's work is done by written communication. For many, work means dealing with e-mail, memos, reports, promotional mailings, proposals, research studies, evaluations, news releases, or policy reviews.
- *Writing is the central medium of the public dialogue.* It is the arena where ideas clash that matter to us as citizens and voters. Articles, books, editorials, and letters to the editor focus on issues like election reform, embattled schools, managed health, and gun control. Even speeches or oral presentations are typically based on scripts or read off cue cards.
- *Writing is a means of learning about ourselves.* Writing and reading about other people and ourselves, we come to a fuller understanding of people—of relationships, families, lifestyles. We better understand our choices and responsibilities in today's world.

"WHAT MAKES A WRITING CLASS DIFFERENT?" How is it different from classes in the hard sciences, the social sciences, or other fields?

- *The emphasis is on active participation.* You are the writer. A writing class is not something you take; it is something you do. You are the one tackling different and gradually more challenging writing projects. Your own growth as a writer is what counts.

- *Much of your work is likely to be work in progress.* To stay current, you have to be part of the process of formulating assignments, defining issues, and exploring sources. You should be on schedule preparing and sharing drafts. You cannot drift in and out—missing important steps in the development of a paper.
- *You may be working in a workshop format.* Much of your work may involve interaction with others. Your thinking may take shape as the result of classroom exchanges and discussion. In revising your written work, you will be responding to instructor's comments or peer review.
- *You may participate in collaborative projects.* Today, promotional campaigns and research projects are the result of people working together. They learn to relate to others and to reconcile their individual agendas. They make the best possible contribution to the joint effort. You may be collaborating with classmates to prepare panel presentations or investigative reports.

"HOW IS THE COMPUTER CHANGING THE WORLD OF WRITING?" The computer and the Internet are changing the way writers write and think.

- *Writing on the computer develops the writing habit.* For millions, the new technology has made writing a more natural activity, making the computer keyboard almost an extension of the human hand. They send e-mail to long-lost friends and then stay in touch; they forward stories or jokes. Managers write their own memos and letters. Cyberspace is becoming the natural habitat of a new generation, less likely to suffer from writer's block than writers did in the past.
- *The Internet helps writers to become informed.* The Internet offers writers instant access to information. It makes possible an instant background search on current issues; it facilitates both informal and in-depth research. To work up background for a "hot-button" issue, you can turn to online newspapers or newsmagazines. You can consult online encyclopedias for quick background on ethnic strife or religious conflict currently in the news.
- *The computer shortens the distance between writing and thinking.* Writers see their thinking take shape in front of them on the computer screen. They work with trial outlines, and they rearrange or recast material to make allowance for second thoughts. Writing, and then rewriting or revising, are today not so much separate stages in the writing process as parts of a continuum. Though they may print out early drafts, writers today make adjustments or fill in missing links even during final editing or proofreading.

- *The computer fosters the habit of responding to feedback.* Writers today are not likely to work on a topic in isolation. Using e-mail or participating in chat rooms, they have developed the habit of answering questions as they come up. They have learned to deal with objections as they arise. Mental habits learned from the instant feedback of the computer world help writers to think on their feet. They anticipate questions and objections because they have internalized the interaction of the computer world.
- *Using the Internet requires you to evaluate sources.* You become more aware of problems of authorship and authenticity. Much print material comes from sources with an established reputation. It has usually been sifted by editors or reviewers. In using material from electronic sources, you will often have to do your own screening. You may have to sift out anonymous material or material of uncertain origin. You need to be wary of material that was pirated, excerpted, or otherwise changed without acknowledgment.

"HOW MUCH RESEARCH WILL I DO?" How much will you draw on your reading? What library work might be involved?

- *Informal research will go into most of your writing.* You will do much focused reading—tracking material that will be useful for a specific writing project. When working on an investigative paper or a formal research paper, you will try to pull together the best available information and the best current thinking on your subject.
- *You will learn more about how to use and evaluate electronic sources.* In the age of the information highway and the knowledge explosion, a full range of material on any major topic is at your fingertips. You will learn more about how to conduct computer searches that will lead you to the most useful or most relevant sources on the Internet.
- *You may do extended library research.* If your course includes a research paper, you will practice research techniques leading you to useful material in periodicals and books. In documented papers, you will provide publishing information that enables readers to track and verify your sources. You will follow a documentation style appropriate to your subject or your field. Where and how are you expected to identify the author, the publication, and the publisher? What kind of bibliography or final listing will give full information about the sources you have consulted?

"WHAT PROBLEMS SHOULD I AVOID?" What issues cause difficulties for the writing student and the writing instructor? What is a good way of handling them?

- *Pay attention to grading policies.* Are there minimum requirements? Are there penalties for late work or unexcused absences? From the beginning, pay careful attention to suggestions for improvement. If you are concerned about your grades, consult with your instructor and make the extra needed effort.
- *Heed warnings about plagiarism.* Plagiarism means taking over other people's intellectual property without acknowledgment. Authors who plagiarize pass off other people's work as their own. Check out and acknowledge any outside material you feed into your writing. Whether resulting from carelessness or deliberate deception, work that creates suspicions of plagiarism undermines the trust and cooperation that make a writing class successful. Plagiarism can ruin a grade and an academic record. At worst, it gets people expelled from institutions or dragged into court.

WRITING ESSENTIALS

Authorship Standards

Make sure that the writing you submit is clearly the result of your own work. Observe basic guidelines:

1. ***Put all direct quotation in quotation marks.*** Clearly identify as quotation all material you copy word for word.
2. ***When in doubt, credit the source.*** Tell your reader who said what. Acknowledge the original source when you feed into your writing statements made and ideas developed by someone else. Show the source of data and statistics.
3. ***Represent other authors fairly.*** Do not take quotations out of context. Do not ignore strong arguments or evidence on the opposing side.
4. ***Be wary of anonymous secondhand material.*** Unsigned, untracked material from the Internet or other sources may have been tampered with or pirated. Do not present "facts" of uncertain origin for which no one is assuming responsibility.
5. ***Keep track of your research effort.*** In a research log, track your progress, or record the steps in your research. Keep notes and first drafts.
6. ***Practice a full-disclosure policy.*** Talk freely about work in progress in a workshop situation. Talk freely with others about what materials you found and how you are going to use them.
7. ***Acknowledge contributions from collaborators.*** When working with others, size up fairly your own contribution and that of your co-workers.

PART ONE

YOUR WRITING GUIDE

Writers pay much attention to the words, sentences, and commas that are the tools of their trade. Make sure you do not lose sight of the larger issues that challenge you as a writer. What gives your writing shape and makes it worth reading? Ask yourself: Why is this topic important to me? What do I already know about it , and what do I need to find out? Who are my intended readers, and what are their expectations or needs? What is going to be my main point or central message? How can I best lay out the supporting material? How do I get the readers' attention, and how can I leave them with a strong final impression?

1 HOW WRITERS WRITE

Do justice to major stages in the writing process.

What will make you a good writer?

Experienced writers take a writing project through several stages. They focus on the task, clarifying in their own minds what they are trying to do. They work up material, often drawing on material they have already saved for possible use. They size up the audience, taking into account its background, needs, and expectations. They organize and reorganize as they feed their material into one of several drafts. Time permitting, they rewrite, responding to feedback and making allowance for second thoughts. They edit and proofread, making last-minute corrections and improvements.

These stages or phases in the writing process are not like the separate steps in assembling an exercycle. Instead, they blend and overlap. You may be checking out further information, rearranging your material, and thinking about a good way to introduce your topic at roughly the same time.

WRITING ESSENTIALS — A Checklist for Student Writers

A successful paper shows that you have done justice to major dimensions of effective writing.

1 ***What is your purpose?*** You focus on your task. What are you trying to do?

2 ***Who is your audience?*** You target your intended readers. What will it take to reach them? What will it take to make your voice heard?

3 ***Where do you turn for input?*** You work up your material. How good are you at exploring your topic, checking out data, and listening to people in the know?

4 ***What is going to be your central point?*** You push toward a thesis. Are you going to scatter your fire? Or are you going to use your material to support a key idea?

5 ***What is your plan?*** You organize your thinking. You sort out data and lay out information in an accessible format. You line up the steps in an argument.

(continued)

A Checklist for Student Writers *(continued)*

6 ***How solid is your supporting material?*** You feed into your draft key examples, revealing details, thought-provoking quotations, and striking statistics. You keep in mind the reader who says: "Don't just tell me—show me."

7 ***What needs work in an early draft?*** You allow time for revision. How much are you going to learn from feedback? Are you ready for serious rewriting and rethinking?

8 ***How careful an editor are you?*** You allow time for final editing and proofreading. Are your sentences clear and lively? Do they meet today's standards of educated written English? Have you proofread your final copy carefully both on screen and in hard copy?

9 ***Have you followed instructions for format?*** You follow guidelines for manuscript preparation—author identification, layout, spacing, page numbering. Have you followed special instructions for number of copies or submission by e-mail?

10 ***Are you preparing to share your writing with others?*** Writing is meant to be shared and read. Will you participate in arrangements for sharing your paper with classmates, contributing to a desktop class publication, or helping prepare a school publication?

OPTIONS FOR WRITING 1 Writing the Personal Résumé

Writing a personal résumé will give you a chance to take stock of your personal resources. What background do you bring to your writing class? What experiences will you be able to draw on in your writing? What will help classmates and your instructor get a sense of who or what you are? Choose four or five headings like the following, and write a paragraph or more under each heading:

FAMILY BACKGROUND
SCHOOLING
WORK EXPERIENCE
CAREER INTERESTS
SELF-IMAGE
PERSONAL ISSUES

The following are sample entries:

FAMILY BACKGROUND:

Most people my age do not realize how hard it was for the older generation to make a new start in a new country. When my grandfather immigrated to the U.S. from China, he had to buy fake identification papers that said he was younger than he actually was. According to my grandfather, a person under the age of 20 could leave the country, but people over 20 had to serve in the Chinese army and were not allowed to leave. My grandfather was 20 and had to buy fake identification papers saying he was only 18. These papers also changed his name from Cheng to Liu, so they not only changed his age but also gave him a new identity. I guess one could say that he was an illegal immigrant. This was taking a big risk for him because he could have been caught, but he thought it was worth it, just to come to America.

SELF-IMAGE:

When I entered high school, I was a shy, insecure person. It was not hard for me to make friends, but it was difficult for me to feel accepted. I usually camouflaged my real feelings with a fake smile. What helped me to shed the layers of self-doubt was working at the Living Tree Coffeehouse. I spent a year serving mochas and lattes, meeting people, and basically having a great time. The atmosphere was warm and cozy, with antique furniture and velvet couches. People came there not only to socialize but also to listen to good music or study for midterms. There was a real sense of community without everyone only trying to get ahead of everyone else. About the same time, I ran for the Associated Student Body Council, and serving on the council helped me overcome my insecurities. I learned that it is perfectly fine to express my feelings or express dislike toward someone else's ideas.

1a Discovering Your Purpose

Know what you are trying to accomplish.

Writers write for a purpose. What will set your writing in motion? When you know what you are trying to do, you can plan your strategy and mobilize your resources. Here are some reasons to write:

- *You may be writing about yourself.* People write about their lives to understand themselves and others. Perhaps you have made a major move or been involved in a divorce. You may decide to go back over what happened and see what it meant for you. Writing about the experience may give you a chance to sort out the good and the bad; it may help you come to terms with disappointments or resentments. It may help you decide where to go from here.

- *You may be expressing your opinion.* Much writing is part of a continuing dialogue. A writer may attack the destruction of old-growth forests by clear-cut logging. In defense of the lumber companies, another writer may plead the case of the loggers who depend on an economy centered on King Timber. Yet another writer will urge environmentalists and loggers to make common cause against timber companies who in the long run will move their lumber mills to Mexico in search of cheap labor and low taxes. Much writing of this kind is like joining a conversation. The dialogue will continue after you have spoken your piece.
- *You may be writing to explain.* Much writing answers the question: How does it work? It aims at readers who want to know. For instance, what does the term *globalization* mean? Why does an economist say that access to the worldwide global labor market has made labor "dirt-cheap"? On another topic of concern to job-seekers, what is behind buzzwords like *flextime* and *flexibility?* Can an employer call you the evening before if you are not needed and do not need to be paid the next day? On the other hand, do these terms mean that people who cannot work on a fixed schedule will have a chance to be gainfully employed?
- *You may be writing to talk back.* Have you ever been angered by remarks about a group with which you identify? Do you bristle at remarks about women, blacks, Jews, "Orientals," Mormons, or white males? Do you object to being stereotyped—put in the same box with other members of a group? What are you going to say when you talk back to the stereotype? How are you going to correct harmful images or misconceptions?
- *You may be writing to argue a point.* When you argue in favor of longer library hours or more bicycle paths, your audience will want to know why. On a subject like affirmative action you are entitled to your own opinion, but your readers may not take it seriously unless you are prepared to weigh the arguments pro and con. A successful argument respects the readers' intelligence, making them feel that writer and reader together are thinking the matter through.

Start thinking of topics on which you have something to say. Among current issues, or among assigned topics, look for those that have a special meaning for you. If you are assigned a topic, look for the personal connection: How has the issue touched your own life? What difference has it made in the lives of people close to you? Do any of the following make you think: "On this I have something to say"?

Are we relying too much on standardized tests?

Should we bring wolves back into our national parks?

Should race or ethnic background be a factor in college admissions?

Why are some drivers a menace on the road?

Would you encourage young women to enlist for military service?

Why do some young people get into drugs, and others don't?

Would you buy a gun for self-defense?

OPTIONS FOR WRITING 2 Starting a Journal

You may be asked to keep a **journal** or writing log. To help you develop the writing habit, you write once or several times a week, putting down informal observations and comments. You write freely about yourself, about current happenings, or about current issues. You respond to what you see, hear, and read. Some of your entries may serve as materials for future papers and more structured writing. Here are some sample topics:

- a local initiative or development that you are supporting or opposing
- something that has been an issue or a challenge in your family background
- a campus issue on which you have strong feelings
- something that happened at work and proved a challenge or was difficult to handle
- names you or people close to you have been called, or putdowns you have experienced
- a television program or movie that you found disturbing or especially rewarding
- something that used to confuse or annoy you but that you have come to understand better

YOUR TURN 1 A Paper for Peer Review

The following paper grew out of a journal entry about a student's growing up in a rural setting unfamiliar to many fellow students. What made the author want to write? What was on his mind? How

YOUR TURN 1 *(continued)*

well did he accomplish what he set out to do? Where does the writer's message come through most strongly or most clearly? What details or points are you likely to remember? Do you make a good audience for this paper? Why or why not?

Morning Glories

The sun isn't even existent at 3:45 a.m. on a chilly July morning.

The alarm clock by my bed starts singing its song five minutes earlier. I roll unsteadily out of bed, take a deep breath that lets the world know I am awake, and stumble into the kitchen for a bowl of some neon-colored breakfast cereal. There aren't any hot breakfasts that my mother will make on days like this, so I'm on my own. After mechanically forcing myself to eat, I climb into my car and head off to my job at a cropdusting service. After I meet with my boss for the list of jobs that we will be doing today, I walk briskly out to the line, still shaking sleep from my head, and put on the white fabric suit that really doesn't do anything to keep the sulfur off of your skin. After I help my co-workers stack the fifty pound bags of sulfur that will be thrown into the hopper of an aircraft that should be sitting in an aviation museum somewhere, we thunk down onto the bags, sweating in the cool, damp air, and wonder the same thing: What the heck are we doing here? What possessed us to take a summer job like this, anyway?

Around ten minutes later, the first few shaded rays of the morning sun drift across the land, turning the world blue. And then, the catch of an ex-military engine more than fifty years old shatters any thoughts of going to sleep on the suddenly very comfy bags of sulfur. I glance across the cracked and sunbaked asphalt mat at the airplane that is shuddering and buzzing like some large and angry insect, the pale blue flame of its over-enriched exhaust lighting up its entire right hand side. And, as the airplane taxis over to us and the pilot, a friend of all of us, gives us the thumbs-up and a smile through his Plexiglass helmet, we remember why we work here. It's because we like to.

I belong to a highly criticized, highly scrutinized generation. One of the favorite targets of any adult is the almost mythical work ethic. I have heard from more than one adult that kids today don't know honest work, and the ones who do work only do so to spend their money on clothes and compact discs. This is generally right before they ramble on about how their own parents sent them to the diamond mines at the tender age of six. One example stands out especially well in my mind. I was in a bank one time, depositing one of my paychecks. Most of each check went into a checking account, and 15 percent of each check I allotted to myself for spending money. The teller, a middle-aged, predatory-looking woman, quipped that I might as well cash the entire check now, as it would undoubtedly be gone in a week or two.

I am sure that there are a lot of kids who work only for their own wants and desires. What many adults don't realize is how many kids either work to save for college or work as a means of feeling accomplishment. Where I come from, all of my friends had some form of summer employment. Many worked for their own farmer fathers, as I did for five years, and many worked at various other jobs. Many were working to pay their families in some way for their college education. What almost all of us had in common was that we were working because we got something out of it besides the money. I was proud of my job. I know that most people don't see a sunrise even once a year. I saw and honestly enjoyed them every day. I worked with people ten years older than I who treated me as their equal, and I was proud because of it. A paycheck every two weeks was just that much more incentive, and saving most of it honestly felt good. And, as for my friends, they are proud that they are what some would call "hick farmers." Wearing that fact like a badge of honor, they will be quick to tell you that it is the hick farmers who hold the economy of this state together. And whatever you do, don't call any of them lazy or uncaring. Chances are they have seen and enjoyed quite a few more sunrises this year than you.

1b Targeting Your Audience

Size up your intended audience.

Writing is meant to be read. Who is your intended reader? What audience do you have in mind? Your estimate of your target audience will determine what information you have to fill in. It will determine what values you can appeal to or what prejudices you might have to confront. Effective writers often visualize an imaginary reader—who nods, frowns, chuckles, or turns angry at the right (and sometimes at the wrong) moment.

- *Much writing aims at initiating the newcomer or outsider.* A basic skill for every writer is to meet the needs of those who want instructions or want to know. How much background and explanation will you have to fill in? Which technical terms are going to confuse the beginner? For instance, when you explain the jury system to newcomers, what will you have to clarify that insiders take for granted? (What's a grand jury? How do subpoenas work? Who can challenge potential jurors and why? Why are juries sequestered? What's a change of venue?)

- *Much discussion of public issues aims at the concerned citizen.* Newspaper readers who read more than the sports page care about issues like congestion, campaign financing, or pollution. They are likely to be looking for new information, relevant statistics, and the testimony of expert witnesses. When you have done an honest job of sorting out your materials and thinking the matter through, you expect that a receptive reader will take in your facts and give your conclusions the benefit of the doubt.
- *Much writing aims at an in-group audience.* This is the ideal situation for a writer looking for validation rather than confrontation. You may find a receptive audience when you ask women to work for better support and shelters for battered women. Outgunned police officers may welcome your call for restrictions on automatic weapons and armor-piercing ammunition. Fellow students may cheer you on when you attack cuts in student loans.
- *Some writing takes on a hostile audience.* What does it take to persuade an audience that does not share your background or values? How do you change someone's mind who disagrees with you? Remarks greeted by cheers at a union meeting might be greeted by stony silence at a meeting with management. How good are you at finding common ground? What resources of goodwill or shared self-interest can you mobilize?

YOUR TURN 2 Sizing Up the Audience

For each of the following writing samples, who would be the ideal reader? Would you be? Why or why not? What would be the perfect target audience? Would the potential audience be homogeneous, or could it be made up of different groups? How much background knowledge would the reader have to bring to the selection?

1 Solectron, a contract manufacturer that makes computer boards, is expanding rapidly, with entry-level jobs for machine operators, materials handlers, clerical and data-entry workers. A materials handler, for instance, needs good reading and writing skills and basic math. He or she has to calculate inventories and communicate with people on the line about their requirements. To move up to a technician's job, it helps to have algebra. "It's not row after row of people with soldering irons," says Al Cotton, senior director of human resources. Line workers "have to work through persuasion, communicate, read and understand instructions, give presentations to sway your team members, explain a process to team members." Team

members must learn how to analyze problems, so they can contribute to solutions.

—Joanne Jacobs, "Job One: Education," *San Jose Mercury News*

2 For the working-class feminist majority, most of the victories still do lie ahead. True, there have been some gains in opening up the better-paying, blue-collar occupations to women, but one is struck at once by how minute they are when measured against women's advance in the professions. While the percentage of women in professional training rose from 10 to 30 or 40 percent, the percentage of women carpenters, machinists, and mechanics has not even risen to 10 percent. As a result, the average working woman is still pretty much where she always was: waiting on tables, emptying wastebaskets, or pounding a keyboard for an hourly wage in the mid-single-digit wage. When she looks out—at television or the dressed-for-success-style magazines—she sees more fortunate women bounding ahead. But when she looks around, she sees women like herself, going nowhere. Somewhere in this collision of rising expectations and unchanging conditions lie the seeds of the next feminist upsurge.

—Barbara Ehrenreich, "The Next Wave," *Ms.* magazine

3 Today marks the 131st anniversary of the 13th Amendment, which officially ended slavery. On this day, we need to ask ourselves why, in a country that proudly built the National Holocaust Museum (with private donations), we don't yet have a national slavery museum. The first colonist killed in the American Revolution was an African American. The former slave, Crispus Attucks, was killed by the British in the Boston Massacre in 1970. Five thousand black soldiers went on to fight in the Revolutionary War. Yet few are remembered in our history books, in our museums, or consequently, in our society.

—Jesse Kalisher, "A Memorial to Slavery in America," *Marina Times*

4 Your recent article, "A Growing Concern," performed a needed service by raising some important issues surrounding the uses and abuses of biotechnology. Unfortunately, you undermined your credibility by choosing to continue the gratuitous fear-mongering that has characterized the biotechnology debate in the environmental community. Calgene's Flavr Savr tomato is a case in point. Your sidebar "Flavor Saved?" implied that the Flavr Savr contains bacterial genes. This is not so. The only functional difference between the Flavr Savr and ordinary tomatoes is that the Flavr Savr has had a gene removed that makes ordinary

YOUR TURN 2 *(continued)*

> tomatoes turn to mush after they ripen. This allows Flavr Savr tomatoes to ripen on the vine and still make it to the store in one piece. Do environmentalists really prefer tomatoes that are picked, shipped green, and then "quick-ripened" with a shot of ethylene gas just before being put on supermarket shelves? Much more sensible is the outcry over Monsanto's Roundup Ready crops. Here is a product deliberately designed to encourage more use of an herbicide of questionable safety.
>
> —John H. Brandt, "Throwing Tomatoes," *Mother Jones*

1c Working Up Material

Work up a rich fund of material for use in your paper.

How do you work up the material for a strong paper? Ideally, you want to be able to say: "On this topic, I have more material than I can use." You seldom hear experienced writers complain that there is nothing to write about. They tend to have the opposite problem—they have folders of notes that need to be sorted out. They have sprawling computer files that need to be sifted and arranged according to some kind of system. They often have a backlog of possibly useful material to feed into a current project.

1c.1 Using Your Resources

Use the full range of your resources. Effective writing shows that you are a sharp-eyed observer, a good listener, and an alert reader. Remember pointers like the following:

- *Start from what you already know.* Search the memory banks of your brain for relevant materials. Suppose you are focusing a paper on questions about assimilation or mainstreaming of current immigrants. Have you been in situations where this was an issue? Have you witnessed any incidents where someone was treated like a foreigner? Have you watched someone from an immigrant background adopting American ways? Do you remember things people have said on this topic or stories that are part of family tradition? Can you draw on news reports you remember or on a television documentary you recently saw?
- *Draw on your current reading, listening, and viewing.* Bring in material from current newspaper articles or from a much-discussed

current book. Search the Internet for discussion of a current topic. Listen to talk shows focusing on a current issue much in the news. Follow columnists like Ellen Goodman for the *Boston Globe* or Molly Ivins for the *Fort Worth Star-Telegram* or Cynthia Tucker for the *Atlanta Constitution* who are on the alert for news items on trends affecting the well-being of Americans.

- *Draw on informal interviews.* Talk about your subject with friends; turn to insiders. For example, when writing about strained community relations of local police, arrange informal interviews with a relative who is a police officer or with a member of a police review board. Talk with members of the community. Talk with a social worker or a local minister. People will often talk eloquently at length about a subject close to their hearts.
- *Be prepared to do informal or formal research.* Especially on topics of current controversy, say to yourself: "Let me check this out." The following passage by a student researcher puts the current arguments over medical marijuana in a historical context:

> Several states have legalized the use of marijuana to alleviate the suffering of cancer patients and AIDS patients. The editor of the prestigious *New England Journal of Medicine* endorsed the medical use of the drug, calling the campaign against medical marijuana by a timid administration foolish and inhumane. Actually, the criminalizing of marijuana is historically a recent development. In early America, hemp plants were grown on the plantations of our ancestors. George Washington said, "Make the most of the Indian hemp and grow it everywhere." The medical use of marijuana was unchallenged in this country until 1937, when a Prohibition-minded Congress pushed a ban on the mixing of marijuana and alcohol. In 1941, marijuana was removed from the United States Pharmacopoeia and National Formulary, becoming fully illegal. Henry Anslinger's film *Reefer Madness* demonized marijuana as the root of violent crimes, psychosis, and mental deterioration.

1c.2 Note-Taking ***Develop the note-taking habit.*** Build up a file of useful data, striking news items, and excerpts from important articles. Experienced writers are always on the lookout for promising material. They clip articles from newspapers and newsmagazines. They download material from the Internet. They keep up a file of quotable quotes. Start the habit of saving material for future use. Buy or borrow a book that everyone is talking about. Talk to insiders and jot down notes on what they said. Keep up a diary, reading journal, or viewing log.

Here are some sample notes from early in a student writer's exploration of an issue that was a major influence in his growing up:

SAMPLE NOTES:

ideal and reality

beautiful words at cousin's wedding: "till death do us part"

"forsaking all others"

"in sickness and in health"

"man shall not put asunder"

(note: no more wedding march from *Lohengrin*—it's from a "pagan" tale)

check current stats—1 out of 2 marriages end in divorce? (what are the latest figures?)

the high cost of divorce: going to court, lawyer's fees

mother going to work: coming home from school to an empty house and empty

refrigerator

the ongoing hostility: remarried father, badmouthing the other side, children caught in the middle

article by psychologist in Sunday edition of the newspaper: claims that children from split families are more "resilient" than we think and develop "resources of inner strength"—check this out?

1d Using Prewriting Techniques

Use prewriting techniques to generate usable material.

Try techniques that experienced writers use to explore a subject. They have ways to overcome **writer's block**—the tendency to stare at a blank computer screen or to crumple up successive sheets with a few scribbled notes. They have ways to jog their memories. They have ways to map or chart a subject.

1d.1 Brainstorming ***Jot down any ideas, images, or associations that the topic brings to mind.*** Leave the sorting out and following up for later. The human mind works by association—one thing leads to another. Perhaps you believe in fitness but have also recently become concerned with the downside of the current fitness craze. If you mentally push the fitness button, memories and images are likely to tumble out. Try not to edit at this point—let anything that could possibly be related come to the surface:

BRAINSTORMING:

fitness videos at video stores

(started with Jane Fonda and Cher?)

top models with slender bodies and firm tummies

Claudia Schiffer

exercisers and muscle builders advertised on TV

commercials focus on tight buns

health clubs, gyms with high-tech machines

space-age consoles on treadmill

diet Coke, diet Pepsi, diet Seven-up, diet-everything

counting calories

health-wise cookbooks

fat-free Polish sausage

fat-free margarine (health risks of substitutes?)

diet pills—appetite suppressants

crash diets ("60 pounds off in four weeks")

Look over your list and add to it as other material comes to mind: headlines, slogans, commercials, personal testimony of fitness aficionados among your friends. While you are still adding to your preliminary idea inventory, the material may begin to sort itself out. Perhaps you could write a paper with two major parts. You sketch things out in your mind as follows:

Keeping Fit?

- You will first give credit to the *positive side* of the fitness movement. It has made us a more health-conscious nation, with a healthier less fatty diet and an emphasis on exercise and a less sedentary lifestyle.
- You will then warn of the *negative side*. When fitness becomes an obsession, it can endanger our health with crash diets and dubious substitutes. It can make young women neurotically self-conscious about weight. It can lead to diets deficient in essential nutrients and trace elements.

1d.2 **Clustering** *Use clustering or other mapping techniques to follow up connections.* **Clustering** is a mapping technique that traces lines of thought branching out from a central word or concept. For instance, the core idea of "flowers" might first make you think "candlelight dinners—courtship—romance." Then another line of thought might make you think "spring in the South—blooms—wilting in autumn—life cycle—growth and death." A third line of thought might make you trace what it takes to *grow* flowers: "care—pruning—pests—spraying—being a good gardener." Your cluster mapping the symbolic meaning of flowers might look like this:

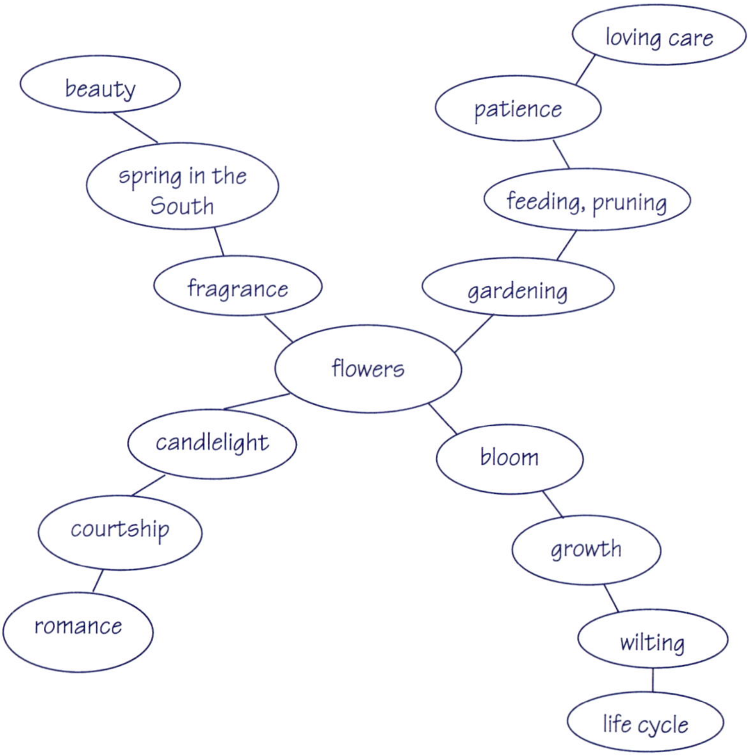

Writers use the clustering technique to generate the thought map for papers, memos, speeches, and advertising campaigns. If you were editing a newsletter for a florists' association, you might use the flower cluster to write an editorial explaining basic points about flowers:

1 The beauty of flowers is an antidote to being stressed out in the pursuit of the bottom line. Flowers reminds us of our capacity for beauty and romance.

2 Flowers are beautiful but they are not permanent. They blossom and eventually they wilt. They go through a cycle, like everything in life. We cherish them because we know they are not for keeps.

3 Wildflowers bloom by the side of the road as if by a miracle. But it usually takes patience and care to make something beautiful grow. The gardener's art is needed—planting, weeding, pruning, fighting pests.

YOUR TURN 3 Mapping the Topic

Do a brainstorming exercise or a clustering exercise on one of the following topics: fads, rap, diets, holidays, cliques, buddy movies, malls, fraternities/ sororities, beauty contests, talk shows, rock. Then write a passage using the material from the exercise.

1d.3 Discovery Frames

Use or adapt a discovery frame. A **discovery frame** is a set of questions that help you generate material on your topic. A computer program for generating a paper on a current issue might lead you through a set of questions like the following:

DISCOVERY FRAME:

1 *What is the issue?* What much-publicized recent incident, striking statistic, or much-discussed publication could dramatize the issue for your reader?

2 *What is the focus of current media coverage?* What are typical current headlines? What comes up again and again in current editorials, favorite columnists, or political cartoons?

3 *What prejudices or misconceptions cloud the issue?* What comes up again and again in angry talk show chatter? What does Rush Limbaugh say?

4 *What are the experts saying?* Who are the experts or insiders on this issue? Do they agree? Or do their opinions divide along party lines?

5 *What are current test cases?* What current cases are or have been before the courts? What election results throw light on popular sentiment or trends in public opinion?

6 *Where has the issue touched your own experience?* What do you know from firsthand observation? Where has the issued touched the lives of people close to you?

7 *What lies ahead?*

What material would fill in the slots when this discovery frame is applied to a current issue? Suppose a reporter for a campus newspaper is investigating the current state of the feminist movement. Has the women's movement slowed down? Filling in the slots, she may start to feed into her article material like the following:

Feminism: Backlash or Second Wave?

1 DRAMATIZING THE ISSUE
Susan Faludi's *Backlash* documented changes in public opinion reversing many of the gains of the women's movement. . . .

2 CURRENT MEDIA COVERAGE
Newsmagazines have headlines asking "Is Feminism Dead?" Columnists talk about "postfeminism." . . .

3 POPULAR PREJUDICE
Talk shows feature angry male callers claiming to have been passed over in favor of women and minorities. . . .

4 EXPERT OPINION
Journalists like Barbara Ehrenreich ask whether feminism has been a middle-class movement with not enough outreach to working class ("pink-collar") women. . . .

5 PERSONAL EXPERIENCE
On campus, controversies over sexual harassment policies have caused hostility and distrust. . . .

6 FUTURE PROSPECTS
Long-range positive trends: increased media coverage of women in sports; men getting used to working under women managers; women achieving parity in enrollment in medical schools and law schools. . . .

YOUR TURN 4 **Using a Discovery Frame**

Use or adapt one of the above discovery frames to generate material on one of the following topics: spamming, globalization, recycling, harassment, hate speech, electronic shopping.

1e Structuring Your Paper

Sort out your material and push toward a thesis.

How are you going to organize your paper? Can you lay out your material in such a way that it will make sense to your readers? Even while gathering your material, you will be sorting it out in a rough preliminary fashion.

1e.1 Using Informal Outlines *Use an informal outline to help you organize your thinking.* Jot down key ideas in a rough preliminary order to see how your paper might take shape. Suppose you are working on a paper about your family history. In your multigenerational family, each generation seems to have a different outlook and lifestyle, reflecting their background and their experiences. As you look over your notes, you find that your material begins to sort itself out under three major headings:

ROUGH NOTES:

the mother: philosophy of independence and moving on to new opportunities, of taking risks

the great-grandmother: like other traditional Japanese American wives, she came as a picture bride from Japan. Bitter because she had to leave her country and marry an unknown and unloving spouse

grandmother (and other older relatives): philosophy of hard work and making do, accepting what is. Cautious and tough like other people who have struggled with hardship and poverty

Your first rough **scratch outline** might look like this:

SCRATCH OUTLINE:

independent self-reliant mother

great-grandmother: the old-country tradition

grandmother's generation: an older America—struggling with hardship

This outline shows that you were struck by the strong contrast between your Americanized modern mother and the more rigid traditional culture. Obviously, the grandmother's generation represents a transitional stage—a link between today and the more distant traditional past. So you start reordering your material, with a definite preview of three major stages. An adjusted **working outline** might look like this. You already include a tentative thesis that would sum up the point of your paper as a whole:

WORKING OUTLINE:

A Tale of Three Generations

TRIAL THESIS: I revel in my family's history because each generation has contributed something important to who I am.

I The old country heritage: struggling against tradition

II An older America: working with what you have

III Americans today: striving for independence

1e.2 **Pushing Toward a Thesis** *Move from a trial thesis to a definitive thesis statement.* Aim at a thesis that will sum up what you have found. What will be the message of your paper as a whole? Try not to start with a ready-made thesis that remains set in cement regardless of where your evidence points.

For instance, you may have followed news coverage of confrontations and court cases involving charges of excessive force used by police. You have material from spokespersons for the community, from ministers, and from families of victims. On the other hand, you pull together the justifications or the defense offered by the officers involved, by police departments, or by an officers' union or association. You look at final determinations by a review board or verdicts in the courts. A rough **working outline** for a paper is already taking shape:

WORKING OUTLINE:

The Police on Trial

I widely publicized charges of police abuses
II defenses offered by the police
III final verdicts by review boards or the courts

What is the point that your paper as a whole will try to prove? What will be your **trial thesis?** Depending on which way most of your evidence points, your tentative thesis statement might be one of the following:

TRIAL THESIS: In spite of denials by police departments and officers' associations, **too many cases of abusive behavior are well-documented.**

TRIAL THESIS: In spite of widely publicized instances of abuses, **it is unfair to stereotype police officers because of abusive behavior by a few individuals.**

Class discussion of the trial thesis may cause you to take factors into account that might make the thesis sound too simple or too unfair. For instance, is it true that newspapers will splash the charges over the front page while reports of officers being cleared are somewhere in the back?

ADJUSTED THESIS: **Although sensational reporting exaggerates charges of police brutality,** too many cases of abusive behavior are well-documented.

The crucial opening section of the paper is firming up: The pointed **title** would bring the issue into focus. An **introduction** highlighting a dramatic recent incident could lead up to the thesis. Then major sections of the paper could present first one side and then the other and lead up to a balanced verdict.

1e.3 From Outline to Draft *Use your working outline as a rough road map as you start writing.* Ideally, you will feed in solid chunks of material from your notes—adapting them as needed and changing everything to complete sentences. For instance, you select and fit in key statistics. You excerpt and fit in quotations you copied earlier. Remember a few points of advice:

- *Keep pushing ahead.* Most editors and writing coaches advise you to keep moving. Don't be a perfectionist at this stage. Don't get bogged down because a key example seems to be missing or because you don't have exactly the right word for a key concept. Come back and attend to it later.
- *Adjust your working outline as needed.* As you move along, you may find that an entry later in your outline should really come first to help explain what follows. Or one of your planned sections may prove to be a detour, distracting from your main argument. By definition, a working outline is subject to revision and adjustment.
- *Feel free to jump ahead or move around.* Some writers start at the beginning, systematically filling in each slot in their outlines. However, others work up first the parts for which they have the best material or that they care about most. Then they fill in the missing links or the more routine parts. Also, many experienced writers write the title, the introduction, and the conclusion last. This way, these can truly lead up to and wind up the paper as a whole—as it actually took shape.

Suppose a student writer has been collecting material on the subject of road rage. She read a cover story in a newsmagazine on how ordinary citizens turn angry and violent in today's congested urban traffic. She has been taking notes under several main headings: How real is the problem? (What statistics, expert testimony, court cases, or local news reporting attest to the extent of the problem?) What are the causes? (Is the young male as the chief menace on the road just a popular stereotype? Can we identify major reasons for growing irrational and violent motorists' behavior?) What is the answer or the remedy? As she starts writing her first draft, her working outline looks like this:

WORKING OUTLINE:

Road Rage

I. Road Rage Headlines
II. Documenting the Trend
  A. AAA statistics
  B. Expert Testimony
III. Explaining the Reasons
  A. Popular Stereotype
  B. Real Reasons
    1. Worsening Traffic Congestion
    2. Growing Time Pressure
    3. Illusion of Power
    4. Defensive Driving Mentality
IV. Changing Our Driving Habits

YOUR TURN 5 A Paper for Peer Review

As you read the first draft of the road rage paper, how successfully does it follow the working outline? Prepare notes to answer the questions that follow the paper.

FIRST DRAFT:

Do We Turn Psychotic behind the Wheel?

Angry driver forces station wagon off the road. Elderly man smashes another man's knees. Attorney attacks pregnant woman. These all sound like extraordinary newspaper headlines, and they are. However, the headlines are not the frightening thing. The frightening thing is who committed these crimes, with what, and why. Ordinary people committed all the crimes. They took these actions in anger, because another person either cut them off, blocked traffic, or bumped cars with them. It seems that many Americans are part of a new driving trend. This dangerous and life-threatening trend is Road Rage. More and more American drivers are taking out their frustrations on other drivers on the road. Taking to the wheel of a car today can become an issue of life and death.

You may think that the first incidents mentioned are extreme and maybe they are, but the ordinary is just as frightening. The American Automotive Association (AAA) did a major study on road rage and aggressive driving. The statistics are appalling. The American Automotive Association defines "aggressive driving" as "events in which an angry or impatient driver tries to kill or injure another driver over a traffic dispute." The AAA found that the rate of aggressive driving has risen by 51 percent since 1990. In addition, 37 percent of offenders used firearms against other drivers, 28 percent used other weapons, and 35 percent used their cars as weapons. Meanwhile, the U.S. Department of Transportation found that two-thirds of road fatalities are at least partially caused by aggressive driving. This clearly shows that aggressive driving may be moving towards becoming the norm rather than the exception. Sandra Ball-Rokeach, who codirects the Media and Injury Prevention Program at the University of Southern California, agrees. She says, "Aggressive driving is now the most common way of driving. It's not just a few crazies—it's a sub-culture of driving."

Why are ordinary people driven to this outrageous behavior? According to the AAA's profile, aggressive drivers are "relatively young, poorly educated males who have criminal records, histories of violence, and drug or alcohol problems." However, regular drivers are showing road rage as well, but in a less violent way. The attorney who hit the pregnant woman because she bumped her car into his clearly does not fit the AAA's profile. Dr. John Larson, a stress expert who specializes in road rage, says, "Everyone is capable of road rage." There are emotional and demographic reasons for a regular driver becoming enraged.

The first and main reason is the number of drivers on the road. Traffic has gotten worse in the last years. Since 1987, the number of miles of roads has increased a mere 1 percent. The number of miles driven has increased by a large 35 percent. The Federal Highway Administration found in a recent study that 70 percent of urban freeways are clogged during rush hour. The traffic jams are not just in the cities. There is an increasing number of workers commuting from one suburb to another suburb. Thus the suburbs are just as congested with traffic. Also, so many people are breaking for lunch that the lunch hour has become a third rush hour. More women in the workplace have caused the number of commuters to increase. Among women the number of drivers increased by 84 percent. But the main problem is that fewer and fewer people rely on public transportation. An amazing 91.4 percent of people drive to work, and carpooling has declined rapidly. So what we have is an increasing number of cars on the roadways. University of Hawaii traffic psychology professor Leon James put it best when he said, "There are simply more cars—and more behaviors—to deal with."

The second reason is stress and time limits. More and more people are leaving less time for driving. Americans are getting more pressed for time, and the roads are more congested. This creates a dangerous situation. We want everything to go the way we plan and when it does not go by our plan, we get hostile. We are too stressed and have too little time to be bothered by incompetent drivers. Dr. Larson says, "Drivers tend to put themselves in a stress bind by constantly trying

YOUR TURN 5 *(continued)*

to beat the clock on their trips. . . . Everything that interferes with our self-imposed time goals becomes an object of frustration and potential rage."

Another reason is that we feel supremely safe and in control in our cars. The larger, heavier vehicles, especially sports utility vehicles, make the driver feel invulnerable. With the false sense of security, the driver is more likely to take risks because the smaller vehicle will be intimidated. The driver has the "illusion [that] he's alone and master, dislocated from the other drivers." The drivers do not realize that it is an actual person in the other car. This attitude leads to the belief that it is a "two-dimensional" world where the other person is not a real person with feelings, but a "jerk."

A final reason may be the emphasis on "defensive driving." Driver's education classes, both for new drivers and old drivers, teach "defensive driving" as the best way to drive. The problem is that defensive driving "teaches an attitude of constant awareness, teaches us to assume the worst, and treat all drivers the same. It's a negative survival technique."

Incidents of violent driving have been increasing about 7 percent a year. To overcome road rage, Dr. Larson suggests that we need to move towards more positive supportive driving. We need to think of other drivers as fellow motorists, subject to the same delays we are. When we think of other drivers as fellow humans, we realize that behavior that is not okay at home or in the neighborhood is not okay in the car either. We can take our minds off the commute by listening to career training tapes or talk radio. If we take a deep breath and relax when caught in a traffic jam, we will eventually get to the place we are going, but we will not get there at all if we wind up in a body bag instead.

How would you answer the following questions about the road rage paper?

1 What does the title accomplish?
2 How does the introduction lead up to the main point of the paper?
3 What sentence best sums up the writer's thesis?
4 How well does the paper as a whole support the thesis?
5 How persuasive is the documentation of the trend?
6 How convincing is the analysis of the causes?
7 What examples are strongest and which seem weakest?
8 What sources are most helpful and which least?

9 How strong or convincing is the conclusion?

10 Do you make a good audience for this paper—why or why not?

OPTIONS FOR WRITING 3 Becoming a Trend Watcher

Prepare a first draft of a trend-watcher's paper. Draw on both your previous experience and current observation. Push toward a central idea or thesis. Bring in detailed supporting examples. Work out an overall plan that your readers can follow. Choose an issue that you think would be of concern to your fellow students.

1 Is hate speech on the increase? Do you hear hateful or abusive language? Should students and faculty be concerned about it? Have you observed attempts to counteract it or curb it? How successful are they?

2 Is romance or young love making a comeback in the movies or in television programs?

3 Are today's young males more sensitive than a previous generation? Are they more attuned to the feelings and needs of others? Or is the new sensitive male mostly a media image?

4 Do people you know tend to be hostile toward the police? Is there a tendency toward mutual antagonism between police officers and the young? What explains it? Should anything be done about it?

5 Are public manners deteriorating? Do you see thoughtless or loutish behavior? Does it represent a general trend, or is it limited to certain groups or individuals?

6 Is race an issue on your campus? Are young Americans becoming more race-conscious or less race-conscious? Do they object to racial classifications? Or are racial divisions becoming stronger?

7 Is there a trend toward unisex clothing among young Americans today? Does everyone dress alike? Does it matter? What does it show about the current generation?

8 Are Asian Americans a model minority? Do they have the fast track in education and business?

9 Has there been a backlash against the women's movement? Leading feminists claim that in some areas of American life the movement's gains are endangered or reversed. Look at one major area of interest to you. Do you see evidence of this trend?

10 How do and your friends feel about the media cult of celebrities? How widespread is it? What explains it? Does it do any harm? Are there celebrities you admire? Do you care about their lives and careers?

1f Revising and Rethinking

Allow time for rereading, revising, and rethinking.

How much time and effort are you going to put into revision? Experienced writers produce rough copy, and then they rewrite until they get it right. When you look over an early draft, keep two questions in mind. What is already in good shape? (What is worth keeping

WRITING ESSENTIALS — Common Revision Tasks

Writing teachers ask for more than cosmetic revision, which only fixes a few surface defects. Here are some typical revision tasks:

STRENGTHENING THE BEGINNING

- sharpening a dull title
- livening up a routine introduction
- leading up more directly to your thesis
- doing more to establish your credibility as a writer

SHORING UP WEAK PARTS OF YOUR PAPER

- adding needed details
- filling in gaps in your evidence
- filling in essential background
- quoting authoritative testimony from experts or insiders
- doing more to define a difficult concept
- explaining a current buzzword

RETHINKING YOUR OVERALL PLAN

- doing more to find common ground early in the paper
- shifting a debatable or controversial point to later in your argument
- doing more to counter possible objections

STRAIGHTENING OUT APPARENT CONTRADICTIONS

- adjusting your thesis to reflect second thoughts
- making sure you did not say one thing first and something else later
- reconciling a strong initial claim and a weak conclusion

LEAVING YOUR READER WITH A STRONG FINAL IMPRESSION

- going beyond a mere rehash of points you already made
- trying to end with realistic suggestions for constructive change
- saving a clinching example or strong quotation for the last

and building up?) What needs work? (What still needs to be done? What are the weak links?) Basically, you strengthen the promising parts of your paper, and you shore up what is weak or fill in what is missing.

1f.1 Learning from Feedback *Profit from feedback by your instructor and fellow students.* Writers do not work in a vacuum. They respond to what others think and say. They bounce ideas off co-workers, roommates, and acquaintances. In the world of work, memos, proposals, and reports often go through several rewrites in response to input from colleagues, supervisors, or editors. In a writing class with a workshop format, you are likely to do one or more rewrites, responding to feedback from an instructor or to peer reviews from fellow students or both. Ideally, feedback serves a double purpose: First, it points out what is good or promising in your paper. It let you know what is worth keeping or building up. However, it should also alert you to problems that need attention. Ideally, it gives you specific pointers on how to improve your work.

INSTRUCTOR'S COMMENTARY Instructors will often provide a **running commentary** asking for clarification, backup, or additional explanation. They will nudge you to look for striking examples, authoritative statistics, expert testimony, or authentic firsthand experience. Here are some sample queries:

> Immigrants today, like my parents long ago, don't come here to freeload off Uncle Sam; they come here to feed their families.
> (COMMENT: How do we know this, really? Include **personal testimony** from your parents or other immigrants?)
>
> Coming into this country is much more of an obstacle race than most people think, involving often a tremendous hassle of paperwork and red tape.
> (COMMENT: Give one or two striking **case histories** of people who went through this process?)
>
> Immigrants are often the most motivated people in the United States.
> (COMMENT: Can you give some official **statistics** on their earnings or the taxes they pay?)

Pay special attention to instructor comments like the following:

> INSTRUCTOR'S FEEDBACK:
>
> *Gossip journalism* is a good term for what you are after. However, you need a striking example of "gossip journalism"

early in your paper. Otherwise this may sound like an unsupported accusation—from someone who is prejudiced against journalists.

You need real examples of news coverage—both the serious stuff and the "sleaze." Quote typical headlines for both kinds? Then give the gist of a few key articles. This way, you give your readers a chance to see and judge for themselves.

PEER REVIEWS Reactions from your fellow students may please you, surprise you, or anger you. They will make you more *audience-conscious*: Something you thought was clear or obvious may not be clear to someone from a different background. Something you thought was funny may not be amusing to someone with a different perspective. Here are some examples of peer comments:

PEER REVIEWS:

1 It's hard to tell what your main point is. You seem to be hedging from the beginning, saying that there is a whole "range of opinion" on the subject. So what are the opinions or viewpoints that we need to take seriously? Is one opinion as good as another? And where do *you* stand and why?

2 I think you belittle the whole issue of sexual harassment on campus. It's no longer good enough to say that "boys will be boys." If a "boy" thinks that insulting or demeaning behavior is permissible, he may find himself subject to expulsion or probation. I think you need to look at some recent test cases either here or on other campuses and try to listen to both sides. Maybe look at some recent court decisions that try to define sexual harassment.

1f.2 Serving as Peer Reviewer *Provide an audience for other student writers.* As a peer reviewer, you help them gauge the response of a cross section of readers to their writing. Formats for peer review vary: You may be asked to participate in class discussion of photocopied student papers. Or you may work in a small group, rotating early drafts for peer response. Or students in your group may share early drafts by e-mail. As your turn comes to study each paper, you may be asked to fill in a response sheet in which you answer a set of questions.

A critical response to others' writing requires you to evaluate what you read. Writers love gracious or appreciative comments. However, welcome as they are, these often do not provide specific pointers for future work. Neither do nit-picking comments by readers who focus only on minor points or inaccuracies. A good critic identifies both strong points and weak points and suggests necessary changes or improvements.

WRITING ESSENTIALS

Questions for Peer Review

Your instructor may ask you to answer questions like the following about an early draft of a paper by a fellow student:

1 ***What was the writer's purpose?*** What did the writer want to do? How successful was the writer in doing what he or she set out to do?

2 ***Does the paper as a whole have a point?*** Does it have a thesis? Where is it most clearly or effectively stated?

3 ***Does the paper have a clear overall plan?*** Where or how do you become aware of it? Can you map major sections or major stages? Do you think the plan could be strengthened or improved?

4 ***How well does the paper support major points?*** Where were examples, supporting material, or quoted material strong or helpful? Do any examples or quotations stick in your mind? Will you remember any striking images or comparisons?

5 ***Where was supporting material weak or missing?*** Were there unconvincing examples? Were there gaps in the evidence?

6 ***How effective are title, introduction, and conclusion?*** Do they help bring the topic into focus, arouse your interest, and leave you with a strong impression?

7 ***Does the writer seem fair-minded?*** Does the paper weigh evidence fairly, or does it tend to leap to conclusions or make wild charges?

8 ***How well does the paper convey its message?*** Was it easy or hard to read? Was it dull or lively? Was it too chummy, too stiff, or just right?

9 ***What did the paper do for you as the reader?*** What did you learn from this paper? What puzzled or confused you?

10 ***Who would make a good audience for this paper?*** Do *you* make a good audience for this paper? Why or why not? Does it seem close to your own experience or far removed from it?

1g Writing/Rewriting Guidelines

rev

Review basic ways to strengthen your paper.

There are no one-size-fits-all instructions for writing or for rewriting. However, some issues come up again and again in teachers' comments and in peer review. Study the following guidelines to help you focus on things that often need attention. Which would help you build on your strong points? Which would help you strengthen the weak parts of a paper?

1g.1 Effective Title *Make your title both informative and inviting.* Seeing your original title, the reader may wonder: What is this paper about? What is going to be the main point? And is this going to be a lively or dull paper?

TOO GENERIC: Immigration Today
(*What about* today's immigration?)

POINTED: **Immigrants Take the Blame**

The New Immigrants: Seeking the Better Life

Illegals: Closing the Gates

✓ ***EDITOR'S TIP:*** Professional writers today often combine a title and subtitle to include *key words* and key information that will guide readers to the article during a computer search:

TRACEABLE: **Mason's "Shiloh": Muscle Building in the New South**

1g.2 Pointed Introduction *Use your introduction to bring the issue to life.* Are you providing an effective lead-in to your main points? Rewrite colorless general introductions. Dramatize the issue by starting with an eye-opening example. Or start with a strong thought-provoking quotation. Or start with a strong opening sentence pointing up a revealing contradiction. Compare the following "before-and-after" introductions to a paper on trash journalism:

WEAK OPENING:

For many there is still a line between the mainstream media and the tabloid media. We expect serious news when we open the daily newspaper or the current issue of a newsmagazine. . . .

DRAMATIC OPENING EXAMPLE:

KIDNAP BREAKTHROUGH—NEW EVIDENCE LINKS MOM TO RANSOM NOTE!!!! This headline from the *National Enquirer* illustrates the kind of tabloid journalism that catches the attention of over 15 million readers. . . .

STRONG STARTER QUOTE:

Is there still a difference between mainstream journalism and tabloid journalism? **"Instead of beating their entertainment and propaganda competitors, many journalists are joining them,"** says Ellen Hume, former professor of journalism at Harvard. **"Substance doesn't sell."**

POINTED OPENING SENTENCE :

Today the sex lives of public figures and sportscasters are front-page news, crowding out news about peace and war. . . .

1g.3 Strong Thesis *Spell out your thesis.* Let your readers know early in your paper where you stand. For instance, don't just say there are issues. Sum up what the most important ones are. Better yet, zero in on the most important one and take a stand.

EVASIVE:

There are many pros and cons to this issue. Yet until a fair solution or possibly a compromise has been reached, illegal immigration will continue to park the emotions of both sides, thus leaving them in a fierce battle of opposing views.
(There are pros and cons on most issues. Where do *you* stand? Early in your paper, give more of a hint or preview of your own position. What kind of compromise do you have in mind?)

STRONGER:

Some would close our borders; other would leave them open to offer refuge to the poor and oppressed. Of the estimated twenty million people who have come into the country over the past thirty years, many were admitted in the name of reuniting families. **A fair compromise may be to limit the reuniting of families to members of an immigrant's immediate family and to families able to support the newcomers when they need help.**

1g.4 Careful Generalizations

Scale back sweeping generalizations. Don't imply that *all* Americans think alike. Don't imply that all members of your generation, of the armed forces, or of the opposite sex think the same. Try to avoid blanket charges—painting all members of a group with the same brush. Scale back general statements that would be hard to defend:

SWEEPING:

In the past, America has welcomed newcomers with open arms.
(But historically haven't there been periods of hostility toward the newcomers?)

SCALED DOWN:

This country has experienced cycles of anti-immigrant sentiment. There has been anti-Irish feeling, anti-German resentment, and anti-Asian prejudice. Even so, **millions of newcomers became an organic part of American society in the span of one or two generations.**

1g.5 Streamlined Organization

Streamline your overall plan. Make your reader see that your paper moves clearly from A to B to C. At an early stage, the seams are likely to show: You may have fed in material that has not been fully integrated into your overall plan. There may be awkward backtracking or repetition, confusing the reader.

Ask yourself: Can I sum up the main points in my proposal or the steps in my argument as a three-point or perhaps a five-point program? For instance, on the occasion of the 150th anniversary of the pioneering feminist meeting at Seneca Falls, you may have found that discussions of the current state of the women's movement touch on many interrelated issues. These range from corporations being asked to provide child care and maternity leave to confusing or contradictory court decisions on workplace harassment. However, just as earlier feminists concentrated on such key issues as the right to divorce and the right to vote, you may decide to focus a new "Declaration of Sentiments and Resolutions" on three high-priority issues:

Seneca Falls Revisited

Priorities for the new century:

1 equal representation (greater participation in the political process)
2 economic equality (equal access and equal salaries for work of equal value)
3 reproductive freedom (free choice in family planning)

1g.6 dev

Strong Supporting Detail *Follow up your points.*

Back them up with striking examples, revealing facts, thought-provoking figures, or firsthand personal observation. If a point is worth making, it is worth following up. Inexperienced writers make a point and move on. Experienced writers make a point and drive it home.

UNDEVELOPED:

I spent a year in Mexico as an exchange student and admired the Mexican culture.
(*What* did you come to admire about the Mexican culture?)

FOLLOWED UP:

I spent a year in Mexico and came to admire the Mexican culture. **The University of Mexico is the oldest university in the Western hemisphere and older than Harvard. The Mexicans threw off European colonialism a few decades after the American colonies and have a fierce pride in their revolutionary history. The great Mexican painters and muralists—Diego Rivera, Frida Kahlo, David Siqueiros—are known around the world. . . .**

✓ ***EDITOR'S TIP:*** Check for *uneven development* of major points. In a first draft, you may have done a good job when you felt confident and had much usable material. However, you may have skimped when parts of the topic were new or confusing to you. Similarly, try to be evenhanded when taking on objections or counterarguments. If you gave only a very abbreviated version of opposing arguments, remember fair-minded readers who expect something closer to "equal-time" treatment.

1g.7 trans

Effective Transitions *Use transitions to build the bridge from one part of your paper to the next.*

Transitions help your reader follow your train of thought. They provide signals that say in effect, "I am now going on to an especially convincing example" or "I am now going to deal with an objection that is often raised" or "I am now going to discuss an important exception to the general trend." Often the way an idea fits into your argument is clear without the need for an added signal. However, well-structured writing often provides a network of links like the following:

Making It to the Big Time

Big-time college sports are often touted as the road to fame and fortune for the players. **However,** at least some of the colleges that are abandoning big-money sports are doing so for the good of the student athlete. . . .

Most important of all, the student athlete often does not really get an education. The pressure of having to win at all costs often leaves too little time, energy, and concentration for academic work. At some institutions, not even 50 percent of the athletes graduate. . . .

Equally deceptive is the promise of glory and admiration from grateful fans. Newspapers play up scandals concerning petty favors—meals, extra trips home, . . .

While players are suspended for accepting small favors, coaches and administrators profit hugely from the big-money sports. Coaches earn more than college presidents and sign lucrative contracts for endorsements. . . .

Finally, while recruiters dangle the lure of a future in the pros, the percentage of college athletes who actually make it is very small. . . .

✓ ***EDITOR'S TIP:*** Replace wordy, roundabout transitions with simpler, pointed phrases:

WORDY: An important example of this situation occurs when zoning decisions take many years. . . .

DIRECT: **For example**, zoning decisions may take many years. . . .

WRITING ESSENTIALS

Transitions: The Missing Link

Transitions may be whole sentences, short paragraphs, or brief connecting words and phrases. Here is a list of common transitional words and phrases. Many of these are used both between and within paragraphs:

GIVING EXAMPLES:	for example, for instance, to illustrate; An especially striking example was . . .
ADDITIONAL SUPPORT:	too, also, moreover, furthermore, similarly; Another more recent case in point is . . .
LOGICAL RESULT:	therefore, as a result, consequently, hence; So we must conclude . . .
RAISING OBJECTIONS:	but, however, nevertheless, on the contrary; In spite of these claims, the evidence shows . . .
EMPHASIZING A POINT:	indeed, in fact, first and foremost, above all; It is no exaggeration to say . . .
GRANTING A POINT:	admittedly, granted, to be sure; While it is true that . . .
WEIGHING CHOICES:	on the one hand, on the other hand; Seen from a different point of view . . .
SUMMING UP:	to sum up, in short, in conclusion

1g.8 Responsible Language *Check for putdowns and name-calling.* Abuses may at times call for strong language—provided you are prepared to support your charges. However, calling your opponents names may only make them more determined. It may also alienate readers who want arguments, not abuse.

> This is a completely ridiculous proposal because . . .
> (Are all those who disagree with you unintelligent or uninformed?)

> Many sexual harassment cases are obviously brought by lawyers trying to make a buck.
> (Why badmouth a whole profession?)

1g.9 **Lively Style** *Use fresh imaginative language.* Use fresh imaginative comparisons to bring places, ideas, and events to life. Do without **clichés**—tired overused expressions like "variety is the spice of life" or "practice makes perfect."

DULL: The call of the coyote is sad and lonely.

LIVELY: The call of the coyote is **lovesick and melancholy, like a good country song.**

DULL: I am known for my assertive personality and extremely strong temper.

LIVELY: My sister describes me as a **fireball** because of my assertive personality and strong temper.

1g.10 **Strong Conclusion** *Strengthen a weak conclusion.* Are you concluding the paper on a strong note? Or is your conclusion a weak repetition of what you just said? If your paper seems to run out of energy at the end, try to finish with a strong punchline. Or save a striking recent example for the last. Or wind up with a clincher quote.

CLINCHER QUOTE:

In the words of Lester Crystal, executive producer at NBC and four-time Emmy Award winner, **"Despite the success of 'tabloid TV' news programs, no one can deny that quality broadcast news accounts for a considerable share of high ratings. The ranks of television news overflow with internationally recognized, widely respected journalists."**

1h Tracking a Sample Paper

Watch a well-developed paper take shape.

Make use of opportunities to see a fellow writer's paper develop and take final shape. Track the following paper from an early draft through feedback and rewrites. What suggestions would you expect classmates reading the first draft to make in a peer review session or in written comments?

FIRST DRAFT:

Divorce

My story is a familiar one in America today. Many of the people I know come from split homes. I understand their feelings and what they have gone through. A large percentage of marriages in this country end in divorce. My parents were divorced after nineteen years, after many quarrels. You might say their marriage was not made in heaven. My mother was religious, and my father had a terrible temper. Often the neighbors came over to see if we were all right after hearing his yelling. However, he did not really hurt me nor my mother physically.

I still remember when my mother announced that my father had left for good. I had never seen such a glazed look in my mother's eyes. Communication had definitely broken down. This was just the beginning of the long drawn out court battles. My mother began working full-time and so I came home to an empty house and often times an empty refrigerator. I grew up without a father in the house, and my lack of social skills showed it. I felt hurt when my father started dating another woman. He eventually remarried and took on two stepchildren.

As the hostility between my parents continued, I often felt caught in the middle. My father had moved away from us to be closer to his dental practice. I saw my dad for maybe one weekend out of the month. I became a messenger between my parents, who never really talked directly to each other. I heard my father bash my mother for talking to their mutual friends and his business contacts. I heard my mother bash my father for leaving his kids and destroying our family. I got yelled at, by both of them, for defending the other. I learned never to say a word, just listen.

I found out later that my father had himself grown up in a broken home with a father who beat his kids more than he hugged them.

I have a brother who shared in many of the same experiences. We became very close and felt we could trust each other. When we were separated, I would call him up at all hours of the night and complain about what my mother said or what my father said. He did not back down to either one of my parents, and he always took care of me. We were the only ones we could trust in our family.

In listening to suggestions during a peer review session or in reading written comments, the writer found himself agreeing especially with comments like the following:

PEER REVIEW 1

I especially liked what you said about your brother and how you two were close and handled the situation together. Maybe you should bring the brother in earlier—he seems to come in as an afterthought after the main story has been told. At first I was put off by your catchall title and a slow start. Maybe you should try to make the people more real, to make your readers care about them more. For instance, tell the story of when your mother made the announcement: Where were you? How did everyone act? You really seem to care for your mother, but she doesn't become very real as a person.

PEER REVIEW 2

You make the reader sympathize with your feelings during the divorce, and many readers are going to remember similar bitter feelings and disappointment. I guess I expected to hear more about how to deal with this kind of situation. What really was the upshot? I think you need to tell more about the divorce settlement and custody and so on to make the situation real and to help the readers imagine themselves in your place. I think for people in a similar situation the main question would be: How did you cope? Are you one of the typical "children of divorce"?

PEER REVIEW 3

For me, your title and your introduction have a real déja-vu feeling. Aren't readers going to say: What else is new? Everyone has heard the bad news and the statistics over and over. What is new or different about your story, or what are we supposed to learn from it? What is the main point? Does your paper have a thesis? Perhaps explain earlier about the father's background—isn't his role in the story central to the whole paper?

Here is a rewrite in which the writer responds to the suggestions made by the peer reviewers. The new version is moving toward a thesis that gives this familiar story its special point. (Where and how?) The writer is filling in the real-life detail needed to make the people convincing and to enable the reader to share in the writer's feelings? (Where and how?) The writer has put the pieces of the story together in such a way that the brother's role and the father's background fit in the right way. (Where and how?)

FIRST REWRITE:

Till Death Do Us Part

My parents were never made for each other. My mother came from a somewhat wealthy and extremely religious family. She practiced the word of the Lord as it should be. I often tease her that she would have been a nun if it hadn't been for my brother and me. My father, on the other hand, grew up in a broken home with a father who beat his kids more than he hugged them. My father's short temper got to the point where the neighbors came over to see if we were all right after hearing his yelling. However, he did not really hurt me nor my mother physically.

My parents were divorced after nineteen years. They had many quarrels, both before and after they divorced. I think it was only by staying close to my mother and my brother that I managed to come out of the experience with a positive outlook. My brother was always there to listen to me when I was discouraged and helped me cope.

You might say my parents' marriage was not made in heaven. I remember walking into the kitchen one bright Thursday morning. I saw my mother sitting in her chair by the window staring without any expression at my dog running around outside. I walked by her and gave her a good morning kiss on the cheek, then sat at my place to eat the scrambled eggs and toast. I felt her watching me eat but paid no attention. My brother then strolled in to tell me to hurry up if I wanted a ride to school. My mother stopped my brother from leaving the kitchen and brought us both next to her. I had never seen such a glazed look on my mother's face. She said, "Your father left last night."

Communication in my family had completely broken down. My mother began working full-time and so I came home to an empty house and often times an empty refrigerator. I grew up without a father in the house, and my lack of social skills showed it. My dad had started to date; as a matter of fact, he began to live with another woman. My father told me that if I told my mother it would upset her, so I didn't. But people talk, and the news of my father's new roommate reached my mother's ears.

As the hostility between my parents continued, I often felt caught in the middle. My father had moved an hour away from us to be closer to his dental practice. I saw my dad for maybe one weekend out of the month. I became a messenger between my parents, who never really talked directly to each other. I heard my father bash my mother for talking to their mutual friends and his business contacts. I heard my mother bash my father for leaving his kids and destroying our family. I got yelled at, by both of them, for defending the other. I learned never to say a word, just listen.

When the divorce finally became official, my mother had custody of me, and my dad agreed to pay child support and alimony, even though alimony was not mandatory in our state. In return, I would spend every other weekend with him and his girlfriend and her two sons. I quickly realized this arrangement was going to hamper my social life. With my father living an hour away from me, he also lived an hour away from my activities. Soccer and basketball games, parties, and time spent with my friends, who did not understand my situation, were memories that will be lost forever, because my father had no respect for what I did.

After continuous court battles, whose attorney fees could have bought me the best car on the market, and the inability to live in the same metropolitan area, my mother decided to move away, at the end of my eighth-grade year, and I joined her. My dad, who by this point had a new wife and two new stepchildren, could not understand my decision, and neither could I. Staying with my father would have brought me all the luxuries I could ever want, except for a sense of home. After spending two of the worst years of my life, I had to start over too. I have never regretted that decision to this day.

The student's instructor might offer advice like the following for a second revision:

INSTRUCTOR'S COMMENT:

This is turning into a strong candid account of your feelings and your way of dealing with them. Here are recommendations for your final draft:

- Keep feeding in real-life details about the people, as your peer reviewers suggested.
- The emphasis on the solidarity or strong bonds uniting the remaining family members makes for a strong positive thesis. To lead up to it, I think you should move the story of your mother's announcing the split-up to the beginning of your paper for a dramatic start.
- You need to watch for clichés: "till death do us part," "marriage was not made in heaven," "communication had broken down," "caught in the middle." These make your feelings sound canned or average. Concentrate on putting your own personal contradictory feelings into words.
- I think you should consider adding a conclusion where you relate what you have experienced and what you have learned to your reading or to the experiences of other people. Help readers see that this is not just one person's story.

Study the following second rewrite. How effective is the more dramatic opening? Does it lead up to the thesis? How effective is the added conclusion? (Does it reinforce the initial thesis?) What details seem most authentic or lifelike? How do you personally react to the finished paper?

SECOND REWRITE:

Till the Courts Do Us Part

I remember waking up that bright Thursday morning and getting ready for school. When I walked into the kitchen, I saw my mother sitting in her chair by the window staring without any expression at my dog running around outside. I walked by her and gave her a good morning kiss on the cheek, then sat at my place to eat the scrambled eggs and toast. I felt her watching me eat but paid no attention. My brother then strolled in to tell me to hurry up if I wanted a ride to school. My mother stopped my brother from leaving the kitchen and brought us both next to her. I had never seen such a glazed look on my mother's face. She said, "Your father left last night."

My parents were divorced after nineteen years. They had many quarrels, both before and after they divorced. I think it was only by staying close to my mother and my brother that I managed to come out of the experience with a positive outlook. My brother was always there to listen to me when I was discouraged and helped me cope.

My parents were never made for each other. My mother came from a somewhat wealthy and extremely religious family. My father, on the other hand, grew up in a broken home with a father who beat his kids more than he hugged them. My father's short temper got to the point to where the neighbors came over to see if we were all right after hearing his yelling. I can say this, though: He never did one thing to hurt me, my brother, or my mother physically. However, for me and everyone else, this marriage of nineteen years lasted too long.

From that day until now, my brother and I have been caught in the middle of a war. My brother started college in the fall in the city where we lived. My father had moved an hour away from us to be closer to his dental practice. I saw my dad for maybe one weekend out of the month. I became a messenger between my parents, whose only words directly to each other were, "Is Eduardo there?" when they called looking for me. I heard my father bash my mother for talking to their mutual friends and his business contacts. I heard my mother bash my father for leaving his kids and destroying our family. I got yelled at, by both of them, for defending the other. I learned never to say a word, just listen.

My brother and I became closer and depended on one another to keep the other sane. I would call him up at all hours of the night and complain about what my mother said or what my father said. I respected him because he did not back down to either one of my parents and he always took care of me. We were the only ones we could trust in our family.

As the date of the infamous court case neared, I became an adult trapped in a seventh-grader's body. My mother began working full-time and so I came home to an empty house and often times an empty refrigerator. I grew up without a father in the house, and my lack of social skills showed it. My dad had started to date; as a matter of fact, he began to live with another woman. My father told me that if I told my mother it would upset her, so I didn't. But people talk, and the news of my father's new roommate reached my mother's ears. I felt as though I had let her down by accepting my dad's new relationship.

When the divorce finally became official, my mother had custody of me, and my dad agreed to pay child support and alimony, even though alimony was not mandatory in our state. In return, I would spend every other weekend with him and his girlfriend and her two sons. I quickly realized this arrangement was going to hamper my social life. With my father living an hour away from me, he also lived an hour away from my activities. Soccer and basketball games, parties, and time spent with my friends, who did not understand my situation, were memories that will be lost forever, because my father had no respect for what I did.

After continuous court battles, whose attorney fees could have bought me the best car on the market, and the inability to live in the same metropolitan area, my mother decided to move away, at the end of my eighth-grade year, and I joined her. My dad, who by this point had a new wife and two new stepchildren, could not understand my decision, and neither could I. Staying with my father would have brought me all the luxuries I could ever want, except for a sense of home. After spending two of the worst years of my life, I had to start over too. I have never regretted that decision to this day.

In his "Memoir," the American playwright David Mamet describes a childhood marred by the cruelty and callousness of unfeeling parents. He explains that his father had himself been the son of a loveless mother who declared him a failure and gave him lasting feelings of bitterness. Perhaps staying close to my mother and my brother can help me break the cycle of bad parenting—not passing on the tradition of blame and resentment to the next generation.

The following might be an instructor's or a student reader's final comment:

FINAL COMMENT:

In this version, several points come through strongly: the conflict in a mismatched marriage, the sense of being torn between conflicting expectations. However, the strong points also come through well: the loyalty to the mother, the sense of solidarity with your brother, and the conviction of having steered the right course in a difficult situation. Many readers will like the honesty of your emotions. The paper moves well from the split-up through the working out of the conflict to your estimate of what the experience has meant to you. The conclusion about breaking the cycle ends the paper on a strong positive note.

1i Final Editing

Recognize high-priority items for final editing.

How much editing will your writing need? Final editing is the fine-tuning that makes your message reach the reader without static. Teachers and editors fine-comb manuscripts to ensure that published writing meets standards of written English. Written English or published English is more permanent and more carefully worked out than casual talk. Areas that may need attention range from accurate word choice through level of formality to effective sentences and correct spelling. Remember: *Proofread, and proofread again.* Text looks deceptively clean on your monitor screen. Proofread your text again after you print it out as hard copy.

✓ ***EDITOR'S TIP:*** Editing software is becoming more sophisticated. **Computer programs** range from highly usable spelling checks to questionable rules of thumb for editing sentences. Remember that the computer program does not read sentences for meaning, although it can flag recurrent patterns for you that might need attention.

WRITING ESSENTIALS

An Editor's Checklist

In editing your work, ask yourself questions like the following:

1 Is *word choice* anywhere too loose or inaccurate—wrong word, misleading term, badly defined key concept?

2 Is the *level of writing* too chatty and informal for a serious topic? Or, at the other extreme, is it too stiff and impersonal?

3 Does the writing follow the conventions of *written English,* such as complete sentences, subject-verb agreement, and clear pronoun reference?

4 Are hastily written or *improvised sentences* a problem? Do some of your sentences seem too casual or too loosely put together? Do they mix different ways of constructing the sentence, use excessive shortcuts, or shift in time?

5 Is *awkward sentence structure* a problem? Are any of your sentences too heavy-handed or roundabout? Will the reader lose track of who does what or what goes with what?

6 Have you checked for sexist or *offensive language?* Do you need to reword objectionable references to gender, race, national origin, or disability?

7 Are you using an overly *aggressive style?* Is the wording at key points in your paper too insulting or condescending? Will it alienate readers who might otherwise take your arguments seriously?

8 Is your *punctuation* doing its job? Or will it seem confusing or distracting to the reader? Are you observing basic comma rules? Have you double-checked your punctuation of quotations?

9 Have you double-checked for familiar touchstones of literacy: *it's/its;* apostrophe with possessives (the *day's* events, the *parents'* consent)?

10 Have you spell-checked for familiar *spelling demons*—from *believe* and *receive* to *definite* and *perform?*

What help will you get with your editing needs?

- To give you quick help with high-priority items, your instructor may provide **marginal glosses**—quick mini-lessons in the margin of your paper. If you wrote "*todays* students," you may find a notation like the following. Copy notes like these, and include them in your personal list of Minimum Editing Essentials.

MARGINAL NOTE: **today's** students, **yesterday's** paper, **tomorrow's** meeting

- Teachers and editors processing many pages of manuscript use **editing symbols**—abbreviations like **ap** (for missing or misused apostrophe) or **DM** (for dangling modifier). These symbols flag familiar editing needs that surface in early drafts by both the pro and the beginner. Here are some of the most frequently used:

agr for agreement
ref for pronoun reference
frag for sentence fragment
sx for sexist language
sp for spelling

- To direct you to help with these and similar problems, your instructor may use a code guiding you to the right section of a style sheet or handbook. *The Access Handbook* provides a **numerical key**—with a code number like **9** steering you to a general section. Code numbers like **9a** or **11c** direct you to help with a more specific problem. Your instructor may add a third-level subdivision like **9b.3** or **29b.2**.

    Either the numerical code or the editing symbol, or both together, will help you target words and passages that need work. Here are some sample sentences with both number key and editing symbol. The original version is *italicized*. The edited version appears in **boldface**.

WORD CHOICE

6a **ww** wrong word	The commission was not fully *convicted* / **convinced** of the accuracy of the report.
6c **w** wordy	The launch was postponed *due to the fact that* / **because** the weather pattern had changed.
6b **inf** too informal	Working as a computer specialist in the electronics industry *is not all it's cracked up to be* / **does not always live up to its billing.**
6d **sx** sexist	Modern science has created weapons that could destroy *mankind* / **humanity.**

SENTENCES

11 agr agreement	The typical diet article in women's magazines *treat* / **treats** food as if it were a foreign agent.
14b DM dangling modifier	*Sitting on top of an animal* / **As the cowboy sits on top of an animal** filled with furious energy, the gate suddenly opens.
12 ref reference	Today's young woman does not expect Prince Charming to take care of *their* / **her** every need.

MECHANICS

29a cap capitalization	Alice Walker's prize-winning *The Color Purple* was read by millions *of americans* / **of Americans**.
29c ap apostrophe	Stations use enticing "newsbriefs" to catch *the viewers* / **the viewers'** attention.

YOUR TURN 6 Editing a Manuscript

Suppose you are a member of an editorial committee working on papers to be included in a class publication. You and the members of your group have been asked to do final editing of the following student paper. Which of the editing issues identified in the paper do you recognize? Be prepared to explain the problem and to show how you are going to solve it. (If you are working in a small group, you may arrange to farm out parts of the paper to the members.)

Honor Labor

At a bank in California, all tellers' jobs were reduced to part-time status and their health plan canceled. The president of Boston University said this week that there was nothing wrong with teachers being paid less than garbage workers, due to the fact that teaching was "attractive work." An investigation into a plane crash in Florida revealed that important maintenance had been outsourced. Workers who had no loyalty to the airline verified safety checks they had not done. (Outsourcing is when companies take work from their employees and farm it out to entrepreneurs using cheaper labor.)

Stories like these in the curent news points to major sources of disatisfaction among American workers: lack of loyalty, lack of recognition, and they feel they are not needed. Employees do not count, what counts is "shareholder value." In my first job I was not identified by my name but by my employee number. There was no social contact and personal communication between the managers and the office workers. The workers hardly spoke to each other. No one ever bothered you.

In my next job I worked hard as a paralegal. I don't remember hearing a word of recognition or praise. One day I was asked at the last minute to copy important court papers. And deliver them to one of our lawyers at the Municipal Court. I had one hand on the keyboard, one on the printer, and one in my briefcase looking for my car keys. When I arrived at the court building with one minute to spare, I was asked, "Why are you so late? Was there a lot of traffic?"

My next job was an office manager. At first I enjoy each day. I helped employees organize their schedules and handle the workload. Each one had their own section. After six months, I was introduced to my new replacement. "It's our new computer," said the person I knew only as the systems analyst. "It can organize files at several times the speed of the old system." This was the first time I experienced the feeling of being declared redundant. The feelings of inadequacy were real hard on my sense of self-confidence.

The writers in the business section of the newspaper talk about cost-cutting, flexible scheduling, and downsizing. They write about cost-cutting CEOs with names like Chainsaw McNaughty. However, as more "Help Wanted" ads and "Now Hiring" signs appear, employees may be able to be pickier about their jobs. Managers in high-tech industries from Silicon Valley to Austin Texas already complain that qualified workers are hard to find.

1j Sharing and Publishing

Find outlets for your writing.

Who is going to read your writing? What are going to be the outlets for your writing? Using the photocopy machine, sharing papers by e-mail, having papers on disk, and scanning them electronically all facilitate wide informal sharing of student papers. Your aim should be to have by the end of a term at least one paper that you would want to publish or contribute to a class publication.

- Ideally, you share the last rewrite of a paper with your classmates—whether it is photocopied for them, circulated among them in the original, read to them, or shared by e-mail.
- Desktop publishing makes it easy for your class to publish an informal **class publication**—published periodically during the term or gathered at the end. You might contribute to a class publication or to a schoolwide collection of student writing.
- You may want to volunteer to serve on the editorial committee of a class publication that would provide an outlet for the best or most representative writing from your class. The committee would set up guidelines and handle the logistics. It would farm out tasks that might range from editing for mechanics to designing a cover to including student-generated graphics.

2 WRITING YOUR PARAGRAPHS

¶
no ¶

Use your paragraphs to develop your ideas one step at a time.

Effective paragraphing helps you make your points. Breaking a paper up into paragraphs is one of the customs of the writing trade—a widely observed practice, like wearing something other than a tie-dyed shirt to a job interview. However, paragraphs are more than just a habit. A paragraph of just two or three sentences will look skimpy—unless you use it to make an especially important thought stand out from the rest of your paper. A long sprawling paragraph going on for most of a page or more may make your reader wonder if you really brought your material under control.

Well-developed paragraphs enable your reader to take in one idea at a time. They help the reader focus on one part of a larger picture and see if you are doing it justice. You may be focusing on one of several reasons, staying with it so readers have a chance to see what is involved. You may zero in on one stage in a process, focusing on what has to be done at this point to make the process work. Or you may focus on an important step in an argument, shoring up one key point instead of rushing on.

PARAGRAPH ESSENTIALS — Paragraphs and the Reader

In a well-written paragraph, you answer several questions in the reader's mind:

FOCUS — *Focus on one limited point or issue:*
What are you talking about at this stage in your paper?

KEY IDEA — *Make a statement, summing up the key idea:*
What is the point?

EXPLANATION — *As needed, explain the key idea or a key term:*
What do you mean?

SUPPORT — *Back up the key point with examples or other supporting material:*
What makes you think so?

TRANSITION — *As needed, provide signals steering the reader's attention:*
How is the paragraph laid out?

2a Focusing Your Paragraph

foc

Focus your paragraph on a main point.

A well-written paragraph makes a point. Often you will state the point in a key sentence or **topic sentence** early in the first paragraph. Often the topic sentence will be your very first sentence. Often it will be your second sentence when your first sentence raises the question or provides the link with what came before.

The following paragraph focuses on one central issue: How do we relate to the animals that share the planet with us? In answering that question, the paragraph makes one key point: Our fellow creatures on this planet were not created for us to "use and abuse." The rest of the paragraphs then develop this idea. The idea of abuse then stays in focus throughout. Like the ringing of a bell, the key idea echoes throughout the paragraph. The writer keeps adding examples that all point in the same direction. The readers are likely to start thinking: "I see what you mean. I get the point!"

KEY IDEA AND EXAMPLES:

Animals were not created to be used and abused by human beings. They share the earth with us and have a right to live with us on this planet. It is true that many of us are still unaware of the **conditions** under which **chickens are caged** or **calves are pent up** in all their short lives in order to feed our appetite for meat. However, public opinion has changed about our **hunting down and poisoning** such creatures of the wild as **wolves and coyotes**. There has been a revulsion against the **trapping of fur-bearing animals** or the **clubbing of baby seals** for their pelts. Dog fanciers have changed their standards to make traditional practices like **ear-cropping** obsolete.

Often you will follow your topic sentence with a sentence or two of **explanation**. A brief pointed topic sentence makes the key point, making it stand out and giving it a chance to sink in. Then you elaborate: The next sentence or two explain what you mean and do not mean. Then the paragraph goes on to supporting examples or data.

IDEA—ELABORATION—SUPPORT:

State lotteries are exempt from laws that require truth in advertising. State lottery commissions are government bodies and are not subject to regulation by the Federal Trade Commission. Lotteries therefore have much leeway in what they tell players, who include large numbers from among the poorer and less educated members of society. Sophisticated advertising techniques mislead players about the chances of winning. (The statistical odds against winning big are higher than they are against being struck by lightning or finding a pearl in an oyster.) Often upbeat slogans and marketing techniques create unrealistic expectations concerning how lotteries will help support and improve education. (States that do not have lotteries on the average spend ten percent more on education per capita than states that do.) Lottery officials tend to mislead the public about the money that goes into state coffers, supporting government programs. (Only about 34 cents for every dollar taken in goes to the state treasury.)

Sometimes you will take up the key idea again and reinforce it by a **clincher sentence** at the end. The following example starts with the key idea. It goes on to support it with details or examples. It then drives it home with a strong final restatement of the main point.

IDEA—SUPPORT—CLINCHER SENTENCE:

In spite of the fitness craze that has swept the nation, we are less fit today than we were ten years ago. Four or five out of ten best-selling books in any one year may be fitness books. Exercise videos sell by the tens of thousands, and several television channels on any given night are likely to sell home exercise equipment. However, recent surveys show that 80 percent of Americans still do not get enough exercise. Young people grow up on a fast-food diet rich in fat and sugar. According to studies published by the Department of Health and Human Services, American children are more likely to be overweight than twenty years ago. Only 36 percent of children today can pass minimum fitness standards set by the Amateur Athletic Union. **While watching lifeguards with perfect bodies running on a beach, the viewers are in danger of becoming overweight couch potatoes.**

✓ ***EDITOR'S TIP:*** A paragraph may vary the more common pattern and give the **topic sentence last.** The writer has decided to give data or examples first. The paragraph asks readers to take in data or examples and think about them. It then leads the readers up to the right conclusion.

TOPIC SENTENCE LAST:

Ticket buyers stand in endless lines, buying at a single newsstand at the rate of 8,000 a day. Citizens put a portion of each minimum wage payment or unemployment check into lottery tickets, often buying five or ten at a time. On talk shows, people talk about what they will do—the maids they will hire, the cruises they will take—if they hit big. Lottery outlets flash the latest numbers on rising million-dollar jackpots. When the jackpot of a state lottery approaches 30 or 40 million dollars, frantic ticket buying raises the payoff to astronomical heights. **Lottery fever has become an American obsession, with lotteries taking in billions of dollars.**

YOUR TURN 7 Writing the Topic Sentence

What topic sentence would best sum up the main point for each of the following paragraphs? Write a topic sentence for each paragraph, and compare your entries with those of your classmates.

1 ______________________________. Activists trying to protect whales steered their small boats between the hunted whales and the sailors of catcher boats attempting to harpoon the animals. Other volunteers harassed sealers on the harp seal breeding grounds on the ice of the Magdalen Islands. They sprayed baby seals with organic dye that would make their pelts worthless for the hunters who club the defenseless cubs and then strip them of their fur. In one widely reported incident, an American released dolphins caught and penned up for slaughter by crews of Japanese fishing boats as threats to their catch.

2 ______________________________. Many companies now employ private security guards to protect business property. The sales of burglar alarms and security systems for private homes have increased steadily over the years. Locksmiths do a booming business fitting entrance doors with multiple locks, dead bolts,

and the like. In high-risk neighborhoods, stores and government offices look like fortresses with barred windows and with bullet-proof cages for cashiers or agents dealing with the public. Increasing numbers of private citizens buy handguns intended for self-defense and for last-ditch protection of their families.

3 ______________________. The spines of cactuses were once leaves at an earlier stage of evolution. The bulb of an onion is really a cluster of specialized leaves. Thorns of spiny plants and tendrils of climbing plants are often modified leaves. The needles of pine trees have taken the place of the leaves shed by deciduous trees that are their cousins. The hard, woody sheathing of palm trees is a modified leaf, so large in one Amazonian plant that local tribes use it as a makeshift canoe.

4 ______________________. Benjamin Franklin started as a printer's apprentice, and the freedom to print independent opinions was one of the cherished rights the American colonists sought to protect. Tom Paine stoked the fires of the American Revolution in a series of pamphlets that were considered high treason by the British crown. Among nineteenth-century writers, Henry David Thoreau wrote "On the Duty of Civil Disobedience" in an unjust war. Early American feminists from Sojourner Truth to Susan B. Anthony and Elizabeth Cady Stanton claimed the right to voice unpopular opinions on subjects including abortion and divorce.

2b Developing Your Paragraph

dev

Develop your paragraphs with solid supporting material.

When writing your paragraphs, remember: A point worth making is a point worth following up. Feel free to state an opinion, to make a claim, or to make a charge. But then follow through: Give examples, furnish evidence, or explain why. It's the backup you provide that will make your writing instructive or convincing.

2b.1 Lining Up Examples *Line up several related examples to drive home a point.* The basic workhorse paragraph offers a limited generalization. For instance, you might make a point about disruptive noisy behavior in college dorms, about spamming or unwanted e-mail, or about "dress for success" advice in women's magazines. You then follow up with **examples** showing that what you are saying is not just a superficial impression. Instead, it is grounded in what you have observed or experienced at first hand.

MULTIPLE EXAMPLES:

The influx of women into the corporate world has generated its own small industry of advice and inspiration. Magazines with titles like *Savvy* or *Working Woman* offer tips on everything **from sex to software**, plus the occasional instructive tale about a woman who rises effortlessly from managing a boutique to being the **CEO of a multinational corporation.** Scores of books have told the aspiring managerial woman **what to wear**, **how to flatter superiors**, and, when necessary, **fire subordinates.** Even old-fashioned radicals like myself, for whom "CD" still means civil disobedience rather than an eight percent interest rate, can expect to receive a volume of second-class mail inviting them to join their corporate sisters at a **"networking brunch"** or to share the privileges available to the **female frequent flier**.

—Barbara Ehrenreich, "Strategies of Corporate Women," *New Republic*

2b.2 Using a Key Example *Develop a single outstanding example in detail.* Sometimes a single example, followed up in detail, is especially instructive. Your readers may learn more from taking a closer look at one key incident or a single test case than from several shorter examples.

CASE IN POINT:

Today, we see many of America's mythical national heroes in a different light. For several generations, **a legendary figure like Buffalo Bill** could serve as a symbol of the gallant, reckless, sturdy independence of the Western frontier. At the same time, he was celebrated as a show business genius who made his Wild West show the most famous spectacle of its kind. Today, however, his name reminds us above all of the heedless destruction of Native Americans and of American wildlife. "Indian fighters" like Buffalo Bill were implicated in the extermination of the native population. Whereas the Native Americans had regarded the buffalo with almost religious reverence, hunters like Buffalo Bill started the wholesale slaughter that decimated the herds and that destroyed the livelihood of the Native Americans. Hides were shipped by the tens of thousands and the carcasses left to rot on the plains.

2b.3 Downshifting *Zero in on one of several related examples.* A writer may use several briefly summarized examples to put the reader in an assenting mood. Then the paragraph downshifts—it slows down to look at one key example in detail. This example becomes detailed enough to convince a reader who might still have doubts.

DOWNSHIFTING:

Employees are increasingly subject to electronic supervision in the workplace. Airline companies track the work patterns of booking agents, including the time they take out for coffee breaks and private conversations. Companies check whether employees are sending private e-mail or using the company's e-mail for offensive messages. **New technologies allow employers to check whether employees are wasting the company's time at recreational Web sites. A software package called LittleBrother allows companies to monitor the use their workers make of the Internet. The software uses a database of 45,000 Web sites that are classified as "productive," "unproductive," and "neutral." The program identifies the most frequent users and the most frequently visited sites. Employees are then rated according to their browsing habits.**

2b.4 Assembling Statistics *Bring together and interpret related statistics.* Often a well-written paragraph assembles statistics that all support the same point. It links them to reputable sources and makes them detailed enough so that they seem grounded in actual research or reliable surveys. The opinion stated in the topic sentence then is no longer "just your opinion." Instead, it is an opinion anchored in facts and figures that are hard to brush aside.

SUPPORTING STATISTICS:

Signs of a strong interest in religion are everywhere today. According to a recent survey in *Psychology Today*, **nine out of ten** American adults believe that there is a God, and **eight out of ten** consider themselves Christians. The latest edition of the *Encyclopedia of American Religions* lists **more than 2,100 religious groups,** a figure **double what is was** twenty years ago. Many forms of Christianity and Judaism are active. In addition, Islam has been spreading rapidly, claiming about **3.5 million followers** according to some sources. Among other non-Western religions, Buddhism counts about **750,000 believers,** including **100,000 American converts.** Buddhism has been called the country's fastest growing faith.

2b.5 Feeding In Quotations *Quote authorities or insiders to support your point.* Often a well-written paragraph brings together revealing quotations or authentic testimony from qualified observers. Listening to firsthand quotes, readers can feel that they are witnessing the give-and-take on a live issue rather than hearing about what is happening at second hand.

FIRSTHAND QUOTATION:

Courts today tend to recognize the employer's right to monitor employees. They honor what one lawyer specializing in employee monitoring calls **"the employer's business justification for monitoring."** An employee of the Pillsbury corporation charged that his privacy was violated when he was fired after his employer read several e-mails he had sent to his supervisors. In one electronic message, he had threatened to **"kill the backstabbing bastards"** in sales management. The court ruled that the employee had **"no reasonable expectation of privacy"** even though the company had assured employees that e-mail was confidential. The court ruled that the corporation's interest in preventing **"inappropriate and unprofessional conduct"** outweighed the privacy rights of the terminated employee.

✓ ***EDITOR'S TIP:*** Sometimes a one-sentence or two-sentence paragraph will set off an important point that the writer wants to stand out. A **highlight** paragraph showcases a key point, making it stand out like a banner headline:

HIGHLIGHT PARAGRAPH:

In today's world of corporate surveillance nothing is confidential. Nothing is private.

Sometimes a one-sentence or two-sentence paragraph will serve as a **bridge paragraph** from one important point to another:

BRIDGE PARAGRAPH:

Most employees understand that their current e-mail and files can be monitored. **However, they do not understand that sophisticated equipment can retrieve material that they thought they had deleted or destroyed.**

YOUR TURN 8 Building Up the Paragraph

How would you build up each of the following paragraphs with supporting material? Adjust the topic sentence so that it reflects your own view. Then complete the paragraph—fill in additional examples, or one key example developed in detail, or supporting statistics or quotations.

1 At one time, African Americans were hardly visible in the media, except as stereotypes—the worker in the cotton field, the maid. **This picture has changed (greatly) (somewhat) (only superficially) over the years.** Bill Cosby—as the wise-cracking detective, as the kind sensitive Dr. Huxtable—was one of the first black entertainers to become a huge success by playing nonmenial roles. ______________________________
____
____
____.

2 **Americans (ignore) (resent) (have become used to) homeless people begging everywhere in their cities.** They see a homeless person with a sign saying "HOMELESS VETERAN—PLEASE HELP" by the on-ramp as they start their daily commute. __________
____
____
____.

3 **Gunplay is (a common) (by far the most common) form of television entertainment.** Flipping the channels, the viewer on any given night sees real and imaginary cops and lawbreakers in shoot-outs maiming and killing the just and the unjust. __________
____
____
____.

2c Transitions as Thought Links

trans

Use transitions or thought links to steer the reader's attention.

A well-developed paragraph often helps us follow the writer's train of thought. It provides **transitions** or thought links that keep us on track as we follow the author's thinking. Transitions may be single

PARAGRAPH ESSENTIALS

Using Thought Links

Here is a list of common thought links or **transitions** and the signals they give to the reader:

GIVING EXAMPLES:	for example, for instance, to illustrate
ADDITIONAL SUPPORT:	too, also, moreover, furthermore, similarly
LOGICAL RESULT:	so, therefore, as a result, consequently, thus
RAISING OBJECTIONS:	but, however, nevertheless, on the contrary
EMPHASIZING A POINT:	indeed, in fact, above all
GRANTING A POINT:	admittedly, granted, to be sure, it is true that
WEIGHING CHOICES:	on the one hand, on the other hand
SUMMING UP:	to sum up, in short

words like *however* or phrases like *on the other hand* (or sometimes whole sentences). They serve as directional signals that let us know "example follows" or "additional support to come." They steer us through an argument by letting us know "several reasons coming here" or "objection follows" or "logical result coming next."

In many well-written paragraphs, the three or four sentences after the topic sentence are obviously giving examples—even without a *for example* or *for instance*. However, transitions can help you make sure that your readers will not miss a turning point or a change in direction. The transitions in the following paragraph signal the change, first from positive news to a **countertrend** and then to some limited **exceptions** to the negative trend.

> **Commercial fishing around the world can barely keep up with the growing demand for scarce protein.** In a recent year, the total catch amounted to 74 million tons, which works out to 16 kilograms per person for the world, or almost a quarter of all animal protein consumed. More than a hundred species of finfish and shellfish are harvested commercially around the world, and 22 species provide 100,000 tons or more. **However,** per capita catches have been slowly dropping during the last decade. At

least eleven major fisheries have been depleted to the point of collapse, ranging from the anchovy in Peru to the Alaska crab. **In fact,** only squid and the Antarctic krill are still underfished, since harvesters find it hard to make them palatable to new consumers.

In the following paragraph, a transition alerts readers to an important **contrast** between two different methods employed by state governments to raise money:

> **Lottery income targeted for, say, education, represents money that the state does not have to come up with from the tax-supported general fund.** The thirty-eight state lotteries have been enormously successful at raising money. Last year, they raked in $35 billion. Overwhelmingly, lotteries draw their players from the poorer and less educated members of society, those least able to contribute to the state's coffers. The states could raise this money openly through taxes, but taxes make voters angry. Lottery players, **on the other hand,** don't get angry because they choose to purchase tickets. They choose this because they believe that playing the lottery might really lift them from poverty and drudgery.
>
> —Robyn Geary, "The Numbers Game," *New Republic*

In the following paragraph, several logical links help the reader follow the writer's train of thought. They announce **examples,** introduce the **problems** these present, and signal the **logical results** of what has been described.

> **Doctors have found that the way a drug is given can be important.** The commonly prescribed antibiotic tetracycline is **one example.** It is completely absorbed when injected in a vein or muscle and fairly well absorbed in pill form on an empty stomach. **But** because the presence of food in the stomach interferes with absorption, patients are advised to take tetracycline before meals. **Further**, drugs are not absorbed equally after injection into different muscles. **Therefore**, doctors now pay more attention to the site at which drugs are injected. **For example**, in the case of a drug called lidocaine, which is used in the treatment of heart rhythm abnormalities, studies have shown that it was absorbed faster following its injection into the deltoid muscle in the arm than into a muscle in the leg.
>
> —Lawrence K. Altman, "Drugs—How Much Is Enough?" *New York Times*

YOUR TURN 9 **Filling In Thought Links**

What thought links would help readers follow the train of thought in the following paragraph? After the number of each blank space, write a transition that would best steer the reader's attention.

> Initiatives to reduce energy consumption in the United States have had only limited success. (1)________, few motorists have been persuaded to abandon their cars for public transportation. (2)________, freeways are clogged, whereas bus companies reduce service. (3)________, the current popularity of minivans and other large vehicles is raising rather than lowering gasoline consumption. (4)________, motorized water skis and snowmobiles rely on gasoline rather than muscle power to move vacationers. (5)________, bicycle clubs and major bicycle events have given many health-conscious Americans a chance to enjoy free time without burning fossil fuels.

2d Revising Your Paragraphs

¶ no ¶

Use stronger paragraphs to structure unsorted, unfocused material.

Much news writing works on the ticker-tape principle. It keeps feeding the audience information in bite-size chunks. The flow of information can be cut short whenever available space is filled or time is up. There may be a continuous flow or a sequence of short informal unstructured paragraphs. A different kind of paragraphing is needed when readers start asking: "What does it all mean?" Effective paragraphing maps out patterns in the flow of information. If your first draft reads too much like an unsorted sequence of material, you need to break up the flow and organize the material around key points.

2d.1 foc

Unfocused Paragraphs *Focus paragraphs that bring together loosely related material.* Everything in the paragraph may be more or less on the same topic. However, the writing disappoints readers who want to know: "What is the point? How does it all add up?" Can you see any connecting thread in the following sentences about a student's family history?

UNFOCUSED:

In many of my classes, teachers have asked me about my Irish heritage. Without my telling them that my father is Irish, they assume I am Irish from merely looking at my name. Many people admire the "fighting Irish" of the Notre Dame football team. On Irish holidays like St. Patrick's Day, many Americans share in the nostalgia for old customs and the old songs. Newspaper articles about the Irish often dwell fondly on their folklore and their love of song and story. However, newspapers also dwell on continuing stories of sectarian violence in Northern Ireland.

In revising the paragraph, the student writer might highlight the common thread in these remarks as follows:

REVISED:

Without my telling them that my father is Irish, many of my teachers assume I am Irish from merely looking at my name. **Being reminded of my Irish heritage often leaves me with mixed emotions.** Many people admire the "fighting Irish" of the Notre Dame football team. On Irish holidays like St. Patrick's Day, many Americans share in the nostalgia for old customs. Newspaper articles about the Irish often dwell fondly on their folklore and their love of song and story. **However**, stereotypes about the boisterous and hard-drinking Irish continue and are reinforced by the holiday. One of the oldest Irish pubs downtown finally closed on St. Patrick's Day because of large unruly crowds. The news from Northern Ireland has long brought stories of continued violence as Catholics and Protestants try to reverse a long history of hatred.

2d.2

no ¶

Choppy Paragraphs *Pull together material scattered in choppy paragraphs.* When you write choppy one-sentence or two- sentence paragraphs, you readers will feel that you fail to follow through. You throw out ideas but do not stay with them enough. When you revise, you try to fit ideas and details together in a pattern that shows how they add up. The following paragraphs provide scattered information:

CHOPPY:

A bicycle plant in Ohio shut down production this year after 44 years in business in the same small town. Workers are picking up unemployment forms to fill out. In a town of 10,000 people, 650 workers will be laid off.

In the future, the company will bring in most of the bicycles it sells from Mexico and Asia. Most Americans know that their running shoes are made in foreign countries. The Nike company has been criticized for running sweatshops using poorly paid women and child labor.

The workers in Ohio blame the closing down of their plant on free trade agreements. Globalization means that American workers must be competitive with foreign labor paid a fraction of what they are paid.

The company will continue to produce some bicycles at a nonunion plant in a different state. . . .

How could the student writer make these choppy paragraphs part of a coherent story?

REVISED:

Most Americans know that their running shoes are made in foreign countries. The Nike company, for instance, has been criticized for running sweatshops using poorly paid women and child labor. However, **globalization means that American workers in many other areas are losing their jobs.** With global free trade, American workers must be competitive with foreign labor paid a fraction of what they are paid. A bicycle plant in Ohio shut down production this year after 44 years in business in the same small town. In a town of 10,000 people, 650 workers will be laid off. Their story follows a familiar pattern: First, half of the workforce was laid off. Then the union accepted a 20 percent pay cut. Now the company will continue to produce some bicycles at a nonunion plant in a different state. However, most of the bicycles it sells already come from Mexico and Asia.

2d.3 ¶

Missing Paragraphs Breaks *Break up long stretches of unsorted material.* Watch out for big chunks of material without a paragraph break. When your paper goes on for two-thirds of a page or more without a new paragraph, your readers may feel that you have not sorted out your material. You have not mapped the territory, enabling them to complete one leg of the itinerary at a time. Give them a break.

In a stretch of material like the following, an editor might recommend paragraph breaks at the indicated points:

BLURRED:

. . . The opening of Japanese-owned automobile plants in the United States produced a culture clash in factory towns where townspeople used to burgers and barbecued ribs had their first exposure to chopsticks and raw fish. Stereotypes about the Japanese work ethic and intense management techniques proved at least partly true. ¶ Japanese managers were incredibly serious about business. Plant ceremonies celebrated milestones such as the installation of a new furnace or the production of one million of an engine part. The rejection of a faulty muffler led to meetings several hours long exploring all angles of the breakdown in quality standards. Every setback was treated as a learning experience. ¶ A major challenge to competing American companies was the relentless cost engineering, producing efficiencies that American car makers found hard to match. Japanese managers had a hatred of waste that made them redesign a front bumper assembly, for instance, from 20 to 13 parts. They continuously experimented with ways to reduce the cost of materials. They reduced the time needed to assemble a car to several hours below the average at Chrysler or GM. Workers felt the continuous pressure to do more for less. ¶ A challenge to workers with a long tradition of union membership was the insistence of Japanese managers on nonunion shops. . . .

OPTIONS FOR WRITING 4 Writing Practice Paragraphs

A paragraph can tell only part of a story—but it can be an important part. Choose one or more of the following writing tasks for practice in writing well-focused, well-developed paragraphs.

1 Write a paragraph in which you use solid examples to *support a claim* or a charge. Study the following paragraph as a possible model:

So-called convenience foods are damaging to our health. These expensive, elaborately packaged, highly processed products are usually a combination of many ingredients, some of which have nothing to do with nutrition. Often the extra ingredients are there to provide long-term preservation and to improve coloring, texture, or taste. Refined sugar is one example of an often unnecessary ingredient. We eat too much sugar without realizing that much of the sugar we consume is hidden sugar. Almost every processed food stuff contains sugar in some form: honey, molasses, sucrose, corn syrup, dextrose, and the like. Too

OPTIONS FOR WRITING 4 *(continued)*

much sugar plays a role as a cause of heart disease, diabetes, and high blood pressure. Salt is also abundantly used in processing beyond what is necessary for good health. The biggest argument against processed convenience foods is that during processing and packaging many of the original nutrients are lost and then artificially replaced by additives called "enriching."

2 Write a then-and-now paragraph that traces a *contrast* between old and new customs or a traditional and a current pattern of behavior. Study the following paragraph as a possible model:

> **We have lost contact with many of our traditional rites of grieving. In the past,** in a more rural America, everybody had a role in the rites of death. Farm women dressed the body while the men built the casket. The body was buried on the family's land or in a nearby cemetery, by community members. Mourners wore black, or black armbands, for a long time—often a full year. The mourners would say, "I'm grieving; be gentle with me." **Now,** mourners are invisible. If a bank teller is short with me, there's no way to know that he is upset because his mother just died. For most of this society, grieving is set aside after a few days. Companies give three days' bereavement leave for the death of an immediate family member, no time for the death of a friend. After three days, we are supposed to come back and perform as usual.

3 Write a paragraph that shows readers the *other side* of a familiar idea, a familiar occupation, or a familiar institution. Study the following paragraph as a possible model:

> Like any other job, police work falls into set patterns: patrol this sector, cover this assignment, check this complaint, interview this man, this woman, this child, investigate this company, work on this case. **But always the unexpected, the sudden violent event, is also part of the routine.** If there is an undue hardness in the voice of a traffic cop stopping an offender for a minor violation, it might be because she remembers, in some deep part of her brain, hearing or reading of some cop, somewhere—stopping a light-jumper, a speeder, an improper turner—a cop who, summons book in hand, was shot dead for no reason. If there is a dictatorial tone in the command of a police officer who tells a group of curious onlookers at some unusual event to move on, it might be because he has seen a curious crowd grow into a menacing mob.
>
> —Dorothy Uhnak, *Policewoman*

4 Write a paragraph that *pays tribute* to a role model or pioneer of a movement. Study the following paragraph as a possible model:

Textbooks should do more to honor the memory of founders of the women's rights movement in America. Women alive today remember older relatives who chained themselves to light posts in the struggle to get women the right to vote. Granddaughters of some of the fiery early leaders use stationery with the slogan "Riots Not Diets." Among unsung early feminists, Sarah Armstrong Wallis (1825–1905) died in poverty and was buried in an unmarked grave. However, in the 1870s she was the leader of the California State Woman Suffrage Educational Association. She and her husband, Judge Wallis, founded a town in an area that is now part of Palo Alto, home of Stanford University. In their home, they entertained Susan B. Anthony and Elizabeth Cady Stanton.

3 MOBILIZING YOUR RESOURCES

Draw on the full range of sources available to a writer.

Where do you turn for material for your writing? Much effective writing is anchored in firsthand experience and observation. At crucial points, the writer brings in a personal account to move the discussion beyond theory or hearsay. At the same time, many writers are compulsive readers. They explore the range of views on an issue. They know where to turn for reliable information, insiders' testimony, or useful statistics. More and more, writers turn for input to the World Wide Web, spending hours exploring the universe of electronic sources. Finally, writers bring in oral sources, drawing on conversations and on informal and formal interviews with people in the know or with special access to information.

3a Writing from Experience

Draw on personal experience to make your writing real and convincing.

Much strong writing has roots in personal experience and authentic firsthand observation. On your own experience, you are the authority. For instance, you can write with conviction about your family background—focusing on a topic like good or bad parenting or on close ties with or alienation from siblings. If you or your parents came to this country, you can write from firsthand experience about the obstacles and successes people encounter when pursuing the American Dream.

Do not limit your use of personal experience to autobiographical writing. Much strong writing about public issues shows that the writer has a personal connection with the topic. At some point, the writer includes a personal story or personal testimony, saying in effect, "This I have witnessed with my own eyes."

3a.1 The Connecting Thread *Trace a connecting thread in a series of events.* Our lives can be miscellaneous or disjointed, with sometimes many things going on at the same time. To write a unified paper, think about a major issue that has played a role in your life. Or focus on a challenge that helped make you what you are. For instance, are you someone who tries to blend in? Or are you proud to be your own person? Here are examples of how fellow students found the connecting thread in events that mattered in their lives:

- *What has been your experience with parents or family?* Growing up, some people go through a period of conflict or rebellion, until they finally reach their own personal declaration of independence. Others may write about going the opposite way. One student writer slowly came to understand and accept the commitment of her missionary parents:

My Parents' Career

When a teacher asks a student what his or her parents' occupation is, you would think it would be easy to answer. Usually their answers ranged from a lawyer to a nurse but my answer was always different, confusing, and unexplainable. For many years of my life, I couldn't explain it to myself. It was even hard for my parents to explain to others that they are missionaries who move around evangelizing, going from place to place forming religious communities and spreading the Word. It took me a long time to accept the job that my parents took up almost twelve years ago. Growing up as a traveling child had its hardships. I would walk into a different class full with staring children, who unlike me had already settled down for the year. . . .

- *How has your background affected your life or your outlook?* Many young people go through a phase when they become interested in family history. What traditions and customs helped shaped their outlook and their lives? A Chinese American student said that she had grown up knowing little about the Chinese culture and language. However, she became interested when she went to a large funeral done in the traditional style. She met many family members who helped her study her family history and the traditional emphasis on work and study and respect for authority.
- *Have you ever been stereotyped as a member of a group?* People of Irish extraction may be sensitive to the stereotype of the hard-drinking Irish. Correcting the stereotype, a student from an Irish American family wrote about growing up as an Irish Catholic—the large family meals with everyone in attendance, the pride in Irish history and culture, the humor and story-telling and love of life.

3a.2 From Journal to Draft Often a revealing incident brings a key issue into focus. The following *journal entry* made the student writer think about obstacles she encountered as the daughter of immigrants. It made her think about what had helped her overcome them.

JOURNAL ENTRY:

I attended Oakhill School, which was not considered to be one of the best schools, to say the least. After graduating from elementary school, I attended one of the wealthier schools, Johnson Middle School. When I left Oakhill School, I was recommended to go into Pre-Algebra, a course taken by many of the students from the wealthier schools. When the middle school teacher asked me what school I was from, I simply responded, "Oakhill School." The teacher told me with a cold heart, "Oh well, then you're not ready." Having her tell me I was not ready for a class simply because of the school I came from was wrong, and I was not going to accept her decision.

Following up the connecting thread, this student wrote a paper tracing a classic pattern from encountering obstacles to overcoming them.

FIRST DRAFT:

A Journey Full of Ordeals

While I was growing up, Spanish was my first and only language. Our neighbors had been in the United States longer than my family. The kids living in the apartment next to us took advantage of the fact that I did not know English. My not knowing English was the greatest form of entertainment these kids could have ever had. As soon as I went downstairs to play with my new, shiny rainbow-colored plastic ball, all of the kids gathered around me. I remember feeling trapped with nowhere to run to—not even to my mother, for she was upstairs making one of her wonderful dishes with the aroma of at least five different spices. The ball was kicked out of my hands while they were making fun of me.

Throughout our struggles, our family has always remained together. I remember my mother's favorite line: "The only thing that will help us get through this is that we remain united as a family." While we were growing up, there were only a few very important values that were above all the others. One of the values was family; family was all that we would have at the end of the day. Family was home; family would always be there no matter what happened, whether good or bad. Family was love. My sisters and I were taught to look out for each other and to care for one another no matter what the situation is. Loving my family is part of my nature and something I do not have to think about. We are a very close family; all the obstacles that we have faced and will continue to face have only made us come together even more. The love of education is another value that was instilled in us since we began kindergarten. Our parents have always told us that school is what will allow us to become someone in life. Lastly, another value instilled in us was the respect we should have for others. Regardless of the people's sex, race, or religious preference, they are people and they are entitled to be respected by others, they have feelings as I do and they should not be treated any different. My kindergarten teacher always told us, "Treat others the way you want to be treated."

I attended Oakhill School, which was not considered to be one of the best schools, to say the least. After graduating from elementary school I attended one of the wealthier schools, Johnson Middle School. When I left Oakhill School, I was recommended for Pre-Algebra, a course taken by many of the students from the wealthier schools. My mother made an appointment to talk to the middle school teacher about my math level. The teacher said that she would change me to Pre-Algebra only if I could bring a letter of recommendation stating that that was the adequate math level for me. Promptly, my mother delivered the letter herself the following week. When the teacher asked me what school I was from, I responded, "Oakhill School." The teacher told me, "Oh well, then you're not ready."

My mother talked to the school principal, who scheduled me for a test the next Monday. That weekend I got together with my sixth-grade teacher to study for my math test. The weekend was filled with math problems that seemed endless. Monday morning came, and as I worked through my test I could hear my pencil writing madly on the paper on the wooden table. Time was up and my test had to be turned in. I exited the library, and a few minutes later the Pre-Algebra teacher approached and gave me the news. I was to be transferred into the Pre-Algebra math class.

From that test, I learned that determination counts. Since then, I feel that I am competing with other students who might have had better academic opportunities than I had, but I feel that I am competing on the same scale. Obstacles such as these are what make my life, my journey, more fulfilling.

3a.3 **Feedback and Revision** Peer reviewers of this paper responded with comments like "A good account of what you had to face growing up" and "You seem like a very determined person." The following might be the instructor's suggestions for a revised second draft:

INSTRUCTOR'S FEEDBACK:

Your account of your childhood experiences as the weird new kid on the block and as the immigrant child in school are told in vivid detail. However, in the second paragraph, your paper turns very ambitious and sweeping. You talk about family, education, and respect. Each one of these is a large *general* topic, and these are things that are easier to say than to show. Take these up one at a time? Focus here on the strong family ties—perhaps add one vivid incident where you and your sister or other family members really stuck together? *Then* go on to the importance of education, leading up naturally to the obstacles you encountered. (This way you could get a stronger *transition* to the incident concerning the pre-algebra class.)

Your philosophy of respect for other people should perhaps go to the end and form a stronger *conclusion* than you now have. Maybe you need some incident where you yourself showed your respect for or understanding of another person. Quoting something you or the other person actually said might make a strong punchline.

In the following excerpts from a revised draft of the paper, strategic changes have been bold-faced:

REVISION:

(Added Thesis) I first came to this country when my father had saved enough money from working in a restaurant and from gardening and had a place for us to live. **From early childhood I learned that opportunity doesn't mean anything if you don't tackle the obstacles in your path.**

(Paragraph Focused on Family) Throughout our struggles, our family has always remained together. I remember my mother's favorite line: "The only thing that will help us get through this is that we remain united as a family." Family was all that we would have at the end of the day. Family was home; family would always be there no matter what happened, whether good or bad. Family was love. My sisters and I were taught to look out for each other and to care for one another no matter what the situation is. **I remember the time my sister and I got lost during a bus trip. . . .**

(New Separate Paragraph on Education) **From the time we began kindergarten, our parents instilled in us the love of education. They always told us that school would allow us to become someone in life. They prepared us to deal with the obstacles that students from a minority background might encounter in their path.** I attended Oakhill School, one of the poorest schools in the district, which was not considered to be one of the best schools, to say the least. After graduating from elementary school, I attended one of the wealthier schools, Johnson Middle School. . . .

(New Conclusion) **One of the most important things I learned from my family was the respect we should have for others. At home, I never heard anyone called an insulting name.** My kindergarten teacher always told us, "Treat others the way you want to be treated." . . .

3a.4 The Personal Connection *When you write about public issues, don't leave your personal experience behind.* Issues come to life when you relate them to the stories of real-life people. When you write about immigration, you can dramatize the issues by talking about a classmate whose family was among the boat people fleeing Vietnam. Or you can talk about a neighbor's struggle to reunite a family separated in the turmoil of civil war. Joe Mianowany, a columnist writing about current issues, said:

> Often, people who responded to my columns had personal experiences to share that illuminated the debate far more than any government statistic you might read or political speech you might hear. People's stories are what issues are all about.

YOUR TURN 10 A Paper for Peer Review

What use has the author of the following student paper made of personal experience? What is the connecting thread in this experience paper? Where does it come through most strongly? What details or examples are you likely to remember? Do you make a good reader for this paper? Why or why not? If you were to write a letter to the student author, what would you say?

Urban Monster

My life has been altered by several people and places. Yet no other situation has shaped my life more than my urban childhood. I grew up in San Francisco, the "City by the Bay," where the streets were packed with varieties of ethnicities, each one separated and by itself in a city so diverse in background and culture. The aimless walking of millions

YOUR TURN 10 *(continued)*

of strangers strangling themselves, cold businessmen who don't glance twice, youth armies who fight over a street corner, drug dealers and the so-called "Guardian Angels"—this is San Francisco. The cold attitude runs through each of these people, protecting them from the urban jungle. The harsh environment that San Francisco was had forever changed me into a defensive, tough urban monster.

My friends were tough, strong guys who wouldn't cry if their lives depended on it. They ran, kicked, bit, and spat better than anyone. As children they were perfectly suited for urban life. They knew how to handle the gangs and the slums. They talked with pride and strength in the face of opposition. When told, "Shut up!" they would talk even louder. I learned to become one of them: wearing the clothes, sporting the grin, and, most importantly, harboring an attitude of "If you touch me I'll kill you!" I had it down. I could handle the mean streets with the rest of them. Anything less was subject to severe violent treatment or even worse, criticism for not being tough in a tough society. I could match threats with threats of my own. To be out of this urban, cultural norm would be to declare suicide unless you stayed home in your closet.

School presented to me its share of problems. Everyone belonged to a separate social clique, or, more accurately, ethnic clique. Hispanics, a majority in my school, stuck with their own, leaving all other ethnicities to establish their own cliques. The Chinese hung out with the Chinese and so on. Being the only (part) Filipino or only (part) Japanese person in class, I had to fend for myself. I sat on the wet benches with the food I had waited endlessly in line for while the others sat in their reserved dry seats with lunches that had priority "cut in line" services. Alienation from the rest of these students compelled me to live a secluded life. Fraternizing became taboo. This antisocial attitude carried on throughout my elementary school years.

My neighborhood presented me with similar attitudes of animosity. Gangs with their booming cars and even louder voices had strength enough to scare even the police. Tattooed arms, revealing tank tops, Ben Davis jeans, cigarettes, and weapons ranging from bats to knives to guns—this was the typical street thug in my neighborhood. They ruled our street with force, compelling me to retreat to an antisocial attitude toward others. When passing by them on the street, I had to make sure I didn't have any valuables for risk of forced "contributions." They had imprinted in me the idea that outward kindness and courtesy were things of weakness and subject to violence.

Clearly my urban life has influenced much of my behavior. I realize that I've grown to avoid public socialization and value reserved attitudes. When I arrived in college, a stranger came up to me and asked me how I was and what my name was. I only paid attention to her long enough to sneer and grumble my name. By the standards here, my defensive personality seems awkward or even rude. Instead of demonstrating friendliness and trust, my urban tendencies shine through as I demonstrate suspicion and mistrust of all that is foreign to me. I surely must adjust to the lifestyle of this friendly place and give up those urban tendencies to shun friendly advances.

OPTIONS FOR WRITING 5

Write a paper focusing on a key issue or major strand in your personal experience. How did it help shape who or what you are? Bring in real-life experiences that will make the issue real for your reader. Bring the people involved to life with lifelike detail. Stay focused on the connecting strand.

1 What was your experience in your previous schooling? Some people look back on their school years as the best years of their lives. For others, school may have been an ordeal or affliction. Focus on one major issue or strand in your school experience. Use detailed real-life examples from your schooling.

2 How much did your family background shape who you are? Did your family fit any familiar stereotypes? Were you a child from "a nuclear family"? Were you one of the "children of divorce"? How did your family experience influence your personality? What about it was most important to you as a person?

3 Are young people more influenced by their peer culture than by family or school? Was this true in your case? How important were buddies, friends, a youth group, or a clique? Did you adopt their values, their lifestyle? Why or why not?

4 Did any one person become a dominant influence in your life? Great works of world literature center on a conflict between father and son or mother and daughter or on a powerful attachment to a mentor or guru. Focus on a person who was important enough to have a lasting effect on your life and personality.

5 How did you learn about gender roles? What were you taught about what it means to be a girl or a boy? How do you define yourself as a woman or a man? Was there a central issue or conflict for you? Bring in real-life memories or key incidents to make the issue real for your readers.

6 How close to the immigrant experience were you during your growing up? Did you experience a "meeting of cultures"? Was loyalty to old-country values or nostalgia for old-country ways an issue in your home? Try to focus on key experiences that helped shape your own sense of identity.

OPTIONS FOR WRITING 5 *(continued)*

7 Did you grow up with a strong sense of group identity? For instance, do you identify strongly with an ethnic, racial, or religious group? Have you ever tried to leave group labels behind? Has ethnic, racial, or religious background played a major role in your upbringing? Or do you think of yourself more as an individual or even a loner?

8 Have you experienced being an outsider? For instance, have you had trouble trying to adjust to an institution like the military, a large corporation, or a church? In retrospect, what was most important for you about the experience?

9 What role did money or social status play in your growing up? What difference did it make? How did it affect your outlook or your values?

10 Have you ever felt that a dramatic or traumatic experience was turning your life around? Write a paper focused on such a turning point and what it meant in your life.

3b Drawing on Your Reading

Draw on your reading in papers presenting a well-informed opinion.

Effective writers draw on their reading. They read up on a subject. Their reading helps make the difference between an opinion and an informed opinion. On many subjects, we have opinions—to which we are entitled, but which no one has to take seriously. However, when a writer presents an informed opinion, readers have to take it into account as they agree or disagree. The writer knows some of the history of the issue, has checked out relevant facts, or is aware of arguments pro and con. Where needed, the writer can marshal supporting evidence that is hard to dismiss out of hand.

Have you developed the reading habit? Are you ready to prove pundits wrong who claim that students today have a short attention span? Is it really true that students today need to have information presented in a jazzed-up format and in bite-size chunks?

3b.1 Reading the Clues *Develop the habit of close attentive reading.* At first reading, you may skim an article to see what it covers and how. However, to make good use of your reading, you will often read more purposefully. You look for the clues that will give you answers to questions like the following: What is the author setting out to do? What is the issue? Where does the author stand? How does the author lay out key steps in the argument or sort out supporting material? What examples or what kinds of evidence are most crucial? What major objections or complications does the author have to address?

The following might serve you as a rough guide as you read an article on a current issue:

READING GUIDELINES

Basic Reading Skills

Look for answers to questions like the following as you work your way through an article or a chapter in a book:

1 ***How informative is the title?*** What hint does it give of the author's intention or major point? How serious or how lighthearted is it? How formidable or informal is the writing likely to be?

2 ***Does the introduction effectively raise the issue?*** Is there an opening example or a key incident that brings the issue to life? Is there a starter quote that brings the issue into focus?

3 ***Early in the article, does the writer sum up the central idea or thesis?*** Is there an overarching point that the rest of the article will support? If not, does the writer sum up the key question that the article as a whole will answer?

4 ***Early in the article, is there a preview of the overall plan?*** Is there a strong hint of how the article as a whole is going to be laid out? Does the writer early set up a general strategy—perhaps a contrast between then and now, or a look at arguments pro and arguments con, or a look at several competing theories to eliminate all but the last?

5 ***What supporting evidence backs up the author's points?*** Are there strong convincing key examples? Are there striking statistics—and where do they come from? Is there expert opinion or insider's testimony? Are there any eye-opening case histories?

6 ***Do important explanations or arguments hinge on key terms?*** How are these explained and illustrated? Are they played off against contrasting terms or different terminology used by others?

(continued)

Basic Reading Skills ***(continued)***

7 ***Does the author acknowledge possible objections or arguments on the other side?*** Does the author belittle opposing ideas? Does the author attack others personally? Or does the writer take objections seriously and provide convincing answers?

8 ***Does the author suggest positive steps or feasible solutions?*** Does the author cite encouraging precedents? Is there any plan for action—are there suggestions for how to rally to a good cause?

9 ***Is there a strong conclusion?*** Does it give added force to a key idea? Does it go in some way go beyond what the author already said? Does the author put the issue in a larger context or address the larger implications?

10 ***Is there anything in the article that relates strongly to your own concerns?*** Does the author speak to issues that are important in your own experience of that of people close to you?

Here are passages you might highlight as you read an article on current twists in the arguments over gun control:

HIGHLIGHTED PASSAGES:

Key Point:

American women are taking up arms. Propelled by a rising tide of crime, more and more of them no longer seem willing to trust their safety solely to their husbands, their neighbors, or the local police. . . .

Supporting Evidence:

. . . Gun ownership among women jumped 53% to more than 12 million, according to a Gallup poll commissioned by gunmaker Smith & Wesson. . . .

The movement to own and carry guns is spread fairly evenly among age groups across professions and around the country. "These are young women, older women; many are professional, but some are housewives," says Barbara Mueller, vice president of the Illinois State Rifle Association.

Contrast with Past Patterns:

Gun owners and sociologists agree that the trend reflects a change of thinking, a rejection of traditional roles. Jerome Skolnick, a professor at the University of California law school at Berkeley, describes the increased gun ownership among women as a "gender revolution."

Shooting instructors observe that women view guns more coldly and cautiously than do men. Some suggest that women make better shots. "Men come in with all sorts of bad habits," says Michael Freire of the Tamiami Range and Gun Shop in Florida. "They see themselves as either Rambo, Roy Rogers, or Daniel Boone." Women, he adds, take their time in learning to shoot. "Discipline is the whole point of training," explains Carol Kolen, a Chicago psychologist who has taken shooting lessons. "It gives me the feeling that I could take care of myself."

Objections and Reservations:

Many law-enforcement specialists fear the residual effects of even broader handgun ownership in a society already saturated with weapons. "The worst reason to buy a gun is solely for protection," says Police Chief Robert Bonneville of Glencoe, Ill., "because guns are very rarely used to stop a break-in. They are most commonly stolen from homes."

—Nancy R. Gibbs, "When Women Take Up Arms," *Time*

3b.2 Focused Reading *Know what to look for as you read.*

You will often be reading with an eye for material that you need to clarify an issue or support a point. Suppose you are exploring the impact of federal guidelines on gender parity in college sports. You are focusing on how the federal regulations known as "Title IX" affect all-male sports like football. In reading a promising article, you take special note of passages like the following—highlighting them or taking notes for future use:

<u>What is Title IX, and what does it require?</u>

Title IX—a law that mandated equal athletic opportunities for men and women at any university receiving federal funding. . . . Title IX did not require a 50–50 split of funding and opportunities. Rather, it said that schools' athletic teams must reflect the gender makeup of the general student body.

<u>What has been the record of compliance?</u>

. . . A full 20 years after Title IX's passage, only one of 107 Division 1-A schools was in full compliance, according to a story in the *Washington Post*. . . . While women made up more than half of the student population, they still accounted for less than a third of all athletes.

What are the arguments in favor of making an exception for college football?

Coaches and athletic directors have often argued that football should not be counted in Title IX figures. A football team costs so much more than any other sport and requires so many more athletes and coaches than any other sport. Because there is no counterpart on the women's side, the argument goes, balancing the gender scales is virtually impossible. Plus, they say, without football, what sport would underwrite all those women's sports that don't generate any revenue?

What are the arguments against exempting college football from the rules?

. . . The biggest myth in college athletics is that football funds the minor sports. Yes, football produces revenue, but most programs don't turn a profit. In 91 percent of all colleges, football programs do make enough money to pay for themselves, according to an NCAA analysis. . . .

—Joan Ryan, "Women Athletes Can Sympathize," *San Francisco Chronicle*

3b.3 **From Reading to Writing** *Feed material from your reading into your own text as part of a "seamless web."* In the following passage, a writer has woven in the links and explanations that help readers see the key points. Note the credit tags that keep reminding the reader of who is being quoted.

DRAWING ON ONE SOURCE:

Twenty years after Title IX mandated equal athletic opportunities for men and women at colleges receiving federal funding, gender parity is still not a reality at many schools. **As Joan Ryan, a columnist for the *San Francisco Chronicle*, explains** in her article "Women Athletes Can Sympathize," Title IX "did not require a 50–50 split of funding and opportunities. Rather, it said that schools' athletic teams must reflect the gender makeup of the general student body." **However, Ryan cites** a *Washington Post* story saying that twenty years later only one of 107 top football schools was in full compliance. In the meantime, women had come to make up more than half of the student population while still accounting for less than a third of all college athletes.

The main obstacle to parity is the resistance of coaches and athletic directors who are fighting to have football exempted from the federal regulations. Football programs are hugely expensive, requiring large numbers of athletes, coaches, and hangers-on. "Because there is no counterpart on the women's side, the argument goes, balancing the gender scales is virtually impossible. Plus, they say, without football, what sport would underwrite all those women's sports that don't generate any revenue?" **Ryan agrees with other critics that** "the biggest myth in college athletics is that football funds the minor sports." Football programs take in large sums of money from ticket sales and television rights, but most don't produce a profit. In fact, "in Division I-A, the big-time football programs, 45 percent lose money." Most other schools just about break even. "In 91 percent of all colleges, football programs do make enough money to pay for themselves, according to an NCAA analysis." **Ryan concludes,** "By the time a team pays for the equipment, the uniforms, the scholarships, the maintenance of the stadium, practice field and weight room, the dozen or so coaches and trainers, the insurance and the travel and food bills, there is usually not enough money left to buy two clipboards and a water cooler."

Often you will be integrating, bringing together, material from several different sources. You can often support a point effectively with quotations from several authorities that all point in the same direction. Try to track the input used by the writer of the following paragraph.

DRAWING ON SEVERAL SOURCES:

The political theater of Luis Valdez focuses on the movement by the Chicanos or Mexican Americans of the West and Southwest to preserve and take pride in their traditional cultural identity. **In an article on Valdez' Teatro Campesino, John Harrop and Jorge Huerta see** Valdez' theater as part of "a strong movement to resist Anglicization and to retain ethnic tradition." In Valdez' plays, the target of satire or the butt of the joke is often the would-be middle-class Mexican American trying hard to assimilate and forget the Mexican heritage. **Guillermo Hernandez, in *Chicano Satire*, says** that "given the sociocultural conflicts encountered by Mexicans living in the United States, their only viable ethical conduct is to maintain loyalty toward their own group in spite of the overwhelming external pressures to turn against their own." **Hernandez points to** Miss Jimenez, in Valdez' *Los Vendidos* (The Sellouts), as the perfect example of "the emerging Mexican American middle class." She works in the governor's office, insists that her Spanish name be given an Anglo pronunciation ("JIM-enez"), and catches herself immediately when she inadvertently slips into Spanish: "Chihuahua . . . I mean, goodness." **In his book, *Necessary Theater*, Jorge Huerta points to** Mingo in *The Shrunken Head of Pancho Villa* as Valdez' first portrayal of a *vendido*. When his father tries to hug him, Mingo offers instead an "American" handshake, and he pretends to the police coming to the family home that he is not part of the family but only rents a room there.

3b.4 Processing Quotations *Study how writers use and introduce material from printed sources.* What works well?

DIRECT QUOTATION In **direct quotation,** you quote verbatim—word for word. You will often use direct quotation for key ideas. You will use it for statements that reveal the author's mindset or attitude. You quote directly when your reader might say: "Show me what the person actually said." A comma usually follows the source tag, or credit tag:

DIRECT QUOTATION:

Alan Buczynski, author of *Iron Bonding*, complains, "The notion prevails that men's emotional communication skills are less advanced than those of chimpanzees, that we can no more communicate with one another than can earthworms."

✓ *EDITOR'S TIP:* You may use a colon instead of the comma before a formal or weighty quotation. Do not forget the *closing quotation mark* showing where your quotation ends.

PARAPHRASE When you **paraphrase** (indirect quotation), you put an author's ideas into your own words. This way you can highlight what you consider important. You can select and condense. At the same time, paraphrase allows you to interpret and explain as you go along:

PARAPHRASE:

Alan Buczynski, author of *Iron Bonding*, criticizes the fashionable view that men are less able to express their feelings than chimpanzees and can no more communicate about their emotions than can earthworms.

PARTIAL QUOTATION When you use **partial quotation,** you can shift back easily between quotation and paraphrase. You weave into your own text quoted words and phrases that add an authentic touch. (The signal you give is: "This is what the author actually said.")

PARTIAL QUOTE:

Jack Balswick, in *The Inexpressive Male*, says that men have been traditionally defined as "independent, task-oriented, aggressive, and inexpressive"—unable to put their feelings into words.

BLOCK QUOTATION Set off more than four quoted lines as a **block quotation.** Reserve block quotations for special occasions—for instance, an author's summing up of a key point or the presentation of key evidence. Indent your block quotation *one inch* or about ten spaces—no quotation marks. In the following passage, the writer quotes in full the original author's summing up of strong condemnations of cult leaders after a mass suicide.

BLOCK QUOTE:

We live in a society that prides itself on tolerance for religious sects of all persuasions. However, perhaps there comes a time when authorities can no longer look the other way when cults turn coercive or homicidal. Elizabeth Gleick in an article in *Time* sums up the views of those who have lost loved ones to cults:

> Cult experts warn that the public should not be taken in . . . by the notion that this was a small number of people exercising their own free will. "I don't consider it suicide. I consider it murder," says Janja Lalich, a cult expert who has been monitoring Heaven's Gate since 1994, when several distraught parents contacted her with their worries about their missing children.

✓ ***EDITOR'S TIP:*** Use no extra margin on the right—and no extra paragraph indentation. (Use the added paragraph indent for any *additional* paragraph of a block quotation.) Double-space as in the rest of your paper. Do not use quotation marks—but keep quotation marks for quotes-within-your-quote.

CREDITING YOUR QUOTATIONS Study the **credit tags** that introduce quoted material in the work of experienced writers. Credit tags keep your readers straight on who said what (and often where). Second, they may show briefly the credentials of the quoted author. (What is this person's background or credibility?) Third, they often sum up the key point. (What is this quotation supposed to show?)

SOURCE:

In an article on "The Culture of Poverty and the Culture of 'Compassion,'" Christopher Lasch attacks "the cynical wisdom that everything has its price."

CREDENTIALS:

Robert Hass, **who is a former poet laureate of the United States and teaches at Berkeley,** said in an interview: "I thought it was irrelevant to talk about what a wonderful thing poetry was if you didn't teach people to read."

POINT:

Gloria Steinem **tries to counteract the distrust of elections widespread among students:** "Voting isn't the most we can do. But it is the least."

The basic workhorse pattern for introducing quoted material is "Author X says . . ." or "Journalist Y reports . . ." To keep this pattern from becoming monotonous, use alternatives like the following:

To quote George Will, "Football is not a contact sport—dancing is a contact sport—football is a collision sport."

The founders of the republic were suspicious of uncontrolled wealth. **In the words of Thomas Jefferson,** small property holders are the "most precious part of the state."

According to Adrienne Rich, feminist and poet, the "drive for self-knowledge, for women, is more than a search of identity"; it is a necessity for survival.

Add **single quotation marks** when the author you are quoting in turn quotes someone else.

QUOTE-WITHIN-A-QUOTE:

In the words of the editor, "New buzzwords quickly become clichés. Comedians make fun of people who say, **'I feel your pain.'**"

✓ ***EDITOR'S TIP:*** *Clearly signal deletions and additions.* Show any omissions or deletions by an **ellipsis**—a set of three periods, or four if the omission occurs at the end of a complete sentence. Word-processing software often uses a single keystroke for three closed-up periods replacing the traditional spaced periods.

ELLIPSIS:

Luis Valdez said in an interview: "I was beaten and kicked and jailed . . . essentially for doing theater."

Square brackets show that you have inserted clarification or comment into a quote:

SQUARE BRACKETS:

As a local columnist said, "Fame is fleeting. The publisher of *American Family* by Dan Quayle **[the former vice-president]** remaindered 85,000 unsold copies."

See **27c** for special uses of brackets to signal an ellipsis in scholarly writing.

QUOTE/ UNQUOTE

Weaving Quotations into Your Text

Effective writers use key quotations at strategic points:

STARTER QUOTE Use a striking quotation to *dramatize an issue*—to bring it to life:

From Cartoons to Courtrooms

In a landmark report, the Surgeon General concluded that "in any one segment of any given cartoon on any network, a child can witness 100 acts of violence."

OPINION QUOTE Quote at first hand a writer's strong personal opinion on a *debatable point*. (What did the person actually say?)

In the words of the Reuters correspondent, "While many see the new open directories as a further step toward democratizing the Internet, it is not hard to see them as unruly systems rife with potential problems and inaccuracies in posted content."

EXACT-WORDING QUOTE For important policy decisions or legal guidelines, quote the *exact phrasing*. (What was the exact wording of an ordinance, a petition, or a ruling?)

U.S. District Judge Ira DeMent struck down an Alabama law that would have allowed "nonsectarian, nonproselytizing, student-initiated, voluntary prayers" at school-related events. The judge said that his barring activities including teacher-led devotionals, vocal prayers at assemblies, and Bible give-aways "does nothing to limit individual exercise of personal religious beliefs."

FOLLOW-UP QUOTE Use an authoritative quote to help explain or define a *key term*. (What does a widely used term really mean?)

Stereotypes have a strong hold on our minds because they help us find our way in a confusing world. We cannot do justice to every separate individual, so we find a way to put many of them in the same bin. As Lippmann says,

> The real environment is altogether too big, too complex. . . . We are not equipped to deal with so much subtlety, so many permutations and combinations. And although we have to act in that environment, we have to reconstruct it on a simpler model before we can manage it.

(continued)

Weaving Quotations into Your Text *(continued)*

BOOSTER QUOTE Quote *authorities or insiders* to show that you are not alone. (Did someone say what you think better than you can?)

> Gun control advocates have been frustrated by the fact that a twelve-year-old can be given a lethal weapon for his birthday that has fewer warning labels than a package of aspirin and that costs less than a set of the *Encyclopaedia Britannica*. In the words of a former West Point student and army marksman writing in the *New York Times*, "It's insanity for military-style assault weapons to be cheaper and more easily obtainable than an American hunting rifle."

CLINCHER QUOTE Conclude with an especially *eloquent statement* in support of your main point:

> Harriet Stanton Blatch, daughter of the lifelong suffrage leader Elizabeth Cady Stanton, summarized the movement's legacy best when she stated: "Their struggle for the ballot took over 70 years of constant, determined campaigning, yet it did not take a single life, and its success has endured. . . . Without firing a shot, throwing a rock, or issuing a personal threat, women won for themselves rights that men have launched violent rebellions to achieve."

YOUR TURN 11 Digesting Quoted Material

From your current reading, pull out two sets of four or five closely related quotations. Then use the material in each set in a paragraph working the material into your own text. Use a mix of direct quotation and paraphrase. Try to vary your credit tags. Hand in your original notes with your finished paragraph.

- For the first set, limit yourself to *one article*. Bring together quotations that all bear on the same point. Then use your material in a well-developed, smoothly written paragraph.
- For the second set, bring together material from *several different sources*. Again, bring together quotations that all bear on the same point. Use your material in a well-developed, smoothly written paragraph.

YOUR TURN 12 A Paper for Peer Review

How did the author of the following student paper draw on her reading? What key ideas does she focus on, and where and how well does she explain them? What key examples or illustrations did she select? How much direct quotation and how much paraphrase does she use? How fair or balanced is her treatment of both sides of the issue? What questions remain in your mind as you finish the paper?

America: A Community of Individuals

Psychologist Henry Murray reasoned that "everyone is in some sense the same as everybody else; everyone is in some sense the same as somebody else; and everyone is in some sense the same as nobody else." These alternatives can serve to clarify the differences between multiculturalism and Daniel Boorstin's "American exceptionalism."

People who think like Boorstin would favor the statement that "everyone is in some sense the same as everybody else." They seek out the similarities in people and not the differences. A self-proclaimed "exceptionalist," Daniel J. Boorstin is one of those who believe that America is unique or exceptional among nations in that it enabled people of different nationalities to live together without ethnic conflict or tribal wars.

Boorstin compares American culture to the Americanized English language in his article "Why I Am Optimistic about America." He first examines the languages of other countries pointing out, "In Europe, languages had made nations. Spanish, Portuguese, English, French, German, and Italian had produced their own literatures—even before there was a Spain, Portugal, an England, a France, a Germany, or a Italy." He emphasizes the distinction of Americanized English: "But the United States was the first great modern nation without its own language. . . . The English language has been invigorated and Americanized by countless importations of words from German, Italian, French, Spanish, Yiddish, and American Indian tongues, among others." He concludes, "The surprising result is that, without a unique national language, our community has developed a language wonderfully expressive of the vitality and variety of our people." Boorstin believes that America is unique in that together we incorporate all of our separate ethnic backgrounds, social beliefs, and personal experiences to create a unique culture of our own.

An analogy that might fit Boorstin's philosophy is that of a patchwork quilt. A patchwork quilt is constructed by sewing an array of leftover cloth and unused material together producing a functional and beautiful quilt. As a "nation of immigrants," we

YOUR TURN 12 *(continued)*

make up a quilt with each individual's culture, belief, and experience. The result is a richly diverse nation—a formidable, colorful quilt. Boorstin's American exceptionalism is based on the theory that the mixture of cultures nevertheless combines to form a unified society. The history of this nation can be traced through the threads of a quilt.

Others do not agree with Boorstin. They argue that such a broad view of American culture lumps everyone together despite the vast differences of American society. They argue that this means individuals surrendering their own cultural, sexual, or ethnic identity. Instead of seeing a beautiful "patchwork quilt," they see a new version of the melting pot theory. The term *melting pot* implies that all will become the same. It does not account for the significant divisions along ethnic, gender, or religious lines. Many feel that this sentiment causes those who differ from the mainstream to feel alienated. As Arturo Madrid states, in "Diversity and Its Discontents," "Being the other sometimes involves sticking out like a sore thumb." Those who share Madrid's feelings believe in a movement toward multiculturalism. Many feel retaining one's cultural, ethnic, and sexual identities is more important than fitting into the mold of society.

Supporters of multiculturalism advocate a change of focus in the schools from the ethnocentric tendencies of historians to the contributions of minority figures in history, attempting to revise the historical record. Critics pounce on examples of "politically correct" teachers going to extremes. In one instance, elementary children were asked who invented the cotton gin. They answered that a white man, Eli Whitney, stole the idea from a woman who was not able to patent it in time. Sue Rinehart, professor at the University of Texas, discussed the problems of multiculturalism in the public school system:

> Attempting to incorporate multiculturalism into the curriculum in our public schools poses an interesting question: How do we determine which culture to focus on? History is infinitely interpretable. We can debate all day long on which aspects of American history have been tainted or distorted due to racist or ethnocentric attitudes of the historians.

George F. Will, a widely read columnist for *Newsweek*, claims to speak for the American mainstream that is becoming increasingly suspicious of multiculturalism. The multicultural movement, he said, "may by now be doing more good than harm because it is producing a libertarian backlash." Sacvan Bercovitch of Harvard University offered this thesis: "America is about possibilities, not certainties. You can (but you don't have to) get rich. America is about promises. Here class divisions do exist, but they don't have to matter. . . . Exceptionalism is the doctrine that justifies that promise."

Supporters for both sides agree that people should not lose themselves in the attempt to "fit in." But those in favor of multiculturalism believe that certain minorities are inevitably left out. Boorstin's "exceptionalism" holds out hope for a society that includes all cultures equally.

OPTIONS FOR WRITING 6

Write a paper in which you respond to your reading. Make extensive use of quotations. Use varied techniques for working quoted materials into your text.

1 "Are Opinions Male?" asked Naomi Wolf, author of *The Beauty Myth,* in an article in the *New Republic.* The editorial pages of the nation's press, she said, were dominated by male journalists. What is the role or influence of widely read female journalists like Ellen Goodman of the *Boston Globe,* Molly Ivins of the *Fort Worth Star,* or Cynthia Tucker of the *Atlanta Constitution?* Study the writing of one widely syndicated female columnist over a number of weeks. Introduce potential readers to the journalist's values or commitments.

2 Respond to an article or editorial that brought out a strong personal reaction in you. Write a paper in which you express your support or argue with the author. Where do you agree with the writer, and why? Where do you disagree, and why? Do justice to the author's point of view and define your own position.

3 Are the views of conservative white male students underrepresented in college courses or college reading? Can you show them that you read columnists or other writers representing a responsible conservative position? Write a paper documenting their position on a core issue or on several related key issues.

4 A book like Herrnstein and Murray's *The Bell Curve,* Naomi Wolf's *The Beauty Myth,* or Gloria Steinem's *Revolution from Within* can create heated discussion and force readers to define their own position on a key issue. Study the treatment of a key issue in a chapter from such a book. Show and discuss the author's (or authors') view.

5 Writers like Ray Bradbury and Ursula Le Guin established a tradition of science fiction that does not deal with monsters from outer space or little green men from Mars. Instead, they made readers look at basic questions about human nature from a thought-provoking new perspective. Write a review-critique of a work of science fiction that you think other readers would find thought-provoking or rewarding.

3c Cyberspace, Internet, e-mail

Use and evaluate material from electronic sources.

In the age of the information highway and the knowledge explosion, anything you might want to know is at your fingertips. On almost any topic, you can call up material ranging from scholarly studies to gossipy news items and to instantaneous responses from a group of concerned individuals. A few keystrokes will call up on your computer screen information about enrollment in private colleges or about a god-king who ruled Egypt four thousand years ago. You can call up definitions of a difficult word from a dictionary on CD-ROM as you are typing a paper. You can call up rich information on the abolitionist movement from an online encyclopedia like *Encarta*, following links to major figures and events in the antislavery agitation.

In the late 1990s, a new translation of Franz Kafka, who made *alienation* a household word, became a publishing event. One student's online exploration of this event and of a renewed interest in the art of translation produced the following items among others. Study the way they show the range of online sources. The two dates for each item show the date it was posted and the day it was accessed. The retrieval code for online material appears in angled brackets.

NEWSPAPER ONLINE:

Coates, Steve. "A Dead Language Comes to Life on the Internet." New York Times on the Web 28 Oct. 1996. 20 Oct. 1998 <http://www.nytimes.com/web/doscroot/ library/ cyber/week/1028Latin.html>.

NEWSLETTER ONLINE:

McCalla, John. "Kafka's Hot and He's Also Funny." Penn News 2 Apr. 1998. 18 Oct. 1998 <http://www.upenn.edu/pennnews/ current/1998/040298/Kafka.html>.

BOOK REVIEW ONLINE:

L., Harold. Rev. of The Castle: A New Translation, by Franz Kafka. Trans. Mark Harman. Philadelphia Inquirer 26 Apr. 1998. 18 Oct. 1998 <http://www.phillynews.com/inquirer/98/Apr/26/ books/KAFKA26.tml>.

REFERENCE WORK ONLINE, WITH VERSION NUMBER AND DATE:

"Kafka." Britannica Online. Vers. 97.1.1. Mar. 1997. Encyclopaedia Britannica. 17 Oct. 1998 <http://www.eb.com/>.

COLLECTION OF MATERIALS ON CD-ROM:

Fresca, Dolores. "Kafka and Patriarchy." The World of Kafka. CD-ROM. New York: Klamm Publications, 1999.

E-MAIL TO THE STUDENT WRITER:

Minusco, Sarah. E-mail to the author. 1 Feb. 1999.

3c.1 **Searching the Net** *Learn to locate material on the net.* Most users of the net have their own favorite search engines, such as Yahoo! or AltaVista or Lycos. They develop their own search techniques.

Are you looking for recent material by an author known for his authoritative comments on current issues (such as Howard Rheingold on virtual reality)? Your instructor or a librarian might recommend AltaVista as the search engine most likely to produce recent publications, reviews, or biographical background. Other frequently recommended search engines have included Infoseek, Lycos, or WebCrawler. In the rapidly evolving world of cyberspace, new competitors will offer ever faster and more efficient ways to help you find your way on the information highway.

You may want to track the same key subject using several major search engines and comparing the results. For instance, is it true that AIDS education for young Americans has been ineffective, with many teenagers practicing unprotected sex? Any large unrestricted label like AIDS is likely to bury you under several thousand listings. So you will start not with the unrestricted key word AIDS but with the narrower and more selective AIDS EDUCATION. People writing on this topic will not all use this exact term, so you may have to be resourceful and ask yourself: "How else would people talk about this topic?" You might then try also SAFE SEX EDUCATION or TEENAGERS AND AIDS or UNPROTECTED SEX.

For a systematic focused search, you are likely to use some variation of the **Boolean** system. It enables you to narrow your key word or phrase to the right point.

- With the Boolean system, you use the **link words** *and, or,* and *not* in order to zero in on your specific concern. For instance, you decide to try

  AIDS *and* education

  You may still receive a sizable list of sources to consult, but they will all be focused more directly on a key question: efforts to alert young people to the threat of the epidemic.

- The link word *not* can screen out entries when your key word has *different meanings* in two large separate areas. If you want to check current research on the relations between AIDS and a failing immunity system, you might try "immunity *not* law *or* legal." This way you would screen out articles about witnesses granted immunity from prosecution in a court of law.
- If you want the computer to search for a phrase, enclose it in **parentheses**: (English Education). This way the computer will not read it as two separate words: English *and* Education.

✓ ***EDITOR'S TIP:*** The way you would actually type in your key words for the AIDS paper or for a paper about regulating the whaling industry might be the following:

AIDS educat*
whal* and regulat*

You type only the root of your key word, followed by an asterisk. This way the computer would search not only for titles and descriptions with the exact word *education* but also with related words like *educating*. If you type *intelligen**, the computer will search for all versions of the word with different endings, such as *intelligent, intelligence, intelligences.*

3c.2 Evaluating Electronic Sources *Evaluate and verify material from Internet sources.* Electronic searches typically generate a wealth of material, presenting you with a special challenge as you sift and evaluate the results. For material put on the net after being published elsewhere, the Internet serves as an **electronic library**—an instant access library. You can often retrieve and check the original print publication. If necessary, you can go back to sources more complete, more permanent, or more carefully checked and verified.

However, increasingly much material is *first* published and often *only* published on the net. The net then serves as a gigantic worldwide **electronic publisher**—minus the army of editors, critics, and reviewers that have traditionally sifted and channeled print materials. As in other areas, the computer increasingly allows you to bypass the middleman, the mediator or facilitator. As a result, "Reader Beware" becomes an important caution.

INTERNET GUIDELINES

Evaluating Electronic Sources

When you draw on electronic sources, keep the following questions in mind:

1 AUTHORSHIP ***Who wrote or assembled the material?*** Is the author clearly identified? Or is the material anonymous or quasi-anonymous? Is there any indication of the credentials or credibility of the author or authors?

2 ORIGINAL SOURCE ***Can you trace the material to an original source?*** Was this piece originally published elsewhere? Who put it on the net? Was it copied, recycled, or pirated from somewhere?

3 INTELLECTUAL PROPERTY ***Who has the rights to this material?*** Is there any indication of copyright?

4 COMPLETENESS ***How reliable is the current version?*** Has it been excerpted or massaged, and by whom? Is anyone responsible for the accuracy and completeness of the current version? Can you trace a more complete original version?

5 PERMANENCE ***How long will this material be accessible?*** Will others be able to retrieve and verify it at a later date?

3c.3 Sample Search Results If you are careful about evaluating your sources, it is hard to beat the speed and convenience of conducting a focused search of major online publications. Suppose you are looking in online newspapers and magazines for material to help answer the question: Is there a new sensitive male in American movies? Have the movies discovered the new sensitized male who has left crude machismo behind? The following might be a part of your results:

SEARCH RESULTS:

New York Times on the Web—Movie Review:

"The action heroes are changing, although their movies still have huge budgets and much violence. Arnold Schwarzenegger said about one of his recent movies that he would play a 'vulnerable' action hero."

Washington Post Online—Columnist:

The new male hero is still an outdoor type "who builds camp fires" and "smears his face with mud." However, he does so in search of "a primitive but more soulful culture living in closer harmony with the earth." In general terms, "He is a friend to the red and black man. He is a spiritual traveler, a visionary outsider."

New York Times on the Web—Movie Review:

"Audience tastes seem to be moving away from the Sylvester Stallones and their crude violence to actors like Harrison Ford, who look thoughtful and intelligent. They portray dedication and perseverance rather than brute muscle strength. However, men are still shown as the controlling people in relationships with women."

Los Angeles Times—Feature Article:

"During reruns of old movie favorites, audiences can see Jimmy Stewart, the original sensitive male. In an early classic, he is shown wearing an apron and working in the kitchen just before the comeuppance of the stereotypical Western outlaw bullying and terrorizing the town."

Local Newspaper Online—Media Critic:

"Movies are not going to go as far as the shaving cream commercial that offered sensitive-skin shaving gel for sensitive men. However, some upcoming movie favorites have played in films where they are shown as handsome and very masculine but also as capable of feeling pain and learning to express emotions."

Remember that teachers and editors warn of relying too exclusively on Internet sources. You will bolster your credibility by bringing in related material from publications not on the net. These might include special interest magazines and perhaps a book of collected reviews by a prominent movie critic. They might include publications known for their searching movie reviews, like the *New Yorker* and the *New Republic*.

YOUR TURN 13 Keeping Up with the Movies

Search major online newspapers or magazines for current movie reviews or articles on trends in Hollywood. Focus on a current trend or issue of special interest to you, such as strong women as action heroes or reexaminations of American history (*Amistad*).

3c.4 Changing Communication Styles *Remember the benefits and possible downside of changing communication styles.* Computers are changing the way we think and write:

- *Computers are shortening the distance between thinking and writing.* As you work at the keyboard, you see a paper take shape as you think the subject through. You can paste in material as you transfer files. You can easily work in second thoughts and new information. You are likely to make better use of the opportunities for ongoing revision and for adapting material to different uses.
- *Writing is becoming more interactive.* Writers are becoming used to the instant reply. Participating in the electronic conversation is likely to make you more audience-conscious—more aware of your readers and what is going on in their minds, even if they are merely **lurking** rather than actively sharing in the give-and-take. One researcher estimated that at peak times members congregate in as many as 19,000 **chat rooms**, representing "a staggering diversity of hobbies, political interests, geographical regions, shared diseases, and sexual tastes."
- *At the same time, writing may turn more simple and choppy in order to fit the small screen.* Are we becoming too used to sound bites—to bit facts and stray comments? We are getting used to glossy bits of gossip in newsmagazines. Instructions for creating **websites** that tout products and services encourage the authors to cut back on print content and concentrate on attractive layouts and graphics. With so many bite-size pieces of information, you may have to make a special effort to establish the connections and to see the larger picture.

OPTIONS FOR WRITING 7

Search the Web for current discussions of one of the following Cyberspace issues or a similar current issue. Is there a developing consensus on the issue? Are there major opposing positions? Write a paper summing up your findings, presenting evidence from your sources. Choose one:

1 attempts to control or censor material on the Web
2 use of unacknowledged sources—pirating, plagiarism
3 copyright protection and remuneration for authors
4 calls for the use of blocking software in public libraries
5 efforts to control spamming, or unsolicited e-mail

3d Drawing on Interviews

Learn to draw on oral as well as printed sources.

Interviews can range from a casual conversation to a carefully scripted question-and-answer session. They give you a way of tapping into what people really think and feel. A first-rate writer is often a first-rate listener. Powerful writing about poverty, the changing family, or the "savage inequalities" of American education has been done by interviewers like Jonathan Kozol, Richard Coles, Studs Terkel, and Mike Rose. These are admirably patient, committed listeners who get Americans to talk eloquently and without pretense or ulterior motives about the things that truly matter in their lives.

Material from interviews can add a special human dimension to your writing. It enables you to bring in live authentic material not found in press releases, agency policy statements, or carefully edited public announcements. You might add an authentic human touch to a paper by **field work** like the following:

- talking to fellow students who did campaign work for a local candidate about what they learned about the political process
- talking to friends who have done volunteer work for homeless shelters or kitchens for the homeless about their observations of the homeless
- talking to a spokesperson for a police officers' association about the dangers of police work
- talking to a social worker about "latchkey kids" who are often alone without their working parents
- talking to a faculty member with a special interest in child care

Experienced interviewers often come to an interview with a set of **prepared questions**. However, they are also ready to depart from the script and follow through when a question produces an exceptionally candid or interesting response. Here is a set of sample questions you might bring to an interview focused on how older people deal with retirement:

INTERVIEWER'S QUESTIONS:

1 What did you do before you retired?

2 Were you ready for retirement?

3 What do you like best about retirement?

4 What do you like least about retirement?

5 What do you think about mandatory retirement?
6 What advice would you give to younger people planning for retirement?
7 If you could turn the clock back twenty or thirty years, what would you do differently?
8 Do you think retired people are a privileged group in our society?
9 Do you think retired people are a political force?

Take notes during the interview, ask for permission to tape, or write down your recollections as accurately as you can afterwards. Sometimes a writer will write up the results of an interview in a **question-and-answer** format. The following is part of an interview with a woman who is successful in a profession that was long dominated by males. Do any of her answers surprise you? What follow-up questions would you have liked to ask?

SAMPLE INTERVIEW:

Q: What is your background and what or who inspired you to become an engineer?
A: After high school graduation, I began college as a pre-med student. During the summers, I held jobs in electronics and mechanical assembly that had to do with lasers. The summer jobs extended over two years, and I switched to an engineering major. . . .

Q: In advanced science or mathematics courses in college, did you find that you were the only female or just one of a few?
A: No, actually in the engineering classes about a third of all the classes had women in them. These women included majors in general engineering, mechanical engineering, industrial engineering, and civil engineering.

Q: Have you had to overcome any specific obstacles in reaching your goal to become an engineer? Has anyone ever turned you down for a job because of doubts that you could do the job?
A: No, actually I find that most women engineers in my field find the opposite. Some people might call it reverse discrimination because there are not very many women engineers around, so for many companies it is a feather in their cap to get a woman on their staff.

Q: Why is that?
A: Equal opportunity requires a number of minorities and women on the staff, and women engineers are considered a minority. As for obstacles, there are a number I have seen. I don't know that they have been obstacles because I have found ways to get around

them. One of the obstacles is the older male engineers who make you feel that you have to work twice as hard as your male counterparts to prove that you know what you are doing. With the younger engineers, closer to my age, I find there is more acceptance because they have gone to school with women students, so they don't have the same bias. . . .

YOUR TURN 14 A Paper for Peer Review

How well do you get to know the subject who was interviewed for this paper? How pointed or fruitful are the interviewer's questions? What is most revealing or thought-provoking about the answers? How well does the material add up? What questions would you like to ask the subject or the interviewer?

Picking Up Garbage

Gabriel was born the youngest of thirteen children. He grew up in the old country and has been in the United States for three years. Every morning he goes to his job in the waste land-fill area. When I ask him about his work, he says: "I used to pick up papers in the area. Everybody starts out with that job. Some people are able to save some money that way. Then they go back to the old country, drink and relax for a few months, and then, when they run out of money, come back here. They will always be picking up papers. I don't want to go back. I drive a truck now, and I crush the garbage. I save money."

I ask him about the place where he lives. He is not living with family. "It is a small place with fifteen people living there. I feel bad because we all sleep together in two rooms. I am the first one to go to work in the morning. So when my alarm goes off at 5:30 a.m., everybody is disturbed. I feel bad that everybody wakes up because of the noise from my alarm. But what can I do? I have to work."

Gabriel spends little time at the place where he "lives." He usually works more than five days and goes to school four evenings a week. What does he like least about his job? He says that he does a lot of thinking while he drives the truck. "You know that the American people throw out many things. Much of it is good stuff. I see toys that are brand new. I see radios that are not broken. I see many things that I would like to send to people in my own country. But I cannot pick up any of the things. There is a rule. The driver is not allowed to get out of the truck."

I assume that the company is trying to protect the drivers' health by not letting them handle items from the garbage cans. But Gabriel says that the rule is intended for the drivers' safety: Once a driver who climbed out of the truck to pick up something was run over by another driver who did not see him. "A few times," Gabriel says, "I have taken the chance of losing my job. I got out and picked up a tape recorder once. I brought it home, and it worked perfectly. The Americans throw away so many things like that. It's like throwing away money. Americans are very rich. The people in my country are very poor. Every day I see good things thrown away, and it breaks my heart to crush them. I am destroying what my people could use."

I am looking at the job of the garbage collector from a different perspective since I talked to Gabriel. I used to think that the filth and the smell would bother me most about the job. I found that what bothers Gabriel most is the idea of looking at "waste" all day.

OPTIONS FOR WRITING 8

Pull together and interpret the results of interviews or conversations on a current topic. Try to identify a major trend or major trends in what you have found. Make use of revealing or thought-provoking quotations. (Your instructor may ask you to write up one of the original interviews in a question-and-answer format.)

1 What role models are there for young people in our society? Is there a shortage of heroes—male or female? Conduct an extended interview with one young person, or talk to several young people. Do they find it hard to find people to admire or to model their own lives on?

2 Why do immigrants come to the United States? What are their motives, their hopes, their fears, their aspirations? Interview immigrants or children of immigrants. Are there recurrent patterns in their life stories? Or conduct an in-depth interview with one individual.

3 Are public figures entitled to privacy in their personal lives? Or does the public have a right to know about their personal lives in order to judge their character? Interview fellow students.

4 Can you find someone who is willing to be identified as an angry white male, a committed feminist, a libertarian, or a representative of another group known for strong views? What are the person's views? How true is the individual to a type or a stereotype?

5 Is there a religious revival or spiritual awakening among college students? Talk to counselors, campus ministers, and interested faculty members about their observation of students they know. Do they agree on overall trends or issues?

4 WRITING/THINKING STRATEGIES

Employ strategies for organizing your thinking and writing.

As a writer today, you have instant access to information, and you can tap into a wide range of opinion and commentary. How will you process your information? What thinking will give shape and direction to your writing? What strategies will help you sort out and make sense of your data? How will you evaluate your options or line up opposing arguments?

The thinking that goes into writing is part of a continuum. You will be thinking the subject through whether you are marking off stages in early humanity's use of tools, or whether you are sorting out different kinds of immigrants, or whether you are weighing the pros and cons of a proposed teenage curfew. Writers do not at some point put on their thinking hats and say: In this paper, I will be logical. In this paper, I will do some systematic reasoning. Instead, writers sort out, compare, generalize, and balance off opposites as part of what it means to be a writer.

The following is a sampling of thinking-and-writing strategies that will help you organize your writing. In a short paper, one of these will often provide the ground plan for your paper as a whole. In a longer paper, first one and then another may help you organize your writing. Think of these strategies not as set formulas but as dynamic processes that you adapt for your own purposes.

- *Line up related examples to show a trend.* This is the thinking that underlies the classic thesis-and-support paper. Sorting out your material often means bringing together evidence that points in the same direction. To document the trend toward "distance learning" (or off-campus learning), you may be able to marshal personal observations, media accounts, revealing statistics, and insider's testimony. Is it true that students will graduate without ever having set foot on an actual campus? As a question of strategy, you may have to decide whether and where to acknowledge obstacles or exceptions. You may have to decide how to defuse objections from readers who disagree.
- *Use comparison and contrast to guide your readers' choices.* This is the kind of thinking that tests your ability to show the connections between different sets of data. For instance, you may be comparing two competing products or ways of thinking or ways of doing business. Each year more shoppers do their shopping over the Internet. You may decide to chart the contrast as follows:

The Electronic Mall

1 shopping the conventional way
  - fighting your way through traffic
  - trying to find parking
  - trying to have a clerk help you to find merchandise
  - standing in line for the cashier

2 shopping the electronic way
  - staying home to shop
  - checking an easily accessible catalog
  - entering your order and credit card information
  - having purchases delivered to your home address

- *Help your readers choose among several alternatives.* A zoning commission or the city council may be weighing the merits of proposals for dealing with a downtown movie palace that has been deteriorating over the years. A basic strategy for influencing such a decision is to look at several alternatives and find them wanting, clearing the way for the solution the writer supports. A well-argued paper may first eliminate the first two choices and then strongly support the third:

  - tear down the building and allow a developer to build an office tower
  - continue subsidies to art and drama groups using the building
  - support a major redevelopment effort to make the building the cornerstone of a new cultural center

- *Mark off stages in a chain of events.* When you trace a process, major stages or waystations may already seem to be built into your subject-matter. Or you may help your readers find their way by identifying major links in a chain of development. The following might be the rough outline of an article tracing the itinerary of an observation satellite that for thousands of years will continue to travel into ever more distant space:

The Ten-Thousand Year Journey

purpose of the mission

equipment for observation

exploring the neighboring planets

first closeup of the more distant planets

leaving our solar system behind

As you become a more experienced writer, you become more aware of the thinking that goes into an effective piece of writing. You become better at using familiar thinking strategies in shedding light on a challenging subject. You learn how to structure a convincing argument, using lines of reasoning that have often proved effective.

4a Tracing a Comparison

Use comparing and contrasting to organize your thinking.

Comparing and contrasting are basic strategies for processing information. When you present new information or explain a difficult concept, the basic questions in the reader's mind typically are: "How is this *similar* to what I already know? And how is this *different* from what I already know?" Writers who show similarities and differences help us size up new developments and make important choices.

Writers often use **comparison and contrast** to make a major point. For instance, they often develop a contrast between then and now or between newcomer and insider. The following passage makes an important point about learning to write by playing off rookie against pro:

The Reluctant-Writer Syndrome

THESIS:

Manuals and guides for writers are full of advice, but one step is basic: You have to overcome the "reluctant-writer" syndrome.

ONE SIDE:

Reluctant writers put the job off till the very last minute, and even then their heart isn't in it. They write the first and only draft late at night before a paper or a project is due. In the words of one disillusioned teacher, the one incentive that keeps them going is that "the thing is due at 9:30 Monday morning." What with the pressure of college work, outside work, and social life or family obligations, the reluctant-writer syndrome is a very easy pattern to slide into. It is also totally different from how real writers work.

OTHER SIDE:

Real writers become involved in a subject. They begin to think about it and worry about it. They are thinking about it when they pretend to be listening politely to what you are saying about dorm food or the Big Game. They start working up the subject—they "read up" on it; they start collecting clippings and quotable quotes. They start talking about it, getting into arguments with a roommate or spouse. While working on a first or intermediate draft, many of them experience a "writer's high"—a feeling of excitement or elation as the paper or article begins to take shape.

When you think a subject through, you will often be following up both similarities and differences. There are different ways to organize the comparison. You might focus first on how two things are alike—and then show how they nevertheless differ in important ways. Or you might decide to focus on how they compare on the points that seem most important to you.

Suppose a student has attended both private and public schools and decides to share an insider's perspective as a contribution to the current debate over public vs. private education. An early scratch outline might look something like this:

homogeneous vs. diverse student body

more parent involvement and arguments over grades in private school

well-behaved and docile private school students?

private schools emphasize the "basics"

A fully worked out **point by point** comparison might be structured as follows:

	PRIVATE SCHOOL	PUBLIC SCHOOL
1 Student Body	student population tends to be homogeneous, often from the same religious or cultural roots (Catholic, Baptist, Jewish)	students tend to come from many different ethnic and cultural backgrounds (like Asian and Hispanic)
2 Academic Preparation	students tend to be well-grounded in traditional academic skills	preparation varies widely from very poor study skills to adequate preparation
3 Parent Involvement	parents worry about grades and badger teachers about subject matter and methods	students are often on their own, with little teacher-parent contact
4 Student Attitudes	students have been trained to respect authority and do as they are told	students are often independent, ready to question authority

Spelling out how such a detailed comparison adds up is a challenge. The thesis pulling together the writer's findings might read like this:

THESIS: **Private schools tend to prepare students well academically, while public schools may prepare them better for life in a diverse and challenging society.**

A writer choosing a different approach might decide to give readers a better feeling for each kind of schooling by covering first the one and then the other as a whole. However, to make readers see the contrast, each half of the paper would take up the same major points in the same order. The following would be the rearranged outline for such a **parallel order** comparison:

1 PRIVATE SCHOOLS
   Student Body
   Academic Preparation
   Parent Involvement
   Student Attitudes

2 PUBLIC SCHOOLS
   Student Body
   Academic Preparation
   Parent Involvement
   Student Attitudes

GUIDELINES FOR WRITING AND REVISION

Tracing a Comparison

In writing and revising a comparison paper, keep guidelines like the following in mind:

1 ***Clarify the purpose of your comparison.*** What are you trying to show? In a paper on city vs. country, are you merely going to line up half-jokingly one more time city slicker vs. country folk? Or are you going to look seriously at reasons for leaving city life in search of a more healthful lifestyle? Are you perhaps focusing on the concerns of parents trying to decide if city or country provides a better environment for growing up?

2 ***Check the flow of ideas.*** Reviewing your outline of the "private vs. public" paper on the schools, you may decide that it has a logical progression that will make sense to your readers:

students—who they are

preparation—what they bring with them

parent interest—who keeps track of them

student attitude—what the end product is

Nevertheless, you might decide that one essential link is missing: Who does the teaching? Between "preparation" and "parent interest," do you need a section on the faculty? Maybe one kind of school promises more personal attention from teachers with a common purpose. The other kind might offer less personal attention but a range of faculty from different backgrounds and points of view.

3 ***Provide thought links to help your readers see the connections.*** For instance, in the second half of a parallel-order comparison, you are likely to need **transitions** reminding readers of what went before and helping them see the connections:

Whereas private schools often have students from the same religious community or cultural background, public schools often bring together the true range of today's society. . . .

Whereas private schools pride themselves on traditional education in the basics, public school students may have had only spotty preparation in basic skills. . . .

Whereas parents in private schools often take a strong interest in grades and teaching methods, teachers in public schools may hear from parents only on rare occasions. . . .

However, while private schools often turn out better model students, public schools often do more to foster independence of mind. . . .

4 ***Try to provide pegs that help readers focus on key concepts.*** See if you can give your readers labels that help them remember major points. For instance, in writing about the schools, consider sharpening key contrasts by lining up pairs like the following:

solidarity vs. **diversity**

the **concerned parent** vs. the **absentee parent**

the **model student** vs. the **independent thinker**

YOUR TURN 15 A Paper for Peer Review

Study the following fresh look at an age-old topic for comparison and contrast. What is the purpose of the comparison? Where or how does it become clear? What are the major points of comparison? How well are they followed up? Can you chart or schematize the overall plan? For you, is the paper well-argued or convincing? Suppose you were sending an e-mail to the student author. What would you say to the writer?

No Escape from the City

We Americans have come to associate country life with everything that's wholesome. We believe that country life is slow-paced and simple and full of good times and good feelings. Advertising agencies constantly capitalize on this folklore. They sell us everything from cars to cigarettes by placing their products in rural settings. They show us hearty outdoor types sitting by mountain streams drinking beer. They know we love cowboys and mountains. However, this nostalgic idealized view of rural life is not consistent with reality.

I know several young couples who dream of escaping the fast-paced urban lifestyle. They're tired of spending hours each day on congested highways. They're tired of fighting for parking spaces when they get to their destination. They're tired of irritable fellow motorists always on the verge of road rage. They're really tired of worrying about their children in unsafe schools. They feel threatened by the high odds of becoming victims of crime—muggings, burglary, "random violence." They dream of living in the country where life is easy and good.

I'm a reverse migrant. I grew up in Idaho in a rural community. My parents, grandparents, and many relatives live there still. I've watched as the meat-packing plant my father and brother and nearly a hundred others worked for went bankrupt and closed down. I've watched, for years, while neighbors have tried to sell their land. Their acreage is worth less now, fifteen years after they bought it, than they paid for it. I've spent hours talking to a friend about the run of dead-end jobs her husband has had, about their frustration with feeling stuck, about their lack of hope and fear of the future.

While certain city people strike out in search of space and quality in living, certain rural dwellers head for the city. Both are looking for an improved quality of life. City kids ride tricycles on litter-strewn sidewalks, play ball on asphalt-paved parking lots surrounded by tall apartment buildings, and stand in line in crowded parks to slide on slides or swing on swings. All this happens while a grown-up watches for safety's sake.

Children do need to breathe clean and smoke-free air, they do need to be safe and have room to play, and they do need to be surrounded by natural, living things. Overall-clad or jean-clad children in the country, making forts in haystacks and mazes in tall over-the-head weeds, running in open pastures, riding horses, or feeding chickens and cattle and sheep are certainly in touch with living things. These children can often play for hours safely without adult supervision. Therefore, the rural environment does seem to be better suited to the rearing of children.

However, studies show that children raised in rural areas often suffer from economic, social, and educational deprivation. There are few schools and the ones there are often lack curriculum diversity. They lack modern facilities—gymnasiums, pools, computer labs, multimedia centers, libraries. In rural areas, there are traditionally high rates of school dropouts, youth unemployment, and delinquency. In addition, rural youth may grow up with low educational and occupational aspirations. Consequently, they aren't prepared to deal with today's world, where even agriculture uses sophisticated technology and modern management techniques.

Community life is often different in small towns where people take the time to get to know one another and become involved in each other's lives. Some people move to rural areas to find this sense of community. They want to escape the isolation of city life. In reality, in many rural settings, there is great distance between houses. People who move to these areas trade psychological isolation for actual physical isolation. The answer is for city dwellers to band together in a real community spirit. Cities like New York City and San Francisco have revitalized neighborhoods where small shops, local restaurants, and small theaters give people almost a small-town feeling. This will happen in any environment where people take the time to get involved with each other.

OPTIONS FOR WRITING 9

Set up a comparison/contrast that could help guide your reader's choices. Concentrate on the most significant similarities or differences. Make sure your reader can see your overall strategy for setting up the comparison.

1 Compare and evaluate two comparable institutions. For instance, look at two child care centers, two fitness centers, or two jails. How much difference is there? How significant are the differences? What accounts for them?

2 How much difference is there between public and private education? Why do parents send their children to private schools? Can you compare two schools, one from the public and one from the private sector?

OPTIONS FOR WRITING 9 *(continued)*

3 For potential users, compare/contrast two kinds of communication or of doing business. For instance, write about using the telephone vs. relying on e-mail. Why do some people swear by the one method and other people by the other?

4 Have you worked for or known both a small business and a large corporation? Are family-type small business operations a relic from the past? Are large corporations soulless? What would you recommend to your readers if they had a choice?

5 Should we think more about what we eat? Health-oriented Americans are committed to organic food. What makes organic food different from ordinary food? What are basic criteria? What is wrong with ordinary food?

6 Some observers claim that a bad marriage is worse for children than a divorce. What is it like to grow up with parents who quarrel but stay together—as against growing up with parents who have divorced? Can you compare and contrast the effect on children, drawing on your own observation or reading?

7 Have you had experience with an alternative kind of medicine? How was it different from standard or orthodox medicine? How open should people be to new therapies or medical perspectives?

8 Do you have the technical background to compare and evaluate two kinds of software or two operating systems or two search engines for the Internet? For instance, is one more user-friendly than the other? Is one more technically sophisticated than the other?

9 Have you observed different ways of dealing with discipline problems or with poor performance in school? What were the differences in philosophy? What was the difference in results? What advice would you give to people in need of help?

10 Have you ever made a change from one kind of religious outlook or spiritual orientation to another? What made you change? What did the new outlook have to offer that the other didn't?

4b Writing to Classify

Set up categories that help your readers find their bearings.

Classification is the thinking strategy we employ when we ask: "What goes with what?" We set up categories that enable us to sort out data and get a handle on confusing situations. Institutions and organizations of all kinds use systems of classification. They need to know what group to put us in, so they can tell us what rules or insurance rates or fee schedules apply to us. They ask us to check off married, single, or divorced. They classify us as minors, adults, or seniors. Sometimes such ready-made categories are useful or helpful, but sometimes they seem to box us in or put us in the wrong bin.

A writer good at sorting things out can help us make sense of what is happening. Changing realities require us to set up new categories or to update existing ones. Once everyone knew what a family was. Now we know that there are different kinds of families. Young people often find themselves in confusing situations, unsure of their roles. One student writer sorted out changing family arrangements for them as follows:

Do You Have Family?

1 The **traditional nuclear family** centered on a provider and a homemaker. (The traditional family according to some estimates is now down to 17 percent.)

2 As families needed added income, women increasingly went to work outside the home. The result was the **two-wage-earner family.**

3 With the rising incidence of divorce, children found themselves increasingly growing up in a **single-parent family.**

4 As their parents got remarried, the children often found themselves with a new parent and new siblings in the **step-family.**

5 As society began to recognize alternative lifestyles, politicians started to wrestle with the concept of the **domestic-partner family.**

6 As traditional family ties weakened, close family friends became substitute uncles and substitute grandmothers in a new kind of **extended family.**

We classify for a purpose. Family counselors or judges in juvenile courts might think in terms of categories different from those the student writer listed but more relevant to their work. Their system of classification might be something like this:

functional families

dysfunctional families

broken homes

single-parent families

We often establish categories by setting up different levels, like *upper class, middle class,* and *lower class*. Like society as a whole, an institution or profession is often a hierarchy—a stratified, layered system where one group of people ranks above the other. Often the challenge for a writer is to revise a traditional think scheme to make it fit new facts. Journalists and sociologists, for instance, have added a new level below the traditional *working class*—a permanently unemployed, welfare-dependent *underclass*. Others are looking for a new term like *overclass* for a new elite of supermanagers, mega-athletes, pop music idols, and top models with dazzling earnings and privileges.

GUIDELINES FOR WRITING AND REVISION

Setting Up Categories

1 ***Make sure readers see the basis for your classification.*** What criteria are you using to put things in one bin or another? Sometimes we sort people out simply by age or academic level—but usually we rely on a combination of factors. As you divide sports into upper-class, middle-class, and lower-class sports, you may be able to show that the way the fans dress and behave, the cars they drive, and the advertisers who cater to them are all part of the package.

2 ***Provide detailed convincing examples for each category.*** Show that your system of classification actually accommodates much of what your readers can observe and verify.

UPPER-CLASS SPORTS

At a tennis match in an exclusive neighborhood, fans arrive in big expensive cars but many in Volvos, Saabs, and Porsches. Attendance is limited and fans wear casual white shirts tucked into cotton slacks. If a player swears after a bad call, a disapproving murmur passes through the crowd. . . .

MIDDLE-CLASS SPORTS

At a football game in a major city, the fans arrive early for tailgate parties, driving Ford, Dodge, and Chevrolet wagons and vans as well as Hondas and Toyotas. Dress ranges from polyester blends from J. C. Penney's and Sears for pants stretching over substantial waists to Levi's 501 jeans for the younger crowd. Commercials for television viewers are heavy on burger chains, muffler shops, and light beer. . . .

LOWER-CLASS SPORTS . . .

3 ***Try to do without hypothetical, made-up examples.*** Perhaps you are describing an imaginary couple that illustrates perfectly one typical kind of male-female communication. (No wonder—you made them up!)

YOUR TURN 16 Setting Up Categories

The following summary of an article or longer paper works its way down the scale of professions ranked according to income and privilege. How well defined or convincing are the categories? Do any of them make you change your own thinking? What examples or counterexamples can you cite for each category?

Winners and Losers: The Changing Workforce

THESIS: **While economists and politicians sing the praises of prosperity, working Americans in several major categories are falling behind.**

I PROFESSIONALS Members of the professions range from doctors with incomes in the six figures and with effective professional representation to teachers with eroding salaries and status. Many physicians that were once top earners have seen their income reduced as a result of the trend toward managed care. Increasingly, undergraduate teaching in American universities is done by disenfranchised part-timers with no job security or benefits.

II MANAGEMENT Compensation for top management that once might have been at ten times the income of a worker has risen to astronomical multiples as the result of huge salaries, bonuses, stock options, and golden parachutes for executives. At the same time, middle management jobs are endangered as computers take over many management and accounting functions.

III SALARIED EMPLOYEES Premium salaries or commissions go to highly skilled individuals in key areas of today's economy—from computer specialists to money managers and advertising wizards.

IV WAGE EARNERS As manufacturing jobs moved across the border or overseas and as labor union power was decimated, the era of high wages and ample benefits for American workers came to an end. Trends like the shift to service sector jobs and to outsourcing left many workers in nonunion employment with limited or no benefits. Many Americans took second jobs to make ends meet.

V TEMPORARIES Recent estimates put the number of temporary workers without health benefits or pension rights at one-third of the workforce. Many are "on call"—called in for work only as needed ("flexible scheduling").

VI ILLEGALS It is hard to estimate the extent of the underground economy that employs illegal immigrants working in sweatshops in the garment industry, on construction jobs, as migrant labor in

YOUR TURN 16 *(continued)*

the fields, or as gardeners, maids, and nannies for affluent Americans. Illegals are at the risk of raids and deportation proceedings and seeing their children barred from schools and health facilities.

OPTIONS FOR WRITING 10

Write a paper sorting out things that are often grouped together. Can you make them less confusing to outsiders? Set up your own major categories—or examine and revise existing ones. Provide convincing examples or cases in point.

1 Can you help students and faculty understand the makeup of the campus population? Everyone wants to be recognized as an individual. Nevertheless, do you tend to identify fellow students as members of a group or representatives of a type? What sets people on campus apart—age? economic background? ethnicity? group affiliation? Can you set up major categories?

2 What makes a movie a winner? Can you set up three or four winning categories of current Hollywood movies—for instance, buddy movies, monster movies, disaster movies? For the movie buff, define each genre and look at outstanding current examples. Is there a common denominator?

3 A writer trying to coax you into reading beyond books assigned in your college courses might set up three basic categories: required reading, reading for personal growth, and reading for sheer enjoyment. Can you set up similar categories for a topic like uses of the computer, unrequired elective courses, or different areas of your personal life?

4 What are major lifestyle choices for Americans of your generation? For instance, would you include the single life, casual relationships, married without children? Set up your own system of classification, and provide real-life examples for each category. Is there an overall trend?

5 Have you ever felt that a familiar bipolar classification—like true and false friends, or bad and good parenting—is too simple? Can you set up a scheme of classification that makes allowance for shades of grey?

6 Can you help friends with little knowledge of politics find their way in today's political landscape? Political labels are often umbrella labels, with many different individuals lumped together as liberal or as conservative. For one such large umbrella label, can you set up major subgroups, with feminists for instance ranging

from radical to moderate or conservatives ranging from neoconservative to archconservative?

7 Students of American politics point out the growing use of initiatives or referendums. Do such exercises in direct democracy tend to fall into major categories? Are there major types, classifiable by sponsorship or intended purpose? Help potential voters understand the system.

8 There has been a large increase in religious programing. Are there major types, ranging perhaps from old-fashioned televangelism to more contemporary formats?

9 A prominent conservative nineteenth-century political leader described England as "two nations"—the rich and the poor. What major layers in the American class structure do you think he would identify today? For instance, would he include both a working class and a nonworking underclass? Would he include a new-rich superclass?

10 Should people be more knowledgeable about how to recognize different kinds of teachers, doctors, ministers, employees, or the like? Can you write guidelines for what kinds to look for and which to avoid?

4c Tracing Cause and Effect

Help your readers understand causes and results.

Much writing about current situations concentrates on **cause and effect**. Confronted with a problem, we ask: "How did this come about? What are the causes? If we continue on our current course, what will be the results? If we change course, what will be the effect?" If we understand cause and effect, we can show what caused a problem and how it could be solved. We can show what brought about current needs and what would produce desired results.

A student writer probing the causes of homelessness sorted out major possible factors as follows:

Americans on the Street

I FAMILIAR ALIBIS The familiar stereotype of the mentally ill homeless long served as an alibi. However, fewer of the patients forced onto the streets after the closing of mental hospitals survive, while the army of the homeless grows.

II RISING EMPLOYMENT REQUIREMENTS Lack of a minimal education or relatively slight disabilities disqualify marginal individuals for even subsistence level jobs. These people do not figure in unemployment statistics because they are the "unemployables." They include many veterans too alienated or disoriented to seek assistance that might be due to them.

III LACK OF AFFORDABLE HOUSING The government "got out of the housing business" while at the same time low-income housing and hotels for elderly citizens made way for luxury condominiums. In many urban areas, even substandard housing is out of reach for single adults working for minimum wage. Sudden layoffs or downsizings can force even white-collar middle-class Americans without a financial cushion into homelessness.

IV ALCOHOL AND DRUG ABUSE A chicken-and-egg argument revolves around whether alcoholism and drug addiction cause homelessness or whether poverty and despair drive people into alcoholism and drug abuse. Treatment programs for alcoholics and addicts, like other social services, have been cut during the rejection of the "welfare state."

GUIDELINES FOR WRITING AND REVISION

Tracing Cause and Effect

Watch for traps like the following in writing or revising a cause-and-effect paper:

1 ***Guard against oversimple explanations.*** People looking for simple solutions love to point to a single cause that explains everything.

2 ***Consider long-range causes.*** Try to distinguish between surface causes and underlying causes. A minor accident may trigger an outbreak of homicidal road rage on the part of one of the drivers. But perhaps an earlier disappointment in love or business was the underlying cause. An earlier personal disaster had pushed the person who went berserk close to the edge.

3 ***Guard against the* post-hoc *fallacy.*** *Post hoc* is Latin for "after this"—short for "it came after this; therefore it must be because of this."

4 ***Guard against scapegoating.*** It is often tempting to blame our problems on an easily identifiable villain. Typically we scapegoat people outside our own group. We blame our problems on illegal aliens, Korean shopkeepers, Jewish merchants, or militant unions. Other whipping boys include intellectuals, the CIA, bureaucrats, and big government.

OPTIONS FOR WRITING 11

Write a paper tracing causes and effects to help your readers understand current predicaments. If you can, help them chart courses of action. Draw on possible sources including your observation, viewing, and reading. Bolster your analysis with real-life examples, case histories, and expert opinion.

1 What explains a student's academic success? What counts most—intelligence? family background? study habits? personality? other factors? What should a counselor or mentor or concerned parent keep in mind? Examine a key factor or key factors and show how they work.

2 Are young Americans natural-born conformists? Do they run with the crowd in matters of dress and appearance? Who or what causes them to wear similar running shoes, caps, or jackets?

3 Why do some advertising or political campaigns seem particularly effective? What makes others seem routine or disappointing? If you were serving as a consultant to advertisers or promoters, what appeals would you identify as particularly effective? How or why do they work? What do they have in common? (Or you might want to focus on the causes of failure. What ploys are likely to fail?)

4 Is it true that there is a communication gap between the sexes? Is it true that women are from a planet with much caring and supportive talk while men are from a silent planet? What causes any gender gap in communication? What are striking examples? Can people learn to deal with it?

6 Are you a fatalist about violence? Have you given thought to the roots of violence—in the family, in the neighborhood, or in school? Focus on one area, and try to show the mechanisms at work. Does any kind of intervention or prevention work?

7 To judge from your observation and reading, what are key causes of homelessness or of poverty? Is there one root cause? Have you seen anyone turn a history of poverty around? How?

8 Every so often, a new fad sweeps the world of popular music. What does it take? What makes it work?

9 Some people turn their lives around in mid-career. Have you seen it happen? What are some of the major factors at work?

10 Political parties look for candidates who have charisma. What is it? How can you tell if someone has it or not? How does it work?

4d Weighing Alternatives

Help readers weigh options and reach a balanced conclusion.

We start thinking critically about an issue when we realize that there is more than one point of view. There is more than side. For a problem that concerns us, there is more than one possible solution. We then start going from "on the one hand" to "on the other hand." We take a serious look at different options. Much effective writing sorts out the alternatives, helping readers make up their minds.

4d.1 Weighing the Options *Guide your reader's choice among major options.* An effective oral or written presentation will often line up major choices. It then examines the merits of each. What are the choices? What should guide the listener's or reader's decision? Suppose you are tracking the strategies parents might use to block children's access to sexually explicit materials. In each section of your paper, you are likely to focus on "how it works"—and on what the unsolved problems are:

Cleaning Up the Internet

1 LEGISLATING AGAINST INDECENCY

<u>how it works</u>: Lawmakers have passed legislation designed to punish providers for putting on the Internet material later found to be indecent or offensive or harmful to minors.

<u>what the problems are</u>: The legislation has been challenged in court as too broad and ill-defined and as unconstitutional on First Amendment grounds.

2 PARENTAL BLOCKING BY KEY WORDS

<u>how it works</u>: Specially designed software can rapidly scan tens of thousands of titles for a whole range of key words that seem to indicate sexual content.

<u>what the problems are</u>: Many seemingly innocuous or ambiguously named sites will fall through the cracks. (And access to anything to do with human sexuality or sex education will be blocked.)

3 PARENTAL BLOCKING BY HUMAN CENSORS

how it works: More discriminating blocking software will combine the results of an automatic search with the work of human censors familiar with code words or advertising come-ons.

what the problems are: Human censors can check out only a limited amount of material and may be drowned by the flood of sexually oriented material on the net.

4 VOLUNTARY LABELING BY PROVIDERS

how it works: Voluntary labeling by Internet providers would follow the example of the movies and television, making possible software that would block sites with restrictive labels.

what the problems are: The question is whether enough of the vast range of providers on the net can agree on and implement a generally binding system of warning labels.

Often a paper weighing options goes through a process of elimination. It looks at the first option and finds it wanting. It goes on to the second and rejects it also. It then goes on to the alternatives that are the better choices. On a censorship issue, the overall pattern of the paper might be: legislation (no)—censorship (no)—self-censorship (maybe)—education (yes).

4d.2 Balancing Pro and Con *Help your readers balance pro and con.* On many issues that really matter, you encounter strong arguments on one side—but then you discover powerful arguments on the other side. Your assignment as a writer then is to weigh contrasting views and reach a responsible conclusion. Some people view pro-and-con thinking as confrontational—as if it were a contest where one side has to win and another to lose. However, the most productive pro-and-con thinking does not *polarize* opposing position—but takes them into account. You may in the end lean to one side or the other. Ideally, you present a balanced conclusion that honors the concerns of both sides.

You may state your own position early in the paper as your thesis. But then you retrace the steps that led to your decision. The main body of your paper will go from statement to counter statement. It will go from assertion to reply or rebuttal. There are different ways to organize the play of pro and con: Perhaps you will first present and discuss the advantages of a proposed law or new procedure. Then you will review the disadvantages. Or you may take arguments pro and con up one at a time—presenting one major point at a time, and then showing how the other side tries to shoot it down.

Here are requirements for an effective pro-and-con paper:

- *Listen to the other side.* If you lean to one side in a controversy, what are the people on the other side really saying? What are their major arguments? What is their strongest evidence? Why are they committed to their cause? For instance, you may in principle be in favor of a minimum wage—and of adjusting it for inflation to guarantee low-wage workers a minimum standard of living. Then why are many economists hostile to raising the minimum wage? What are they saying?
- *Line up opposing arguments.* To clarify your own thinking, try lining up key arguments on either side in two facing columns. A few years ago, arguments flared up in several states about the proposed medical use of marijuana to counteract the extreme nausea and discomfort experienced by cancer patients or AIDS victims. A chart like the following can help bring the opposing arguments into focus:

PRO	CON
1 Much *personal testimony* supports the therapeutic effect of marijuana in combating the retching and drastic weight loss associated with chemotherapy, for instance.	1 "Medical marijuana" is used as a wedge by people trying to *legalize marijuana generally*.
2 *Medical precedents* exist. Morphine has been used as a pain killer since World War I to ease the hellish pain of war wounds.	2 No *scientific studies* exist supporting the medical uses of the drug; it would take years to get reliable results.
3 *Legal precedents* exist. Virginia was among the first states to legalize medical marijuana.	3 All the evidence shows that the use of marijuana is a *first step* toward addiction to "hard drugs" like heroin or cocaine.
4 Much opposition to legalization stems from *politicians* scared to be seen as soft in the "war on drugs."	4 The pharmaceutical industry is developing synthetic drugs promising relief for cancer patients and AIDS patients.
5 *Humanitarian or religious values* compel us to relieve human suffering.	5 The war on drugs can only be won with "zero tolerance."

GUIDELINES FOR WRITING AND REVISION

Weighing Alternatives

Keep cautions like the following in mind:

1 ***Observe the equal-time principle.*** Try to give roughly equal space to competing arguments or to arguments on the other side. Your paper will seem biased or slanted if you present the arguments of one side in loving detail—and then give short shrift to the other.

2 ***Don't brush off opposing views.*** You defeat the purpose of reviewing the options if you simply label the views of one side foolish, ridiculous, cynical, or corrupt.

3 ***Push toward a balanced conclusion.*** Try to suggest some reasonable or responsible course of action. The following might be the balanced conclusion of a paper on the topic of affirmative action:

> Affirmative action may need to be updated rather than abolished. Today, women do not need a path to get into business so much as they need a way to get up in business. According to a Department of Labor survey of 94 random selections from the Fortune 1,000 companies, only 16 percent of managers were women, and only 6.6 percent of executives. Minorities were only 2.6 percent on the executive level. Getting hired may no longer be the problem—assuring fairness in retention and promotion may be the real challenge.

YOUR TURN 17 **A Paper for Peer Review**

Does the following student paper succeed in making you weigh both sides in a current controversy? Does the issue come clearly into focus? How would you outline the arguments pro and con examined in this paper? Has the student writer observed the equal-time principle for pro and con writing? Do you think both sides are fairly represented? Or is the paper slanted toward one side or the other? Has the writer tried to reach a balanced conclusion? How convincing or useful is the ending of the paper?

YOUR TURN 17 *(continued)*

"Say Goodbye"

During my freshman year in high school, I watched a movie on endangered animals called *Say Goodbye*. The narrator stated that "in nature, each creature takes only what it needs to survive." For most nonhuman creatures, this is true. However, humans have tended to deplete the earth's resources beyond what they truly need. This is the issue in the current arguments over whether loggers should be allowed to cut old-growth forests. Should these old-growth forests be sacrificed for human "needs"?

Those that argue that old-growth forest logging should be banned have several strong arguments. For some, these forests are a spiritual place. A recent article in *Business Week* mentioned that in the California Lost Coast the redwoods serve as a home to a monastery. Mother Myriam explained, "We came to this place to turn ourselves toward God. God is not just a spirit within but is also in nature. Nature is a gift to be respected, not exploited." Even the owner of a local construction company opposed clear cutting and said, "That a tree is big and old doesn't mean it should be cut."

Perhaps these old trees are even more special than younger ones. Many animals reside only in old-growth forests. The most famous example was the spotted owl, which faced extinction if the loggers removed their homes. A *U.S. News & World Report* article, "A War in an Ancient Forest," by Michael Satchell, describes the Tongass National Forest and the adjoining coastal waters as teeming with "bald eagles, seabirds, grizzly bears, wolves, humpback whales, and migrating salmon. The Tongass is one of the world's most diverse and fecund ecosystems." Indeed, forests are homes to many different species of animals and plants. The older trees play a vital role in this delicate ecosystem.

Some environmental activists view the whole world as a delicate ecosystem. An organization called Earth First! believes that we must place the "Earth first in all decisions, even ahead of human welfare if necessary." The preservation of wilderness is their fundamental goal. These activists argue that the environment as a whole is more important than human welfare. Consequently, the loggers' jobs should be sacrificed for the greater good of the environment.

Those who oppose the ban on logging argue that thousands of jobs will be lost. These loggers have been logging all their lives and don't have another trade to fall back on. Many of these loggers have families to support. Why should human families suffer for the sake of "a few old trees"? The logging industry has played a vital role in our economy. This ban would hurt the economy and cause the unemployment rate to go up. Additionally, many of these logging companies have legal, binding contracts that allow them to cut the trees.

Ironically, the loggers may be doomed even if they are allowed to clear cut the old-growth forests. Peter H. Raven from the Missouri Botanical Garden and author of *Environment 1995* says that "if the industry continued to log at its 1980s rates, all of the old-growth forest would disappear within 20 years." These loggers will be forced to either find new jobs or focus on tree-harvesting as opposed to clear cutting old-growth forests.

Modern technology has treated the non-human realm, which includes animals, plants, and trees, like moldable wax. The wax is here for our purposes, and humans may shape it however they like. Therefore, the trees are here for us to do with as we see fit. If cutting the trees for timber will benefit humans the most, that is what should be done. Humans need timber for shelter and for many other purposes—trees can grow back.

It is clear that there is no easy choice. A biology professor who teaches "Endangered Ecosystems" says, "In the real world, there are no easy answers; priorities need to be determined and tradeoffs have to be made." Often in compromises, neither side is happy with the result. Perhaps the old-growth forests should be saved; so much of our wildlife has already been destroyed. Possible solutions to the logging problem include retraining the loggers in a different field of work, perhaps one that will help to preserve the environment. A more practical solution may be to force more lumber companies to practice tree-harvesting. Tree-harvesting is similar to running a tree farm, where the trees are grown especially for lumber. Both of these possible solutions will preserve the diverse forests while allowing the loggers to continue supporting their families. I learned a very simple, yet important lesson in watching that movie my freshman year. Perhaps the most powerful line was the last one, "Share, or say goodbye."

OPTIONS FOR WRITING 12

Write a paper helping your readers weigh alternatives or sift arguments pro and con. Try to do justice to different points of view. Aim at a balanced or reasonable conclusion.

1 What teaching format helps you learn best—traditional lecture class? group discussion? distance learning by e-mail or over the net? Weigh the merits of different kinds of pedagogy or formats of instruction.

OPTIONS FOR WRITING 12 *(continued)*

2 How open-minded are you about dress codes or regulations affecting appearance? Weigh the pros and cons in a test case, such as school uniforms for children, regulations banning beards or ponytails for police officers, beach restaurants ruling out bare feet, or restaurants requiring jackets and ties for male patrons.

3 Will traffic come to a standstill in the new millennium? Alternatives advanced by traffic planners to avert strangling traffic congestion include new urban freeways, car pool lanes, expanded bus transportation, trolley car systems, and new subways. Which of these are realistic? Weigh their merits for the benefit of planners and voters.

4 New safety devices or new safety precautions sometimes have unexpected negative results. Argue the pros and cons of one of these, such as airbags, special car seats for children, or motorcycle helmets.

5 What is the answer to discipline problems in schools? What alternatives have you seen tried? With what results?

6 Examine a current movement or initiative. For instance, examine the merits of a proposed new smoking ban or of new "sin taxes" on alcohol. Or weigh the merits of proposed changes in the legal drinking age or similar legislation.

7 What is the best way to deal with sexual harassment in an educational institution or in the workplace? Is there a point in confronting the harasser? What is the merit of complaints to management, educational programs for the workforce, or lawsuits? Are there other alternatives?

8 Are you for or against school prayer? What are key arguments on either side? Is there a middle ground?

9 In your area or community, have there been recent gun control initiatives? If you can, focus on a specific initiative like a proposed ordinance to ban the sale or manufacture of Saturday Night specials—cheap handguns. Weigh the arguments pro and con. Or weigh the merits of an initiative moving in the opposite direction, like making it legal for ordinary citizens to carry handguns.

10 Do you live in an area or community locked in a struggle over whether to promote or slow down further growth? What are key arguments of pro-development and anti-development forces?

4e Structuring an Argument

Show that your position has the force of logic on its side.

The purpose of a logical argument is to move the discussion of an issue beyond personal preference, beyond likes and dislikes. If statistics show a correlation between smoking and heart disease, and if I am a smoker, I may still decide to smoke. However, I may no longer have the option of denying the risk to my health. When writers present a serious argument, they are asking their readers to listen to reason. They have thought the matter through, and they ask their readers to do the same.

4e.1 Styles of Argument *Decide on an aggressive or on a less direct style of argument.* Many current discussions of argument map out three requirements: First, you need to formulate your *claim* clearly in your own mind: What point are you trying to prove? Second, you need to have ready the data or the evidence that you have gathered to support your claim. Third, you prepare to take your reader through the logical steps that connect your claim and your data and thus *warrant* your conclusions.

What is the best strategy for taking your reader along?

- *A traditional style of argument encourages strong assertion.* Perhaps you support liberalized immigration regulations allowing highly qualified foreigners to come into the country. You start with a strong plea. Then you document case after case where highly skilled immigrants have proved an asset in areas like medicine or computer programming. In fact, the countries of origin of such highly skilled newcomers often complain about a "brain drain." Building as strong a case as possible, you "pile on," as a commentator at a football game might say. Your basic strategy might be charted as follows:

  STRONG CLAIM: . . .
  REASON ONE: . . .
  REASON TWO: . . .
  REASON THREE: . . .

- *On the other hand, people sounding too aggressive and self-righteous may defeat their own purpose.* A more modern style of argument stresses the need for establishing common ground. Before you come on strong, you ask yourself: What are the people on the other side thinking? How about first showing them that you respect their right to their own opinion and that you honor their commitments? Then, once you have shown you are sensitive to their concerns, you ask them to listen to yours.

The result may be a **"Yes, but"** style of argument, with phrasing like the following:

> **It is true that** exemptions to immigration laws for special interest groups tend to set a bad precedent. . . .
>
> People opposed to a stepped up importation of highly skilled newcomers **express important reservations.** For instance, free access for foreign graduates may lead Americans to neglect building up their own graduate schools and funding of high-tech research. . . .
>
> **Nevertheless, the basic fact remains** that highly skilled immigrants can be an important asset in the fiercely competitive global struggle. . . .

4e.2 Arguing from Principle *Argue on the basis of shared values and assumptions.* Regardless of how you decide to approach your reader, on an important issue you will often be arguing from principle. You take your stand on assumptions that you expect your intended readers to accept:

> All young Americans are entitled to a quality education.
>
> Money should not be the deciding factor in finding a defendant innocent or guilty.
>
> The U.S. Constitution guarantees citizens the right to bear arms.

You then apply these principles to a specific situation. You show how the principle applies to a new proposal for funding schools, or a widely-publicized court case, or a proposed gun control ordinance. When building an argument on such shared assumptions, you face two basic tasks. First, you need to state your basic assumptions carefully and convincingly enough so that they will put your readers in an assenting mood. And you need to build an argument on these assumptions that has the force of logic.

The basic reasoning pattern is "If A is true, and if B is true, then C will also be true." For example, if only children of low-income parents are eligible for a scholarship, and if your parents earn over the limit, then it follows that you are not eligible. The same basic pattern structures many arguments on public issues:

IF:	The U.S. Constitution separates church and state, religion and government.
AND IF:	The nativity scene is a religious symbol.
THEN:	The nativity scene should not be displayed at city hall.

Such arguments present conclusions already implied in the premises. You merely draw out or deduce what is already implied. The arguments are examples of **deductive** thinking. The shared assumptions are your **premises**—they provide the foundation on which the argument rests. A successful argument takes the reader from accepted premises through a chain of reasoning to a valid conclusion. A three-step argument, moving from two accepted premises to a justified conclusion, is called a **syllogism**:

FIRST PREMISE:	All full-time students are eligible for the loan program.
SECOND PREMISE:	You are a full-time student.
CONCLUSION:	Therefore, you are eligible.

FIRST PREMISE:	No undocumented aliens will be hired.
SECOND PREMISE:	I am an undocumented alien.
CONCLUSION:	Therefore, I need not apply.

FIRST PREMISE:	No one with an arrest record will be hired.
SECOND PREMISE:	I do not have an arrest record.
CONCLUSION:	Therefore, I am eligible.

In each of these arguments , the first premise specifies what it includes or rules out. The conclusion necessarily follows because the premise includes or rules out *all* members of a group. In practice, many arguments are not true syllogisms. Arguments that use *some* or *many* instead of *all* or *no* in the first premise are less airtight. They lead to a *probable* conclusion:

IF:	Most members of the Achievement Club are business majors.
AND IF:	Maria is a member of the Achievement Club.
THEN:	Maria is likely to be a business major.

As you put together a logical argument, prepare for challenges from readers who remain unconvinced:

- *An argument may rest on doubtful assumptions.* Check for **questionable premises.** When you present an argument like the following, your readers may challenge your premises rather than your conclusions:

IF:	Students learn best in a relaxed, supportive atmosphere.
AND IF:	The present system of exams causes tension and anxiety.
THEN:	Exams work against true learning. (But do not at least some students perform better under pressure?)

- *Your readers may refuse to go along with your argument because of unstated assumptions.* Check for **hidden premises.** When you bring these out into the open, you have a chance to reexamine them and revise them if necessary.

PREMISE:	My economics teacher is from a middle-class background.
CONCLUSION:	She cannot be expected to sympathize with the poor.
HIDDEN PREMISE:	(People cannot sympathize with someone from a different class?)

- *An argument may look logical and yet produce the wrong result.* For instance, the first premise may start with the **nonexclusive *all*.** It is then easy to draw a wrong conclusion. The word *all* includes everyone in a group—but it does not *exclude* others. It often means "all of the above—*and* maybe others."

FIRST PREMISE:	All Marxists admire Karl Marx.
SECOND PREMISE:	Professor Darien admires Karl Marx.
WRONG:	Therefore, Professor Darien must be a Marxist. (Like other non-Marxists, she may admire Marx but disagree with many of his conclusions.)

FIRST PREMISE:	All pigeons have feathers.
SECOND PREMISE:	My canary has feathers.
WRONG:	Therefore, my canary is a pigeon.

4e.3 Recognizing Logical Fallacies *Avoid familiar kinds of shortcut thinking.* Advocates of straight thinking warn against familiar **logical fallacies**—predictable ways of reaching the wrong conclusion.

THINKING STRAIGHT

A Checklist of Logical Fallacies

Guides to straight thinking warn against shortcut reasoning like the following:

1 **scapegoating** Politicians may blame an unpopular group for loss of jobs or a lost war. Factory workers may blame immigrants or "affirmative action hires" rather than automation or foreign competition for the loss of highly paid factory jobs.

2 ***ad hominem*** *Ad hominem* arguments aim "at the person" instead of at the issue. Rather than discussing a candidate's proposals regarding school vouchers or health care, an opponent might call attention to a divorce, an alcoholic relative, visits to a psychiatrist, or sexual orientation.

3 **hasty generalization** We should not make sweeping generalizations about "what the American people want" or "the world view of the younger generation" after talking to only friends and family. We should not generalize about "how Asians think" after knowing only a few Vietnamese or Filipino students.

4 **unrepresentative sample** You cannot determine student sentiment on current issues by talking only to students in your own living quarters. You may have to listen as well to coop dwellers, people living on their own close to the campus, and commuters. You should probably talk to re-entry students, minority students, and part-time students.

5 **false dilemma** A true dilemma puts us in a tight spot and leaves us only two ways out—both bad. A true dilemma may face medical researchers conducting animal experiments. Should they abandon experiments that torture animals? Or should they continue experiments that benefit suffering human beings? A *false* dilemma narrows your choices to two—so that you will shun the obviously bad one and opt for the one favored by the writer. A false dilemma sets up an either-or choice: Either let a downtown area deteriorate, or raze the area and rebuild. A third alternative, hidden from view here, might be to restore and renovate.

6 **false analogy** An analogy is a detailed, systematic comparison between two things that are similar in several ways. A false analogy stretches the similarities between two things too far. Is our nation like a lifeboat—with only so many spaces? Would it be swamped if we allowed a large number of the people to climb

(continued)

A Checklist of Logical Fallacies *(continued)*

aboard? No nation has unlimited resources, and absorbing too many immigrants might "swamp" institutions. However, sooner or later the analogy breaks down. Immigrants have often brought new talents and developed new resources (which newcomers to a lifeboat don't do).

7 **rationalization** When you rationalize, you go for explanations that make you look good or feel good. When a supervisor treats you poorly, the reason may well be that the supervisor is prejudiced against your group. But the reason may also be that your job performance is inadequate, regardless of what group you represent.

8 **slanting** Interested parties tend to slant data or suppress damaging evidence. They may exaggerate everything that favors their cause and leave out contrary testimony. Skeptical readers ask: Who on this issue has an ax to grind? Who has an interest in tampering with the evidence?

9 **bandwagon** Advertisers and public relations experts try to sway us by letting us know that "everybody does it" or "everyone thinks so."

10 **smokescreen** Propagandists may hide damaging information behind a verbal smokescreen. When the cutting down of trees is described as "harvesting," the word *harvest* suggests that in a few years the trees will grow again (though old-growth trees may have taken centuries to grow).

YOUR TURN 18 Checking Your Logic

Which of the following arguments are logical? Which illustrate common fallacies? How would you argue in support of the writer? On what grounds would you take issue with the writer?

1 Vincent Nolan left town a few days after the police started a crackdown on drug pushers. Nolan must have been involved in the narcotics trade.

2 Where there is smoke, there is fire. When a high-ranking city official is accused of financial irregularities, you can assume something was going on.

3 Alcoholism is an addiction, like a heroin habit. Therefore, beer should not be sold on college campuses.

4 Students study because they hope for good grades or fear bad ones. When there is no tough grading system to offer reward or punishment, students have no incentive to learn.

5 A law has to be approved by a majority of the people before it becomes the law; therefore, everyone should obey the law.

6 Scholarships at this college can no longer be awarded on the basis of race or ethnic origin. Therefore, special scholarships for African American students will be a thing of the past.

7 Since the mayor's crackdown on street crime, six weeks have passed without a homicide in the city. This proves that criminals respect the language of force.

8 The police department continues to enforce a minimum height requirement for new hires. The human female tends to be less bulky and less tall than the human male. Therefore, the police department policy discriminates against women.

9 My history teacher spent four class hours on the history of the Mormon religion. She must be a Mormon.

YOUR TURN 19 A Paper for Peer Review

Do you agree with the premises bold-faced in the following reprinting of a student paper? Can you chart the student writer's arguments according to the *if-and if-then* pattern? Are you prepared to follow the argument from the principles stated to the logical conclusion?

Justice Denied

"On the subject of crime, all politicians are demagogues," says a columnist in a recent issue of the *New Republic*. Playing to the public fear of violent crime, legislators everywhere are advocating stiffer sentencing laws and more and bigger prisons. The death penalty, which was in abeyance in the seventies and eighties, has made a comeback. The courts are shortening the appeals process that has kept many convicted criminals on death row for ten, twelve, or fourteen years. However, in spite of the strong grass roots support for the revival of the death penalty, capital punishment violates basic principles underlying the American system of justice.

The weakness of passionate last-minute appeals for clemency is that they tend to focus on the special circumstances of the individual case. A murderer was the victim of child abuse. A rapist suffered

YOUR TURN 19 *(continued)*

brain damage. By focusing on the individual histories of those waiting on death row, we run the danger of losing sight of the principles at stake when a civilized society reinstitutes capital punishment.

Most basic to our legal system is the commitment to even-handed justice. **We believe that equal crimes should receive equal punishment.** However, the death penalty has always been notorious for its "freakish unfairness." In the words of one study, "Judicial safeguards for preventing the arbitrary administration of capital punishment are not working." Some murderers walk the streets again after three or five or seven years, whereas others—because of ineffectual legal counsel, an ambitious prosecutor, or a hanging judge—join the inmates waiting out their appeals on death row. Judges and juries apply widely different standards. In one celebrated case, two partners in crime were convicted of the same capital crime on identical charges. One was executed; the other is in prison and will soon be eligible for parole.

We believe that all citizens are equal before the law. Justice should be blind to wealth, race, or ethnic origin. However, poor defendants are many times more likely to receive the death penalty than wealthy ones. Rich defendants are protected by highly paid teams of lawyers whose maneuvers stymie the prosecution. Defendants with millions to spend bring in an array of experts who baffle the jury. Minority defendants convicted of capital crimes have a much higher statistical chance of being executed than white defendants. . . .

Finally, fairness demands that the judicial system correct its own mistakes. If someone has been unjustly convicted there should be a mechanism for reversing the verdict and setting the person free. No one doubts that there are miscarriages of justice. Witnesses admit to mistaken identification of suspects. A convict confesses on his deathbed to a crime for which someone else was convicted. A woman withdraws a rape charge years after the accused was sent to prison. However, in the case of the death penalty, any such correction of error is aborted. The judicial system buries its mistakes. We are left with futile regrets, like the prosecutor who said: "Horrible as it is to contemplate, we may have executed the wrong man."

OPTIONS FOR WRITING 13

On which of the following questions would you take a stand on principle? Choose one for your own paper. You and your classmates may want to stage a panel discussion exploring the principles at stake in one or more of these.

1 Should officials have the right to set aside car pool lanes on highways financed by taxes from all taxpayers? (Are commuters in single-occupant vehicles being discriminated against?)

2 Should funding for college scholarships for male student athletes be matched by equal funding for female college athletes?

3 Should employers have the right to ban romance in the workplace? (Should they have the right to rule out dating or romantic relationships among employees? among managers?)

4 Do smokers have rights? Does government have the right to ban smoking in public buildings? in airports? in private homes with small children? Where do you draw the line?

5 Should employers or government agencies have the right to regulate appearance—for instance, banning facial hair (like beards for police officers), veils for women (required by the woman's religion), or turbans for men?

6 Do you find cigarette advertising directed at women and using a slogan like "It's a woman thing" objectionable?

7 Are coed dorms a mistake?

8 Are you in favor of lowering the drinking age in your state or community?

9 Do you favor legislation to block material considered harmful to minors on the Internet?

10 Who should decide if life support systems of terminally ill patients can be disconnected—the patient? the family? a doctor? the courts?

4f Tracing a Process

Trace a process through its major stages.

In much technical and scientific writing, tracing a process is a major part of the assignment. Two key questions in process analysis are "How does it work?" and "What *makes* it work?" A biologist may trace the stages in the life cycle of an insect—from the larva to the caterpillar to the butterfly. An economist specializing in what we eat may trace an example of modern food processing—from the harvesting machine snuffling up whole tomato plants to the sorting and cooking and flavoring that produces the ketchup. A student of automotive engineering may chart the many-branched manufacturing process that feeds many different components and preassembled parts into a computerized and heavily accessorized state-of-the-art car.

In a paper tracing a process, you are likely to use or adapt an overall plan like the following:

PROCESS ANALYSIS:

value or benefits of the process or procedure

preconditions for success

needed material or support

initiating the process

major stages or phases

important cautions

prospects for future improvements

In a classic essay, a writer traced the life cycle of the salmon. She followed the mythic journey of the salmon upstream to the spawning grounds, through the laying and fertilizing of the eggs, to the swarming of the fingerlings, and finally to their proceeding downstream to live first in the fresh water estuaries and then in the salt water of the ocean—until the cycle begins again.

Marking off major stages and doing them justice one at a time will help you make your readers understand processes not only in nature or in manufacturing but also in our social and political world. For instance, what were milestones in the movement toward greater representation of women in college sports? You might decide to organize your paper as follows:

The Joy of Women's Sports

- the days of big-time male college sports
- pioneering women's teams
- collegiate women's teams with national visibility

OPTIONS FOR WRITING 14

Americans have become used to not doing things for themselves. Write a how-to paper that would help your readers become less reliant on others. Try to mark off major stages and fill in the details needed to make the process work. For instance, you might motivate them to do one of the following and show them how:

1 baking their own bread

2 starting their own business

3 doing clown shows for children
4 training dogs for the blind
5 working on a family history
6 publishing a zine
7 building a website
8 raising award-winning show animals
9 training to do car repair or VCR repair
10 becoming a bodybuilder

5 RESPONDING TO LITERATURE

Discover the challenges of imaginative literature as a reader and writer.

How does imaginative literature work its magic? It brings your imagination into play, it stirs your emotions, and it makes you think. It can make you share in the thoughts and feelings of others. It can give you a fuller sense of what it means to be human.

5a Reading Imaginative Literature

Become an alert, attentive reader of fiction, poetry, or drama.

To respond to what literature has to offer, you need to become a willing and alert reader. You need to pay attention—weighing the author's words, taking in striking details, seeing how a story or a poem takes shape. What do you need to look for when reading a short story, a poem, or a play?

5a.1 The Dimensions of Fiction *When reading a short story, pay careful attention to detail.* Short stories are not meant to be skimmed. Prepare informal reading notes: Highlight or copy striking details, revealing key quotations, and major turns in the road. Alert readers are prepared to respond to major dimensions of a story:

SETTING *Where does the story take you?* What kind of world does it create for you? What circumstances, what history, or what traditions will play a role? For instance, much American fiction takes you to the immigrant world—with older people still rooted in old-country traditions while a younger in-between generation is forging its own course. Other stories may bring into play the allegiances and divided loyalties of a shared history. An Irish writer may take you among proud people marked by a history of poverty and oppression. Characters in the story or play may be torn by conflicts between those ready to make peace with the English and those committed to an ongoing struggle.

CHARACTER *Who are the people?* What makes them the people they are? (What do others say about them? What do they say about themselves? What do you learn about them by the way they act in test situations?) Many readers are fascinated by the interplay of setting and character: How much are the people shaped by their setting? Are they a "product of their environment"—how or to what extent? To what extent is each his or her own person? Are people doomed to be trapped or hemmed in by where and how they live? Or do they have a chance to become individuals—to realize their own human potential?

PLOT *What happens in the course of the story?* You are likely to read modern fiction with little external action—no car chases, sensational heists, or alien invasions from outer space. There may be a conflict that builds up to a high point; there may be a climactic encounter or confrontation. However, much of what happens in the story may take place in the characters' minds. Do the characters develop or grow in the course of the story—why or how? The story may be a story of initiation—with a central character moving on to a new or challenging phase in his or her growing up.

POINT OF VIEW *Through whose eyes do we see the people and events?* Who is telling the story—from what point of view? Is it the traditional all-knowing storyteller, telling us what goes on each character's mind? Is it the main character—telling his or her own story? Is it an objective observer—bearing impartial witness? Mark Twain's great classic *Huckleberry Finn* is told by a runaway boy, traveling down the Mississippi on a raft with his friend Jim, an escaped slave. We see the adult world through the eyes of a boy abandoned by his abusive father and resisting the well-meant efforts of a guardian trying to "sivilize" him. Why make us look at the world through the eyes of a poorly educated country boy? Maybe we as adults have become too blunted and callous to be appalled the way Huck is by the scams, violence, and vindictiveness of the adult world.

SYMBOL *What objects or events have a larger meaning beyond themselves?* In "Swaddling Clothes," a story by the Japanese writer Yukio Mishima, a doctor shows his disapproval of a newborn child conceived out of wedlock by wrapping it in old newspapers rather than in the traditional flannel cloth. Later, the woman who is the central character and who felt guilt and shame at watching the callous treatment of the child, walks in a park where what looked like traditional white cherry blossoms are really pieces of paper. Dirty old newspapers strew the walkways, and a homeless person covered with newspapers sleeps on one of the benches. The soiled newspapers become a symbol of how our hopes for beauty and human dignity may be disappointed in a careless callous world.

THEME *Does the story have a theme?* Does the story as a whole give an answer to a central question it raises? Traditional writers of fiction felt free to comment, to teach, or to preach. Modern writers usually do without editorializing—they do not spell out the message or the moral of a tale. Instead, they involve their readers in the lived experience of the story. In Bernard Malamud's "The Magic Barrel," a rabbinical student with no social life feels loved by no one and is doubting his vocation. Told he should have a wife if he wants to be chosen by a congregation, he goes through a series of sad and funny misadventures with candidates lined up by a down-at-heels Jewish matchmaker. In the end, however, he falls desperately in love with a young woman, although he was told she was totally ineligible as a rabbi's wife. What is the theme of the story? Maybe the story is saying that people who seem emotionally deprived and spiritually exhausted may actually have the same potential for beauty and passion that the rest of us have. It may just take a "magic" encounter or special circumstances to activate their emotional being.

THE READER'S RESPONSE *Does the story have a special meaning for you personally?* Often a story that has a special impact relates to something you yourself have experienced or felt. Suppose you are reading a story about a character torn between conflicting influences and searching for his or her own identity. Does the story in turn make you ask: Where do *I* myself come from? What has made *me* what I am? How far have *I* come from the setting or the circumstances in which I grew up?

5a.2 The Language of Poetry

Be prepared to linger over a poet's words and images. Poets are in love with words. They use more of our shared language than others do, and they use it more deliberately. In a short poem, every word, every image, and every detail counts. Look especially for the following:

IMAGE *What does the poem make you see?* Poets respond more to the shapes and colors and movements of the world around us than other people. It is as if they are saying to us: "Look! Listen! You are missing much of the colorful spectacle of life!"

METAPHOR *What key metaphors play a role in the poem?* A **metaphor** is an imaginative comparison. It allows the poet to bring into the poem feelings and associations that might otherwise be hard to bring to life. Calling the sun a "furnace" can make us feel the searing heat of a desert setting. A metaphor comes into a poem unannounced—with no introductory tag such as *like,* or *as,* or *as if.* The poet simply equates one thing with another. May Swenson's poem "Question" starts like this:

> Body my house
> my horse my hound
> What will I do
> When you are fallen
>
> Where will I sleep
> How will I ride
> What will I hunt

How is our body like a house? (It houses our mind and spirit; it keeps out the wind and the rain; it shelters our thoughts and feelings from prying eyes.) How is our body like a horse—"all eager and quick"? (It moves us quickly to where we need to go; it allows us to jump out of harm's way.) How is our body like a hound—a sleek hunting dog, a "good / bright dog" that lets us know whether "in thicket ahead / Is danger or treasure"? (It equips us with alert senses to help us scout danger and opportunity.) Is there a common thread in these three body metaphors? How does the poet's way of looking at the body differ from more familiar ways? What metaphors would *you* choose to communicate how you feel about your body?

SIMILE AND PERSONIFICATION *Does the poet use other kinds of imaginative comparison?* We group such imaginative comparisons together with metaphors under the general heading of *figurative language.* A **simile** is a close cousin of metaphor that is signaled by a word such as *like* or *as.* "What happens to a dream deferred?" asked the African American poet Langston Hughes. "Does it dry up / *Like a raisin in the sun?*" **Personification** is a metaphor or simile that treats an object or a plant as if it had the thoughts and feelings of human being. In a poem by Emily Dickinson, considered by many America's greatest poet, the frost becomes a "blonde assassin" who kills "a happy flower" that was innocently "at its play." Looking at the frost and the flower as if they were actors in a human drama, the poet injects human questions of purpose and of guilt into the impersonal workings of nature. (Is anyone responsible for a killer frost? Are we wrong if we accuse nature of being cruel?)

THE LANGUAGE OF SYMBOLS *Does the poem center on a unifying symbol?* Symbols are often rooted in age-old shared human experience. Green has long been a color with powerful symbolic associations.

After the long near-death of a winter of ice and snow threatening famine and despair, the first budding green becomes a sign of the return of spring. It signals the return of the life-giving sun, the promise of crops on which human life depends, the renewed fertility of livestock, and the renewal of love. In David Wagoner's "The Other House," a boy has grown up in a household where father and mother were always silent. No one ever sang or expressed emotion. But the boy would often sneak out to an abandoned house with frogs in a flooded basement. During the winter, all seemed frozen and dead. However, once the ice melted, there would at first be some stirrings of life. And then

> finally April would come pouring
> Out of their green throats in a green chorus

Green, the color symbolic of rebirth and renewal, is central in the poem about this boy who is starved for song and emotion and finds them in "the other house" where life "sang all night."

METER AND RHYTHM *Does the poem have a strong regular rhythm?* The **meter** of traditional poetry regularized the varied rhythms of ordinary speech. It set up an underlying beat over which the actual lines of the poem could play variations. The following opening lines of a Shakespeare sonnet show the basic five-beat line (iambic pentameter) of much poetry written in English:

> That tíme of yéar thou máyst in mé behóld
> When yéllow léaves or nóne or féw do háng
> Upón those bóughs which sháke agáinst the cóld

In much modern poetry, the beat has become much less regular, although you can still beat out the rhythm with your hand in a poem like Wendell Berry's "The Peace of Wild Things":

> When the despáir of the wórld grows ín me
> and I wáke in the níght at the léast sóund
> in féar of what my lífe and my chíldren's life may bé
> I gó and lie dówn where the wóod drake
> résts in his béauty on the wáter, and the gréat héron féeds.

The still strong but more varied and natural rhythm of this poem helps calm the spirit of the poet who looks in the "presence of still water" and in "the peace of wild things" for the antidote to the fears and apprehensions that make us restless in our anxiety-ridden modern world.

RHYME AND PATTERN *Does the poem use rhyme?* Much traditional poetry measured off regular lines bonded by end rhyme. The final sounds of one or more syllables at the end repeated or echoed the final sounds of an earlier line: "The grizzly bear whose potent HUG / Was feared by all is now a RUG" (Guiterman). Much unrhymed modern poetry uses other kinds of patterning. For instance, in Marge Piercy's "Simple song," the second set of lines, or **stanza**, dances out exactly the same pattern as the first. It makes the second set a mirror image of the first, playing off exactly opposite ideas:

> When we are going toward someone we say
> You are just like me
> your thoughts are my brothers
> word matches word
> how easy to be together.
>
> When we are leaving someone we say:
> how strange you are
> we cannot communicate
> we can never agree
> how hard, hard and weary to be together.

PERSONA *Who is speaking to you in the poem?* Many poems are autobiographical. When Anne Sexton writes a poem about the fruitless "activities" in a psychiatric clinic, we read the poem as a bulletin from her own struggle with mental illness. However, often the speaker in a poem assumes a different identity—close perhaps to the real person of the poet but maybe also very different. We call the assumed identity the **persona**. Walt Whitman often speaks to us with a grand sweep in his public role as the nineteenth-century poet of democracy: "I am with you, you men and women of a generation, or ever so many generations hence, / Just as you feel when you look upon the sky and the river, so I felt." Only rarely does Whitman talk quietly about private emotions that as a gay poet in a largely hostile society he usually keeps from public view.

IRONY AND PARADOX *What is the tone of the poem—bitter, happy, mournful?*

- **Irony** makes us respond with a wry smile when reality goes counter to what we might expect or had hoped for. In Lorna Dee Cervantes' "Refugee Ship," the Mexican American poet feels "orphaned" from her Spanish name and from the language and religion of her parents and grandparents. (The words have become "foreign, stumbling on my tongue.") However, she is reminded of her heritage every time she sees her reflection in the mirror:

"bronzed skin, black hair." The irony is that people looking at her type her as Mexican, but she has become estranged from her Mexican heritage. She is not fully at home or fully accepted in either culture—like a refugee whose ship is shunted from one country to another.

- A **paradox** is a contradiction that makes sense on second thought. "Every poem is the same; and every poem is unique," says the Mexican poet Octavio Paz. How can all poems be the same and yet be not alike? Each poem is different—creating its own world of thought and feeling. But each poem is basically the same—because all poets ask us to take in more of life, to be less superficial about it, to value or ponder it more.

5a.3 The Workings of Drama *Imagine a stage performance as you read a play.* Reading a play, you bring the playwright's script to life in the theater of the mind. You visualize how major encounters or confrontations would play on an actual stage. In a stage performance, a director (or directorial committee) charts a course. Directors may bring out strongly what they consider most significant. Or they may find new meaning in what others have overlooked. Actors create their characters, entering into their mannerisms, thoughts, and feelings. The audience plays its role: The spectators share the illusion of being witnesses at the events of the play. The reactions of a live audience create a special kind of interaction, as the spectators experience amazement, indignation, or shared laughter.

Take mental or written notes on major dimensions of a play:

SITUATION *Early in the play, what clues point to future developments?* What do you learn about the characters' past history? Are there hints of scores to be settled? Are there signs of conflict—resentments or remembered slights? Do you learn about hopes or ambitions that might bear fruit—or be disappointed? Are there challenges that the characters might surmount or that might defeat them?

CHARACTER *What do you learn about the major characters?* How much can you tell about them from what they say, from what they do, or from what others say about them? Is there a lead character or **protagonist**—in the ancient Greek tragedies or in a Shakespeare play often a dominating figure larger than life? Is there an **antagonist**—a worthy opponent? What is the role of minor characters—like a friend the hero takes into his or her confidence, or a shady character from a half-forgotten past?

CONFLICT *Is there a central conflict?* A play may line up rebels against an established order. Or it may pit idealistic youth against corrupt elders. It may play off two ways of doing business, two ways of looking at life, or different ways of committing to a marriage. The events of the play may build up to a climactic confrontation, or they may leave a basic issue unresolved, leaving the audience to wonder about the future.

DIALOGUE *How closely do you have to pay attention to what is said?* Although some plays use spectacular stage effects, the heart of a play is words spoken on the stage. Through dialogue, the characters define who they are. They challenge, defy, or convince others. In **soliloquies**, or solo speeches, a major character may bare her soul or weigh his options at a fateful point in the play. In **repartee**, characters may trade quick-witted remarks or high-spirited insults.

GENRE *What conventions, or customary patterns, does the play observe?* Much modern drama mixes the serious and the comic, as does real life. However, much traditional drama followed the conventions of two major **genres**, or kinds, of theater: the solemn world of **tragedy**, and the happy world of **comedy**.

- *Tragedy acts out the drama of human limitations.* It may center on a fateful decision, on a fatal quarrel, or on disappointed hopes. A strong or ambitious central character—man or woman—may be brought low by fate, by powerful outside forces, or by flaws in the person's own character. In *Antigone*, a play that is still powerful theater 2,500 years later, the Greek playwright Sophocles put on the stage a young woman who defied the power of the state. In a culture where honoring the dead was a central religious duty, the king had denied her brother a decent burial because the brother had died fighting as a rebel against his own native city. Antigone asserts her duty to the gods over her duty to the state. Although she is destroyed, she has over the ages inspired many who put allegiance to conscience above allegiance to state or country.
- *Comedy restores our faith in good fortune.* It makes us believe in lucky breaks, young love, and goodwill. It keeps alive the spirit of celebration, of revelry, of good times. It make us laugh at bumbling fellow humans and harmless fools. In Moliére's *The Would-Be Gentleman*, a *nouveau-riche* (newly-rich) merchant wants to rise in society. He hires a tribe of personal tailors, music teachers, dancing teachers, mentors, and personal trainers so he can ape upper-class sophisticates and marry his daughter to an aristocrat. While his new employees unmercifully exploit him, the young lovers in the play find a way to override the father's veto. When the laughter of comedy acquires a sharper bite, we enter further into the world of **satire**, and meanness and hypocrisy may be exposed to ridicule.

STYLE *How formal or informal is the style?* The language of a play may range from the soaring poetry of Shakespearean verse ("Ah! She doeth teach the torches to burn bright!") to a modern playwrights's everyday prose, laced with insult or vulgarity. In ancient Greek tragedy, the **chorus**, a group of supporting characters, set a solemn mood of foreboding. At regular intervals, it made its choreographed entrances to recite measured odes expressing its comments, warnings, or predictions. The performers wore special tragic masks and used grand gestures. At the opposite end of the spectrum, low comedy, or **farce**, survived through the ages, with pratfalls, comic misadventures, and bawdy jokes.

OPTIONS FOR WRITING 15 The Creative Dimension

For a journal entry about your reading, prepare a response that brings your own imagination into play. How well do you get into the spirit of a story? How well do you take in the pattern that a poem dances out on the page? How fully do you enter into the world of a play? Choose one of the following:

1 *Use your imagination to write a sequel or update to a short story.* (Have you ever felt dissatisfied at the end of a story?) Study the following update as an example. Shirley Jackson's "The Lottery" told the story of an annual ritual stoning of a fellow villager, as if an ancient tradition of human sacrifice had survived in New England. The victim was chosen by lot, as if to remind us that people become victims through no fault of their own—because they happened to be Jewish, because their parents had been captured by slavers, or because they had contracted a mental illness that made society push them out into the street. Does the student writer's update help convince you that the story is not ancient history?

Winning the Lottery

Over the years, many of the old buildings have been torn down to make room for Seven Elevens and a large SUPER-mart with a cafeteria. . . . People are remodeling, improving, and accessorizing their homes, their bodies, and their televisions. The annual lottery has been moved to the large SUPER-mart parking lot. This year, it's—Mr. Stanfield! He was a pretty good man, and he watched television regularly too. The crowd moves to his home and dismantles it piece by piece. Pictures of his family are distributed, clothing passed around, and patterned dishes lovingly packed in bubble wrap. He wanders slowly down the road, past the store where he used to rent movies and the station where he used to put gas in his car. . . . He dejectedly holds on to a hand-lettered sign that says he'll work for food, but he knows it's against the rules for anyone to help him. Every morning he leaves the old cardboard that's his cover during the nights under the overpass and stands in line at the Bureau with the other lottery winners of years past. The lone window opens for a short span at ten. The person working the window tells the waiting line of winners that the forms they need to get sustenance stamps were delayed at the printers but that they can expect them any day.

2 *Do a re-creation of a favorite poem.* One way to enter into the spirit of a poem is to write a similar poem of your own—playing with the same basic format and tone. This way you get to know the poem "from the inside"—the way you are no longer a passive spectator when you play an instrument or act in an amateur performance. Wallace Stevens' "Disillusionment of Ten O'Clock" is a poem that invites imitation:

The houses are haunted
By white night-gowns.
None are green,
Or purple with green rings,
Or green with yellow rings,
Or yellow with blue rings.
None of them are strange,
With socks of lace
And beaded ceintures*
People are not going
To dream of baboons and periwinkles**
Only, here and there, an old sailor,
Drunk and asleep in his boots,
Catches tigers
In red weather.

Why is this poet "disillusioned"? What is funny about the idea of these houses being "haunted"? Why does the color of people's nightgowns matter in this poem? Has the following student-written re-creation captured the mood and intention of the original? How close is it to the original in pattern or form?

*Fancy sashes
**Cone-shaped snails

OPTIONS FOR WRITING 15 *(continued)*

Try your hand at a similar creative effort, inspired by this or another poem you have read.

Disenchantment at the Dance

The dance is crowded
With blue denim.
There are no dresses
Of shiny, red satin
Or shimmering silk.
No bright feathered hats
No rhinestone buttons.
People aren't dancing
The foxtrot or cha cha.
Only, once in a while,
A few underclassmen
In T-shirts and jeans
Clap their hands
Shuffle their feet.

3 *Comment on major events as seen by a minor character in a play.* For instance, tell the story as seen by a character who is the trusted friend of the hero or who is the sister of a strong heroine. Or write a diary entry that starts, "I, Polonius, counselor to the king, . . ."

5b Writing about Literature

Write a paper that combines close reading of the literature and your personal response.

When you write a short paper about a story, a poem, or a play, keep in mind basic requirements: Focus on a key issue or central question. Push toward a unifying overall idea or thesis. Work out a plan that you can outline for others and that your readers can follow. Support all general statements or claims you make with telling detail or revealing short quotations from the story. Steer a middle course between a chatty chummy style and a hyperformal jargon.

5b.1 Live Introduction *Start with an imaginative, thought-provoking introduction.* Imaginative literature stirs the reader's emotions and bring the reader's imagination into play. A dry introduction will not help the reader get into the spirit of what you have read. Start with a striking image, incident, or quotation to bring the story or the play to life. Make a live introduction lead up to your key issue.

Broken Spirit: Alice Munro's "Boys and Girls"

If a wild horse is to be used on a ranch, it must first be broken. That is, the horse must be taught obedience against its will. The horse is placed under physical restraint and allowed to struggle for its freedom until it realizes that its attempts to be its own master are now futile. When the horse can no longer fight, it will surrender to the human will. In the same way that the horse is broken in against its will, the young woman in Munro's "boys and Girls," is in a way broken in against her will to submit to society's rules. **Her family, as a representation of society as a whole, forces her to conform to the proper gender role in her struggle to achieve adulthood.**

5b.2 **Programmatic Thesis** *Push toward a thesis that gives a preview of your paper as a whole.* Try to make the thesis set up the program for the paper. The following paragraph followed the introduction to a paper about a short story set in Japan. The paragraph states the student writer's thesis and charts the directions for a paper that explores the meeting of Japanese and American cultural expectations—but that does not simply line up opposing American and Japanese ways:

Toshiko, the main character in Yukio Mishima's "Swaddling Clothes," lives in a culture that honors tradition, where any deviation from the traditional mold could bring disgrace not only to herself but to her family. **She is outwardly the traditional Japanese wife, humble and loyal to her husband; but on the inside she has her own strong feelings and opinions which make her husband seem "almost a stranger."** Both her crude superficially Americanized Japanese husband and the traditional Japanese doctor treat the newborn child, born out of wedlock, with callousness and contempt. Toshiko does not outwardly challenge them, but her sensitive nature makes her experience acute feelings of shame and guilt and sets her on her independent and in the end fatal course.

5b.3 **Meaningful Plan** *Make your readers see the flow of ideas in your paper.* In the thesis for the paper about the Mishima story, three waystations for the paper are already sketched: The writer will show first that the men in the story, whether traditional or superficially Americanized, share a callousness shocking to the wife. A second major section of the paper will show the stereotypical outward conformity of the wife bound by tradition. The final section will trace the central character's inward rebellion and ultimate fate.

5b.4 **Strong Follow-Through** *Use striking detail and pointed quotations to support your key points.* Don't merely follow the story or the play along as in a plot summary. Instead pull out from different parts of the story or play relevant events and revealing quotations that support the claims you want to make.

> **The young woman in Munro's story grows up in a society that almost unanimously supports the limitations on what she can be and do.** No one speaks up for her or supports her resistance to the world and its stereotypical role for women. When the father jokingly introduces his proud daughter-helper as "my new hired man," the feed salesman replies, "Could of fooled me, I thought it was only a girl." Fighting to get her to do more of the domestic chores in the house while acting as her greatest nemesis, the girl's mother and grandmother fulfill their roles as disciplinarians, criticizing her unfeminine behavior. "Girls don't slam doors like that." "Girls keep their knees together when they sit down." Henry, hired help on the farm, warns her against fighting her younger brother, saying, "Oh, that there Laird is going to show you one of these days."

5b.5 **Personal Connection** *Explore the personal connection when your reading has a special meaning for you.* Finding the tie-in with your own experience can help show the human relevance of a poem or story beyond its limited setting or point in time. (A *classic* is a work that speaks to us today across distances in time, place, and culture.)

> Growing up on a farm was much the same lesson in stereotypes for me as it was for the young woman in Alice Munro's "Boys and Girls." I was never told outright that something was "man's work" or "woman's work." I simply worked with my father, and my sister worked with her mother. My sister was encouraged to participate in sports, earning an athletic scholarship, and I was allowed to cook. But these things took place during recreational time; when work needed to be done, we knew our place. I idolized my father and was constantly seeking ways to make him proud of me. Unfortunately, I was very small growing up (under five feet until high school), and I was sub-par at many "manly" tasks that required strength or size. My father always praised me for my accomplishments, but I knew I was never really living up to his idea of what a young male should be.

When reworking an early draft in response to feedback from your instructor or peer reviewers, you may want to keep the following checklist posted next to your computer:

GUIDE TO REVISION

Revising a Critical Paper

1 ***Be prepared to reread.*** In response to feedback from your instructor and peers, go back to a story or poem to check out details. Verify quotations or clear up debatable points.

2 ***Do more to avoid the appearance of a plot summary.*** Show more clearly that you are not just paraphrasing the poem or retelling the story step by step. In the same paragraph, bring together evidence from *different parts* of a poem or story.

3 ***Go back and reexamine your thesis.*** Should you adjust it in the light of points that came up later in your paper? Do you need to spell out more clearly something that confused your readers?

4 ***Build up evidence for key points.*** Develop a key example that you used too briefly. Whenever you can, drive a point home by adding a second or third example.

5 ***Bring life into grey homogenized general passages.*** Splice in more vivid images and attention-getting quotes—give your readers things to visualize and to react to emotionally.

6 ***Save block quotations for support of important points.*** Big chunks of undigested quoted material may make your readers lose sight of key points (and may tempt them to skip). Break up big chunks so you can weave interpretation and personal reaction more naturally into your text.

7 ***Strengthen transitions from one point to the next.*** Show logical connections instead of using weak links of the *and-then* type. Instead of saying "At this point in the story" start a new paragraph with a transition like "The *other side of her character* shows when . . ."

8 ***Watch out for stereotypes.*** A label like *tomboy* or *meek Asian woman* may be too much of a stereotype—there may be more to the person than shows under the stereotypical surface.

9 ***Cut out weak repetition.*** Especially in your conclusion, do not just restate points you have already made clear (although you may want to sum up clearly a point on which you presented evidence pro and con).

10 ***Strengthen your conclusion.*** Add a striking final example or a clincher quote. Or conclude with a striking relevant anecdote from your own experience. Or bring in a strong supporting quotation from another story or poem by the same writer, highlighting the same theme.

YOUR TURN 20 Questions for Peer Reviewers

Here are suggested questions for peer reviewers. Use them as a guide in responding to the following student paper or to papers from your classmates.

1 What does the paper as a whole accomplish, or what is the point of the paper as a whole?

2 How well does the writer get you into the spirit of the poem or story or into the world of the play?

3 Does the writer focus on key images or a central symbol or bring a central theme into focus? Or does the writer perhaps highlight a central conflict or focus on a play of opposites?

4 What is the overall plan, or what are major stages or waystations in this paper? Is the plan easy or hard to follow? Are there clear signposts or transitions?

5 Does the writer support major points with key details and revealing quotations? Which are most striking or thought-provoking?

6 If you have read this work yourself, does the writer read it the way you do or differently? Why or how?

7 Does the writer seem to have a personal connection with the story, poem, or play? Does it have a special personal meaning for you?

8 What questions does the paper leave in your mind, or what issues would you like to see addressed?

The Blowing of Free Spirit in the Wind

Life on Native American reservations is often viewed in a negative light. Louise Erdrich grew up on a reservation herself. In her short story "The Red Convertible," she counteracts negative associations of reservation life by showing the strong relationship between two brothers and vividly displaying the power of the free spirit. Contrary to widespread stereotypes, the two brothers, Henry and Lyman, were able for a time to satisfy their hunger for life beyond the confines of the reservation. The red convertible Olds that they bought on an impulse was for a time their ticket to freedom and also allowed for the strengthening of their brotherhood.

Adventurous, lucky, and loyal are just a few words that describe Lyman, the younger brother. He prides himself upon his one outstanding talent—he "could always make money." This characteristic, as Erdrich says, was "unusual in a Chippewa." Lyman was the "only kid let into the American Legion Hall to shine shoes . . . and one Christmas sold spiritual bouquets for the mission door to door." At age fifteen he was managing the Joliet Cafe and eventually became the owner at sixteen, working his way up from simply being a dishwasher. He was constantly defying the odds. He was thirsty for adventure, living through an experience that would catapult him from his confining environment and redefine who he truly was.

Henry, the older brother, was similar to Lyman in that he too sought out the unknown, curious as to how life was elsewhere, beyond the scope of his own two eyes. He was funny and spontaneous and like a comic; "he always had a joke." He brought smiles to his younger brother's face and set wonderful examples for him as well. Henry was free spirited, constantly eager to try something new and exciting. Picking up a hitchhiker during a long carefree trip in the brothers' red Olds, Henry wondered what it "felt like to have long pretty hair" and placed the young woman upon his shoulders, "twirling this way and that so that her hair was flung out from side to side."

The combination of these two passionate and exceptional young men made for an amazing spirit of brotherhood. The desire of both to experience life at first hand beyond the reservation became a reality with the purchase of the red Olds. They gave in to their impulsiveness for the sake of something unique, something out of the ordinary. They were simply walking the streets of Winnipeg when they saw it, parked "large as life . . . really as if it was alive." They both emptied their pockets and had barely enough money for the tank of gas to get them home, but it didn't matter; "they went places in that car." They took off and drove one whole summer spanning the nation from Montana to Alaska, observing and appreciating everything they encountered. They were together, sharing all of the memories together without putting up the top of the convertible once. The red Olds was the defining symbol of their brotherhood. It allowed them to exercise their freedom, to escape the monotony of the reservation, and to laugh together.

The joy and laughter ended abruptly with the end of the short Alaska summer and the deployment of Henry to Vietnam with the Marine Corps. The three years of separation forever altered the relationship that was molded while the brothers were cruising in

YOUR TURN 20 *(continued)*

the red Olds. Henry came home "very different . . . the change was no good." His comic tendencies had been replaced with silence and stillness. The vivid images of death and outright disgust of the war had sucked Henry dry, stealing the free spirit and fervor that had defined him. His behavior was difficult for Lyman to cope with, watching for instance at dinner as Henry bit through his lip with the "blood going down his chin." Despite Lyman's valiant attempts to bring back what he and Henry once shared, Henry could not be helped; the war had stripped him of his will to live.

Eldrich's story plucks at the heart strings of anyone who is privileged to share the joy of life with a sibling. Lyman and Henry defied the life that they were supposed to have led. The bond that they strengthened while their hair blew in the summer wind was utterly destroyed by the horrors of war. They had owned the red convertible Olds together until Henry made an end by walking into the flooded river on a windy night. His "boots filled with water " and he disappeared in the waves, with Lyman sending the car after him, saying, "He bought out my share."

OPTIONS FOR WRITING 16

Write a critical paper about a literary selection (or literary selections) with a special meaning for you. Focus your paper on a central question that the literature you have read is likely to raise in the reader's mind. Support your points with striking details and revealing brief quotations from your reading. Show evidence of your close first-hand reading, and bring your own personal reactions as a reader or spectator into play.

1 Explore the interplay of setting and character in a short story where the setting looms large. How much does the setting or cultural environment shape the character(s)? How much is environment? How much is the individual's character or temperament? For instance, explore the role of the New South in a story by Bobbie Ann Mason, of the reservation setting in a story by Louise Erdrich, of the old South in a story like William Faulkner's "Tall Men," or of Puritan New England in a story by Nathaniel Hawthorne.

2 Trace the growth of a central character in a story of initiation like Alice Munro's "Boys and Girls." What are the major stages in the character's growing up? Or what are the major forces in the character's spiritual growth?

3 Explore the role of a central symbol in a short story like John Steinbeck's "The Chrysanthemums" or Charlotte Perkins Gilman's "The Yellow Wallpaper." How does the symbol become important in the story? Are there different ways of interpreting the symbolic meaning of the story?

4 Study one or more poems by a poet whose poetry has a strong personal or autobiographical dimension. For instance, select from the poetry of May Swenson, Sharon Olds, Anne Sexton, or Sylvia Plath. Or choose a poem like Li-Young Lee's "Persimmons." What voice do you hear in the poem or poems? What person is speaking to you? How do you relate to the person?

5 Study several poems by a poet whose work has a strong regional identity or is rooted strongly in a part of the country, such as Robert Frost's New England or William Stafford's Midwest. What is the role of the poet's roots or favorite setting in the poetry?

6 Study several poems by an engaged or committed poet with a strong allegiance to a group or a cause. For instance, study the role of social conscience or a sense of mission in poems by Gwendolyn Brooks or Denise Levertov.

7 Focus on one or more plays whose central character or protagonist is a strong woman. For instance, study Sophocles' Antigone, Henrik Ibsen's Nora in *The Doll's House*, or the matriarch in Lorraine Hansberry's *Raisin in the Sun*. What are the sources of the character's strength or pride? Are there major stages in the development of her self-image or self-esteem? What role does she play in the lives of others?

8 Select a play that centers on what Shakespeare's Hamlet calls the clash of "mighty opposites." What are the sources of the conflict? How does it develop? How is it resolved? What does it show about the playwright's perspective on human nature or attitude toward life?

9 The ancient Greek tragedies and Shakespeare's tragedies focus on a great figure—a heroic or admirable character, although the character may have fatal flaws. It is often said that modern plays from Ibsen onward could not be tragedies or rise to a tragic level: The central characters were unheroic everyday people. Compare

OPTIONS FOR WRITING 16 *(continued)*

the human stature of the central character in a traditional tragedy and in one of the classics of the modern stage. In each, how does the audience relate to the central character?

10 Study a major shift or reversal in the reputation of an American classic. Why have critics re-examined and sometimes drastically re-evaluated writers such as Ernest Hemingway, Walt Whitman, Mark Twain, or Emily Dickinson?

PART TWO

EDITING FOR WORDS AND SENTENCES

Rewriting is a familiar part of every writer's job. Teachers and editors will encourage you to do real revision—to go beyond a few surface changes and strengthen the overall effectiveness of your paper. At the same time, they will stress final editing to make your writing meet the standards of educated written English. They will expect you to do careful line-by-line editing for effective word choice, well-built sentences, and up-to-date punctuation. They will ask: Is this the right word? Does this sentence really say what you want it to say?

6 WORKING WITH WORDS

Make the choices that will best serve your purpose.

What makes a good writer? The most basic answer is likely to be: Good writers are seldom at a loss for words. They seem to have the right word at their fingertips. They use more of our language than others do, and they use it better. In much editing, you will respond to feedback asking you to reword something to say it better—to say it more accurately or more clearly. You may be rewording a chatty informal passage to make it less casual, more likely to be taken seriously. You may be rewriting a murky roundabout passage in plain English. You show that you respect the feelings of readers who may have found your original wording insulting or condescending.

6a Choosing the Right Word

ww

Improve the range and accuracy of your vocabulary.

Effective writers use the word with the right shade of meaning or the word calling up the right picture in the reader's mind.

6a.1 **Tracking New Words** *Keep track of new words—new to you, or new to the culture.* In your reading and writing about current developments, you are likely to encounter words like the following. As a word watcher, you take a good look at how they are used and make them part of your own working vocabulary. You look at how they are used in **context**—in a sentence, in a paragraph, in a situation.

laser	In various new kinds of microsurgery, *highly concentrated light beams* are used with millimeter precision.
meltdown	As the result of a breakdown in the cooling system, for instance, a *runaway nuclear reaction* may turn a nuclear plant into a catastrophic environmental hazard.

globalization	National trade barriers erode with the trend toward a *global economy* where not only products but also labor must compete on a world-wide scale.
disinformation	Agencies or governments may put *purposefully wrong information* into circulation in order to mislead the public and damage political opponents.
workfare	In an attempt to counteract "welfare dependency," states are experimenting with new ways of creating *jobs for welfare recipients.*

YOUR TURN 21 Keeping Up with Words

Write *capsule definitions* for five new or difficult words from a fast-changing area with which you are trying to keep up, such as media, fashion, medicine, high-tech, or electronic communication. For instance, explain to your classmates *digital, zero-sum, bionics, distance learning,* or *EQ.*

6a.2 Distinguishing Synonyms

Among several related words, choose the one with the right shade of meaning. The English language is rich in **synonyms**—words that mean almost the same but not exactly the same. For instance, notice differences in degree: A **lucid** explanation is clear, but it is *exceptionally* clear, making something intelligible that may have been murky before. Build up your range of choices in sets like the following:

SET 1

brief	short but often to the point
terse	intentionally very brief, as if fending off nosy questions
curt	brief to the point of being impolite

SET 2

danger	a risk of harm
hazard	a constant lurking danger, an accident waiting to happen
menace	something threatening us with evil intent

SET 3

doubtful	outcome or right decision subject to honest doubt
dubious	raising serious doubts about shady dealings
questionable	vulnerable to serious questions about its wisdom
problematic	likely to cause problems for whoever tackles it

YOUR TURN 22 Choosing the Right Synonym

What differences in meaning set apart the related words in each of the following sentences? Write brief *capsule definitions* for the boldfaced words in five of the sets.

The Language of Revolution

1 A full-scale **revolution** is more than a **mutiny** on a ship or a **rebellion** in a limited region.

2 The American revolutionaries included **idealistic** leaders who had a **visionary** or **utopian** blueprint for a new society.

3 Often the revolutionaries fight against authorities that label **dissent** as **treason** or **heresy.**

4 During the French Revolution, **extremist** elements steered the revolution in a **fanatical** or **doctrinaire** direction.

5 A new **authoritarian** or **totalitarian** government may replace the old **paternalistic** regime.

6 Critics warn against turning **education** into **propaganda** or **indoctrination.**

7 Sometimes **liberation** of the oppressed takes the form of peaceful **emancipation.**

8 Political movements may aim at **reform**, **overhaul**, or **abolition** of the old system.

6a.3 Recognizing Connotations *Become more aware of attitudes and judgments built into words.* Some words offer only neutral, objective description. However, many other words carry with them attitudes of approval or disapproval. They suggest something desirable or even admirable, or they suggest something to be feared or shunned. We call the added freight of attitude or emotion that a word activates its **connotation.**

dagger/sword	Both are lethal weapons. However, a **dagger** can be concealed and suggests treachery or treason. A **sword** suggests open honorable combat.
entrepreneur/ tycoon	Both build large commercial empires. **Entrepreneur** suggests a person with vision who boldly takes risks, contributing to general prosperity. **Tycoon** suggests someone who ruthlessly exploits employees and rides roughshod over the competition.

Connotative words are a powerful tool for shaping the attitudes of the audience, but they are also easily abused. They may be used too glibly to put the other side in the wrong. Terms like *special interests, lobbyist,* or *union bosses* put down people who look after the interests of those they represent, regardless of whether their activities deserve praise or blame. Terms like the following make serious charges. They do not simply point to people; they point the finger. If you feel justified in making these charges, be prepared to back them up.

TERM	CONNOTATION
mercenary	a soldier who hires himself out for pay with no commitment to country or ideals
demagogue	a politician who exploits the voters' fears and prejudices, leading them by the nose
speculator	an investor who aims at making a big unearned profit as the result of turns of events that might be harmful to many other people
bureaucrat	a public servant who does the job badly and puts obstacles in other people's path
cynic	someone who pays lip service to values or ideals but basically assumes that only crude self-interest counts

✓ ***EDITOR'S TIP:*** Angry emotionally charged words easily turn into insults that alienate fair-minded readers. Do without heavily weighted words like *gun nut, fem libber, crony, Uncle Tom, skinhead, commie,* or *fascist.* They may signal to your readers to expect little fair-minded discussion of the issues.

YOUR TURN 23 Managing Connotations

What differences in connotation set apart the italicized words in each sentence? What attitudes, feelings, or judgments does each word bring into play?

The Power of Words

1. The media have the power to *shape, slant, or manipulate* the news.
2. Action by an official may be called *courageous, rash, or foolhardy.*
3. Dissenters may be said to *protest, complain, or whine.*
4. A new law may be labeled *tough, severe, or punitive.*
5. Resistance to change may be called *caution, delay, or obstruction.*
6. A governor may be said to take advice from *friends, intimates, or cronies.*
7. Social programs may be called *compassionate, sentimental, or misguided.*
8. An unconventional proposal may be called *bold, novel, or far-fetched.*
9. A response to a threat from abroad may be called *temperate, timid, or abject.*
10. News reporting may be called *aggressive, sensational, or inflammatory.*

6a.4 ww

Inaccurate Words *Replace the wrong word—or the right word used the wrong way.* When writers expand their range of vocabulary, they may use a word that is almost right but that for some reason does not fit. At times they may use a word that is just plain wrong. When making new words your own, try to take in exact accurate meanings:

	GENERAL MEANING	SPECIAL ASSOCIATIONS
precarious	risky	already tottering on the brink
incongruous	out of place	standing out in weird or ridiculous fashion
spurious	false	claiming to be genuine but actually completely fake

Edit sentences like the following:

WRONG WORD:

Young people today get married without *consenting* their parents. (without **consulting** them or **getting their consent**)

Critics *contribute* the drop in crime to doctored statistics. (**attribute** or **trace**)

Students *lost their appeal for* the Greek life. (the Greek life **lost its appeal for** them)

The news about the stolen funds was first *exposed* in May. (the news was **revealed** or the theft **exposed**)

YOUR TURN 24 Finding the Right Word

What is wrong with the words italicized in the following sentences? Find a better word for each.

1 Working parents often do not have time to *adhere* to their children's needs.
2 Difficult choices *affront* students choosing their majors.
3 The new owners discovered the difficulties *coherent* in serving diverse customers.
4 Their idealistic parents were trying to raise healthy *opinionated* children.
5 In Platonic love, sexual relations are *illuminated*.
6 Her traditional parents placed a high *standard* on education.
7 The driver *braved* her life trying to save the passengers.
8 Work in the sweatshops was sheer *trudgery*.
9 Their *analogy* of our marketing plan exposed its strengths and weaknesses.
10 Psychologists criticized the strict rules of *authoritative* parents.

6b Formal/Informal English

inf

Move on the right level of formality for serious writing.

Learn to move from the casual English of talking with friends to the more formal English of writing for a larger public. Effective writers shift gears without effort from informal speech to more formal written

English. Much serious discussion of issues or ideas and much interpretation of data move on a middle ground between friendly, chummy talk and stiff formality. Most **edited written English** is moderately formal (semiformal), with an occasional informal touch.

INFORMAL: Talk radio gives people a chance to shoot off their mouths and is as American as apple pie. In a democracy, you can't shut people up.

MIDDLE GROUND: The public's right to know and the right of the individual to privacy have long been on a collision course, with aggressive prying journalism more and more eroding privacy protections for people in public life.

VERY FORMAL: There is a heavy legal presumption against prior restraint of journalists, making most censorship initiatives futile undertakings.

The following is a sample excerpt from discussion of current issues in newspapers and newsmagazines. The writer uses edited written English formal enough to be taken seriously—but not too technical or stiff for lively public debate. The passage was first published when an unprecedented heat wave in the Southwest revived discussion of the theory that our failure to control the emission of industrial gases will produce catastrophic global warming:

> We continue to report global warning as though it were a "debate" among scientists. It is not. What we mistake for a debate is actually a public relations campaign by the American Petroleum Institute, which has recruited and funded a few scientists who question the whole phenomenon. They, in turn, are given equal weight by the media, as though they were precisely as objective as the 2,500 scientists who work with the United Nations' Intergovernmental Panel on Climate Change. According to *USA Today*, when fourteen energy industry lobbyists gathered in April to work out the details of a $6 million lobbying plan on global warming, they targeted Congress, the news media, the public, and . . . schoolchildren.
>
> —Molly Ivins, "Don't Say It's Global Warming," *Fort Worth Star Telegram*

Key words in this passage are plain English but a cut above the level of chatty informal talk: *phenomenon, precisely, objective, targeted.* Although Ivins is a columnist known for her strong opinions and biting wit, she says that the Petroleum Institute "recruited and funded" its line-up of scientists (rather than that it "dug up and bankrolled" them).

6b.1 Editing Informal English

Edit for informal English that will sound too casual, chummy, or folksy to your readers. Words like *kids, folks,* and *sis* are all right mostly in an informal family context. Unless you are on close friendly terms with the person, you are getting too familiar when you call a police officer a *cop,* a teacher a *prof,* or your physician *doc.* When you switch from talk to writing, edit out catchall labels that might sound gushy or superficial, such a *cute, terrific, wonderful, great,* and *nice.*

Much of the small change of casual conversation will be too informal for your writing:

INFORMAL	FORMAL	INFORMAL	FORMAL
buddy	friend	boss	employer
brainy	intelligent	bug	germ
broke	penniless	flunk	fail
picky	fastidious	butter up	flatter
stuck up	conceited	hassle	problem
snooze	sleep	hustle	try hard
snoop	pry	stump	baffle

You can usually adjust the level of formality a notch by going for the more formal choice in pairs like the following:

INFORMAL	FORMAL	INFORMAL	FORMAL
ad	advertisement	mad	angry
mess	disorder	skimpy	meager

✓ ***EDITOR'S TIP:*** Informal **contractions** like *don't, isn't,* and *can't* are usually all right in shorter papers but even then they should not be overused. Some teachers and editors advise against using them altogether. These informal shortcuts often cause spelling problems: Double-check **don't, doesn't, they're** (not *their* or *there*).

YOUR TURN 25 Rewriting Informal English

The following advice to parents imitates the brash shirtsleeve style of some popular columnists. Rewrite the passage in a less informal style for use in serious discussion.

Daddy Is a Wimp

Instead of being strong family leaders, parents have become wimps who are too wishy-washy to enforce rules. They have been told not to be bossy with the brats. If your kids get in your face, you aren't supposed to lose your cool and yell at them. Blowups like that are considered bad for the kid's self-esteem. As a result, we're turning out a bunch of really smart-mouthed kids who are in for a big shock when they get out into the real world and find it's not owned by Mom and Dad. Some experts figure that maybe the inmates shouldn't be running the asylum after all. Kids who can't yet tie their own shoe laces shouldn't have an equal say-so in the family democracy.

6b.2 sl

Restricting Slang *Use slang or extremely informal language only in very special situations.* Slang is colorful and uninhibited, and writers may use an occasional slang term like *gas guzzler, couch potato,* or *loan shark* to liven up their prose. Some words move from slang to standard: *disc jockey, joystick, workaholic, panhandler.* However, most slang is brash and disrespectful. When you use terms like *jalopy, clunker,* and *lemon* in a paper, your readers may feel you are showing disrespect not only for the subject but also for your audience. Most slang is too crude or insulting for serious writing.

TOO SLANGY: hick, crony, jock, lush, computer nerd, bimbo, jailbird, pothead

Although common in informal speech, words like the following are too crude for serious discussion:

SLANG	FORMAL	SLANG	FORMAL
bitch	complain	*bug*	annoy
gyp, shaft	cheat	*shrink*	psychiatrist

6b.3

Avoiding Hyperformality *Keep your writing from becoming too stiff and impersonal.* If you are criticized for using informal language, you may go to the opposite extreme. The writing then may become too stiff and formal for a live discussion of an issue. Your writing turns hyperformal when it moves too far away from vigorous natural everyday English. Don't go out of your way to prefer a more formal or unusual word over a plain word that says the same thing.

VERY FORMAL: Our *institutions of higher learning* should not *divulge documentation* of a student's *academic performance*.

PLAIN ENGLISH: **Colleges** should not **give out grade records to outsiders.**

VERY FORMAL: High-tech corporations *tender extraordinary inducements* to employees from abroad with *the requisite expertise* in mathematics and science.

PLAIN ENGLISH: High-tech corporations **offer extraordinary incentives** to employees from abroad **with the necessary background** in mathematics and science.

Unusual words by themselves do not make your writing stilted. Often the more unusual word offers a shade of meaning important to what you are saying. For example, *aspersion* is more than blame. When we cast aspersions we seem to be making damaging and perhaps groundless charges in a mean-spirited way. Similarly, *recrimination* is the right word for an unusually intense and hostile putting of blame on another. However, your writing will sound stiff and artificial when you often needlessly seem to reach for the more unusual word:

VERY FORMAL	PLAIN	VERY FORMAL	PLAIN
commence	begin	*sojourn*	stay
remuneration	pay	*demise*	death
pulchritude	beauty	*astound*	amaze
nuptials	wedding	*accolade*	tribute

6b.4 Recognizing Jargon

Prefer plain English to inflated language. Writers use **jargon** to make themselves sound more important than they are. Jargon is designed to make trivial things sound important and average ideas impressive. It uses technical-sounding or scientific-sounding terms for everyday matters. Childhood becomes *preadolescence;* food becomes *dietary intake;* methods become *methodology*.

JARGON:	Verification of time completed is mandatory as you leave your workstation.
PLAIN ENGLISH:	**Punch your time card when you leave.**
JARGON:	Testing of personnel for controlled substances may be implemented without prior notification.
PLAIN ENGLISH:	**We may administer drug tests to employees on short notice.**

Plain-English consultants in law, business, and social science help writers look for tell-tale signs of inflated language. They warn against the routine use of objective-sounding terms like *factors, aspects, phases, facets, phenomena, elements,* and *strata.* They warn against fashionable new-fangled *-ize* words and the overuse of *-ation/-otion/-ition* words:

-ize	maximize (develop to the fullest), prioritize (rank)
-ation, -otion, -ition	conceptualization (thinking), utilization (use)

Jargon tends to be impersonal, making us lose sight of who does what:

JARGON	PLAIN
reference was made	**the researchers mentioned**
the hypothesis suggests itself	**we might conclude**

All of the words in the following list are good to know, and they all have legitimate uses. However, when you use too many of them instead of plainer words, readers may start to find your writing pompous:

ELABORATE	PLAIN	ELABORATE	PLAIN
magnitude	size	*prevalent*	common
parameter	limit	*imperative*	necessary
interrelationship	relation	*outcomes*	results
corollary	result	*divulge*	reveal
extrapolate	extract		

YOUR TURN 26 Plain English, Please

Rewrite the following sentences to bring them closer to plain English.

1 Careful consideration of desired outcomes is imperative.

2 The senator was instrumental in instituting new parameters for facilitating access to public parks.

3 Further insight into the article discovered that the writing insinuated a connection between the acquittal and the socioeconomic status of the accused.

4 Sensitivity to stereotypes and avoidance of ethnic slurs have become important factors in the communication situation between police and the minority community.

5 A recurrent paradigm in the context of the youth culture is the media icon who succumbs tragically.

6 It was felt that an element of deception was present in the speaker's words.

6b.5 Resisting Euphemisms *Avoid the deceptive use of euphemisms.*

Euphemisms are "beautiful words"—language more uplifting or reassuring than the reality they describe. Some familiar euphemisms show respect for the feelings of others. We may refer to a family member as a **problem drinker** rather than an *alcoholic*. We may prefer to say that a friend was **dismissed** rather than *fired*. In education or law enforcement, we use euphemistic language to neutralize traditional stereotypes and deal with problems in a constructive fashion. We talk about **substance abuse** rather than drug addiction, about **underachievers** rather than academic failures.

However, euphemisms become a problem when they become fuzzy or intentionally misleading. Euphemisms serve for verbal upgrading of institutions and occupations. Often the new label sounds vaguely complimentary, while leaving the reader wondering exactly what the people do. Garbage collection becomes *waste management;* the department of physical education becomes the *Department of Human Performance;* an interpreter becomes a *language facilitator;* a plumber becomes a *sanitation engineer*.

Euphemisms may be used to gloss over harsh realities. Much management talk is designed to make current business practices sound more human. The cutting down of centuries-old trees is called *harvesting*. *Flexible scheduling* puts a positive spin on calling on employees only when they are needed instead of giving them steady work. *Outplacement* used to be called firing. Imitations of management talk that are widely circulated among employees make fun of euphemisms like *left to pursue other interests* (was let go) and *between assignments* (out of a job).

Effective writers know when to be polite and when to be blunt:

EUPHEMISM	BLUNT
negative economic growth	**recession**
streamlining operations	**layoffs**
lack of proper health habits	**dirt**
deteriorating residential section	**slum**
below the poverty line	**poor**

YOUR TURN 27 **Euphemisms and Blunt Language**

How would you answer the following questions, and why? If your answer is "that depends," on what does it depend?

1 Do you prefer *memorial park* or *cemetery?*

2 Do you prefer *correctional facility* or *penitentiary* or *jail?*

3 Do you prefer *secretary* or *office worker?*

4 Do you prefer *under the influence* or *intoxicated* or *drunk?*

5 Do you prefer *illegitimate child, born out of wedlock,* or *child of a single mother?*

6 Do you prefer *juvenile delinquent, young criminal,* or *young person in trouble with the law?*

6c Reducing Wordiness

w red

Aim at vigorous plain English with a minimum of static.

Use the words needed to carry your meaning, but don't load down your sentences with unnecessary verbal baggage.

6c.1
w

Reducing Padding

Cut out padding, filler, or empty words. Look for mouthfuls that you could replace with shorter, more pointed language:

WORDY	BRIEF
at the present time	**now**
due to the fact that	**because**
at a point in time when	**when**
it is an unfortunate fact that	**unfortunately**
the question whether	**whether**
under the prevailing circumstances	**as things are**

Words like *aspect, situation, area,* and *angle* are often mere filler. So are conversational tags like *kind of* and *sort of.*

WORDY: In our *situation* in society today, the *area* of early childhood education is an important *aspect.*

TRIMMED: **Early childhood education is important.**

WORDY: Lauren *kind of* aspired to be the class clown, which *sort of* embarrassed his friends.

TRIMMED: **Lauren aspired to be the class clown, which embarrassed his friends.**

6c.2
red

Editing for Redundancy

Edit for direct duplication of meaning. Free gift is **redundant** because gifts are supposed to be free. *Consensus of opinion* is redundant because a consensus is already a reconciling of opinions, a meeting of minds.

REDUNDANT	BRIEF
basic *fundamentals*	**basics**
in the future *to come*	**in the future**
academic grade record	**grade record**
new innovations	**innovations**
anticipate *in advance*	**anticipate**
return *back*	**return**
true facts	**facts**

Edit for redundancy in sentences like the following:

is a complete misconception.
REDUNDANT: This *misconception* is completely *erroneous.*

As a rule, judges hesitate
REDUNDANT: *As a rule*, judges *usually* hesitate to treat young offenders as criminals.

YOUR TURN 28 **Cutting Down on Wordiness**

Rewrite the following sentences to make them less wordy.

1 In due course, our offices will eventually move to the newly renovated building.

2 Re-entry students often get good grades academically due to the fact that they have definite goals to aim at for the future ahead.

3 Another aspect we need to consider is the consumer relations angle in terms of an aging baby boomer population.

4 Dissatisfaction with our schools is peaking at a high point at a point in time when politicians are reverting back to stressing basic fundamentals.

5 It is an unfortunate fact of life today in our current news business that the true facts are often overlooked in the rush to scoop the competition.

6d Sexist and Offensive Language

sx
off

Become sensitive to sexist and other offensive language.

Fair-minded readers are alienated by language that mirrors prejudice. Most institutions and government agencies have guidelines for avoiding language that slights people because of race, religion, sex, national origin, sexual orientation, age, or disability.

6d.1 **Racial and Other Slurs** *Stay clear of the vocabulary of hate speech.* Educated readers have zero tolerance for *fag* and *faggot; greaser, beaner, gook,* and other ethnic slurs too ignorant and ugly to mention. (Members of one of the groups concerned may at times use a normally offensive label as a form of rough kidding or of defiant self-assertion, as when rappers use the N-word as a badge of group identity.)

6d.2 Sexist Language

Edit for sexist language. Most organizations and publications have guidelines for avoiding language that demeans women or locks them into traditional gender roles:

- *Avoid terms felt to be belittling or condescending.* Use **young woman** instead of *girl*, **office staff** instead of *the girls in the office*, and **female student** instead of *coed*. Avoid terms like *chick flick* or *lady Ph.D.*

- *Avoid gender bias in labels for occupations.* English has many gender-neutral terms for occupations: *manager, physician, scientist, artist, carpenter, professor, mechanic*. Replace gender-specific words that seem to lock women into traditional roles, especially words ending with *-man* or *-ess*. When you say that we need more *policemen* walking our streets, you make it sound as though all police officers are or should be male.

GENDER-SPECIFIC	GENDER-NEUTRAL
policeman	police officer
congressman	representative
mailman	mail carrier
fireman	firefighter
foreman	supervisor
chairman	chair, chairperson
businessman	merchant, businessperson
spokesman	voice, spokesperson
stewardess	flight attendant
waitress	server

✓ ***EDITOR'S TIP:*** Use references to gender or marital status not at all or in evenhanded fashion. Use **Ms. Claire Bergen** instead of *Mrs.* or *Miss* in addressing correspondence unless you know that a woman prefers to be addressed as *Mrs.*

UNEVEN: Fred Brewster, local builder, and Sarah Firth, mother of three, are running for City Council.

BALANCED: Fred Brewster, father of two, and Sarah Firth, mother of three, are regulars in the cheering section at the Junior Hockey League.

- *Use updated generic labels. Mankind* and *the history of man* were supposed to include both men and women, but **human beings, humanity,** and **humankind** are more clearly gender-neutral. *Manpower* has become **labor force** or **workforce.**

6d.3 Nonsexist Pronouns *Deal with the pronoun dilemma.*

English does not have a gender-neutral pronoun for *he/she* or *s/he*. Unless you are clearly referring to a specific man or woman, avoid the traditional gender-specific pronouns. Avoid using *he (him, himself)* in reference to doctors, judges, managers, CEOs, police officers, coaches, or generally people with authority or money. Avoid using *she (her, herself)* when talking about office workers, nurses, medical technicians, teachers, flight attendants.

SEXIST: *A doctor* should give *his nurse* specific instructions.

You usually have three options: Use the **double pronoun** *he or she (him or her; himself or herself)*. Note that several double pronouns in a row can make a sentence wordy and awkward. You can try changing the sentence to the plural, since a *they* referring to several doctors or judges is gender-neutral. Often you can eliminate the pronoun (and possible reference to gender) altogether.

DOUBLE PRONOUN: A doctor should give **his or her nurse** specific instructions.

PLURAL PRONOUN: **Doctors** should give **their nurses** specific instructions.

NO PRONOUN: A doctor should give **a nurse** specific instructions.

YOUR TURN 29 Editing for Sexist Language

In each of the following sentences, rewrite the part that uses sexist language. Compare your rewrites with those of your classmates.

1 On Secretaries' Day, a manager should show his appreciation by taking the girls in the office to lunch.

2 A doctor usually knows his patients less intimately than his nurse and her coworkers do.

3 Trying to defuse a violent situation, a policeman risks losing his life but also losing his job if charges of excessive force are brought against him.

YOUR TURN 29 *(continued)*

4 As long as you are a paying customer, the young lady waiting on you should at least be polite.

5 It's hard to get through to the CEO of a company if his receptionist employs her usual delaying tactics.

6 Early man's use of weapons and other man-made implements gave him an edge over his fellow creatures of the wild.

7 A movie director should not show his impatience when dealing with a temperamental leading lady.

8 A defendant in a criminal case and his lawyer usually know better than to badger the judge to change his rulings.

9 The average user of the Internet spends hours at his computer.

10 A mayor, congressman, or senator spends more of his time running for reelection than serving his hard-working constituents and their wives.

6e Clichés and Buzzwords

Use fresh language to replace clichés and buzzwords.

Clichés are tired ready-made expressions, worn out from overuse. They make it sound as if your thinking is canned, making it hard for you to take a fresh look at an issue. Clichés make writing too easy; they seem to type themselves: *few and far between, to say the least, cart before the horse, in the final analysis, do more harm than good.* When you first encounter a cliché (*the tip of the iceberg; walk the walk*), it may seem fresh and colorful, but you soon discover everyone has used it before you.

Your writing software may soon include a cliché detector that zaps expressions like the following. Most of these are *as old as the hills, to coin a phrase*:

this day and age	last but not least
believe it or not	better late than never
beyond the shadow of a doubt	easier said than done
let's look at the facts	the last straw
let's face it	crying shame
Mother Nature	off the beaten track

pride and joy	rude awakening
shot in the arm	sink or swim
sneaking suspicion	to all intents and purposes

Special areas of interest have **buzzwords** that are constantly used and overused for a time. Much current business talk keeps up a buzz of expressions like *look at the bottom line, cost-efficient, user-friendly, market share, shareholder value, window of opportunity, cutting edge, downside.* Many people tune out pep talk that seems to paste together the same tired old phrases: "For a while it seemed as if things were falling apart, but when our backs were to the wall and the chips were down, everyone in the group seemed to come through and did a great job."

Try to phrase your ideas freshly in your own words:

CLICHÉ: My parents never talked to me about *the facts of life.*

FRESH: My parents never talked to me about **questions that confuse young people.**

CLICHÉ: The coach *let us have it, straight from the shoulder.*

FRESH: The coach **spoke to us urgently, like a scout just returned from the enemy camp.**

YOUR TURN 30 Editing for Fresh Language

Rewrite each sentence to replace clichés with language fresh enough to get the reader's attention.

1 When all is said and done, sports organizations are not going to penalize players who are the apple of the public's eye.

2 Instead of giving foreign competitors a run for their money, American CEOs tend to throw in the towel.

3 Legislators who are forced to play ball with special interests are no longer able to look at the big picture.

4 In the fast-moving world of today, candidates have to be willing to give their all and walk the extra mile.

5 Businesses unable to make the quantum leap into the new century will miss the bus and fall by the wayside.

6 Raising standards for students from the other side of the tracks is easier said than done.

7 Voters from every walk of life will have a chance to stand up and be counted.

8 When we try to give the economy a shot in the arm, appealing to self-interest is our best bet.

6f Effective Word Choice

d Choose words that make your writing vivid and informative.

Push toward language that is exact, vivid, and informative. **Barometer** is more exact than *gadget for measuring air pressure.* **Loophole** is more vivid than *special provision of the tax code.* **Cement truck** is more informative than *vehicle.* Vivid informative language helps your readers see the world as if through an open window. Overly general and colorless language is like a befogged windshield that gives them only a blurry view of reality.

6f.1 Blurry and Exact *Trade blurry or roundabout words for words that carry exact information.*

the crew
BLURRY: The skipper and *the people working for him on the boat* were lost.

in a snowed-in mountain pass.
BLURRY: The Donner Party was stranded *in difficult terrain.*

Use exact **technical terms**, but help your readers with terms that may be new or difficult for them. Provide capsule definitions like the following:

TECHNICAL: The climbers **bivouac, spending the nights in a temporary encampment in the open, with only tents for shelter**.

While most participants in a chat room join in, others **lurk, listening in without revealing their presence.**

The **primates—the big apes that are our closest biological relatives**—are wired for emotions like anxiety and apprehension the way humans are.

6f.2 Abstract and Concrete

Writing becomes too abstract when we can no longer see what ideas mean in practice. **Abstract** words are words for general ideas like *consent, eligibility,* or *representation.* Some stand for sweeping large concepts: *liberty, happiness, excellence.* **Concrete** words take us to the opposite end of the scale. They move close to the world we take in with our senses. They give us things to visualize, hear, and touch. To make your writing more real and vivid, try moving down a step or two on the scale of abstraction. Move closer to actual sights and sounds.

GENERAL: Rodeo artists lived a *strenuous life*, *eating poorly*, always *exposed to injury*.

CONCRETE: Rodeo artists **lived off hot dogs** at county fairs and **ruptured their intestines** while **twisting the necks of steers**.

GENERAL: Yuppies are people who are *always in a hurry*, *never staying long in one place*.

CONCRETE: Yuppies are people who are **on the go so much that their answering machines answer their phones more often than they do.**

Try the following to make your writing more vivid and informative:

- *Call things by their names.* Instead of using a colorless general label, use names that call up shapes, textures, and colors.

COLORLESS	MORE REAL
weed	dandelion, crabgrass, tumbleweed, thistle
small animal	gopher, squirrel, opossum, chipmunk, raccoon
tree	birch, elm, pine, fir, eucalyptus, poplar, cypress
building	mansion, bungalow, warehouse, tenement, shack, cabin

- *Use concrete words—words that appeal to our senses.* Concrete words bring us close to sights, sounds, smells, textures, and motions. Here are some all-purpose general words with the more concrete choices that could take their place. What does each of these concrete words add to the general idea? What does it make you see or hear?

GENERAL	CONCRETE
walk	stride, march, slink, amble, shuffle
look	stare, gaze, ogle, peer, squint
take	seize, grab, pounce on, grip
throw	hurl, heave, pitch, toss, dump, flip

6f.3 mm

Mixed/Effective Metaphor *Use imaginative language to bring color and life into your writing.* Effective writers use imaginative comparisons to bring ideas to life. They make use of language that gives us a vivid image: **whistle-blower, deep pockets, brain drain, population explosion, hiring freeze.** They use their imagination to bring in the right vivid comparison. A comparison signaled by *like* or *as if* is called a **simile:**

SIMILE: Growing up is **like ski racing.** When we are eighteen, our parents push us out of the starting gate and we are on our own.

In these stories, language is **like signals from ships in distress,** telling us of desperate needs.

Getting complete sentences out of him was **like trying to put together *homo sapiens* from a few bones in a cave.**

—Anita Strickland

An imaginative comparison without a signal such as *like* or *as if* is a **metaphor:**

METAPHOR: Star players in basketball and baseball earn **stratospheric** salaries. The Chicago Bulls paid Michael Jordan $33 million in one single year.
(The salaries are not *literally* up in the stratosphere, but they are up there compared with the earnings of ordinary mortals.)

The salaries of the lowest-tier athletes are being **squeezed** by the huge salaries of the mega-stars.

Skyrocketing salaries are driving up ticket prices for ordinary fans.

- Revise **mixed metaphors,** which result when the parts of a comparison don't go together (the virgin forest where *the hand of man* had never *set foot*). Metaphors are consistent when everything is part of the same picture:

CONSISTENT: Everyone **holds dual citizenship, in the kingdom of the well and in the kingdom of the sick.**

—Susan Sontag

Any number of people have been **through earthquakes** in their private lives that haven't even **made a crack in the walls** of their philosophy.

—Ellen Goodman

Metaphors become mixed when the ship of life jumps the tracks (on the trackless sea) or the trial balloon blows up on the launching pad.

make grow.

MIXED: The family *plants seeds* that teachers *build upon.*
(we don't build on seeds)

new energy

Immigrants bring *new blood* to help us *recharge our batteries.*
(batteries don't run on blood)

- Revise **distracting metaphors,** which result when you strain too hard to give your readers a vivid image.

DISTRACTING: The supermarket is filled with the stuffed carts that will *fill the growling stomachs* of the customers.

Many people are unaware of the *gut issues that are propelling them forward.*

YOUR TURN 31 Strengthening Imaginative Language

Rewrite the following sentences to take out mixed or distracting metaphors and make better use of imaginative language.

1 Sarcasm is a kind of armor that helps us stay afloat in the hostile currents of life.

2 A racial slur is often the spark that sets a fatal train of events in motion.

3 The roots of prejudice have become deeply entrenched in many people.

4 Again the jagged teeth of terrorism have bitten deeply into the tender flesh of the community.

5 Distrust and paranoia will take over the cities the way bacteria do our bodies if we do not harness them.

6 Words that carry heaping servings of anger short-circuit thought.

7 Today glad-handing, back-scratching politicians no longer automatically hit the bull's eye in the political arena.

8 They refused to bring up the rear on the treadmill of life.

6g Using the Dictionary

Discover the resources of your college dictionary.

Today's college dictionaries, available both as 1,500-page books and on CD-ROM, catalog the meanings, uses, and histories of maybe 150,000 words. Dictionary makers compete in covering the leapfrogging advances in science and technology (*quasars, dark holes, gene splicing, microsurgery*). They track the rapidly changing vocabularies of electronic communication (*hackers, spamming, lurking, flaming*). They try to keep up with popular culture (*punk, heavy metal, media event, break dancing, infomercial*).

A typical dictionary entry crams much information into a small space. Before you come to the meanings of a word, you get information about

- spelling (for instance, listing both **catalog** and **catalogue**)
- division into syllables (how to divide a word at the end of a line: **au•di•tion**)
- pronunciation, transcribed according to a code that varies from dictionary to dictionary (for instance, stress on the second syllable may be marked as follows in **dia'meter**)
- part of speech (use as part of a sentence, for instance **adj.** or adjective for "the *heavy* burden" but **n.** or noun for *heaviness*)

Major competing dictionaries promise that they will "help you understand and use the language as no other dictionary can." If you are looking for consumer information, you may want to follow up leads like the following:

- *Webster's New World College Dictionary* often comes closest to giving you plain-English definitions of difficult words.

  dichotomy a division or split into opposites, "especially when these are sharply distinguished or opposed"

  interface detailed "interaction between two systems, disciplines, groups"

- All major dictionaries draw on citation files that record actual uses of words. However, the Merriam Webster data bank has long been considered the "national archives of the language." For students fascinated by our evolving language, the *Merriam Webster's Collegiate Dictionary* gives dates of first recorded use in addition to extensive information on word history. For instance, *mea culpa*, for a "formal acknowledgment of personal fault or error," was first recorded in 1602.

- Some users go to the dictionary mainly to settle an argument over the spelling, pronunciation, or correct use of a word. The *Random House Dictionary* has a record of giving especially full **usage notes** warning against expressions often labeled wrong, illogical, or substandard.

6g.1 **Range of Meanings** *Go through different listed uses of a word to find the one that fits.* Dictionaries provide sample phrases or sentences to show the meanings of a word in different contexts. Your dictionary may give the most *common* meaning first—and go on to less common meanings or special applications. Or it may give the *earliest* meaning first—and then show how the word branched out from its original uses. For a common word like *heavy*, your dictionary may list more than twenty meanings, with another dozen uses in combinations like *heavy-handed* and *heavy-duty*.

USING YOUR DICTIONARY

The Range of Meanings

heavy (adjective, also sometimes used as a noun)

BASE MEANING

1 hard to lift (going back to an Old English word for lifting)

RELATED MEANINGS

2 especially weighty for its size
3 of above normal or average weight

EXTENDED MEANINGS

4 above normal amount (a *heavy* turnout)
5 hard to do (*heavy* work)
6 hard to bear (*heavy* taxes)
7 hard to digest (a *heavy* meal)
8 striking with great force (a *heavy* blow)
9 violent or intense (a *heavy* sea)

SPECIAL USES

10 *chemistry:* of more than normal atomic weight (*heavy* water)
11 *theater:* a bullying villain (he played the *heavy*)
12 *slang:* serious and depressing (something *heavy* came down)

6g.2 **Synonyms and Antonyms** *Let the dictionary help you distinguish among words with similar meanings.* **Synonyms** are words with nearly the same meaning—that nevertheless may differ in how they are used. Here is a typical set of synonyms that your dictionary will help you tell apart:

freedom	most general term for lack of shackles, confinement, or restraint (*freedom* of the press)
liberty	often used for freedom fought for and gained after a period of oppression (civil *liberties*)
license	often used for freedom not granted to everyone (fool's *license*) or freedom being abused

Antonyms are words with nearly the opposite meaning. They can help you pinpoint a word by playing it off against its opposite. As antonyms of *freedom*, your dictionary may list **repression** and **constraint**. As antonyms of *authentic*, it may list **spurious**, **counterfeit**, and **sham**.

6g.3 **Usage Labels** *Check usage labels for words with a limited range.* For instance, the word *lorry* is **British English** for *truck*. Your dictionary may label *heavy breathing* **colloquial**—chatty or very informal for fake passion in soap opera and movies. It may label *heebie-jeebies* as **old slang.** (It's a term remembered by people who listen to oldies stations.) *You-all* may be labeled **Southern**—Southern informal speech. Here are some additional usage labels:

archaic	old-fashioned and surviving only in special uses (*brethren* for *brothers* is still used by some religious denominations)
obsolete	still found in earlier texts but no longer used today (*fain* for *gladly* and *nice* for *foolish* have gone out of use)
dialect	part of a local or regional variety of English (*kirk* is Scottish dialect for *church*)

6g.4 **Word History** *Let word history sensitize you to meanings and overtones.* Often a capsule history of a word will help you understand its special uses or associations. The basic structure of today's English goes back to **Old English** (after A.D. 450), the language that Germanic tribes brought to England across the sea. Much of our basic vocabulary is still close to similar words in sister languages like German or Dutch: *father, mother, daughter, heart, blood, water, rain, cold.* For much of the Middle Ages (roughly A.D. 1100 to 1500), England was ruled by Northern French (Norman) overlords. During the **Middle English** period English gradually absorbed an extensive overlay of French words. Some still remind us of the lifestyle of the French rulers and landowners: *castle, court, glory, mansion, noble, servant, treason, war.* The language of the church was for many centuries Latin, giving us words like *mass, altar, candle,* and *shrine.* The languages of learning and science were Latin and Greek, giving us words like the following:

LATIN: history, intelligence, legal, mechanism, rational, individual, dissent

GREEK: politics, democracy, chaos, cosmos, crisis, atmosphere, dialogue

Dictionaries have their own formats for **etymologies**—brief tracings of the roots of words. They will trace names like *Chicago* or *Massachusetts* to the original Native American languages. They will trace terms like *canyon, manzanita,* and *hacienda* to the period of Spanish colonization in the Southwest. A detailed etymology will often trace a typical family tree, sometimes going back all the way to the assumed common Indo-European parent language of most European languages. A sample etymology may give you information like the following in highly abbreviated form:

complain <from

ME (Middle English = medieval English) *compleinen* <from

OFr (Old French = medieval French) *complaindre* <from

VL (vulgar Latin = late popular Latin) *complangere,* "beat the breast" <from

L (earlier Latin) *plangere,* "strike" + prefix *com-,* "much or hard") <from

IE (Indo-European) root also seen in an ancient German word for "cursing" (*fluchen*) and an ancient Greek word for "striking" (*plessein*)

6g.5 Latin and Greek Roots

Let your knowledge of a shared root help you understand and use related words. Dictionaries highlight Latin and Greek roots like the following, especially if these are still active in the formation of new words:

ROOT	MEANING	EXAMPLES
arch-	rule	patriarch, matriarch, anarchy
bio-	life	biochemistry, biomass, biofeedback
chron-	time	chronological, synchronize, anachronistic
phon-	sound	euphony, phonograph, phonics
urb-	city	urban, suburb, urbanization

Prefixes and **suffixes** are exchangeable attachments at the beginning or end of a word. Prefixes account for the different meanings of *prewar, postwar, prowar,* and *antiwar.* Suffixes account for the different uses of *organize, organic,* and *organism.*

PREFIX	MEANING	EXAMPLES
bi	two	bicycle, bilateral, bilingual
mono	one	monogamous, monopoly, monolithic
multi	many	multinational, multiethnic, multimillionaire
post	after	postpone, postwar, postscript
pre	before	prearranged, precedent, prenuptial

YOUR TURN 32 Going to the Roots

1 What is the difference between *benevolent* and *malevolent?* between a *benefactor* and a *malefactor?* between a *benediction* and a *malediction?*

2 What is the difference between *intramural* and *intermural?* between an *introvert* and an *extrovert?*

3 What is the common element in *extraneous, extradition,* and *extraterrestrial?*

4 What is the common element in *circumference, circumscribe,* and *circumnavigate?*

6g.6 Encyclopedic Information *Turn to your dictionary for quick identification of names, places, and events.* College dictionaries include capsule information about people, places, historical events, or intellectual movements. Much of it is part of the general alphabetical listing. Some of it (as in the *Merriam Webster Collegiate)* may be in separate biographical and geographical listings. Sample entries will identify *Fujian* as a province of China; *Heidelberg man* as a branch of our evolutionary family tree; *Voltaire* (remembered for his biting wit) as a French eighteenth-century writer.

7 UNDERSTANDING SENTENCES

Make words work together in a sentence.

Your basic tool as a writer is the sentence. You use it to make statements: "We are running out of time." You also use it to ask questions: "Are we running out of time?" You can also use it to make requests: "Give us more time!" Sometimes a single word makes a point, like "Nonsense!" or "Cool!" However, usually you put the right words together in the right order. English grammar is the system that enables you to take a list of just words and turn them into a sentence:

JUST WORDS: writers are words in good with love

SENTENCE: **Good writers are in love with words.**

To chart English sentences, you need a minimum of technical language. (Teachers or authors of guidelines will also often describe features of a sentence in plain English or use common-sense labels to make instructions more self-explanatory.) You need grammatical terms when facing questions like the following:

- *How does a good sentence work?* What features help a good sentence make its point? What makes the reader say: "That is a good sentence"? Look at model sentences and see how well they use our common sentence resources.
- *How do you improve sentences that need work?* Some sentences are poorly designed, with ill-fitting or missing parts. Some are cluttered with material that gets in the way. Editors and teachers suggest effective ways of correcting problems with sentence structure.
- *How do you shift from speech to written English?* Many sentences in need of editing use the informal expressions of relaxed conversation. If your writing sounds too casual, your readers may think that you are not taking your topic seriously. Editors and teachers will help you making your writing more formal—but not stiff or *hyper*formal.
- *How do you shift from local varieties to standard English?* In your neighborhood or region of the country, people may use English with a strong local flavor. They may use the language of the turf or a down-home dialect. In your written work, you may have to shift to the standard English that is the language currency good in all parts of the country.

- *If English is your second language, where does your writing show the influence of another language?* What features of English grammar are strange for writers whose first language was Spanish, Chinese, or Vietnamese? Does your writing show that sometimes you still think in another language—and then translate mentally into English? Guidelines for ESL students (using English as a Second Language) could be helpful to you.

7a Basic Sentence Parts

Look for the subject and a complete verb.

English sentences are rich and various. They are short and long, simple and elaborate, pointed and roundabout. We use them to give the simplest instructions and also to develop the most challenging ideas. Nevertheless, most English sentences are variations of a few basic sentence models. They employ the same basic building blocks over and over—using them in new combinations, putting them together in fascinating ways.

To understand English sentences, we can start by looking at the most basic building blocks of a sentence and the way they combine in an elementary bare-bones sentence. We can strip most English sentences down to a basic underlying one-two structure. The minimum sentence has two parts the way most cars have four wheels. The first part, the **subject**, brings something into focus: *birds, speed, money.* The second part, the **verb**, goes on to make the statement:

BARE-BONES: Birds **sing.**

Speed **kills.**

Money **talks.**

Grammarians and language scholars (or linguists) spend much of their time trying to show how we get from such minimum sentences to the fully developed mature sentences that we use every day in speech and writing:

DEVELOPED: With the coming of spring, **birds** returning from warmer climates **sing** again in the trees.

In spite of pleas and warnings, **speed kills** hundreds of celebrating teenagers each year.

In the current corporate economy, **money talks.**

7a.1 **Recognizing Nouns** *The subject slot in a sentence is most often filled by a noun.* Traditionally, grammar study has focused on kinds of words (**parts of speech**) and the slots they fill in a sentence. Nouns fill the subject slot (but they also have other important uses in English sentences). Key features will help you recognize nouns:

- *Many nouns stand for things you can count.* Such **count nouns** can signal a change from one (**singular**) to several (**plural**) by a change in the word itself: (one) bird/(several) **birds**. The most common plural signal for nouns is the *-s* ending: car/**cars**, building/**buildings**, idea/**ideas**, condition/ **conditions**, investigation/ **investigations**. However, some English nouns signal "more than one" in other ways—or not at all. Some, like **sugar** or **flour**, are used only in the singular, except in unusual situations.

PLURALS OF NOUNS

How Nouns Show Number

Nouns can signal "one" or "more than one."

REGULAR PLURALS:	cars, buildings, laws, regulations, exceptions
IRREGULAR PLURALS:	men, women, children, teeth, mice
UNMARKED PLURALS:	people, cattle, offspring, deer, sheep
SINGULAR ONLY:	happiness, courage, disarray, chaos, sugar

! *LITERACY ALERT:* Watch for spelling changes: one **woman** but several **women**, one **freshman** but several **freshmen**; one **family** but several **families**, one **city** but several **cities**; one **potato** but several **potatoes**.

- *Many nouns come after a noun marker.* A **noun marker** signals that a noun is about to follow. Three kinds of words commonly serve as noun markers. One of the **articles**—*the, a,* or *an*—may serve as a signal that a noun is ahead: **the** car, **a** ticket, **an** application. Other words that may serve as noun markers are the **pointing** pronouns (demonstrative pronouns): *this (these)* or *that (those):* **this** map, **these** charts; **that** file, **those** folders. Still other possible noun markers are the **possessive** pronouns. They show where something belongs: **My** relatives, **your** exam, **his** application, **her** interview, **their** excuse.

NOUN MARKERS: **The** play closed.
This effort will succeed.
Our newsletter arrived.

- *Pronouns can take the place of a noun in a sentence.* A **pronoun** like *he, she,* or *it* (singular) or *they* (plural) can substitute for a noun in a sentence. Pronouns are shortcut words: *He* can take the place of *President Clinton; they* can take the place of *the United Nations. You* can take the place of *dear brother*. Words like *I, you, he, she,* and *they* are called **personal** pronouns because they point to specific persons. Words like *everybody, anyone, somebody,* and *nobody* are called **indefinite** pronouns because they do not point to anyone in particular. Pronouns serve as subjects in the following minimum sentences:

PRONOUNS: **We** agree.
She objects.
Everybody has contributed.
Nothing helped.

! *LITERACY ALERT:* Watch for a special spelling: **nobody** (one word) but **no one** (two words).

7a.2 Recognizing Verbs *The verb makes a statement about the subject.* Often the verb sets the subject in motion: Somebody **acts**. Something **happens**. Sometimes the verb simply signals something just being there: Something **exists**.

- *A verb can show a change in time.* This is the key feature that sets verbs apart from nouns and other kinds of words. You can signal a change in the timeframe by a change in the word itself. Often the *-d* or *-ed* ending signals a change from present to past: works (now)/**worked** (then); agree (now)/**agreed** (then); investigate (now)/**investigated** (then). Often a change other than the added ending signals the change in time:

I **know** it now. I **knew** it then.

They now **buy** only organic food. They **bought** only organic food even then.

By plane, the trip **takes** five hours. By ox cart, it **took** three months.

- *Often the main verb is part of a longer complete verb.* It comes after **helping verbs** (also called **auxiliaries**). These include *will (would), can (could), may (might), shall (should),* and *must:* **will** arrive, **can** enter, **may** happen, **should** end, **must** cease. The words in this first set point to the future, show a possibility, or signal an obligation. They set up different perspectives on an action—looking at an action as future, possible, or required. (They are often grouped together as modal auxiliaries, or **modals** for short.)

  Other auxiliaries beside *will* can signal a change in time: she **has** agreed; they **had** promised. More than one auxiliary may come before the main verb: **should have** known, **has been** cir-

TENSES OF VERBS

How Verbs Show Time

Verbs are words that can place events in time:

PRESENT—now or usually:

The supervisor **knows**.

Many workers **work** at home.

PAST—over and done with:

As a boy, he **worked** in the fields.

At Columbia, she **studied** law.

PERFECT—completed recently or still true:

We **have changed** the code.

They **have** always **supported** you.

PAST PERFECT—prior to other past events:

The rates **had changed**.

The fire **had burnt** out.

FUTURE—still to come:

The law **will change**.

The jury **will reconvene**.

FUTURE PERFECT—prior to other future events:

The law **will have changed** by then.

The judge **will have retired**.

cling, **would have** succeeded, **might have been** killed. Together with the change in the word itself, auxiliaries help us set up different timeframes or **tenses** of the English verb:

- *A special set of verb forms signals action in progress.* These **progressive** forms show that a situation is continuing. Or an action is still taking place: He **speaks** English well (off and on). He **is speaking** English (at this moment).

PROGRESSIVE: I **am** still **waiting.**

They **are checking** the files.

The FBI **has been looking** for a second suspect.

✓ **EDITOR'S TIP:** Another special set of verb forms shows that the subject is no longer the active part of the sentence. Instead, it has become the target of the action. "The police **arrested** the protesters" has become "The protesters **were arrested** by the police." The verb has changed from active to **passive**—with the former subject "acted upon" by somebody or something else: The protesters **were arrested**. The veto **had been upheld**. The new members **will be sworn in** on Monday.

See **18A** on choosing between active and passive.

- *The dividing line between nouns and verbs is not airtight.* **Verbal nouns** are verbs that have crossed over to become nouns. They then serve as noun substitutes. They can take the place of a noun. The verbs in *I swim* and *we meditate* have turned into verbal nouns in the following sentences:

VERBAL NOUN: **Swimming** tones the muscles.

Meditating relaxes.

Commuting can become a nightmare.

The *to*-form of verbs (**infinitive**) also crosses over to take the place of nouns:

INFINITIVE: **To win** is sweet.

To lose hurts.

To be ignored can be painful.

MORE ON GRAMMATICAL TERMS: The main part of a combined verb is traditionally called a **participle** when it follows a form of *have* (*has, had*) or *be* (*am, is, was, were, has been*). The main part of a progressive verb (always the *-ing* form) is the **present participle**:

Third-graders are **communicating** by computers.

Colleges have been **putting** courses on CD-ROM.

The main verb for the perfect tense (also used to make up the passive) is called the **past participle**:

Volunteers have **linked** many schools to the Internet.

The White House has **taken** the lead in this effort.

Many schoolrooms have been **wired**.

YOUR TURN 33 Tracking English Verbs

How many verbs do you know that can follow a subject and make a complete sentence—without any added material? For instance, birds **soar**. Birds **swoop**. Birds **peck**. Birds **hop**. Birds **twitter**. Boxers **punch**. They **feint**. They **jab**. They **clinch**. In each of the following frames, fill in several additional verbs (two or more) that could make a complete sentence.

(Combinations like **break up** or **break down** are also used as verbs, but here limit yourself to single words.)

1 Cars start, __________, __________.

2 Artists paint, __________, __________.

3 Horses can run, __________, __________.

4 Audiences may applaud, __________, __________.

5 Athletes may succeed, __________, __________.

6 Planes arrive, __________, __________.

7 Winners may celebrate, __________, __________.

8 Losers may cry, __________, __________.

9 Workers may organize, __________, __________.

10 Politicians compromise, __________, __________.

7b Basic Sentence Patterns

Recognize basic patterns of the complete English sentence.

Several common patterns set up the basic structure of a complete English sentence. Some sentences are complete with only two basic parts. Others need a third and perhaps a fourth basic part to make a complete statement.

Officers arrest ________. (whom?)

Officers arrest **suspects**.

The President sent the Prime Minister ________. (what?)

The President sent the Prime Minister **congratulations**.

Sometimes a verb alone completes the sentence: Speed **kills.** Money **talks**. Such an **intransitive** verb "is not going anywhere." It can tell the whole story. All the following bare-minimum statements are complete sentences:

S-V: Accidents **happen**.

Experiments **fail**.

Her license **had expired.**

The nation **will survive.**

Often, however, in order to complete the sentence, you have to continue after the verb. Often you will specify the target or the result of the action. A **transitive** verb carries the action across to an **object**: Coyotes kill **sheep.** Logging endangers **wildlife.** (Here the sheep and the wildlife are targeted; the action in the sentence is aimed at them.)

S-V-O: Nurses assist **patients.**

Accountants keep **records.**

Oswald shot **Kennedy.**

The U.S. bombed **Iraq.**

With verbs like *give* , *send*, or *promise*, the sentence may take a detour to show first the receiver or destination—the **indirect object:** A stranger had sold **the suspect** the gun. (We are told not only *what* was sold but first also *to whom*.)

S-V-IO-O: The customer wrote **the company** a letter.
The store gave **its employees** a discount.
The college had awarded **these athletes** scholarships.

Not all verbs signal actions or events. **Linking verbs** pin a label on the subject. The most common linking verb is the special verb *be* (with forms including *is, am, are, was, were, has been,* and *will be*): Gorillas are **apes.** Wolves are **predators.** Other linking verbs include *become, seem,* and *turn:* Friends became **enemies.** In these and the following examples, the label is a noun:

S-LV-N: Chimpanzees are **our cousins.**
The project had become **a liability.**

The label following a linking verb may be an **adjective** instead of a noun: The judge was **sympathetic.** The weather turned **cold.** Adjectives can tell us which one or what kind (the *red* convertible, a *sympathetic* judge). Most adjectives can show degree: *fast/faster/fastest; cold/colder/coldest; dangerous/more dangerous/most dangerous.* They fit in after *very:* very fast, very dangerous. The following are all complete English sentences:

S-LV-ADJ: The audience turned **hostile.**
Our software had become **obsolete.**

In two other common sentence patterns, a verb like *call* or *consider* pins a label on the object. We first pinpoint an object or a target. Then we go on to attach a label. The label may again be either a noun or an adjective.

S-V-O-N: The prosecutor called **the defendant a menace.**
Her lawyer considered **the verdict a vindication.**

S-V-O-ADJ: The mayor called **the charges ridiculous.**
It makes **me angry.**

Just as pronouns and other noun substitutes can replace nouns in the subject slot, so they can replace nouns after the verb:

PRONOUNS: Management considered **him** expendable.
The decision made **everybody** happy.

VERBAL NOUN: The report called **skateboarding** dangerous.

In real-life sentences, more than one noun may fill the subject slot, just as several verbs may follow the same subject. Nouns may double up to form a **combined subject** or combined object. A series of adjectives may follow a linking verb.

SUBJECTS: **Conventions and sales fairs** attract crowds.

VERBS: Computers **store, organize, and analyze** information.

OBJECTS: Think tanks produce **studies, graphs, pie charts, and policy analyses.**

ADJECTIVES: Home computers became **cheaper, faster, and more user-friendly.**

MORE ABOUT TERMS: The statement that the verb makes about the subject is traditionally called the **predicate.** The verb and all other material the verb carries with it make up the complete predicate:

> Pioneers **invented today's computers in a garage in California.**

YOUR TURN 34 Tracking the Pattern

The basic patterns set up the sentence frame the way the steel frame of a high-rise sets up the structure of a tall building. In the typical sentence, additional material comes into the sentence to flesh out the skeleton. In the following sentences, can you still track the basic patterns? Choose the right label for each sentence:

S-V	S-LV-N	S-V-O-N
S-V-O	S-LV-ADJ	S-V-O-ADJ
S-V-IO-O		

Censorship Lives

1 Americans dislike censorship.
2 Free speech is a constitutional right.
3 The press promises its readers honest reporting.
4 Censors continue their activities.
5 Artists have been prime targets.
6 A city council may commission modern art.
7 Angry citizens object.
8 Senators label avant-garde art degenerate.
9 Some citizens call all sexual material pornography.
10 The V-chip promises parents protection.

7c Filling In Modifiers

Use modifiers to fill in the simple sentence frames.

Simple sentences give us basic information: **The plane was late.** Modifiers come into a sentence to tell us more. They tell us which one? or what kind? They answer questions like when? where? how? and why? (**Usually** the **small** plane **to the upper peninsula** was late.) **Modifiers** expand, limit, or otherwise modify the meaning carried by the stripped-down minimum sentence.

SIMPLE: The woman ran.

EXPANDED: **Recently** the **young** woman **in the blue jumpsuit** ran **in the traditional Bay-to-Breakers race.**

Several kinds of modifiers build up simple sentences:

7c.1 Using Adjectives

Adjectives often answer questions like which one? or what kind? They often come before a noun: the **red** car, not the **black** one. Adjectives are words like *red, black, sweet, heavy, difficult, futile,* and *complex.* They often have typical adjective endings like **-ous** *(obvious, courageous);* **-ful** *(beautiful, wonderful); or* ***-some*** *(handsome, awesome).*

Unlike nouns and verbs, most adjectives can show **degree**: *sweet/sweeter/sweetest; wonderful/more wonderful/most wonderful.* We use the plain (or **positive**) forms when comparing things similar or alike: as *good* as gold, as *sweet* as honey, as *popular* as a tax cut. We use the **comparative** forms to compare two things that are different: *better* than cash, *sweeter* than wine, *more popular* than popcorn. We use the **superlative** for the top rank in comparing more than two: *best* of seven, the *sweetest* of the several varieties, the *most popular* of the three candidates.

Several adjectives in a row may modify the same noun to help bring ample information into a sentence:

ADJECTIVES: The **small** tree produced **marvelous sweet juicy** oranges.

He preferred his **gnarly green sour** apples to **tasteless store-bought** fruit.

The **new** software differed from the **simpler earlier** version.

7c.2 **Using Adverbs** *Adverbs answer questions like when? where? and how?* Many show the *-ly* ending: *quickly, obviously, immediately, reluctantly.* Others are words like *soon, again, outside, alone, today, tomorrow, anytime, downtown, upward,* and *downstairs.* Expressions like *each morning* or *most evenings* are also used like adverbs. Some adverbs show **degree:** ran *faster,* moved *more rapidly,* arrived *earliest.*

Several adverbs may come into the same sentence to specify when, where, or how something is done:

ADVERBS: The market reacted **cautiously.**

She will travel **upriver alone early tomorrow.**

Recently he has been practicing **most evenings.**

Adverbs most commonly modify verbs (drove **recklessly,** stopped **suddenly,** reported the accident **immediately.**) However, they also modify adjectives or other adverbs:

ADVERB + ADJECTIVE: The **surprisingly** inexpensive new modem replaced a **considerably** older one.

ADVERB + ADVERB: The new arrangement worked **incredibly** well.

7c.3 **Using Prepositional Phrases** *Prepositions bring in the same kind of detail that adjectives and adverbs do.* Prepositions are words like *at, on, in, by, for, with, without, before, after, about,* and *around:* **at** the end, **in** transit, **by** mistake, **with** luck, **without** a permit, **around** the corner. They start **prepositional phrases** that tell us either which one (like an adjective) or how, when, and where (like an adverb).

WHICH ONES? Students **with special passes** may register early.

Students **without passes** are out of luck.

HOW? WHEN? WHERE? We notified everyone **by e-mail.**

The park opens **at sunrise** and closes **after sunset.**

We met **near the front gate.**

Often a string of prepositional phrases fills in details:

The van **with the band from Florida** was involved **in a head-on collision on a country road.**

7c.4 **Using Noun Modifiers** *Another noun may replace an adjective that would usually modify a noun.* The result is a noun-noun combination: a **car** payment, a **student** loan, a **government** subsidy, a **distress** signal.

NOUN MODIFIERS:	The **security** guard had locked the **administration** building.
	The voters favored **tax** cuts, **lobbying** reforms, and a **welfare** overhaul.

7c.5 **Using Verbals as Modifiers** *A modifier may be a special form of a verb.* The verb used as a modifier is then called a **verbal**. One of these is the *-ing* form of a verb: the **acting** governor, a **visiting** professor, an **ongoing** experiment. The versatile *to*-form of verbs (**infinitive**) can take over the job of both adjectives and adverbs:

AS ADJECTIVE:	The bride **to be** liked food **to go**.
AS ADVERB:	The agent often stopped in **to talk.**

Although these verbals no longer serve as the main verb in a sentence, they may still carry their own objects or other materials:

The poet **visiting the campus** met with faculty and students.

Her agent called **to cancel the performance.**

! *LITERACY ALERT:* In the basic English sentence, modifiers are accessories. They do not by themselves make complete sentences. When you set them off after a period, the result is not a sentence but only a sentence **fragment**.

	compensation within reasonable limits.
FRAGMENT:	The company offered compensation. *Within reasonable limits.*
	scholarship to play volleyball.
	She was awarded a scholarship. *To play volleyball.*

See 9 for more on correcting fragments.

YOUR TURN 35 Recognizing Modifiers

Can you still track the underlying simple structure in the following fully developed sentences? How would the sentence read without the modifiers that flesh out the sentence skeleton? For each sentence, write the stripped-down basic structure that would still make a complete sentence.

EXAMPLE: A nonprofit group provides training materials for young entrepreneurs.

STRIPPED-DOWN: A group provides materials.

Becoming a Student Entrepreneur

1 Programs in local high schools offer young entrepreneurs seed money.

2 Instruction in basic business skills improves the self-confidence of alienated students.

3 Several national organizations are providing help with starting a small business.

4 Students in these programs may run their businesses from a garage or out of their backpacks.

5 They develop financial skills by using calculators and tracking expenses.

6 Often making a profit is difficult for the beginner.

7 A new business may fail after a promising start.

8 Some ventures into the world of business have been very prosperous.

9 Students have continued a clothing or cosmetics business after graduation.

10 Apparently the teachers in these schools consider these programs a success.

YOUR TURN 36 Building Up the Simple Sentence

How far can you stretch the simple sentence? Each of the following student-written sentences still has only one subject and one verb. However, each student writer has made exceptionally full use of the resources of addition, expansion, and substitution that help us get from simplified basic statements to fully developed real-life sentences.

YOUR TURN 36 *(continued)*

For each sample sentence, write a similar sentence of your own that is also packed with details.

1 In *Jurassic Park*, an eccentric gentleman makes a major investment to revive the long dead DNA of the dinosaurs only to create horrific bloodthirsty merciless marauders.

2 According to Naomi Wolf in *The Beauty Myth*, on any day 25 percent of women are on a diet, with 50 percent finishing, breaking, or starting one.

3 Racism evokes a wide array of feelings: hatred, resentment, pride, anger, fear, inadequacy, confusion, frustration, or any combination of the above.

4 Listening to a baseball game in the bottom of the ninth with the best hitter on the team up and the go-ahead run on third is a pleasure.

5 Swerving all over the road while speeding and yelling "donut-eating pig" at a highway patrol officer is a mistake.

SAMPLE RESPONSES:

1 In *The Joy Luck Club*, the daughter of a recently passed away immigrant mother recalls the troubles and tribulations of her mother and her friends as Chinese immigrants in the United States.

5 Cheating on a test instead of studying like the rest of the class is a mistake.

8 COMBINED SENTENCES

Join simple statements in a larger sentence.

To build up your sentences and to punctuate longer sentences, you need to know how we link statements in a larger whole. When a shorter statement becomes part of a larger whole, we call it a **clause.** A clause has its own subject and verb, but it links up with other statements in a larger combined sentence.

COMBINED:

When **their visas** (S) **expire** (V), foreign **students** (S) **are expected** (V) to leave.

By working several statements into the same sentence, you can spell out circumstances and conditions. In each of the following combined sentences, several clauses have their own subjects and verbs:

Many **Americans realize** that **their ancestors were** immigrants.

Many **immigrants who were** in the country illegally **were granted** amnesty.

Americans tend to believe that **their forebears were welcomed** by those **who were** already here.

8a Avoiding Comma Splices

CS Use the semicolon to join two closely related statements.

When two statements are part of the same picture, you may simply put them next to each other. The result is a one-two pattern, without any connecting word or verbal link: "This is true; that is false." The two statements are part of the same story. However, they could easily be unhooked again; they remain **independent** clauses. Use a **semicolon** between the two closely related statements. Think of it as a *semiperiod*—stronger than a comma, but weaker than a period.

SEMICOLON:

Apple was struggling; IBM continued to grow.

Rap took over popular music; it spread to Europe and Japan.

Three thousand students applied; twelve hundred were turned away.

When you put only a comma between two independent clauses, the result is a **comma splice.** It leaves the two statements loosely spliced together. Use the semicolon to correct comma splices. A period—followed by a capital letter—would also be correct.

COMMA SPLICE:

patients; others
Some doctors inform their *patients*, *others* keep them in the dark.

miracle drugs; they
Doctors are wary of *miracle drugs*, *they* may have side effects.

ALSO CORRECT:

Doctors are wary of **miracle drugs. They** may have side effects.

See **22c** and **23d** for more on using semicolons.

! *LITERACY ALERT:* When you run together two statements without any punctuation or added link, the result is a **fused sentence.** Find the point where the fusion occurred. Insert a semicolon:

FUSED:

the third time; this was
They were taking the test the third time this was their last chance.

her father; he had died
She hardly knew her father he had died in an accident.

8b Using Coordination

CO

Use coordination for equally important ideas.

Coordination makes things work together. When a **coordinator** (short for *coordinating conjunction*) links two related statements, the added link spells out the relationship. The words that may be used as coordinators are **and, but, so, for, yet, or,** and **nor.** The two statements being joined are still **independent** clauses. Each clause is inde-

SENTENCE ESSENTIALS

Kinds of Connectives

Joining two or more statements in a larger combined sentence is a key step in moving from simplified bare-bones statements to real-life sentences. Sometimes we simply juxtapose two closely related statements: "Wild geese migrate; they seek a warmer climate." However, often one of the following kinds of connectives provides the thought link from one statement to the other:

COORDINATORS:

and, but, so, for, yet, or, nor

SUBORDINATORS:

Single Words if, unless, when, whenever, while, before, after, since, until, as, because, provided; though, although, whereas

Phrases so that, as if, as though; no matter how, no matter what

CONNECTIVE ADVERBS (adverbial conjunctions):

Single Words however, therefore, moreover, accordingly, furthermore, nevertheless, besides, indeed, consequently, instead, otherwise, hence, thus

Phrases in fact, on the other hand

RELATIVE PRONOUNS:

who, whom, whose; which, that

SPECIAL CONNECTIVES (for noun clauses):

that, why, whether, how, where, who, what, whoever, whatever

pendently true, and each is equally important. Use the **comma** to punctuate coordinators.

Unemployment declined, **and** inflation remained low.

Oil was becoming cheaper, **but** gasoline prices remained high.

Banks posted record profits, **so** their stocks rose.

The stock market fluctuates, **for** investors panic.

The new regulations did not lower taxes, **nor** did they simplify them.

See **23a** for more on punctuating coordinators.

8b.1 **Effective Coordination** *Use effective coordination to line up ideas that are equally important.* Coordinators—*and, but, so, for, yet, or, nor*—join two ideas that remain on an equal footing.

EFFECTIVE: Big-league teams bring a multimillion dollar payroll to a city, **and** [equally important] they are a source of civic pride.

New downtown arenas can revitalize a city, **but** [equally important] they bring traffic congestion and a parking nightmare.

8b2 **co** **Weak Coordination** *Correct weak coordination that merely adds instead of showing connections.* Check for sentences that merely use *and* when readers should focus on the logical connection.

WEAK: New hires may take a test and pass it, *and they will then be exempted* from taking the training course.

STRONGER: New hires will be exempted from taking the training course **if they pass a test.**

✓ *EDITOR'S TIP:* Avoid falling into a loosely joined "and then . . . and then" pattern.

WEAK: Each year at the same time the whales leave the arctic North, *and they* swim south toward warmer waters, *and then they* bear their young there.

STRONGER: Each year at the same time the whales leave the arctic North, **swimming south toward warmer waters and bearing their young there.**

8c Using Subordination

sub

Use subordination to tighten relationships.

Use subordination to specify when, where, how, or why. A **subordinator** (short for *subordinating conjunction*) subordinates one clause to another—the main clause. To show time, you may add a second clause starting with **when, while, before, after, until, as,**

since, whenever, and **as soon as.** To specify conditions, you may use **if** or **unless**. To give a reason, you may use **because**. The added clause is called a **dependent** clause—what the one statement means may depend on what the other statement says.

DEPENDENT: The planet will overheat **unless we change our ways.**

A dependent clause can no longer be easily separated from the main clause. Punctuation depends on how the added clause affects the meaning of the whole sentence. Use no comma if the point made by the main clause applies *only* under the conditions specified. The added clause is then **restrictive;** it limits or restricts the meaning in an essential way.

ONLY IF: Some college athletes will become ineligible **if** academic standards are raised.

Prices drop through the floor **when** investors panic.

The pilots will strike **unless** their demands are met.

Use a comma if the point made by the main clause is true regardless of what was added. For instance, to set up a contrast, you may use *whereas* or *although*. The added clause is then **nonrestrictive.** It does not change or limit the first point made, although the main point is what the two statements say together.

TRUE REGARDLESS: Tuna are fish, **whereas** dolphins are mammals.

To verify that the link you are using is a subordinator, try switching the two clauses. Reversing the order does not work with coordinators or other kinds of connectives. If you reverse the order, use a comma to show where the main clause starts.

When investors panic, prices drop through the floor.

If standards rise, some athletes may be forced out.

! *LITERACY ALERT:* A dependent clause causes a sentence fragment when you mark it off as a separate sentence.

dropped after affirmative action was banned.
FRAGMENT: Minority enrollment dropped. *After affirmative action was banned.*

See **23b** for more on punctuating subordinators.

8c.1 Effective Subordination *Use effective subordination to specify logical relationships.* Subordinators—*when, while, if, unless, because, although, whereas*—specify time and place. They set up conditions, show cause and effect, or pinpoint contrasts. Often they signal that a statement is truly *only if* or *only when* specified conditions are met.

EFFECTIVE: Experienced investors buy stocks **when** [only when] **prices are low**. Investors make money in the long run **if** [only if] **they ride out the ups and downs of the market.**

Investors buy newsletters, **although the gurus are often wrong.**

8c.2 Missing Subordination *Spell out connections that are merely implied.* When ideas are too loosely strung together, use improved subordination to show the connections.

LOOSE: Dolphins can send distress signals to other members of their group. *They communicate by beeps and clicks.*

TIGHTENED: **Because they communicate by beeps and clicks,** dolphins can send distress signals to other members of their group.

LOOSE: The term democracy originated in ancient Greece. *It has been used to describe very different political systems. Many people still use the term today. They often think it has only one meaning.*

TIGHTENED: **Since it originated in ancient Greece,** the term democracy has been used to describe very different political systems, **although the person using it often thinks it has only one meaning.**

8c.3 Excessive Subordination *Avoid piling up confusing or apparently contradictory conditions.* Rewrite seesaw sentences like the following:

OVERLOAD: *If students do well on college placement tests,* they can usually get into the college of their choice *if they have good grades.*

CLEARER: Students can usually get into the college of their choice **if they do well on college placement tests, provided they also have good grades.**

8c.4 **Upside-Down Subordination** *Rewrite to adjust unintended emphasis.* When you tie in one idea with another, the wrong idea may seem to stand out. Weigh choices like the following:

> **Local women signed on for sweatshop wages,** although they were not enough to live on.
> (emphasis is on the women signing on)
>
> **The sweatshop wages were not enough to live on,** although the local women signed on nevertheless.
> (emphasis is on the inadequate wage)

YOUR TURN 37 Combining Sentences

What would be the best way to link the two statements in each of the following pairs? Join the two statements, using effective coordination or subordination. (Compare your answers with those of your classmates.)

Our Love Affair with the Gun

1 Gunplay accounts for most of the murder rate.
We don't seem to have the answer.

2 Children are gunned down in class or on the playground.
There is a public outcry.

3 Gun control laws are often voted down.
Many voters support them.

4 Assault weapons should be banned.
They serve no recreational purpose.

5 A gun control ordinance passes.
The NRA mobilizes its supporters.

6 The organization is well-financed.
Political candidates respect its wishes.

7 Movie ratings warn us of adult material.
There is no G rating for gunplay.

8 The legislature may pass a bill requiring trigger locks.
The governor may veto it.

9 Guns don't kill people.
People with guns kill people.

10 We will have the highest murder rate in the world.
We change our attitude toward guns.

8d Using Connecting Adverbs

Use connecting adverbs to show logical connections.

Connecting adverbs (also called *adverbial conjunctions*) are common links in writing that argues seriously with the reader. In arguing your points, you may use connecting adverbs like **however** and **therefore**. Other logical links in this group are **nevertheless, furthermore, moreover, consequently, accordingly,** and **indeed.** Combinations like **in fact** and **on the other hand** work the same way in a sentence.

OBJECTION: Fossil fuels pollute the atmosphere; **however**, nuclear energy presents pollution hazards of its own.

RESULT: Spent nuclear fuel remains radioactive; **therefore**, storage is a major problem. (drawing a logical conclusion)

CONCESSION: The safety hazards are horrendous; **nevertheless**, some countries rely heavily on nuclear reactors. (admitting that something else is true)

Like other adverbs, connecting adverbs move more freely in a sentence than other words. You are using a connecting adverb if you can shift the word to the middle or the end of the second clause.

Women fill more management positions;
however, they are still rare in boardrooms.
they are still, **however**, rare in boardrooms.
they are still rare in boardrooms, **however**.

A **semicolon** shows where the two statements join—even if the *however* or *therefore* appears later in the sentence. The two statements or clauses remain independent. (They could easily be separated again by a period.) Conservative writers use a comma to separate the connecting adverb from the rest of the second statement. (They use two commas if the link splits the second clause.) Avoid comma splices: Do *not* use a comma to replace the semicolon.

energy; however,
COMMA SPLICE: Investors put up billions for nuclear *energy, however* many of the plants were never finished.

See **23d** for more on using semicolons with connecting adverbs.

YOUR TURN 38 Avoiding Comma Splices

In each of the following pairs, write down the last word of the first clause and the first word of the second clause. Put a semicolon between them when a semicolon is needed. Put a comma between them if a comma is sufficient.

EXAMPLE: Lawrence is in Kansas Kansas City is in Missouri.

ANSWER: **Kansas; Kansas**

1 America is a land of many nationalities it is a nation of nations.

2 Swedes went to Minnesota and Czechs settled in Nebraska.

3 Early settlers traded with the natives however relations deteriorated.

4 The Spaniards colonized California the Anglos came later.

5 The Irish encountered prejudice they prospered nevertheless.

6 The War liberated African Americans many moved north.

7 Many Jews assimilated rapidly but others remained orthodox Jews.

8 Politicians exploited anti-foreign sentiment immigration laws therefore excluded Asians.

9 America was the promised land so millions of immigrants came from eastern and southern Europe.

10 Many Italian Americans live in Boston many Polish Americans live in Chicago.

8e Using Relative Pronouns

Bring added information in after *who, which,* or *that.*

Often a link like **who (whom, whose), which,** and **that** will bring added material into your sentence. These **relative pronouns** tie (or relate) the added information to a specific part of the sentence: the detective **who** found the glove; the testimony **that** swayed the jury. Like subordinators, relative pronouns can help you tighten relationships. The resulting **relative clause** is often inserted or folded into the main clause rather than just attached at the end.

LOOSE: Some investors have no access to inside information. They are taken by surprise by mergers or selloffs.

EFFECTIVE: Investors **who have no access to inside information** are taken by surprise by mergers or selloffs.

A relative clause that you use to single out or identify is restrictive: no comma.

WHICH ONE? The detective **who found the glove** later pleaded guilty to perjury.

A Chicago dating service **that helps clients improve their image** charges $1,250 a year.

The defense had attacked the testimony **that swayed the jury.**

A mere "add-on" relative clause that is not needed to narrow down a larger group is nonrestrictive—it requires a comma or commas.

Pitbulls, **which terrorize neighborhoods,** have ardent defenders.

Gloria Steinem, **who founded *Ms.* magazine,** wrote a book on self-esteem.

A restrictive pronoun is often left out in sentences like the following:

The reforms [that] **voters approve** may serve special interests.

See **23c** for more on punctuating relative clauses.

8f Using Noun Clauses

Use noun clauses to vary basic sentence structure.

A dependent clause may *replace* part of the main clause rather than link up with it. Such **noun clauses** take the place of one of the nouns in the original sentence:

NOUN: The company denied **the charge**.

NOUN CLAUSE: The company denied **that the plant was unsafe.**

NOUN: The governor explained **the reason.**

NOUN CLAUSE: The governor explained **why he vetoed the bill.**

NOUN: **The cause** has never been determined.

NOUN CLAUSE: **What caused the blackout** has never been determined.

In these sentences, noun clauses become *part* of the basic structure. They are not just added to it. Do not separate them from the rest of the basic structure by a comma.

of the Maya remains

NO COMMA: What caused the decline *of the Maya, remains* unknown.

✓ *EDITOR'S TIP:* In real-life sentences, more than two clauses often combine. The many different arrangements that result make possible the incredible variety of actual English sentences. Language scholars say that no two English sentences are exactly alike. The following examples combine three or more clauses.

> **Before** school begins in September, the college offers an orientation program **that** orients new students to academic life.
>
> Students **who** need financial aid can find out **whether** they are eligible for loans or grants.
>
> **When** employers pay students' tuition, students **who** get low grades may have to repay the money **that** they received.

YOUR TURN 39 Writing Relative Clauses and Noun Clauses

Study the way the following model sentences use relative clauses and noun clauses. For each model, write one or more similar sentences of your own. You need not follow the sentence structure of the original in all details.

1 Energy is the power that drives every human being.

—Germaine Greer

IMITATIONS: Greed is the disease **that** infects many landlords.

Compatibility is the glue **that** keeps a marriage together.

YOUR TURN 39 *(continued)*

2 The person who jumps to conclusions often lands on unfirm ground.

IMITATION: The enthusiast **who** dives into unknown waters crashes on the shallow bottom.

3 Corporations have discovered that buying software is cheaper than hiring consultants.

IMITATION: Growers discovered **that** hiring aliens is cheaper than paying Americans.

4 Ethnic cleansing, which means the removal of minorities, is a polite word for genocide.

IMITATION: Downsizing, **which** means reducing staff, is a polite word for layoffs.

5 Parents wonder why their offspring don't talk to them.

IMITATION: Teachers wonder **why** their students listen to the Sex Pistols.

9 CORRECTING FRAGMENTS

frag

If possible, tie sentence fragments into a preceding sentence.

A **sentence fragment** is not complete enough to stand alone as a separate sentence. Fragments happen when you close down a sentence too early. You go on after the period to add material that is not a complete separate sentence.

9a Diagnosing Fragments

Check for sentence fragments.

Complete English sentences include at least a subject and a complete verb: **E-mail** (S) **travels** (V) incredibly fast. Many **users** (S) **have abandoned** (V) snail mail. Fragments result when a possible subject or verb is missing. Sometimes there is only part of a verb—like *processing* instead of **were processing**, or *given* instead of **had given**. One way to correct a fragment is to tie it into the preceding sentence. In the following sample fragment, a subject was missing. (Who or what destroyed the town?)

NO SUBJECT:

unexpectedly and destroyed half of the town.

The tornado struck *unexpectedly. Destroyed half of the town.*

(*Tornado* can serve as the subject for both verbs)

Another way to correct a fragment is to add a missing subject or verb, or both.

NO SUBJECT:

unexpectedly. It destroyed half of the town.

The tornado struck *unexpectedly. Destroyed half of the town.*

(The pronoun *it* supplies the missing subject)

In the following sample fragment, there was no verb to make a statement about the snowmobiles. The snowmobiles should be tied into the previous sentence:

NO VERB:

vehicles, like snowmobiles and dirt bikes.

The county banned off-road *vehicles. Snowmobiles and dirt bikes.*

In the following sample fragment, there was only part of a verb—*spilling* instead of **was spilling** or **had been spilling**. (Also, who or what did the spilling was in the previous sentence.)

PART OF VERB:

overturned, spilling toxic waste.
The truck *overturned. Spilling toxic waste.*

In the following sample fragment, there was no subject or verb to show who did what on the dirt roads.

NO SUBJECT OR VERB:

lives on dirt roads and super highways.
Speed limits save *lives. On dirt roads and super highways.*

EDITOR'S TIP: Requests or commands are the exception to the subject-and-verb requirement for the complete English sentence. In verb-only sentences like "Run!" or "Back off!" the subject (namely *you*) is implied or understood.

9b Modifiers as Fragments

frag

Correct fragments added as modifiers.

Many fragments are modifiers added after a period to give the reader further detail. Don't keep them separate as afterthoughts. Make them a part of the sentence to which they belong.

9b.1 Adverbs and Phrases **Adverbs** answer questions like how, when, and where: how? *reluctantly;* when? *always;* where? *outside*. **Prepositional phrases** start with words like *in, at, on, by, for, with, without, before,* and *after*. They can tell the reader what kind or which one (the guard *at the gate*). They can also tell the reader how, when, and where (the riot *after the game*). You can usually tie the added modifier into the preceding sentence without any comma or other punctuation.

the request repeatedly.

ADVERBS: The judge denied *the request. Repeatedly.*

against foreigners in many cases.

PREP. PHRASE: Juries were prejudiced against *foreigners. In many cases.*

9b.2 Added Adjectives Added **adjectives** answer questions like what kind or which one. When you add them to a sentence as an afterthought, they are usually optional detail. (They give added-on information that helps us understand but is not essential to make the point.) Use a comma instead of a period:

choice, colorful but ineffectual.

ADJECTIVES: Her lawyer was the wrong *choice. Colorful but ineffectual.*

9b.3 Appositives Nouns that come into a sentence as added labels are called **appositives.** Do not mark them off with a period—use a comma or a colon instead:

musicians: a violinist from Japan.

APPOSITIVE: The conductor married one of the musicians. *A violinist from Japan.*

9b.4 Thought Links Correct fragments caused by links like **especially** and **such as** or by links like **for instance, for example, namely.** Use a comma before but not after *especially* and *such as.*

COMMA: The school attracted many foreign **students, especially Chinese.**

Americans learned to accept religious **minorities, such as Mormons and Quakers.**

✓ ***EDITOR'S TIP:*** Conservative editors expect a second comma after *for example* and *for instance.* The second comma is left out in the **open punctuation** found in many current publications.

TWO COMMAS: New immigrants are building their own houses of **worship, for example, Buddhist or Islamic temples.**

9c Verbals as Fragments

frag

Correct fragments caused by verbals—the *-ing* form and *to*-form especially.

Verbals are parts of verbs. They are not being used as complete verbs but instead do other jobs in a sentence. The following sentences have complete verbs: The crew **is preparing** for departure. My friends **were taken** to the terminal. *Preparing* (and other *-ing* forms) alone could not make a complete verb. Forms like *taken, given, applied,* and *investigated* are not complete verbs when applied to what has been or is being taken or investigated: **Investigated** by the FBI, the suspect left the country.

The following fragments use only verbals—only parts of verbs. Tie such verbals into the previous sentence. Use no comma if the main point is in the added material:

teams playing in the World Cup.

VERBALS: Millions of fans watch their *teams. Playing in the World Cup.*

trains touted as safer than air travel.

Accidents have derailed high-speed *trains. Touted as safer than air travel.*

Use a comma if the verbal brings in merely optional or dispensable added information.

VERBALS: Brazilian soccer fans invaded the sleepy little **town, drumming and dancing late into the night.**

In these sentences, both the *-ing* verbals and the *-en/-ed* verbals are used as **participles**—they are not used as complete verbs. The *to*-form (**infinitive**) of verbs also does not serve as a complete verb. *Food to go* and *things to do* are not complete sentences. Do not add an infinitive to a sentence after a period as belated explanation. Tie it into the sentence without punctuation:

Europe to watch the World Cup.

INFINITIVE: Brazilian soccer fans traveled to *Europe. To watch the World Cup.*

west to escape persecution.

The Mormons kept moving *west. To escape persecution.*

9d Subordinators and Fragments

Correct fragments caused by subordinators.

Some fragments have their own subject and complete verb. However, they start with a link meant to tie them to another sentence. When the connection is broken, a sentence fragment results.

9d.1 *If/when* **Subordinators** (subordinating conjunctions) like *if, when, unless,* and *because* are links in a one-two set of statements. An *if*-clause makes us ask, "If this is true—then what?" Do not separate the two parts of the proposition by a period. Words like *if, unless, when,* and *while* specify conditions, times, or locations. The main point is true *only if* or *only when* something else applies. Join such essential specifications to the main sentence with no comma or other punctuation.

permitted if it is safe to turn.

IF-CLAUSE: Right turns on red are permitted. *If it is safe to turn.*

working when we are asleep.

WHEN-CLAUSE: Our brains keep working. *When we are asleep.*

9d.2 *Whereas* The subordinator *whereas* causes especially noticeable fragments. Tie *whereas*-clauses to the main sentence with a comma. The second point is true regardless of what came earlier.

analytical, whereas the right brain is creative.

WHEREAS: The left brain is *analytical. Whereas the right brain is creative.*

9e *Who/which* and Fragments

Correct fragments caused by *who* or *which*.

Relative clauses starting with *who (whom, whose)* or *which* often cause fragments—because writers use them to add something they had forgotten earlier. Use a comma (a slight pause) rather than the period.

governor, who had long been popular.

WHO-CLAUSE: Voters turned against the *governor. Who had long been popular.*

education, which had received much negative publicity.

WHICH-CLAUSE: The voters rejected bilingual *education. Which had received much negative publicity.*

✓ ***EDITOR'S TIP:*** Often sentence fragments show a combination of familiar types. For instance, a fragment may start with an added label, followed by a *who*-clause.

by Booth, an actor who supported the Rebel cause.

FRAGMENT: Lincoln was assassinated *by Booth. An actor who supported the Rebel cause.*

9f Acceptable Fragments

Experiment with permissible fragments in special kinds of writing.

Especially in description and narration, writers use permissible fragments for a thinking-out-loud effect:

> On the left, a bank of elevators. **Straight ahead, a long burnished corridor, spooky as a lit tunnel.**
>
> —Cynthia Ozick

> There he is: the brother. **Image of him. Haunting face.**
>
> —James Joyce

YOUR TURN 40 Checking for Subject and Verb

The following headlines include many that were chosen by editors as the most important of the twentieth century. Some of these headlines are complete sentences—complete with a subject and a verb. Many others do not include a complete verb. Mark each C (for complete) or I (for incomplete). After the C for *complete*, write the complete verb.

Headlines of the Century

1 U.S. Sues Microsoft
2 Hitler Takes Power in Germany
3 Bolshevik Revolution in Russia
4 Japanese Bombing of Pearl Harbor
5 Lindbergh Flies Across the Atlantic
6 Roosevelt Inaugurated as President
7 Germany Surrenders
8 Peace Comes to Northern Ireland
9 The Nightmare Again—War in Europe
10 Scientists Split the Atom
11 Astronauts Land on the Moon
12 President Kennedy Dead
13 Nixon Will Resign
14 Berlin Wall Coming Down
15 Earthquake Devastates Mexico City

YOUR TURN 41 Correcting Sentence Fragments

Rewrite to correct all sentence fragments. Put S (for satisfactory) after the number of a pair of complete sentences.

EXAMPLE: The speaker was Sandra Day O'Connor. The Supreme Court Justice.

ANSWER: The speaker was Sandra Day O'Connor, the Supreme Court Justice.

The Language of Politics

1 Reformers attacked campaign financing. Without success.
2 The senator was a states rights advocate. Always championing local control.
3 Attack ads attack political opponents. Accusing them of supporting higher taxes and being soft on crime.
4 Immigration became a sensitive issue. Candidates started to criticize welfare for immigrant families.
5 The Second Amendment guarantees the right to bear arms. It talks about a well-regulated militia.

YOUR TURN 41 *(continued)*

6 The court objected to gerrymandering. Drawing up districts to favor one party.

7 Many senators represent thinly populated states. For example, Wyoming and Montana.

8 Successful politicians have come from the South. Bill Clinton built up a national following.

9 The memorial honored John Brown. Who led the raid on Harper's Ferry.

10 The group started a movement. To unionize restaurant workers.

10 WATCHING VERBS

vb

Use the right verbs—words that can show a difference in time.

Verbs are like clocks—they can show a difference in time. Watch the change in the timeframe in a series like the following:

> **It snows** (now); **it snowed** (in the past); **it has snowed** (more recently); **it had snowed** (farther back, in the more distant past); **it will snow again** (in the future)

The different timeframes are called the **tenses** of a verb. English verbs show a change in time by a change in the word itself: **answer** (now)/**answered** (then). Or they show a change in time with the help of an **auxiliary** (or helping verb). Auxiliaries include *have* (or *has* and *had*): **has answered, had answered.** They include words like *will*: **will answer.**

10a -*s* for Third Person Singular

Use the form with the added -*s* for third person singular.

Use the plain or unmarked form of the verb for most present action: I **exercise** daily. You **exercise** too little. My friends **exercise** every day. However, add the -*s* ending when you are talking about *one* single person or thing, with action now: George **exercises** every day. He **exercises** most mornings. His sister **exercises** at the gym. She **exercises** most days. Special equipment **exercises** your calf muscles. In all these examples, you are talking about a **third person**—a single third party (or thing), with action now. You are using the third person singular, in the present tense.

THIRD PERSON SINGULAR (-*s* ending):

> E-mail **reaches** people instantly. Often the other person **responds** right away. Snail mail **takes** almost a week. It sometimes **gets** lost. My cousin **corresponds** with several friends regularly. He **exchanges** news and gossip. So **does** my best friend. My sister **communicates** mostly by voice mail. She **checks** it twice a day.

ALL OTHER (unmarked):

I myself **use** e-mail regularly. You probably **do** too. E-mail messages **reach** people the same day. Letters **take** several days. Some researchers **communicate** daily by electronic mail. They **exchange** their latest findings.

Make sure to use **doesn't** or **does not** (not *don't*) for third person singular:

THIRD PERSON SINGULAR:

Their trainer **doesn't** tolerate absences. She **doesn't** like excuses. She **does not** like weak alibis.

ALL OTHER:

Coaches **don't** like alibis. They **don't** make exceptions.

! *LITERACY ALERT:* Note spelling changes: **apply/applies, reply/replies, notify/notifies.**

10b *-d/-ed* for Past Tense

Use the *-d* or *-ed* ending that shows past tense.

Verbs using the *-d* or *-ed* ending to show past time are called **regular** verbs. When writing about the past, do not leave the ending off in hasty writing.

PAST: Columbus **entered** the figures in the ship's log.

Portuguese ships **circumnavigated** the globe.

Columbus **organized** a second expedition.

! *LITERACY ALERT:* Note spelling changes: **apply/applied, reply/replied, notify/notified; occur/occurred, prefer/preferred, submit/submitted.**

10c Verbs with *have* and *be*

Use the *-d* or *-ed* ending for verbs starting with a form of *have (has, had)*. Use it also when appropriate with a form of be *(am, is, are, was, were, has been).*

Check for the right form of regular verbs for the different **perfect** tenses—combinations using *have* (*has, had*) to show different relationships in time. Make sure you use the *-d* or *-ed* ending:

Geneticists **have identified** genes responsible for illnesses.

Scientists **had suspected** that genetic defects cause disease.

Use the *-d* or *-ed* ending also in combinations using *be (am, is, are, was, were, has been)* to form a **passive** verb. A passive verb follows a subject that is "acted upon" or the target of an action:

PASSIVE: The experiment **was described** in an earlier issue of the journal.

The results **have been analyzed**.

Questions **should be submitted** in advance.

A main verb ending in *-ing* may follow a form of *be (am, is, are,* and so on). The verb then shows action in progress, not yet finished.

PROGRESSIVE: I **am** still **working** on my degree.

He **was living** with his parents.

The police **has been asking** the family questions.

! ***LITERACY ALERT:*** Never use the *could of, might of,* or *should of* spelling:

RIGHT: It **could have** happened.

She **should have** exercised.

He **might have** called.

10d Irregular Verbs

Use the standard forms of irregular verbs.

Some very common English verbs do not use the *-d* or *-ed* ending. Instead, the whole word changes: **go** (now), **went** (in the past); **throw** (now), **threw** (in the past); **take** (now), **took** (in the past). Many of these **irregular** verbs have a third different form for use after *have (has, had):* **has gone, had thrown, might have taken.** The different combined forms using *have* are called the **perfect** tenses.

> I **go** to the gym today but also **went** yesterday. I **had gone** also last week.
>
> She often **takes** students to the theater and **took** us to a play this week. She **had taken** us twice before.
>
> We **know** much about the universe. The ancient Greeks **knew** the world was round. Astronomers **have** long **known** about comets.

The third form is also used in combinations using a form of *be* (*am, is, was,* and so on) to make a passive verb:

PASSIVE: The verdict **was thrown** out. The issue **had been taken** to a higher court.

Pay special attention to the second and third forms in the checklist on the following page.

✓ ***EDITOR'S TIP:*** Written English keeps the hypothetical *were* (**subjunctive**) for an unlikely possibility or wishful thinking:

SUBJUNCTIVE: If I ~~*was*~~ **were** a politician, I would have to please rich contributors. (but I am not really)

We all wish the election ~~*was*~~ **were** over. (but it isn't)

ENGLISH ESSENTIALS

A Checklist of Irregular Verbs

PRESENT	PAST	PERFECT
begin	**began**	have **begun**
blow	**blew**	have **blown**
break	**broke**	have **broken**
catch	**caught**	have **caught**
choose	**chose**	have **chosen**
come	**came**	have **come**
dig	**dug**	have **dug**
do	**did**	have **done**
draw	**drew**	have **drawn**
drink	**drank**	have **drunk**
drive	**drove**	have **driven**
eat	**ate**	have **eaten**
fall	**fell**	have **fallen**
fly	**flew**	have **flown**
freeze	**froze**	have **frozen**
get	**got**	have **got** (or **gotten**)
go	**went**	have **gone**
grow	**grew**	have **grown**
know	**knew**	have **known**
lead	**led**	have **led**
run	**ran**	have **run**
sing	**sang**	have **sung**
speak	**spoke**	have **spoken**
steal	**stole**	have **stolen**
swing	**swung**	have **swung**
take	**took**	have **taken**
tear	**tore**	have **torn**
throw	**threw**	have **thrown**
wear	**wore**	have **worn**
write	**wrote**	have **written**

✓ ***EDITOR'S TIP:*** Forms like *knowed, growed, drownded* (for **drowned**), *catched, brung* (for **brought**), *drug* (for **dragged**), and *busted* (for **burst**) are used in rural or down-home American dialects. Do not carry these forms over into standard written English.

10e Problem Verbs (*lie, sit*)

Check the forms of problem verbs: *lie/lay, sit/set.*

In standard written English, **lie-lay-have lain** and **lay-laid-have laid** are two different verbs. Sun worshipers on the beach *lie* or *are lying* in the sun; in the past, they *lay* or *have lain* in the sun. However, when we place something, we *lay* it down (now) or *laid* it down or *have laid* it down (in the past). **Sit-sat-have sat** and **set-set-have set** are also two different verbs: We *sit* somewhere now (or *sat* in the past). However, we *set* something down (or *set* it down in the past).

YOUR TURN 42 Building the Habit

Put verbs through their paces. How would you fill in the slots in the following sets? Each set starts with the plain or unmarked form. Fill in the *-s* form (third person singular); then the form for past tense; then a form that fits after *have* or *be*; and finally a form that fits after *do not (don't)* or the like. Read the completed sets over to help the patterns sink in.

How Do You Like College?

1 Many student **apply** to different colleges. Sometimes one student __________ to a dozen different schools. Most of my high school friends __________ to colleges nearby. My younger brother has already __________ to a local college. Some students do not __________ until it is too late.

2 Some colleges **notify** applicants early. However, sometimes a college __________ applicants late. One college __________ me too late to make plans. My sister had been __________ earlier. Some schools did not __________ those not accepted.

3 Many students **go** to private schools. A friend's sister still __________ to a Catholic high school. Her parents also __________ to parochial schools. In my family, everyone has always __________ to public schools. Too many students in high school don't __________ to class regularly.

4 Classes **begin** early at my school. My first class __________ at seven thirty. Last term, my last class __________ at four in the afternoon. When I arrived yesterday, the class had already

__________. Most students prefer classes that don't __________ at dawn.

5 Some students **choose** their classes carefully. Sometimes a student __________ at the last minute. A former friend of mine always __________ the easiest classes. This year several of the classes I had __________ were closed. Many students do not __________ a major the first year.

6 Many instructors **schedule** regular exams. The college usually __________ the final exams. My high school teachers __________ frequent tests. Many long papers are __________ for late in a term. Teachers fond of surprise quizzes don't __________ exams in advance.

7 Spiral-bound manuals **lie** open on the desk. The book __________ flat. My previous roommate's books always __________ on the floor. By exam time, several of his textbooks had __________ unopened for weeks. My own books don't __________ unopened in a corner.

8 College students **write** more than they used to. A friend __________ a paper a week. Last term, I __________ several papers for science classes. This week, I am __________ a draft for a social science paper. A plagiarized paper is a paper the alleged author did not __________.

9 Students often **collaborate** on a project. A student who __________ with others learns about group dynamics. In one class, students __________ on a study of the local homeless population. Students have __________ on miniproductions of scenes from a play. The traditional competitive student did not usually __________ with others.

10 Arguments over controversial topics **lead** to heated discussion. An instance of hate speech often __________ to angry calls for action. Last month, a friend __________ a group of anti-logging protesters. In recent years, budget cuts have __________ to campus protests. Activists believe that mere talk does not __________ anywhere.

YOUR TURN 43 Following Up

Write similar sets of five for five or more of the following verbs: *take, divide, accept, break, assimilate, organize, resign, condition, delay, believe.*

11 CHECKING AGREEMENT

agr

Make the verb agree with the true subject of the sentence.

Agreement is the use of matching forms for the most basic sentence parts—subject and verb. Subject and verb agree when they are both singular or both plural. Most nouns have different forms for one and more than one: **law/laws, regulation/regulations, officer/officers, question/questions, woman/women, child/children, foot/feet.** Verbs give us a similar choice in the present: (one) **asks**/(several) **ask**; (one) **runs**/(several) **run**; (one) **investigates**/(several) **investigate.** The *-s* ending does double duty: It serves as a plural-signal for most nouns, but it serves as a singular-signal for verbs.

SINGULAR: The **bus stops** here.
The **conductor makes** change.
The **map shows** the route.
The **train does** not run on Sundays.

PLURAL: The **buses stop** here.
The **conductors make** change.
The **maps show** the routes.
The **trains do** not run on Sundays.

Observe agreement especially also in sentences using a form of **be** (is/are, was/were) or of **have** (has/have). One **is** late/several **are** late; one **was** defective/several **were** defective. One **has** left/several **have** left.

SINGULAR: The **train was** late.
The **license has expired**.
The **schedule is changing**.

PLURAL: The **trains were** late.
The **licenses have expired**.
The **schedules are changing**.

YOUR TURN 44 Agreement at Work

In the following sentences, change *both* subject and verb from singular to plural. Focus on agreement—try not to make other changes.

Teaching Science

1 The physics teacher explains the structure of the atom.

2 The biology teacher teaches evolution.

3 The scientific theory about the origin of life has become controversial.

4 A biology textbook is often revised.

5 Sometimes the chapter about evolution was removed.

6 A politician overestimates the influence of school.

7 An American youngster learns from movies and TV.

8 A life form like the dinosaurs becomes extinct.

9 Sometimes a mad scientist brings extinct prehistoric monsters back to life.

10 A new species like *homo sapiens* evolves.

11a Blind Agreement

agr

Correct blind agreement by finding the true subject.

Watch for agreement problems when the subject does not come right before the verb. Avoid **blind agreement:** Do not make the verb agree with a noun that comes before it—but that is not the subject of the sentence. Ask: In this sentence, who does what? What is described as what?

NO: Arresting the crack *dealers strain* police resources.
(*What* causes the strain?)

YES: **Arresting** the crack dealers **strains** police resources.

NO: The cost of new *stadiums are* enormous.
(*What* is enormous?)

YES: **The cost** of new stadiums **is** enormous.

NO: Large amounts of leftover radioactive *material presents* a huge storage problem.

YES: Large **amounts** of leftover radioactive material **present** a huge storage problem.

Check for agreement when a major wedge comes between the subject and verb. Visualize how the sentence would read without the intervening material:

Even **a small rise** {in average yearly temperatures around the globe} **is expected** to melt the ice caps.

YES: **The deterioration** of aging and poorly maintained Russian nuclear plants **alarms** experts in the West.

YES: **Refugees** who fled their villages after the revolution **were still living** in camps.

Verify agreement especially when you single out one thing (or person) among several, one quality shared by many, or one action affecting several people:

SINGULAR: Only **one** of the components **was** ready in time.

The **efficacy** of the these medications **has been questioned**.

Arresting crack dealers **puts** an impossible strain on the courts.

11b Combined Subject

agr

Check agreement with more than one possible subject.

Check for agreement when several possible subjects come before the verb. The word *and* may combine two singulars to make a plural:

PLURAL: The developer **and** the city **were** unable to reach agreement.

The word *or* may merely give a choice between two singular subjects. When *or* gives a choice between a singular and a plural, make the verb agree with the choice closest to it.

SINGULAR: A passport **or** birth certificate **was** needed to reenter the country.

PLURAL: Money **or** cigarettes **were** needed to bribe the officials.

Expressions like *as well as, together with,* and *in addition to* do not add a subject. What applies to the subject also applies to what these expressions add, but they do not affect agreement.

SINGULAR: The candidate's war **record,** as well as his private life, **was becoming** an issue.

The mayor's **office**, together with other agencies, **is sponsoring** the event.

✓ ***EDITOR'S TIP:*** Sometimes the word *and* joins two parts of a single name (pork and beans **is** a single dish). Or it may join two parts of a single description (the President and chief executive **is** one person).

SINGULAR: Corned beef **and** cabbage **was served** on St. Patrick's Day.

His closest friend **and** advisor **distrusts** journalists.

11c Postponed Subject

agr

Check for agreement when a subject follows the verb.

In some sentences, you may reverse the usual subject-verb order. Make the verb agree with the **postponed subject:**

PLURAL: Inside the envelope **were** several large **bills**.

In *there is/there are* sentences especially, make sure the verb agrees with the subject that comes later:

SINGULAR: **There was** scattered **applause** from the expensive seats.

PLURAL: **There were** loud **boos** from the balcony.

Use a plural verb if a combined subject with *and* follows the verb:

PLURAL: **There were** a ceremonial plaza **and** a temple pyramid at the center of the city.

✓ ***EDITOR'S TIP:*** When a linking verb links the subject and a label, make the verb agree with the subject. Do not make the verb agree with the label as if it were a postponed subject.

SINGULAR: Our chief **problem has been** defective parts.

PLURAL: Defective **parts have been** our chief problem.

11d Logical Agreement

agr

Carry agreement through to other sentence parts.

When the meaning requires it, carry agreement through to sentence parts other than the subject and the verb. Look at all the words that signal "more than one" in the following sentence: **These students are** sending **their** loan **applications** to **their** hometown **banks.**

ILLOGICAL: Some people go through *their whole life* without visiting a museum or attending a concert. [**their whole lives**]

Advertisers target *women who are a wife, mother, and executive* at the same time. [**women who are wives, mothers, and executives**]

11e Singular or Plural?

agr

Check for agreement with borderline singulars and plurals.

Some subjects look plural but are singular and vice-versa.

11e.1 Words in *-ics* *Many words ending in -ics look plural but are singular.* They often name one field or activity: mathematics, physics, aeronautics, aerobics.

SINGULAR: **Mathematics is** a demanding subject.

Modern **physics allows** for uncertainty.

However, some other words with *-ics* can go either way, depending on how they are used:

SINGULAR: **Politics** (the area of politics) **was** their favorite topic.

PLURAL: Her **politics** (political views) **have changed.**

SINGULAR: **Statistics** (the area of study) **is** a large field.

PLURAL: Their **statistics** (statistical figures) **were** incomplete.

11e.2 Indefinite Pronouns *Treat the so-called indefinite pronouns as singulars.* Pronouns like the following point to more than one person—but they make us look at them *one at a time:* **each** counts, **either** is acceptable, **neither** was right, **everybody** knows, **everyone** loves you. Since these pronouns do not point to only one definite person, we call them **indefinite pronouns**.

SINGULAR: **Each** of the applicants (each one) **was** interviewed.

Either (either one) of the candidates **is** acceptable.

Everybody (every single one) **supports** your decision.

11e.3 Sums or Totals *Treat figures giving the whole amount as singular when they record the sum or total.*

SINGULAR: **Twenty-five dollars pays** for the ticket and a beverage.

YOUR TURN 45 **Solving Agreement Problems**

In each of the following sentences, solve an agreement problem by changing the verb or first auxiliary. Write the changed word after the number of the sentence.

Acing the Interview

1 Much preparation, self-confidence, and alertness is required for a successful job interview.

2 Often each of several applicants are equally qualified.

3 Competence or a good track record alone do not guarantee success.

4 Showing interest in the job and the company are essential.

5 Previous experiences relating to the job helps a great deal.

6 However, bragging and stretching the truth is not recommended.

7 Getting interviewers to talk about their own hobbyhorses often bring good results.

8 An insincere answer or too much hesitation have hurt many candidates.

9 There is hidden risks in innocent-seeming employment questionnaires.

10 Questions about politics, sex, or religion generally calls for safe conservative answers.

11e.4 **Irregular Plurals** *Know irregular plurals of English nouns.* Regular English nouns use the -*s* plural: *buildings, tickets, automobiles*. However, some words borrowed from Greek and Latin have kept irregular plural forms: one **crisis**, several **crises**; one **criterion**, several **criteria**. Watch for irregular plurals especially in technical and scientific writing:

SINGULAR	PLURAL	SINGULAR	PLURAL
crisis	**crises**	criterion	**criteria**
thesis	**theses**	phenomenon	**phenomena**
hypothesis	**hypotheses**	medium	**media**
analysis	**analyses**	stimulus	**stimuli**
species	**species**	nucleus	**nuclei**
curriculum	**curricula**	stigma	**stigmata**

Media people and data crunchers use *media* and *data* as singulars (their **data is** obsolete). Outside the media and the communications industry, use both *media* and *data* as plurals to be safe (**these data have** not been verified).

SINGULAR: The artist's favorite **medium was** stained glass.

PLURAL: The **media were turning** the murder trial into a circus.

✓ *EDITOR'S TIP:* Anglicized plurals have become acceptable for **index** (**indexes** replacing **indices**) and **formula** (**formulas** replacing **formulae**). Sometimes the older form survives in a special technical use: the **antennas** of radios but the **antennae** of insects.

11e.5 ***Who, which,* and *that*** *Check for agreement after* who, which, *and* that. A **relative pronoun**—*who, which,* or *that*—may serve as the subject in a *who*-clause or *which*-clause: the clerk **who keeps** the records. The verb then agrees with what the pronoun points back to (the clerk). But the clause may have its own subject, with the pronoun serving as the object: the records that **the government keeps**.

SUBJECT: Young **children who** daily **watch** crime shows on TV see thousands of brutal murders.

OBJECT: The crime shows **that a child watches** on TV blunt sensitivity to violence.

11e.6 Loose Agreement (*these kind, one of those*) *Avoid the loose agreement of informal speech.* Expressions like *these kind* and *those kind* are mixed forms—half singular and half plural. In your writing, use **this kind** or **that kind** for singular and **these kinds** or **those kinds** for plural.

RIGHT: Politicians using attack ads have found that **these kinds** of ads may alienate the voters.

Change expressions like "I am not one of those who **believes** . . ." to "I am not one of **those** who **believe**" (talking about several believers).

RIGHT: She was not **one of those** administrators **who talk** about excellence only at commencement.

✓ ***EDITOR'S TIP:*** Especially in British English, **collective nouns** (or group nouns) are often used as plurals if the writer is thinking not of the whole unit but of several *individual members:*

SINGULAR: The police **has been targeting** drunk drivers. (the police generally)

PLURAL: The police **were interrogating** the suspect. (specific officers)

YOUR TURN 46 You Are the Editor

In the following sentences, which choices are right for edited writing? Click on the right choice by circling the form that is right for written English. Then read the edited sentence, putting extra emphasis on the right choice.

YOUR TURN 46 *(continued)*

Fired Teacher Wins Lawsuit

1 Censorship of written materials **threatens/threaten** a free society.

2 Profane language used by her student writers **was/were** enough to have a teacher fired.

3 A good teaching record and the support of students **has/have** often not saved a teacher's job.

4 The teacher targeted by school board members **incurs/incur** huge legal fees.

5 The courts often in the end **decide/decides** the issue.

6 Students of American history **know/knows** why the founders protected free speech.

7 Control or licensing of the printing press **was/were** a favorite tool of tyrannical governments.

8 Censorship of writers and artists **is/are** as old as the pen.

9 Hitler's Germany and Stalin's Russia **was/were** silencing intellectuals.

10 Today self-censorship in the media **takes/take** the place of government censorship.

11 Statistics on censorship in the schools **is/are** sobering.

12 Often a librarian or English teacher **is/are** at the center of the storm.

13 There **is/are** groups that scan textbooks for offensive material.

14 Classical literature as well as adolescent literature and children's books **has/have** been attacked.

15 The greatest writers of the past century **has/have** been banned at one time or another.

12 PRONOUN REFERENCE

ref

Make pronouns stand clearly for what they replace.

We use pronouns as shortcut words to take the place of something previously mentioned. We then have to make them point clearly to what they replaced. They have to point clearly to the **antecedent**—to what "came before." Otherwise, readers start asking: "Who are *they?* What is *it?* Who is *she* in this sentence?" Pronouns refer clearly to what they stand for in sentences like the following:

> **The redwood trees** inspire awe. **They** are hundreds of years old.
>
> **The law** protected old-growth trees. However, **it** covered only part of the forest.
>
> When **a protester** fights the lumberjacks, **she** may be risking **her** life.
>
> Some protesters **live in the trees. This** practice is dangerous.

12a Ambiguous Reference

Make a pronoun point clearly to one thing rather than another.

When several people have been mentioned, a *he* or *she* may not point clearly to one of them. When several groups of people have been mentioned, a *they* may not point clearly to one group rather than the other. The sentence then remains **ambiguous**; it has two possible meanings. It can be read two ways. You may have to reshuffle parts of the sentence:

AMBIGUOUS: When **the doctor** explained the new procedure to **her assistant**, **she** looked bored.
(*Who* looked bored—the doctor, or her assistant?)

CLEAR: **The doctor** looked bored when **she** explained the new procedure to **her assistant.**

When **the doctor** explained the new procedure, **her assistant** looked bored.

12b Informal Pronouns

Avoid vague informal pronouns.

Substitute more exact references for the informal *they* and *you* of casual speech.

12b.1 Orphaned *they/it* *Spell out implied references.* A *they* or *it* may refer to something that is merely implied: "There were rumors of a drug deal gone sour, but *they* hushed it up." (*Who* hushed it up—the police? the newspapers? the government? friends and family?) Point the finger more directly at what the pronoun stands for.

her teachers
IMPLIED: Sarah wanted to be an engineer, but *they* discouraged her.

the coal dust
The men worked in *the coal mines*, and *it* got into their lungs.

12b.2 Informal *you* *In writing, avoid the informal you.* Avoid *you* when it cannot possibly mean "you, the reader." ("As a top model, *you live* on carrot juice and salads"—how many of us are top models?)

only aristocrats were allowed to vote.
INFORMAL: In ancient Rome, *you had to be an aristocrat to vote.*

12c *This* and *which*

Avoid confusing reference with *this* or *which*.

A *this* or *which* may point back to one of several ideas earlier in a sentence or paragraph. Rewrite the sentence to avoid possible confusion.

VAGUE: The company fired the workers that had started the unauthorized strike. *This* was a big mistake.
(What was a mistake—the firings or the strike?)

CLEAR: The company fired the workers who had started the unauthorized strike. **This retaliation** was a big mistake.

VAGUE: The council refused a permit for the rally, *which* we considered ill-advised. (What seemed ill-advised—the rally, or the council's action?)

CLEAR: The council refused a permit for the rally, **a move** we considered ill-advised.

12d Agreement of Pronouns

Make pronouns and what they stand for agree in number.

Check if a pronoun refers to a singular or a plural, and make the pronoun agree:

MISMATCHED: *Abortions* should not be outlawed because *it is* often required for medical reasons. [correction: **they are**]

12e Sexist Pronouns

Avoid the generic *he, his,* and *himself.*

English does not have a gender-neutral, unisex pronoun for *he/she*. The masculine *he* or *his* used to be defended as a **generic** pronoun. It was said to stand for both male and female in sentences like "**The student** must pay the fee when **he** registers" or "**The driver** should check **his** rear-view mirror." Today teachers and editors require gender-balanced pronouns that cannot be interpreted as ignoring one half of humanity.

12e.1 Gender-Balanced Pronouns *Use gender-balanced or gender-neutral pronouns.* Use the gender-balanced **double pronouns—he or she** or **his or her** (also **himself or herself**). Or you can change the whole sentence to plural to make it gender-neutral:

SEXIST: *A true leader* cannot always please *his* constituents. (Are true leaders always male?)

BALANCED: **A true leader** cannot always please **his or her** constituents.

NEUTRAL: **True leaders** cannot always please **their** constituents.

SEXIST: When *a doctor* entrusts a patient to a nurse, *he* expects *her* to follow *his* instructions.

NEUTRAL: When entrusting patients to a nurse, **doctors** expect the nurse to follow **their** instructions.

Sometimes you can avoid the pronoun dilemma by leaving the pronoun out altogether:

NO PRONOUN: **A true leader** cannot always please **constituents**.

12e.2 Singular *everybody/someone*

Avoid the informal they *after words like* everybody *or* nobody. A special pronoun dilemma is caused by the **indefinite pronouns:** *everybody (everyone), somebody (someone), anybody (anyone), nobody (no one),* and in addition the impersonal *one*. These pronouns do not point to one particular person, and in informal spoken English they are treated as plurals: **Everyone** in the office did **their** best. These pronouns may seem to refer to many different people. However in written English treat them as singular, as if looking at each one of these people *one at a time:*

SINGULAR: **Everyone** on the women's team did **her** best.

Someone in the fraternity had double-parked **his** car.

Agreement becomes a problem when a pronoun like *everybody* or *someone* cuts across gender lines. Grammarians used to require the singular *he* (or *his*), saying that the **generic** *he* stood for both male and female: **Everybody** in the audience rose to **his** feet. Today, teachers and editors require the gender-balanced **double pronoun** *he or she*, or *his or her:* **Everybody** in the audience rose to **his or her** feet. When double pronouns (especially several of them in the same sentence) seem awkward, try to convert the whole sentence to gender-neutral plurals instead: **All** in the audience rose to **their** feet.

GENERIC: *An immigrant* in effect creates a new identity for *himself.*

GENDER-BALANCED: **An immigrant** in effect creates a new identity for **himself or herself.**

GENDER-NEUTRAL: **Immigrants** in effect create new identities for **themselves.**

12e.3 **Representative Person** *Use a singular pronoun to point back to one representative person.* In informal spoken English, *a person, an individual, a typical worker,* and *the average American* make people think of a whole group of people (who are *all* typical or average). In written English, treat these expressions as singular, as if you were looking at one typical or average person at a time. Or change the whole sentence to plural.

INFORMAL: *The average American* no longer leaves *their* front door unlocked.

SINGULAR: **The average American** no longer leaves **his or her** front door unlocked.

ALL PLURAL: **Average Americans** no longer leave **their front doors** unlocked.

YOUR TURN 47 Checking Pronoun Reference

Correct the pronoun reference in each of the following student-written sentences. After the number of the sentence, write the pronoun (or pronouns) that should replace the italicized word in the sentence. Read the edited sentences over with special emphasis on the corrected pronoun.

1 Nonsmokers refused to patronize restaurants because of the smoke *he* might inhale.

2 Today's executive has a computer by *his* desk.

3 Every member had *their* own private reason for joining the fraternity.

4 Many medical students were still white males, although admission policies were already less biased in *his* favor.

5 Colleges often prove a mixed blessing to the town surrounding *it.*

6 Since the bear feeds primarily on roots, *they* would have to be desperate to attack livestock.

7 England had a much lower murder rate because *they* enforced gun control laws.

8 Each person runs differently, depending on *their* body size.

9 The Founders intended that a citizen's religion should be *their* own responsibility.

10 A woman preparing for a career in the theater might find *themselves* acting in hairspray commercials.

13 PRONOUN CASE

ca

Choose the right pronoun for different positions in a sentence.

Several **personal pronouns** give you a choice of forms: *I/me, he/him, she/her, we/us, they/them.* Use the **subject form** as the subject of a sentence. Ask: **Who** does what? **I** read the report. **He** resigned. **She** initialed the contract. **They** have reservations. **We** are on the waiting list. Use the object form as the object of a verb. Ask: **Whom** (or what) are we targeting here? The office paged **me.** The manager hired **him.** The company promoted **her.** The buyer stalled **us.** The delay angered **them.** The variable forms for subject and object require you to select the right form for **pronoun case.**

13a Double Subject/Object

Avoid informal pronouns for subject and object of verbs.

Informal spoken English often reverses traditional rules for pronoun case. Change the pronoun to the right form especially when it is part of a **double subject:**

The sheriff and I
SUBJECT: *The sheriff and me* had a disagreement.

She and the manager
Her and the manager do not get along.

We and they
Us and them see things differently.

Also change a pronoun to the right form especially when it is part of a **double object:**

my partner and me
OBJECT: The judges awarded *my partner and I* first prize.

her sister and her
The accused had sent *her sister and she* threatening letters.

Use the right form in pronoun-noun combinations like **we Americans** and **us Americans:**

SUBJECT: **We Americans** pride ourselves on due process. (Who does? **We** do.)

OBJECT: The French students expected **us Americans** to chew gum and wear baseball caps. (Expected whom? Expected **us.**)

13b Object of Preposition

Avoid informal pronouns as objects of prepositions.

Use the object form of a pronoun as the object of a preposition: for **me**, with **her**, under **him**, near **us**, by **them.** Change the pronoun to the right form especially if it is part of a double object for a preposition:

between you and me.

OBJECT: All this will have to remain strictly *between you and I.*

of her sister and her.

The will made no mention *of her sister and she.*

13c Subject Form after *be*

Use the subject form after linking verbs.

Grammarians require the subject form after a **linking verb**, usually a form of *be* (*is, was, has been, will be*). Use the subject form in sentences like the following:

SUBJECT FORM: It was **she** who always came to our aid.

It was **he** and not his father who had signed the check.

✓ ***EDITOR'S TIP:*** The brief *It is I* and *This is he* are grammatically correct but have so often been ridiculed that most people avoid them.

13d Pronoun after *as/than*

Use the right pronoun form in shortened comparisons and similar situations.

In shortened comparisons using *as* or *than,* fill in enough of what has been left out to see how the pronoun fits into the sentence. Is the pronoun used as subject or object?

SUBJECT: Her siblings felt as neglected as **she** (did).

His fiancée earned more money than **he** (did).

OBJECT: We liked no other candidate as much as (we liked) **him**.

The public distrusts no profession more than (it distrusts) **them**.

Choose the right form when a pronoun is not subject or object but a *label* (or part of a label) that applies to the subject or object. Again fill in enough to see how the pronoun would fit into a separate sentence.

SUBJECT: Only two passengers—**she** and her sister—survived.

Only two passengers survived: **she** and her sister. (Who survived? **She** did.)

OBJECT: The bandits released two hostages: her and her sister. (They released **her**.)

✓ *EDITOR'S TIP:* **Who** is the subject form: **Who** would have known? (*he* or *she* might have). **Whom** is the object form: **Whom** did they choose? (they chose *him* or *her*). **Whom** also goes with a preposition: Do not ask **for whom** the bell tolls (it tolls *for him* or *for her*). However, *who,* used as an all-purpose form, has widely replaced *whom* in current English, and many people trying to use *whom* get it wrong. You can often avoid *whom* altogether:

NO *WHOM:* The coach cut two players [whom] he had signed on last year.

Check how the *who* or *whom* fits into sentences like the following:

OBJECT: Medieval Christians fought the Arabs, **whom** they considered infidels. (They **considered them** infidels.)

SUBJECT: Believers persecuted fellow citizens **who** they thought were heretics. (They thought **they were** heretics.)

YOUR TURN 48 Checking Pronoun Case

Correct pronoun case in each of the following student-written sentences. After the number of the sentence, write the pronoun (or pronouns) that should replace the italicized word in the sentence. Read the corrected sentences over with special emphasis on the right pronoun.

1 We asked his fellow bigots and *he* to lower the volume.

2 Visitors from space might snigger at the technology that *us* earth dwellers have.

3 The losing candidate seemed better qualified than *her*.

4 The letter brought bad news for *she* and her family.

5 Few other nations are as wasteful as *us* Americans.

6 The report cited two other officers and *she* for bravery.

7 We recognized the face; it was *him* who had cruised the neighborhood.

8 This information should remain strictly between you and *I*.

9 He constantly interrupted the conversation of my friends and *I* with sarcastic remarks.

10 *Us* and the manager constantly fought over work schedules and breaks.

14 CHECKING MODIFIERS

adv
DM

Check form and position of modifiers.

Modifiers help us build up bare-bones sentences. They range from single-word adjectives and adverbs to longer prepositional phrases and verbal phrases:

ADJECTIVES:	The **furious** customer called the clause in the **small** print a **cheap** trick.
ADVERBS:	**Often** passengers have to wait **patiently forever** for **really** late buses.
PREPOSITIONAL PHRASES:	A woman **in grimy overalls** was standing **on the ladder.**
VERBAL PHRASES:	**Delayed in slow traffic,** motorists **talking on cellular phones** make good use of time.

When modifiers do their job well, they blend smoothly into a sentence. Electronic grammar checkers of the future may scan sentences to see if the right form of a modifier is in the right place. In the meantime, you will have to check your writing for informal or loosely joined modifiers carried over from everyday speech.

14a Adverb Form

adv

To tell your readers how, select the distinctive adverb form.

Be sure you can tell adjectives and adverbs apart. Adjectives tell us which one or what kind: a **candid** talk, the **terrible** news, an **immediate** reply, a **reluctant** candidate. Adverbs tell us how (also when and where). They tell us how something was done or how it happened: he spoke **candidly**; it hurt **terribly**; she replied **immediately**; they complied **reluctantly**. Often the only difference between adjective and adverb is the *-ly* ending: considerable/**considerably**; cheerful/**cheerfully**; happy/ **happily.**

In written English, avoid the unmarked adverbs of informal English. Use the *-ly* form to tell the reader how. For instance, the engine ran **smoothly.** They drove **cautiously.** We had behaved **badly.**

considerably.

INFORMAL: Rents had gone up *considerable.*

very carefully.

The examiners went over the books *very careful.*

seriously.

At first no one took the new policy *serious.*

✓ ***EDITOR'S TIP:*** A few informal adverbs—*slow, quick,* and *loud*—are becoming widely accepted in writing. However, use the distinctive adverbs to be safe: everyone drove more **slowly;** the mood shifted **quickly;** they talked **loudly** in restaurants.

14a.1 Adverbs without *-ly* *Know special adverbs without the -ly ending.* Adverbs that do not have the *-ly* include *soon, fast, much,* and *thus:* it ended **soon**; they drove **fast**; he loved her **much.** (There is no *muchly* or *thusly*.) **Good** is an adjective (**good** teaching); the adverb is **well** (they taught us **well**).

very well.

INFORMAL: New immigrants often did not speak English *very good.*

14a.2 Adverb with Modifier *Use adverb forms to modify other modifiers.* They then often answer questions like how true or how well: **probably** right, **really** true, **extremely** well. Avoid the informal adverbs of popular speech—*real* popular, *awful* expensive, *pretty* exciting.

truly popular

INFORMAL: The Grateful Dead had been *real popular* for many years.

reasonably well

The new policy worked *pretty good* for a time.

14a.3 Adjective with Linking Verb *Use adjectives after linking verbs.* Not all verbs go with adverbs that tell us how something is done. **Linking verbs** go with adjectives that tell us what something is like. For instance, adjectives follow forms of *be (is, are, was, has been):* spring was **wonderful;** the heat is **oppressive.** Adjectives may also follow words like *seem, become, feel, sound,* and *look:* we felt **bad;** he looked **sad;** it became **obvious.**

felt bad
INFORMAL: His friends *felt badly* after rejecting the invitation.

✓ *EDITOR'S TIP:* Adjectives and adverbs overlap. Some words ending in *-ly* are adjectives: a **friendly** conversation, a **lonely** life, a **leisurely** drive. Some words do double duty as adjectives and adverbs: a **fast** train and traveling **fast;** an **early** class and getting up **early;** an **only** child and having **only** one.

YOUR TURN 49 Editing for Adverbs

In each of the following sentences, change one word to the distinctive adverb form. Write the changed word after the number of the sentence.

1 Macbeth interpreted the prophecies of the witches very literal.
2 The witness testified nervously and very defensive.
3 The new arrivals spoke English good but not perfectly.
4 Since the first deposition, his testimony had changed considerable.
5 Toward the end, everything happened very sudden, as in an action movie.
6 The new system operated more efficient than the earlier model.
7 The fuel-efficient new cars ran good on ordinary gasoline.
8 The gate opened easy, but the driveway was blocked.
9 The new game required players to think fast and logical.
10 We read the instructions as careful as time allowed.

14b Dangling Modifier

DM

Hook up dangling modifiers.

Modifiers are like attachments that are not always properly plugged into the sentence. A modifier is left **dangling** when it points to something left out of the sentence altogether: *Having run for an hour,* the carrot juice tasted great. (Who ran? Who drank the juice?) Often such danglers start with verbals—forms used as only parts of verbs. Often a dangling modifier starts with a form like *driving or having left: Driving home,* sheep blocked the road. (Who was driving home—the sheep?) Fill in the missing connection: **When we were driving home,** sheep blocked the road.

DANGLING: *Dangling from the window ledge, the fire truck* arrived just in time.
(Both the person and the modifier are left dangling.)

FILLED IN: The fire truck arrived just in time **for the tenant dangling from the window ledge.**

Other verbals also cause danglers. In addition to the *-ing* forms, look for forms like *broken* and *repossessed:* not used as complete verbs:

DANGLING: *Repossessed for nonpayment, Rita* went to a lawyer.

FILLED IN: **When her truck was repossessed for nonpayment,** Rita went to a lawyer.

Danglers often start with the *to*-form (infinitive):

DANGLING: *To become a computer specialist, an early start* is necessary.

FILLED IN: **To become a computer specialist, you will need** an early start.

A dangling modifier may be caused by a mismatched **appositive.** An appositive is a second naming or second label for a noun already mentioned: my friend, **the dentist;** pollution, **a constant threat.** You may need to fill in what the appositive is supposed to rename:

DANGLING: The firm had only *one vacancy, a paralegal.*

FILLED IN: The firm had only **one vacancy, a position for** a paralegal.

✓ ***EDITOR'S TIP:*** Some free-floating phrases are acceptable because the missing speaker or writer is implied: **Considering the alternatives**, their plan sounded good. Such phrases are called **absolute constructions:**

> **Generally speaking,** prejudice is on the decline.
> (**the writer** is speaking generally)

> **To be exact,** seven states had already passed strict anti-smoking laws.
> (**the writer** means to be exact)

Other absolute constructions carry along with them the information that could cause a dangling modifier if left out:

> **The fugitives** having scaled the fence, the general alarm went off. **Escape** being impossible, the fugitives surrendered.

14c Misplaced Modifier

MM Reposition misplaced modifiers.

Make sure modifiers appear at the right place in a sentence. Where a modifier appears makes a difference:

> The man **with the parrot** started a conversation.
>
> The man started a conversation **with the parrot.**

14c.1 Misplaced Phrase *Check for misplaced modifying phrases.* A modifier is misplaced when the reader might miss the connection with what it modifies. A **misplaced modifier** seems to point to the wrong thing:

MISPLACED: *Blocking the sidewalk, the officer* arrested the street musician. (The officer was blocking the sidewalk?)

REPOSITIONED: The officer arrested **the street musician blocking the sidewalk.**

14c.2 Misplaced Adverb

Check placement of single-word modifiers. An adverb may seem to point to the wrong part of a sentence:

think Hamlet subconsciously
MISPLACED: I *think subconsciously Hamlet* wanted to die.

Place adverbs like **only** and **almost** carefully:

I **only hinted** to him that I needed advice. (I didn't insist)

I hinted **only to him** that I needed advice. (to no one else)

I hinted to him that I needed **advice only.** (not anything else)

Riots **almost broke out** at every major soccer game. (but they never quite did)

Riots broke out **at almost every** major soccer game. (they did almost every time)

YOUR TURN 50 Reconnecting Modifiers

Rewrite each of the following sentences so that it will say more clearly what the writer apparently meant. Compare your rewrites with those of your classmates.

1 Teen magazines appeal to immature readers with stories of torrid romances.

2 The owner looked at the room we had painted with ill-disguised disgust.

3 Wilting in the heat, Lorenzo watered the plants in the garden.

4 Made of defective material, the builder had to redo the patio.

5 Having always rented an apartment, owning a home is a challenge.

6 After exploding on the Interstate, we had the car towed into town.

7 Unsure of her future, the year abroad sounded good.

8 We watched a movie over the weekend that ended with a massive train wreck.

9 To order plane tickets, the wait for a reservations agent is endless.

10 When riding a bicycle at night, motorists often do not see someone in the bike lane.

15 PARALLEL STRUCTURE

FP
//

Make related sentence parts parallel.

Sentences are **parallel** when similar sentence parts appear in a row: **body** and **soul; red, white,** and **blue; single, married,** or **divorced;** surrounded by **family, relatives,** and **friends.** Grammatically, the elements in such a set are on an equal footing. For instance, they are all nouns, or they are all adjectives. Other sentence parts also are parallel in well-balanced sentences:

VERBS: Squeegee men **swarmed** around the car, **cleaned** the windshield, and **polished** the chrome.

INFINITIVES (*to*-form): Two things a successful ad must accomplish are **to be noticed** and **to be remembered.**

-ing FORMS: She loved the human dimension of the job: **meeting** with people, **listening** to their problems, and **finding** ways to help.

15a Faulty Parallelism

Revise mismatched sentence parts.

Look for parts joined by *and, or,* or *but* and make sure they are parallel. **Faulty parallelism** results when one of the parts seems to snap out of the expected pattern:

NONPARALLEL: They promised *to call and returning* the money. [correction: **to call and return**]

They loved *the wilderness and to backpack* to solitary lakes. [correction: **to explore the wilderness and to backpack**]

You may want to try different rewrites to make a sentence run smoothly:

OFF BALANCE: Her cousin was *tough* in a bargain but *a generous friend.*

PARALLEL: Her cousin was **a tough bargainer** but **a generous friend.**

Her cousin was **tough in a bargain** but **generous as a friend.**

✓ ***EDITOR'S TIP:*** Avoid mixing a noun and an adjective as modifiers: *race and ethnic* quotas (better: **racial and ethnic** quotas). Watch out for other badly matched pairs: *personal and society* needs (better: **personal and social** needs); *hygienic and health* considerations (better: **hygiene and health** considerations).

15b Parallel Series

Check parallel structure in a series of three or more parts.

Three or more sentence parts in a set are called a **series:** Americans were obsessed with **spies, conspiracies,** and **UFOs.** (These are all *nouns.*) Celebrities **practiced** yoga, **hired** personal trainers, and **consulted** psychics. (These are all *verbs.*) Sometimes the second or third part in such a set snaps out of the expected pattern. It derails the reader's train of thought:

tired, lazy, and gloomy.

NONPARALLEL: Days of rain make people feel *tired, lazy,* and *in a gloomy mood.* (should be three adjectives in a row)

loved conversation, good music, and good food.

Our friends *loved to talk, listen to music, and good food.* (could be three nouns in a row)

Sometimes the best way to revise faulty parallelism is to break up the series:

prepare wills and depositions and basically run

NONPARALLEL: As a legal secretary I had to prepare *wills, depositions, and basically run* the office.

15c Paired Connectives

Check parallel structure with paired connectives.

Paired connectives are **either . . . or, neither . . . nor, not only . . . but also,** and **whether . . . or.** What follows the first part of the pair should be on an equal footing with what follows its counterpart.

Check *not only . . . but also* especially: The test of affirmative action was **not only to get** minority students into the colleges **but also to help** them graduate.

whether they should believe him **or try**

NONPARALLEL: Reporters wondered *whether to believe* him *or should they try* to verify his story.

threatened the lawyer with **not only expulsion but also jail**

The judge *not only threatened* the lawyer with expulsion *but also jail.*

15d Phrase and Clause

Avoid switching between phrase and clause for the same thought.

When ideas in a sentence are closely related, we expect them to be lined up in similar form. Avoid shifting gears grammatically when the thought continues on the same track. For instance, the following sentence continues to give reasons, but the first is worded as a prepositional phrase (*for personal reasons*) and the second as a dependent clause starting with *because:*

NONPARALLEL: She left the States *for personal reasons* and *because jobs were scarce.*

PARALLEL: She left the States **because she was unhappy in her personal life and jobs were scarce.**

Be ready to rewrite if an *and who* or *and which* changes the pattern in the middle of a sentence:

who lived in Paris **and had known**

NONPARALLEL: They met a painter *living* in Paris and *who had known* Picasso.

YOUR TURN 51 Working on Parallel Structure

Rewrite the italicized sentence parts to make them parallel.

Space-Age Vampires

1 Fans of vampire movies should neither be committed vegetarians *nor getting sick at the sight of blood.*

2 The traditional vampire lives in a gloomy castle, tricks unwary travelers, *and sucking their blood at night.*

3 Today's vampires *neither totally abandon their blood-sucking ways* nor their costumes.

4 They can read minds *but perhaps unable to use a touch-tone phone.*

5 They deal with a variety of *society and personal issues.*

6 Today's vampire often has a management job, *a late-model car, and is dating someone at the office.*

7 Student vampires party, surf, *and recreation majors.*

8 Gone are *the immigrant vampires from Eastern Europe and who* speak with a heavy accent.

9 The space-age vampire zaps roaches in a microwave, lifts planes into orbit, *and similar high-tech exploits.*

10 Audiences are not sure whether to thrill with horror *or should they laugh at a satire of our modern world.*

16 SHIFTS

sf Revise confusing shifts in time or perspective.

As a writer, you have different options for looking at events. You may be describing them as if they were happening now. ("As we **enter** the village, children **appear** from nowhere. . . .") You may be placing them in the past, or in a more distant past before more recent events. ("When they **reached** the foot of the mountain, they **learned** that three of the climbers **had not made** it back.") You may be quoting someone for whom the events of the past were then current news. ("The president said: 'We **have** nothing to fear . . .'") Whatever your choice, be consistent—try to stay with the timeframe or perspective you adopt.

16a Shifts in Tense

Revise confusing shifts in time.

Verbs have **tense** forms that place events in time. When describing a situation or tracing events, keep track of the verb forms that show time. Avoid confusing shifts in the timeframe.

PRESENT:	Nuclear reactors **pose** frightening safety hazards. (now and ongoing)
PAST:	The U.S. **exploded** the first atom bomb in New Mexico. (over and done with)
PRESENT PERFECT:	World leaders **have warned** against the resumption of nuclear testing. (recent and still important)
PAST PERFECT:	Major powers **had agreed** on a test ban. (before more recent events)

16a.1 Past to Present *Avoid shifting from past to present.*

Do not shift to the present when past events become so real that they seem to be happening now. Be consistent—stay with the timeframe you have chosen:

we heard

SHIFT: The plane *was preparing* for landing when suddenly *we hear* a crunching noise. (all of this happened in the past)

spun around and jumped

The spectators *scattered* as the lead car *spins around and jumps* the barrier.

16a.2 Recent/Distant Past *Signal differences between recent and distant past.* Show the difference between what *happened* in the past and what *had happened* prior to those events.

had been

SHIFT: Carla *was* a copywriter, but she *was* now a vice-president of the agency. (had been a copywriter before then)

had changed

The CEO always *talked* about how computers *have changed* marketing. (had changed marketing up to then)

16a.3 Real/Remote Possibility *Signal differences between real and remote possibility.* Show the difference between factual possibilities (that may really happen any time) and merely hypothetical "what-if?" possibilities. Be consistent—use verb forms for factual possibility throughout, or stay with the **conditional** forms that make the possibility seem more unlikely.

SHIFT: If the refugees *come* here, we *would refuse* them asylum.

FACTUAL: If the refugees **come** here, we **will refuse** them asylum.

CONDITIONAL: If the refugees **came** here, we **would refuse** them asylum.

SHIFT: If terrorists *threaten* to use nuclear weapons, what *would we do?*

FACTUAL: If terrorists **threaten** to use nuclear weapons, what **will we do?**

CONDITIONAL: If terrorists **threatened** to use nuclear weapons, what **would we do?**

16a.4 Indirect Quotation

Adjust the timeframe in indirect quotations. When you quote people directly, word for word, they may be using the present tense for what was happening at the time. (What is now then was then now.) When you change their words to **indirect quotation**, you put what they said into your own words. You then show that they were talking about the past:

DIRECT: President Roosevelt **said**: "We **have** nothing to fear but fear itself."

INDIRECT: President Roosevelt **said** that the nation **had** nothing to fear but fear itself. (had nothing to fear *at that time*)

You may also have to adjust the timeframe when someone was speaking about the future. What was the future at that time may have to change to what *would* have been:

MIXED: Their chosen candidate *said* that if elected he *will not serve.*

DIRECT: Their chosen candidate **said:** "If elected, I **will not serve.**"

INDIRECT: Their chosen candidate **said** that if elected he **would not serve.**

✓ *EDITOR'S TIP:* What someone said in the past may still be true today: Galileo **said** that the earth **moves** and that the sun **is** the center of our solar system. (What the early astronomers said in the past is still accepted as true today.)

16b Shifts in Reference

Revise confusing shifts in reference.

How might you refer to people in a depersonalized computer language of the future? You might use a code like NUMBER ONE PERSON in talking about yourself. You might use NUMBER TWO PERSON to address someone else. You might use NUMBER THREE PERSON to refer to a third party who is not part of the conversation. As of now, in current people language, you will use **I** and **we** to talk about yourself or about yourself and others of your group (**first person**). You will use **you** in talking to your reader or readers (**second**

person). You will use **he** and **she** or **they** in talking about others (**third person**).

FIRST PERSON: **My** family and **I** left the camp, and **we** never saw **our** friends again.

SECOND PERSON: To download this material, **you** need a different browser.

THIRD PERSON: CEOs like an automated system, because **they** prefer dealing with machines to dealing with **their** employees.

When you shift between these different ways of referring to people, your readers will wonder: Are you still talking about yourself? (Who is the *we* in this sentence?) Are you still talking to me—or to someone else? Remain **consistent**—stay with the same way of talking about yourself or others.

SHIFT: To do well in an interview, *applicants* have to research *your* future employer.

CONSISTENT: To do well in an interview, **you** have to research **your** future employer.

SHIFT: If *a student* gets a D, *you are asked* to retake the course.

CONSISTENT: If **students** get a D, **they are asked** to retake the course.

YOUR TURN 52 Editing for Shifts

Rewrite the italicized part of each sentence to eliminate shifts in time, reference, or perspective.

1 When a woman is interviewed, *you should not be too assertive or too quiet.*

2 Often when Carl got impatient, *he suddenly switches to the carpool lane.*

3 The agent said the plane would leave *as soon as the weather clears up.*

4 When a student tried to join a fraternity, *you have to expect some rough horseplay.*

5 The judge cleared the accused *because the plaintiff was not reading the fine print.*

17 CONFUSED SENTENCES

st

Rebuild shaky or confusing sentences.

As a sentence editor, you learn to rebuild sentences that send mixed messages or seem off kilter. They may still send the message to your readers, but they slow them down with double-takes and crossed signals. When a sentence sends mixed signals, you can often straighten out basic relationships by asking: "Who does what? What is compared to what? What causes what?"

17a Skipping and Duplication

Proofread for skipped or duplicated sentence elements.

In hasty typing or keyboarding, you may have skipped some of the small sentence parts that are the mortar among the bricks of a sentence. Proofread carefully for missing little words like *a, the, be, to, we,* or *they:*

on the moon, but we have faltered

SKIPPED: Our astronauts walked *on moon* but *have faltered* since.

Proofread carefully for doubled-up little words like *that* and *of:*

DOUBLED-UP: Americans long had a health care system *of* which they could be proud *of.*

PROOFED: Americans long had a health care system **of** which they could be proud.

DOUBLED-UP: Economists predict *that* with a rapidly aging population *that* the Social Security system will be overburdened.

PROOFED: Economists predict **that** with a rapidly aging population the Social Security system will be overburdened.

YOUR TURN 53 **Proofreading Hasty Sentences**

Flag all omissions or duplications in the following hastily written sentences. Use a ^ to mark an omission; circle duplicated items. Your instructor may ask you to retype the passage with all corrections in place.

1 Some readers look in newspaper for trivia, of which they never tire of.

2 They love read that because of an ancient law that citizens of Lower Liguria not allowed to do laundry on Fridays.

3 They interested in the news that stamp machines in hotel lobbies take three quarters but only fifty cents worth stamps.

4 They love ads for toy sumo wrestlers fight in ring that can be made out package in which they came in.

5 A favorite trivia article said that restaurant in Delaware been serving "marsh rabbits" that really muskrats drowned in ingenious traps.

17b Mismatched Predicate

pred

Make sure subject and predicate go together.

The subject of a sentence brings something into focus (a late-model car, the lead singer, the U.S. Constitution). The **predicate** is the part of the sentence that makes a statement about the subject. It includes the verb and all other material that goes with the verb. (A late-model car **blocked the driveway**. The lead singer **had once been a cab driver in L.A.**) Make sure the statement the predicate makes can logically apply to the subject.

ILLOGICAL: *The choice* of the new stadium site *was selected* by a committee.
(the site was selected, but the choice was *made*)

LOGICAL: **The choice** of the new stadium site **was made** by a committee.

ILLOGICAL: Her new job *was a systems analyst.*
(a systems analyst is a *person*, not a job)

LOGICAL: Her new job **was working as a systems analyst.**

ILLOGICAL: *A couple with two stressful jobs* often *contributes* to a divorce.

LOGICAL: **A couple's having** two stressful jobs often **contributes** to a divorce.

✓ ***EDITOR'S TIP:*** A mismatched predicate may result when a prepositional phrase telling us how follows an *is* or *was*. We expect to learn *what* something is rather than *how* it is done:

was to cross
ILLOGICAL: Their last hope *was by crossing* the mountains before the snow.

17c *Is when/was when*

Rewrite *is-when* or *was-when* sentences.

Is-when sentences are off kilter in statements like "Conservation *is when* we try to save natural resources." Conservation is not a *time* when we do something but a *practice:* "Conservation **means trying to save** natural resources."

is the result of being estranged
IS-WHEN: Alienation *is when* people are estranged from the values of society.

was the process of freeing the slaves.
WAS-WHEN: Emancipation *was when* the slaves were free.

17d Mixed Sentence

Do not mix two ways of expressing the same idea.

Sometimes you will start a sentence one way and finish it another. Retrace your steps: What were the two possible ways of expressing the same idea? Settle for one or the other:

MIXED: Their mother *married* at age eighteen, as *were* many women of her generation.

OPTION 1: Their mother **married** at age eighteen, as **did** many women of her generation. (She **did**, and they **did**.)

OPTION 2: Their mother **was married** at age eighteen, as **were** many women of her generation. (She **was**, and they **were**.)

MIXED: *In case of* obvious inaccuracies in the loan statements *should have been reported* to the regulatory agency.

OPTION 1: **Obvious inaccuracies** in the loan statements **should have been reported** to the regulatory agency.

OPTION 2: **In case of** obvious inaccuracies in the loan statements, **the bank should have filed a report** with the regulatory agency.

17d.1 ***Because/because of*** *Use the combination* because of *as a preposition.* It may be followed by a single word (**because of** rain). However, use *because* alone when you go on to a complete statement, with a subject and a verb (**because** it rained).

MIXED: The class was canceled *because of* not enough students registered.

OPTION 1: The class was canceled **because** not enough students registered.

OPTION 2: The class was canceled **because of** insufficient enrollment.

17d.2 ***Because . . . does not mean*** *Rewrite "Because . . . does not mean" sentences.* They mix a statement telling us *why* something happens with a statement telling us *what* it is. Take out the *because:*

MIXED: *Because* the voters rejected the initiative *does not mean* it was wrong.

STRAIGHT: **That** the voters rejected the initiative **does not mean** it was wrong.

17e Incomplete Structure

inc

Check for excessive shortcuts with items of the same kind.

When a sentence includes several related items in a row, you can omit tags and props that would cause unnecessary repetition. You shorten a statement like "We **were supporting** and still **are supporting** the peace effort." It then becomes "We **were and still are supporting** the peace effort." However, leave out only those forms—like *supporting*—that would cause actual duplication.

17e.1 **Incomplete Verb** *Check for completeness when you shorten one of several related verbs.* Leave out only exactly identical words: The problem **can** [be corrected] **and will be corrected.**

SHORTCUT: The alarm *was sounded* and the safety doors *closed.* (but the doors **were** closed)

COMPLETE: The alarm **was sounded,** and the safety doors **were closed.**

17e.2 **Missing Preposition** *Keep prepositions that are not identical but merely signal a similar relationship.* Keep both prepositions in combinations like the following: admiration **for** and trust **in** the leadership; counting **on** and preparing **for** a recovery.

respect for and faith in

SHORTCUT: Young people have lost *respect and faith in* our leaders.

17e.3 **Shortcut Comparison** *Avoid informal shortcuts in statements making comparisons.* If necessary, spell out more fully what is being compared. Clarify **three-cornered comparisons** like the following. How do the developers fit into the following sentence? Were they also distrustful—or were they also distrusted?

SHORTCUT: The voters distrusted the local government *more than the developers.*

OPTION 1: The voters distrusted the local government more than **the developers did**.

OPTION 2: The voters distrusted the local government more than **they did** the developers.

Fill in **unspecified comparisons** in informal expressions with *more* and *most:*

SHORTCUT: We had *more trouble*, in spite of *the most scenic route.* (more trouble than what? most scenic of what?)

COMPLETE: We had more trouble **than on any previous trip**, in spite of the most scenic route **I had ever traveled**.

✓ ***EDITOR'S TIP:*** Do not leave out the second *as* in comparisons of the "just as good if not better" type:

as good as if not better than

SHORTCUT: Women hired as managers were just *as good if not better than* men.

17e.4 Mismatched Comparison ***Compare things that are really comparable.*** "Her *voice* was as harsh as *a drill sergeant*" compares a voice and a person—instead of comparing two voices. "**Her voice** was as harsh as **a drill sergeant's**" compares two voices.

worse than that of the rest

MISMATCHED: The company's *safety record* was *worse than the rest* of the industry.
(you want to compare two *safety records*)

any other country.

America is more criticized and more imitated than *any country.*
(*any* country would include America)

YOUR TURN 54 **Editing Mixed Sentences**

Rewrite the italicized part of each of the following mixed sentences.

But Is It a Sport?

1 Boxing is more controversial *than any American sport.*

2 In earlier days, fans had *faith and admiration for their heroes.*

3 Young people glorified boxers *more than the journalists.*

4 Today, a fighter's prison record *may be worse than his promoter.*

5 A well-known columnist claims that the moral level of boxing *is as bad as bear-baiting.*

6 *Because some fighters have terrible problems* does not mean that all contenders do.

7 *Stereotyping is when* a few bad apples make us condemn the whole barrel.

18 SENTENCE CHOICES

pass **Make the right choices for effective English.**

With many language choices, the question is not "Is this right or wrong?" The question is "What is most effective in this sentence?"

18a Active/Passive

Use the active voice to focus on who does what.

Most English sentences use **active** verbs. Active sentences focus on who or what is active in a sentence. Who or what takes action? The subject of the sentence tells us who. Then an active verb tells us what is going on: **Poachers slaughtered** the elephant herds. (The verb *slaughtered* is in the **active voice.**) **Passive** sentences focus on the target or the result of an action. In the elephant slaughter, who were the victims? And what was done to them? **The elephants were slaughtered.** Here the target of the activity has been pulled to the front and has become the subject of the sentence. The verb *were slaughtered* is now a passive verb (we say it is in the **passive voice**).

Passive verbs include a form of the helping verb *be:* **is** supported, **are** excluded, **was** broken, **will be** changed, **has been** canceled. In the short passive, whoever or whatever was active has disappeared from the sentence:

ACTIVE:	The police **was interviewing** several suspects.
PASSIVE:	Several suspects **were interviewed** by the police.
SHORT PASSIVE:	Several suspects **were interviewed.**

18a.1 Weak Passive

Avoid the passive when it makes a sentence seem weak or roundabout. Not all passives are bad: The passive is effective when you are putting the spotlight on the result or target of an action. It allows you to pull the target or the victims to the front of a sentence:

EFFECTIVE:	**Millions were uprooted** during the war in Vietnam.
	The city of Warsaw was almost totally **destroyed** in World War II.
	Marijuana laws have been only fitfully **enforced.**

However, many verbs work best when the sentence tells us who does what. When the source of an action is known and important, the passive may make us look at an action from an awkward angle. Passives are weak or roundabout when they seem to play down who does what.

WEAK: *Ulcer-causing delays are encountered* by millions of Americans on the way to work.

STRONGER: **Millions of Americans encounter** ulcer-causing delays on the way to work.

WEAK: With each advance in automated customer service, *more complicated instructions must be followed* by the user.

STRONGER: With each advance in automated customer service, **the user must follow** more complicated instructions.

18a.2 Evasive Passive *Avoid the passive when it seems to hide who is active from view.* In the short form of the passive, the doer or agent has often been omitted: Schools today *are widely criticized* (by whom?). School prayer *is advocated* as an answer to declining morals (by whom?). The governor *has been praised* as a friend of education (by whom?). Fill in the missing source of the action when the shortened passive statement might seem evasive:

ACTIVE: **The religious right is advocating** school prayer as an answer to declining morals.

18a.3 Shifts to Passive *Avoid unmotivated shifts from active to passive.* Do not shift to the passive when the original subject is still active:

SHIFT: We *received* their e-mail in the morning, and it *was answered* the same day. (by whom?)

ALL ACTIVE: **We received** their e-mail in the morning and **answered** it the same day.

SHIFT: After you *complete* the form, it *should be returned* to the agency.

ALL ACTIVE: After **you complete** the form, **you should return** it to the agency.

✓ ***EDITOR'S TIP:*** In much scientific or technical writing, the focus is on the process or the procedure. The description is expected to be **impersonal**—because others should be able to restage an experiment or replicate the procedure. Often the passive has been the conventional style for impersonal description. Even so, today research reports and technical writing are often shifting to a more personal style.

CONVENTIONAL: *Twelve pairs* of whooping cranes *were observed* in their natural habitat.

PERSONAL: **We observed** twelve pairs of whooping cranes in their natural habitat.

YOUR TURN 55 Rewriting for Weak Passive

Convert the following sentences from passive to active.

Your Work May Be Dangerous to Your Health

1 When health warnings are issued by public agencies, they should be taken seriously by concerned citizens.

2 If fish from contaminated waters are eaten, mercury poisoning may be contracted.

3 When living quarters adjoin fields sprayed with pesticide, severe health risks are incurred by the children of migrant laborers.

4 Extended exposure to asbestos was experienced by many workers.

5 Finally the dangers of asbestos contamination were recognized by the public.

6 Today the effects of radiation from electronic equipment are being studied by scientists.

7 Stories of contaminated hamburgers are sensationalized by the press.

8 A panic can be easily created when customers are felled by food poisoning.

9 However, regulations to ensure safety in the workplace are less widely publicized.

10 Industrial safety laws have been strengthened and weakened as legislators follow the winds of public opinion.

18b Strong/Weak Predicate

Restructure weak predicates on the who-does-what model.

The predicate of a sentence makes a statement about the subject. (The predicate of the sentence is the verb and material that goes with the verb.) In a strong sentence, that statement is often direct and to the point: The governor **vetoed the pay raise for public employees.** The voters **voted to end affirmative action.** When sentences seem weak or roundabout, ask: Who does what? Who initiated what? Who is responsible for what?

To strengthen weak sentences like the following, make the subject and the verb answer the question: "Who does what?"

The army did not usually

ROUNDABOUT: *It was not the usual procedure of the army to* pamper recruits.

A store clerk illustrated the trend toward vigilantism by

An example of the trend toward vigilantism was provided by a store clerk running down and killing a shoplifter.

18b.1 Colorless *be* *Convert a weak use of* to be *to a more active verb.* Avoid overreliance on the colorless linking verb *be* and its many forms (including *is, was, were, has been, will be*). Try to substitute a stronger verb that helps your readers visualize who does what or what does what:

TO BE: Excessive tanning *is a cause of* cancer.

NOT *TO BE:* Excessive tanning **causes** cancer.

If you use editing software, it may flag sentences like the following:

joined in

Alice Walker *was a participant in* the early civil rights demonstrations.

keep many groups from

High insurance rates *are a major disincentive for groups* staging public events.

Many American teachers believe in

A basic tenet of many American educators is the Jeffersonian ideal of free universal public education.

18b.2 **-ation/-otion Nouns** *Convert static nouns to active verbs.* Watch for overuse of nouns ending in *-ition, -ation, -otion,* or *-ution.* Much discussion of issues and current developments uses nouns like *attrition, implementation, validation, gentrification, verification,* and *diminution.* However, when you rely too heavily on such words, too much of the action may be in the nouns rather than in active verbs. Try putting the action into active verbs rather than static nouns. Help readers visualize who does what:

STATIC: *Discussion turned to the implementation* of the committee's recommendations.

ACTIVE: **The supervisors began discussing how to act** on the committee's recommendations.

STATIC: There will be an *investigation by the institution of the unauthorized distribution of confidential information* about students.

ACTIVE: **The college will investigate the unauthorized release** of confidential information about students.

18b.3 **Padding and Tags** *Remove grammatical deadwood from your sentences.* If your sentences move slowly or awkwardly, consider trimming sentence parts that serve as props and tags in wordy sentences:

PADDED: *As a doctor, one should* show respect for the patient's wishes.

TRIMMED: **A doctor should** show respect for the patient's wishes.

PADDED: *In my opinion, I was convinced that* this project would prove a turning point in my career.

TRIMMED: This project, **I was convinced,** would prove a turning point in my career.

Trim wordy tags like *the fact is that* (just state the fact) or *the question is whether* (just ask the question).

WORDY: *The fact is that costly new stadiums have* provided few good jobs for the low-income people they displace.

TRIMMED: **Costly new stadiums have** provided few good jobs for the low-income people they displace.

WORDY: *The question is whether* taxpayers who cannot afford tickets should pay for state-of-the-art facilities.

TRIMMED: **Should taxpayers** who cannot afford tickets pay for state-of-the-art facilities**?**

It-is and *There-is* sentences sometimes set the stage for an emphatic statement:

EFFECTIVE: **It is no secret that** taxpayer-financed new stadiums for hometown teams benefit wealthy owners.

There is no excuse for taxing the poor to pay for luxury boxes for the rich.

In weak sentences, however, the *there-is* or *it-is* may be adding unneeded baggage. Unnecessary *who-is* or *who-ares* may also be adding unnecessary weight:

WORDY: *There was* a demonstration participated in by agency employees *who were* denied a pay raise.

TRIMMED: **Agency employees denied a pay raise staged a demonstration.**

WORDY: *It is probable that* the new provisions *that were* approved by the voters will be tied up in court.

TRIMMED: **The new provisions approved by the voters will probably** be tied up in court.

YOUR TURN 56 Highlighting Who Does What

Rewrite the following sentences on the who-does-what model.

1 There is a likelihood that a rebellion against cuts in benefits will take place among the voters.

2 Lack of convenient parking is a cause of shoppers staying away from downtown.

3 Outright condemnation of the exploitation of overseas workers by American companies is rare by mainstream journalists.

4 Active participation in the interaction of the classroom is a must if the stereotype of student apathy is to be overcome.

5 As a social worker, one should try to avoid interference in domestic disputes.

18c Strong/Weak Repetition

rep

Exploit the potential and avoid the pitfalls of repetition.

Repetition can guide our attention and add emphasis, but it can also seem awkward or absent-minded.

18c.1 Intentional Repetition *Use intentional repetition for emphasis.* Deliberate repetition of *a key word or phrase* can help drive a point home:

EFFECTIVE: For many Americans, globalization means the job has gone **overseas,** the car comes from **overseas,** and an **overseas** bank owns the building.

I cannot remember when I was not surrounded by **sports,** when talk of **sports** was not in the air, when I did not care passionately about **sports.**

Repetition of the *same idea* in slightly different form can build up to a high point:

EFFECTIVE: When television constantly presents images of what people have no chance to attain, **frustration sets in, resentment builds up,** and **smoldering rage finally takes over.**

Repetition of a *similar sentence pattern* can add to the impact of related points. In sentences like the following, **parallel structure** gives added force to related ideas:

EFFECTIVE: Commercials try to sell us **cars that** attract women, **scents that** attract men, **seasonings that** flavor our food, and **mouthwash that** will kill the odor later.

We need more patterns of desire. **We need** models of women—and men—who expect everything, and set out to get it. **We need** people in novels as well as in life to show us how to have the courage to walk out.

—Gail Godwin

Parallel structure can line up *opposed ideas* for added impact:

EFFECTIVE: It is better to be **active today** than **radioactive tomorrow**.

Radicals are often accused of being **against everything** and **for nothing.**

YOUR TURN 57 Developing Sentence Rhythm

Write several sentences in which repetition of the same or a similar pattern sets up a strong rhythm or builds up a central point.

EXAMPLE:

If we overfish the oceans, there will be no fish left for anyone; if we overcut the forests, there will be nothing left for the future; if we permit arid land to be overgrazed, it will never come back.

—Molly Ivins

18c.2 rep Awkward Repetition

Edit for unintentional repetition that makes a passage sound clumsy. Unintentionally repeated sounds, words, or phrases can make a sentence awkward. The rewrite of the following sentence eliminates the awkward echo caused by too many *-ation* words:

AWKWARD: Detailed *examination* of the findings of the police *investigation* led to a *reorganization* of the *organization.*

REWORDED: Detailed **study** of the findings of the police **inquiry** led to a reorganization of the **agency.**

The rewrite of the following sentence eliminates the awkward echo caused by too many *-ing* endings:

AWKWARD: *Displaying* nude torsos or *smashing* guitars does not make for *entertaining* and *relaxing listening.*

REWORDED: Displaying nude torsos or smashing guitars does not **entertain** and **relax** the **listener.**

Several *who-is* or *which-are* clauses laid end to end can cause an awkward add-on effect:

officers arresting the protesters who had

AWKWARD: The crowd booed the officers *who had arrested the protesters who had stopped traffic* on the bridge.

19 SENTENCE STYLE

Make full use of the resources of the English sentence.

Good sentences use more of the rich resources of the English sentence than routine plodding writing would. If they are especially well written, we may remember them and want to quote them. Some sentences get the job done, but they strain to do it and are painful to watch. Others have a flair; they make us say "Well done!" "Well said!" They make us say: "That was a pleasure to read."

19a Short/Long

s

Use both short pointed and long well-developed sentences.

Use short sentences to make a point stand out, and use long sentences to fill in detail. Short sentences stand out. They can sum up important points. They are easy to quote and to remember.

POINTED: Our pets eat better than our poor.

A riot is the language of the unheard.

—Martin Luther King

You should write, first of all, to please yourself.

—Doris Lessing

Long sentences fill us in by giving us details, rounding out the picture, and including important ifs and buts. Each of the following well-developed sentences—a snapshot of a workplace, a capsule review of a play—carries a load of information. Each more than carries its weight:

DEVELOPED: The name Bell Labs usually conjures up images of white-coated physicists working in cubicles, equipped with super computers, and subjecting ions to megawatt laser blasts in an effort to improve communication technology.

Sir Thomas More, a man of high position, enjoying the respect of his peers and the friendship of his king, is brought to ruin because he cannot go against his conscience.

Liven up your paragraphs by bringing your readers up short with a pointed sentence that will make them pause and think. Often a short pointed sentence will serve as the key sentence of a paragraph. Then you build up your paragraph with fully developed sentences, each carrying its load of examples and data. Look how short and long work together in the following pairs:

Newspapers give us a distorted picture of the world. They pounce on the unusual: the birth of quintuplets, gang fights, drive-by shootings, celebrities accused of molestation, disowned children of the rich suing their alleged fathers.

Athletic competitions are often praised for building character and bringing out the highest standards of sportsmanship in people. **They often bring out the worst.**

Most of Wyoming has a "lean-to" look. Instead of big roomy barns and Victorian houses, there are dugouts, low sheds, log cabins, sheep camps, and fence lines that look like driftwood blown haphazardly into place.

—Gretel Ehrlich

19a.1 **Choppy Sentences** *Too many short sentences in a row may make writing seem choppy or immature.* One-idea-at-a-time sentences can give us the bare facts. However, they may fail to show the connection between ideas.

CHOPPY: The victim had been goaded beyond endurance. *He finally turned on his tormentors. He shook his fist.*

CONNECTED: **Goaded beyond endurance,** the victim finally turned on his tormentors, **shaking his fist.**

19a.2 **s** **Sentence Overloads** *Rewrite sentences where too many explanations or conditions get in one another's way.* Well-developed sentences often work their way through a whole sequence of ifs and buts. They go from example to example, or from statement to objection and back. But some sentences seem loaded down, sinking under their own weight.

An editor or reviewer might ask you to break up sentences like the following. Too many added-on explanations or conditions seem to get in each other's way:

OVERLOAD: Nitric oxides have an overfertilizing effect on deciduous trees, *which* are trees *that* lost their leaves during the winter, *that* causes them to keep their leaves too far into the winter, *which* makes them sensitive to frost.

BROKEN UP: Nitric oxides have an overfertilizing effect on deciduous trees—**trees that** lost their leaves during the winter. **The excess fertilizer causes them** to keep their leaves too far into the winter **and makes** them sensitive to frost.

OVERLOAD: *When students* are constantly criticized *while they* are learning and *when they* are looking for help in *what should be* a supportive environment they may retreat into a shell.

BROKEN UP: When students are constantly criticized, they may retreat into a shell. **Students who are** learning and looking for help should find themselves in a supportive environment.

19b emp Emphatic/Unemphatic

Change word order for emphasis.

Emphasis makes ideas stand out in the flow of your sentences. Beginnings and endings of sentences are good places for ideas that need special attention:

EMPHATIC START: **Enormous amounts** of time, money, and talent go into commercials.

EMPHATIC END: The most care and the most money are lavished not on programs **but on commercials**.

You can emphasize ideas by pulling them out in front. Changing the normal word order to move something to the front can make it stand out. "I have to see that" is normal. "**That** I have to see" is emphatic.

NORMAL: The networks *schedule blockbuster movies* in prime time.

EMPHATIC: **Blockbuster movies** the networks schedule in prime time. **Public affairs programs** they schedule at obscure hours.

You can emphasize ideas by leaving the most important point to the last:

EMPHATIC: Although Rembrandt died bankrupt, he had been **a successful painter who commanded high fees.** (emphasis on success)

Although Mozart had charmed the aristocrats of Europe, he was buried **in a pauper's grave.** (emphasis on failure)

19c Normal/Varied

var

Vary your sentence rhythms.

The subject-verb pattern is the basic workhorse pattern of the English sentence. It is the normal or default pattern in much workaday writing:

S-V: *Elephants live* in shrinking habitats. *They require* tons of foliage for forage. *The rhinoceros looks* like a tank. *It faces* extinction. *Lovers of wildlife love* these huge lumbering animals. *They look* like survivors from some Stone Age Jurassic Park.

When the basic subject-verb sequence becomes too monotonous, experiment with different positions for modifying or supporting material. For instance, vary your sentence rhythms by putting modifying material up front. Or use it to interrupt the basic pattern. Or work it in at the end.

OPENING: **Requiring tons of foliage for forage,** elephants live in shrinking habitats.

MIDDLE: The rhinoceros, **an animal built like a tank,** faces extinction.

END: Lovers of wildlife love these huge lumbering animals, **looking like survivors from some Stone Age Jurassic Park.**

Try using these ways of varying your sentences in combination:

COMBINED: Passenger pigeons, **once covering the American skies in huge flocks,** are today extinct, **surviving only in the paintings and photographs of early bird watchers.**

YOUR TURN 58 Aiming at Sentence Variety

Write several sets of sentences that play variations on familiar ways of working added material into a sentence. Here are some examples:

1 The University of Mexico is the oldest university in the Americas, **older than Harvard.**

Older than Harvard, the University of Mexico is the oldest university in the Americas.

The oldest university in the Americas, the University of Mexico is older than Harvard.

2 The Acropolis is the ancient temple hill **overlooking the city of Athens.**

Overlooking the city, the Acropolis is the ancient temple hill of Athens.

The Acropolis, **the ancient temple hill,** overlooks the city of Athens.

20 SENTENCE RHETORIC

Practice writing sentences suited for a range of tasks.

When you move from grammar to **rhetoric**, you move from how sentences are put together to what purposes they serve. Rhetoric is the art of purposeful writing, of using the best means to achieve the writer's ends. Not all sentences are suited for every task. For a sentence workout, try your hand at sentence types like the following. Study the purposes they serve. Experiment with using them in current writing assignments.

1 SNAPSHOT SENTENCES Seize on striking details to call up a scene or situation before your reader's eyes. Make your reader say: "Yes, I can see that" or "This sounds like something you observed in real life."

> **A timid-looking young woman sat alone twirling the spaghetti round and round on her fork** while those in the clique whispered and giggled together over their lunches.
>
> **Leather-clad, tattooed, crotch-grabbing** musicians were performing in front of a screaming crowd.

2 EXAMPLES GALORE Effective writers always seem able to think of more than one skimpy example. When you pile on detailed examples, readers don't have a chance to say: "What *are* you talking about?"

> Blue jeans are favored equally by **cowboys, bureaucrats, bankers, fashion designers, deadbeats, and beer drinkers.**
>
> The new cookbooks give recipes for sophisticates: **tofu tornadoes, seaweed supreme, soybean Wellington, and free-range chicken steamed in parchment and garnished with green tomatoes.**
>
> **Applications for credit cards, supermarket coupon books, and come-ons for contests ("You may already be a winner!")** are part of the constant stream of junk mail.

3 INSERTED SPECIFICS Some writers are good at giving readers needed information or key examples on the run. Look at the way writers have *injected* details into a sentence that makes a general point. Listen to the rhythm created by the insertion of added material between the main parts of the sentence.

> The great apes—**chimpanzees, gorillas, orangutans**—are the closest living relatives of human beings.
>
> Sports that promise violence—**boxing, football, soccer, hockey**—attract large crowds.
>
> Trials **for murder, rape, robbery, burglary, vandalism, assault, fraud, and littering** cost communities millions of dollars.

4 DETAILS FIRST Some writers give us a general label—telling us how wonderful or depressing a person or situation is—but don't go on to provide specifics. The remedy is to practice giving the specifics *first.*

> Eager faces pressed against a rusty chain link fence, an overwhelmed cashier trying to make change, rows of fans hoping for that one-in-a-million flyball, Polish dogs and peanuts sold by the ton—**this is an afternoon at the ballpark.**
>
> The smells of espresso, chocolate, and pastries; the whispering of the espresso machine; fattening cookies and pastries in the pastry case; the clanking of the cash register over the soft playing of a guitar—**this is a coffeehouse.**
>
> Smudged tile floors, graffiti on the walls, a dirty mirror, and toilet paper strewn about the stalls—**this is a public restroom.**

5 PARALLEL IDEAS When you make your sentences parallel, you line up related ideas in grammatically similar form. You set up a pattern that the reader can recognize and follow with pleasure. You are signaling to your reader: "Here—compare this with this."

> Knowledge that is **known only to a few** can be **used only by a few.**
>
> —Gloria Steinem
>
> **Being on time** when the rest of the world is behind gives the impression of **being ahead.**
>
> —Jean-Luc Godard
>
> **We read** often with as much talent as **we write.**
>
> —Ralph Waldo Emerson

6 PARALLEL OPPOSITES Sometimes you will line up not similar but opposed ideas in grammatically parallel form. You are signaling to your reader: "Here—*contrast* this with this."

> Scientists have to be interested **in things**, not **in persons.**
>
> —Marie Curie
>
> We must begin **the journey to tomorrow** from **the point where we are today.**
>
> —Garrett Hardin
>
> We have exchanged **being known in small communities** for **being anonymous in huge populations.**
>
> —Ellen Goodman

7 SHORT AND LONG When similar long sentences begin to drone on, you may want to bring the reader up short at a brief pointed statement. Then you use a second longer sentence to explain.

> **Writing is like a mirror.** Whoever goes to the mirror risks a confrontation with the self.
>
> **One writes of one thing only—one's own experience.** Everything depends on how relentlessly one forces from this experience the last drop, sweet or bitter, it can possibly give.
>
> —James Baldwin

8 THE MATURE SENTENCE Some sentences give us only the bare-minimum facts: "Americans work out." Other sentences carry a full load. Try your hand at telling the whole story in one single fully developed, mature sentence, giving us the when, where, why, and how. Start with a minimal statement like "Politicians raise money," "Polluters degrade the environment," or "Americans love pets." Then turn it into a packed sentence.

MINIMAL: Americans work out.

MATURE: **Every day** Americans work out **on specialized equipment in their local health clubs to rejuvenate their deteriorating bodies in hopes of preventing heart disease, strokes, and arthritis.**

MINIMAL: Homeless people have nowhere to turn.

MATURE: Homeless people have nowhere to turn **because they have lost their houses, their jobs, their strength, and their motivation to turn their lives around.**

9 EMPHATIC WORD ORDER What do you do when you want an idea to have special attention? Try pulling a sentence part from later in the sentence up front. Make it stand out for emphasis. For instance, reverse the usual who-does-what order to put the target or the object first. Or reverse the what-is-what sequence to start with a label that usually follows later.

NORMAL: We do not need advice. We can always use volunteers.

EMPHATIC: **Advice** we do not need. **Volunteers** we can always use.

NORMAL: Human prejudice is deeper than a dry well.

EMPHATIC: **Deeper than a dry well** is human prejudice.

YOUR TURN 59 The Range of Sentences

For each of the nine patterns just shown, write two or three sentences that follow a similar pattern. Do not try to follow the original pattern in every detail, and use your own subject-matter. Before you write your own, study the originals and sample responses like the following. Read them out loud, listening for the rhythm of each sentence.

1 SNAPSHOT SENTENCES

The irritated driver **impatiently tapped her fingers on the steering wheel** and **wistfully looked at the clock** while waiting for the light to turn green.

2 EXAMPLES GALORE

The old cookbooks gave recipes **for tuna-noodle casseroles, meatloaf from leftovers, hamburgers made to go farther with Hamburger Helper, and beanie-weanie surprise.**

Turbulence, cramped seats, tiny bathrooms, overly chatty seat neighbors, and bland meals all contribute to the discomfort of air travel.

3 INSERTED SPECIFICS

The big cats of the wild—**cheetahs, tigers, and panthers**—are formidable predators.

Alternatives to traditional sports—**fencing, synchronized swimming, ultimate Frisbee, and dirt biking**—were making their way into the high school curriculum.

4 DETAILS FIRST

Gold coins "valued at ten times the asking price," Vegematics ("Slice 'em and dice 'em"), authentic Ginza knives used by Real Japanese Chefs, and ugly dinettes with instant credit—**this is a mail order catalog.**

Dirty stubble-ridden faces glaring at the dingy cement walls, the antagonizing jingle of the guards' keys, following a schedule planned by higher authority, and fearing for one's life at every meal and during every shower—**this is the average day in jail.**

5 PARALLEL IDEAS

To succeed as a writer, you must have **the perseverance of a used-car dealer, the patience of a saint,** and **the hide of an armadillo.**

Chefs **nourish the body** just as writers **nourish the soul.**

6 PARALLEL OPPOSITES

Politics is the art of **making one's own record look good** and **making the other person's look bad.**

The role models young girls see today in magazines are **ultra-slim models** rather than **healthy women comfortable with their weight.**

Relatives are given, while **friends are chosen.**

7 SHORT AND LONG

Athletes face a thicket of regulations. Track stars have had their track records disallowed for using steroids or wearing shoes with too many spikes.

Golf is a form of exercise. According to an article in *Sports Illustrated*, in years of playing on courses, Jack Nicklaus covered the equivalent of walking across the United States five times.

8 THE MATURE SENTENCE

Polluters degrade the environment every day by **relying on their own cars rather than carpooling, throwing away aluminum cans rather than recycling, and not properly discarding litter and toxins.**

Politicians raise money **during countless fund-raising events and private solicitations to pay for television ads, mass mailings, and voter registration campaigns.**

9 EMPHATIC WORD ORDER

Sadder than an empty wallet is life without experience.

More boring than watching grass grow is a life without risks.

21 FOCUSING ON STANDARD ENGLISH

Shift gears from nonstandard English or a limited dialect to standard English.

Standard English is the language of the media and of school and office. It is also the written language, the language you usually see in print. Like our national currency, standard English is good everywhere. It is in fact good way beyond our national borders as an international medium of communication. As part of the globalization of English, airline pilots, scientists, rock musicians, and computer nerds around the world communicate in English.

Earlier, people in most countries often spoke local varieties or **regional dialects.** Especially in isolated areas, these sometimes drifted far apart. People coming from rural communities learned the national standard when they went to school, moved to the city, or joined the army. In Europe, these regional varieties or dialects were often different enough to be almost another language. (Dutch was once a German dialect.) In this country, the migrations of newcomers and immigrants and the leveling influence of the media have generally kept regional English from becoming a barrier to communication. Yankees can usually tell Southerners by their speech patterns but understand what they are saying.

The language differences that matter in this country are social dialects or **class dialects.** Young people who grow up speaking the language of the local turf or neighborhood need to master standard English when advancing to the mainstream of education or employment. They learn to shift gears from the private English of home or neighborhood to the public English of school and office. To succeed in American society, most immigrants became **bilingual**—they learned English as a second language. Many native-born American students have always been **bidialectal**, speaking and writing standard English as a second dialect.

21a Nonstandard Verbs

std

Work on verbs as key indicators of standard English.

Since every sentence has one or more verbs, nonstandard forms can quickly identify the user as a nonstandard speaker. Generations of rural children were reminded that in standard English there ain't no such word as *ain't*. Other markers of nonstandard English are verb forms like *he don't/she don't* and *had went*. Look out for nonstandard verb forms in editing for standard English.

21a.1 Forms of *be* *Concentrate on standard uses for the many forms of the verb* **be.** Words like *is, are, was, were,* and *has been* are everywhere in English sentences. They are the different forms of the verb *be*. This word with its many different forms is used as a linking verb, helping pin a label on the subject of the sentence (the time **is** ripe; whales **are** mammals). It is also used as a helping verb helping make up complete verbs (the grapes **are ripening;** the leaves **were turning**).

The various forms of *be* are part of the small change of English grammar. They pattern as follows:

am	I **am** ready, I **am** surprised
is	he **is** new, she **is** absent, it **is** obvious; time **is** up
are	we **are** pleased, you **are** welcome, they **are** confused; the rules **are** clear
was	I **was** there, he **was** delayed, she **was** glad, it **was** unfortunate
were	we **were** notified, you **were** invited, they **were** absent

Study the differences between nonstandard and standard forms:

NONSTANDARD	STANDARD
I is, you is, we is, they is	I **am,** you **are,** we **are,** they **are**
we was, you was, they was	we **were,** you **were,** they **were**
I been thinking, he been laid off	I **have been** thinking, he **has been** laid off

If you grew up hearing nonstandard forms from family or friends, go over sets like the following to help the standard forms sink in:

STANDARD: we **are** scheduling an appointment; we **have been** looking for you; they **were** waiting at the airport; I **am** giving you another chance; the gates **were** locked; the ordinance **has been** repealed; you **were** not expected

ORAL PRACTICE 1

Complete sets like the following, and read them over several times. Complete several sets by yourself, or share in a group effort where each participant adds one or more examples.

1 He **was** early; they **were** late.

She **was** friendly; they **were** hostile.

The soup **was** hot; the beans _________.

The night **was** quiet; the days _________.

The concert **was** crowded; tickets _________.

(add other similar pairs)

2 I am single, but **I have been** married.

She was working, but **she has been** laid off.

He was in prison, but he _________.

Her ratings were poor, but she _________.

Buses were often late, but the service _________.

(add other similar pairs)

21a.2 Missing *-s* Ending

For ordinary verbs, concentrate on forms showing singular and plural. Especially, look for changes from one to several for action now (**present tense**): One person **buys** a ticket; several people **buy** a ticket. He **works** late; they **work** together. She **does** the right thing; they **do** the right thing. Be sure to use the *-s* ending for one single thing or person—a third party, with action now (**third person singular**).

THIRD PERSON (one):

the parent **consents,** the minister **preaches,** the instructor **teaches,** the bus **leaves,** the store **closes,** the FBI **investigates,** the answering machine **records,** the attempt **fails,** the plane **takes** off

ALL OTHER:

the parents **consent,** ministers **preach,** attempts **fail;** we **know,** you **owe** us, they **forget**

Look out for **doesn't/don't** as a special indicator of nonstandard or dialect usage: One person **doesn't** care; several **don't** care; he **doesn't** qualify/they **don't** qualify:

THIRD PERSON (one):

the bus **doesn't** stop here; it **doesn't** matter; the news **doesn't** surprise me; **doesn't** it bother you; the rule **doesn't** apply here

ALL OTHER:

the buses **don't** stop here; the differences **don't** matter; we **don't** remember, you **don't** count, **they** don't care

Use the *-s* ending after *he, she,* or *it* (third person). Don't use the *-s* ending after *I, we, you,* or after plural subjects.

know
NONSTANDARD: I *knows* the difference.

forget.
You always *forgets.*

live
We *lives* here.

ORAL PRACTICE 2

Read over the following sample set designed to reinforce the standard form for third person singular. Then run through several similar sets using the *-s* form. Make up several complete sets by yourself, or share in a group effort where each participant adds one or more examples to the same sentence.

EXAMPLE:

On an ordinary day, a police offer **checks** a stalled car, **stops** a speeding driver, **writes** a ticket, **listens** to the driver's excuses, **tracks** down a drunk motorist, **administers** a sobriety test, **gives** a minilecture about felony drunk driving, **answers** an emergency call, **arrests** an abusive spouse, **helps** reroute traffic after an accident, and **doesn't** get off work till after dark.

YOUR TURN:

On an ordinary day, a teacher _________.

On an ordinary day, a worker in a child care center _________.

On an ordinary day, a student in a writing class _________.

On an ordinary day, (fill in a subject of your choice) _________.

21a.3 Nonstandard Past *For some common verbs, make sure to use standard forms for the past.*

Avoid nonstandard verb forms as you shift from present to past with verbs like *grow, know,* and *throw:*

NONSTANDARD	STANDARD
growed, knowed, throwed	**grew, knew, threw**
drug, bursted	**dragged, burst**

Change to a standard past form when a nonstandard dialect uses the same form for present and past:

came
He *come* here all last year.

wrote
They *write* to me last week.

If you grew up hearing nonstandard forms, go over sets like the following to help the standard forms sink in:

STANDARD: the supervisors **dragged** their feet; they **grew** their own corn; no one **knew** the truth; the judge **threw** out the lawsuit; a new star **burst** upon the scene; my last year's roommate always **wrote** letters home; I first **came** here two years ago

See **10d** for a rundown of standard verb forms.

21a.4 Verb with *have/be* *Watch out for verb forms like* had went *and* was tore.

Standard English often uses three different forms of the main verb for different uses in a sentence: We **go** now, we **went** yesterday, we **had gone** before. It **takes** time now, it **took** time before, it **has taken** them a long time. We **are writing** now, we **wrote** last week, we **had written** before that.

In nonstandard English, the second of these forms often does double duty (we *go* to church, we *went* to school—we *had went* to town). Study verbs that require the *different third form* after a form of the helping verb *have (has, has been, had been)* or the helping verb *be (am, is, are, was, were)*.

NONSTANDARD	STANDARD
had *went*, has *wore* off, had *broke*	had **gone,** has **worn** off, had **broken**
was *tore*, had been *froze* earlier	was **torn,** had been **frozen** earlier

ORAL PRACTICE 3

Complete the following sample sets designed to reinforce standard forms of irregular verbs. Read them over several times. Then make up several complete sets by yourself. Or share in a group effort where each participant adds one or more sets using the three different basic forms of a main verb like **begin, break, choose, know, speak, steal, tear, throw,** and **write.**

EXAMPLE: Today the wind **blows**; yesterday it **blew**; it has **blown** all week.

1 My nephew **goes** to Sunday school; I __________ myself at his age; all my siblings have __________.

2 Commuting **takes** time; it __________ longer last year; it has __________ me hours.

3 People who fish **freeze** their catch; we __________ salmon last season; some fish is __________ at sea.

4 My family **grows** wheat; their parents __________ wheat also; the grandparents had __________ other crops.

5 Athletes **break** records; track stars __________ records last month; many records were __________ at the last Olympics.

21a.5 **Missing *be*** *Supply the missing* is *or* was *in statements like* He cute *or* That a lie. In a language like Russian, no linking verb like *is* or *are* is needed in a statement pinning a label: He **actor.** She

politician. That **a big mistake.** In English, leaving out a form of the linking verb **be** (**am, is, are, was, were**) is nonstandard.

NONSTANDARD	STANDARD
Monday *a holiday.*	Monday **is** a holiday.
That number *wrong.*	That number **is** wrong.
The new mayor *a woman.*	The new mayor **is** a woman.

Insert the missing form of *be* in sentences like the following:

His grandfather ∧ **was** a lieutenant in the army.

Puerto Rico ∧ **is** not a state.

Chemistry ∧ **was** his best subject.

All offices ∧ **will be** closed on Monday.

21b Nonstandard Pronouns

std

Recognize common nonstandard uses of pronouns.

Like verbs, pronouns are high-frequency items that can quickly identify someone as speaking a nonstandard variety of English. In rural American dialects, people used to say "That book is *hisn*" (rather than **his**); "the fault is *yourn*" (rather than **yours**). Nonstandard forms like *hisself* and *them UFOs* are still common in popular speech in big cities as well as small towns.

21b.1 ***-self* Pronouns** *Know the standard forms of the -self pronouns, like* himself *(singular) and* themselves *(plural).* These so-called **reflexive pronouns** are often used for emphasis (he told me **himself**). They also in other ways point back to someone already mentioned (they know how to protect **themselves**). Keep nonstandard pronouns like *hisself* and *theirself* from surfacing in your writing.

NONSTANDARD	STANDARD
hisself, meself	**himself, myself**
theirself, theirselves	**themselves**
ourself	**ourselves**

21b.2 ***them* as Pointer** *Edit for expressions like* them youngsters *or* them bureaucrats. Replace *them* when it is used as a nonstandard substitute for the **pointing pronouns** (demonstrative pronouns) **these** or **those.**

NONSTANDARD	STANDARD
how about *them Bears*	how about **those Bears**
we need to move *them barrels*	we need to move **these barrels**

21b.3 **Repeated Pronoun** *Take out the pronoun in noun-pronoun combinations like* the President he. Do without the *he* or *she* that takes up the subject again in combinations like *my father he* or *her grandmother she.*

My father never
My father he never showed emotion.

Her sister wrote
Her sister she wrote regularly.

21c Double Negative

std

Take out the double or triple negatives common in popular speech.

Take out double negatives: it *don't* make *no* difference; they *never* meant *no* harm. Double negatives are expressions that say *no* twice. In today's standard English, the double negative is a no-no. Rewrite to make the sentence say *no* only once: It **doesn't** make **any** difference; they **never** meant **any** harm.

NONSTANDARD	STANDARD
there *wasn't nobody* here	there **wasn't anybody** here
can't nothing top that	**nothing** can top that
it *won't never* happen again	it will **never** happen again

21d Double Comparative/Superlative

std

Avoid doubling up the signals for comparative or superlative.

Avoid nonstandard forms that add *-er/-est* or *more/most* to a word that is already a form used in comparisons: *worser* (should be **worse**); *more better* (should be **better**); *most cheapest* (should be **cheapest**). Most adjectives and some adverbs add either the endings *-er* and *-est* or the words *more* and *most* for use in comparisons. We use the **comparative** form in comparing two or more: **faster, better, deadlier; more** efficient, **more** cautious (also **more** efficiently and **more** cautiously). We use the **superlative** form for the top rank: **fastest, best, deadliest; most** efficient, **most** cautious. Some irregular forms for comparisons include **good-better-best, bad-worse-worst, little-less-least.**

Remember: Do not use *worser, more faster,* or *most rudest.*

21e Standard *a/an*

std

Know when to replace *a* with *an.*

Standard English requires **an** instead of *a* before a word beginning with a vowel (*a, e, i, o, u*): **an** accident, **an** exceptional opportunity, **an** unlikely story.

an **an** athlete, **an** A, **an** earful, **an** inmate, **an** orchestra

Use *a* only before consonants (the remaining letters): **a** briefing, **a** car, **a** year, **a** shareholder. However, go by pronunciation and not by spelling. Make sure the consonant is actually pronounced: **a** house but **an** honest effort, **a** failure but **an** F. Remember that *u* is sometimes pronounced as a consonant (**a** useful hint) and sometimes as a vowel (**an** unnecessary move).

ORAL PRACTICE 4

Insert **a** or **an** as required in standard English. Read the completed set over several times. (For added practice, make up a similar set.)

______ athletic scholarship, ______ unexpected guest, ______ useful address, ______ administrator, ______ A and ______ B, ______ D and ______ F, ______ college, ______ organization, ______ institution, ______ invitation, ______ summons, ______ honest mistake, ______ horrible misunderstanding, ______ honor, ______ new address, ______ old address, ______ Internet address, ______ aunt and ______ uncle, ______ Canadian father and ______ Australian mother

Check the **glossary (Section 37)** for *being as, had ought/hadn't ought to,* and *without.*

YOUR TURN 60 English as a Second Dialect

A. The following sentences are adapted from dialogue in a play reproducing the nonstandard dialect of people in rural New England. What dialect features do you recognize? Rewrite the sentences in standard English.

1 Wait till ye've growed his age.
2 They was chores to do, wa'nt they?
3 He's gone and married again. The preacher from New Dover, he brung the news.
4 I yells "Whar you going?" and his old snake eyes was glittering in the sun.
5 We never had no time to meddle.
6 Why didn't you never do nothing?
7 I ain't like him—I ain't hisn.
8 Let's light out and git this morning.
9 They been stringing ye.
10 I remember it right well.

B. The following sentences are adapted from dialogue in a play reproducing the Black English of African Americans who came north from the South. What dialect features do you recognize? Rewrite the sentences in standard English.

11 I told him you was a preacher.
12 How you get to be a preacher?

YOUR TURN 60 *(continued)*

13 It come to me in a dream.

14 He don't want to hear all that.

15 I went through one of them doors.

16 There was three or four other men standing there.

17 Ain't nobody going to ask you.

18 You sure these size nine?

19 Is they ready for you?

20 I don't care if he black or white.

PART THREE

EDITING FOR PUNCTUATION AND MECHANICS

The appearance of your text on your page is the first thing that strikes the reader. Layout, punctuation, spelling—these meet the eye. When punctuation and spelling do their job well, your readers hardly notice them. However, punctuation slows down the reader when needed signals seem to be missing or unnecessary marks get in the way.

Early writing systems had no punctuation marks. Our own writing system has punctuation marks that regulate the flow of traffic on the page. Some of our punctuation rules are very useful—clarifying meaning and preventing misunderstanding. Others are customary—they reflect what is usually done. When you study the English system of punctuation, you can sort out the functions that punctuation serves under roughly three headings:

- The most basic marks set off complete sentences—**end punctuation.**

- Much punctuation joins statements that are becoming part of a larger combined sentence—**linking punctuation.**
- Much punctuation deals with the many added sentence elements that we can use to build up a single bare-bones statement—**inside punctuation.**

English spelling has been a special challenge for generations of students. Our spelling system is an inheritance from the past. We do not have a one-to-one relationship between sound and letter. For example, several letters in *night* and *through* have not been pronounced in centuries. (If there were a better fit between sound and letter, we might spell the word *phonics* as *fonnix*.) Nevertheless, spelling words correctly is a basic test of an educated person.

PUNCTUATION MARKS A Reference Chart

PERIOD	at end of sentence	22b
	for ellipsis	27c
	with abbreviations	29f
COMMA	before coordinator (*and, but, or*)	23a
	before nonrestrictive clause (*whereas, though*)	23b
	after introductory dependent clause	23b
	with relative clause (*who/which/that*)	23c
	with nonrestrictive modifier	24a
	after introductory modifier	24a
	with connecting adverb (*therefore, however*)	23d
	with transitional expression (*after all, for example*)	24a
	between items in a series	24b
	in a series of parallel clauses	22c
	between coordinate adjectives	24d
	with dates, addresses, and measurements	24c
	with parenthetic elements	24f
	between repeated or contrasted elements	24e
	to introduce a direct quotation	27a
SEMICOLON	between closely related sentences	22c
	with connecting adverb (*therefore, however*)	23d
	before coordinator	23a
	in a series with items containing commas	24b
	outside a quotation	27b
COLON	to introduce a list or an explanation	26a
	to introduce a formal quotation	27a
	between title and subtitle	26a
DASH	to show a break in thought	26b
	before summary at end of sentence	26b
	to set off modifier with commas	26b
QUOTATION MARKS	with direct quotations	27a
	for quotation-within-quotation	27a
	with end marks	27b
	with technical terms	27d
	to set off titles	27e
EXCLAMATION MARK		22a
QUESTION MARK		22a
PARENTHESES		26c
SLASH		26d

22 COMPLETE SENTENCES AND FRAGMENTS

p

Apply basic punctuation rules for the sentence.

Three punctuation marks serve as basic **end punctuation**—they bring something to a full stop. The **period** signals the end of a statement. The writer might go on to a next sentence, but the current statement is complete in itself.

STATEMENT: Space probes have traveled to distant planets**.**

Not all complete utterances are statements marked off by periods. We use **exclamation marks** to signal strong requests or commands. We use **question marks** to turn statements into questions.

REQUEST: Support the American space program**!**

QUESTION: Is there intelligent life in other worlds**?**

When editing for sentence punctuation, look for two common problems. Not everything marked off by a period is really a complete sentence that can stand by itself. Something that should be part of another sentence may have been split off as a **fragment.** At the opposite extreme, two complete statements may be too loosely joined together.

22a Exclamation/Question

/ !
/ ?

Use exclamation marks sparingly; use question marks for direct questions.

The **exclamation mark** signals forceful requests or commands. It also signals strong surprise or other strong emotion. Use exclamation marks only when you want to make a very strong point. (Do not sprinkle your writing with them! And do not use more than one at a time.)

REQUEST: Help save the rain forest**!**

STRONG POINT: Animals that evolved over millions of years are now down to a few dozen surviving specimens**!**

The **question mark** marks questions directly addressed to the reader. Remember to use the question mark when a question has become long or involved.

LONG QUESTION: **Should we allow** wildlife to disappear that has evolved over millions of years**?**

In **indirect** questions, you no longer use the exact wording of the original question. Instead, you are working the information into a larger sentence—which would not be read with a questioning tone of voice. Do not keep the question mark when converting a direct to an indirect question.

DIRECT QUESTION: They asked: **"Is global warming a myth or a real possibility?"**

INDIRECT QUESTION: They asked **whether global warming was a myth or a real possibility.**

22b Sentence Fragment

frag

Make a sentence fragment a part of a complete sentence.

Use the **period** to mark off complete sentences. The period brings a sentence to a full stop. Each of the following sentences makes a full statement.

COMPLETE: The network is reducing the staff in its news division. It is putting added money into sports. Big-name announcers and analysts will be back on the air.

Complete sentences can stand on their own—each with its own subject and verb. Do not carry over into your writing the incomplete stop-and-go sentences of informal speech. If you can, hook up a **sentence fragment** with the sentence of which it should be a part.

on the road fighting the traffic.

FRAGMENT: Commuters spend hours on the road. *Fighting the traffic.*

car pool lanes for families and buses.

Planners reserve car pool lanes. *For families and buses.*

early risers who try to beat the traffic.

Roads are clogged with early risers. *Who try to beat the traffic.*

Sometimes you will decide to turn the fragment into its own separate sentence.

FRAGMENT: The media hail miracle medications. *With unknown long-range effects.*

NEW SENTENCE: The media hail miracle medications. **Sometimes the long-range effects will not be known for years.**

See **9** for full coverage of sentence fragments.

22c Comma Splice

CS

Use the semicolon to prevent comma splices.

Two statements simply put next to each other need a stronger link than a comma. Use a **semicolon** to show that the two statements are closely related. Use the semicolon when there is no link like *and, but,* or *if* to join the two statements. However, you may also decide to use a period to separate the two statements altogether.

problem; it is

COMMA SPLICE: The parking problem is not *a problem, it is* a disaster.

here; they park

COMMA SPLICE: Students no longer park *here, they park* in the garage.

PERIOD: Students no longer park here. **They park in the garage.**

✓ ***EDITOR'S TIP:*** When *more than two* closely related statements appear in a row, commas are acceptable. Three statements that are very similar or parallel in grammatical form may make up a **series.** A set of three like the following drives home an overall point:

COMMAS: The sound system was blaring, the light show was dazzling, the fans were in ecstasy.

See **8a** for full coverage of comma splices.

22d Fused Sentence

FS

Separate two complete statements that have been run together.

If there is no punctuation at all to separate two complete sentences, the result is a **fused sentence**. Supply the missing period. Or use a **semicolon** to show that the two statements are closely related.

FUSED: The meeting *was canceled the insurance* was prohibitive.

SEPARATE: The meeting **was canceled. The insurance** was prohibitive.
The meeting **was canceled; the insurance** was prohibitive.

FUSED: Our candidate *withdrew she was* ineligible.

SEPARATE: Our candidate **withdrew. She was** ineligible.
Our candidate **withdrew; she was** ineligible.

YOUR TURN 61 Editing for End Punctuation

Retype the following sentences to eliminate fragments, comma splices, and fused sentences. Leave satisfactory sentences as they are.

Can Money Buy Your Vote?

1 Voting is the citizen's basic responsibility. In our society.
2 Totalitarian elections are rigged. Ninety percent vote for the leader.
3 Refugees show their view of the system. By voting with their feet.
4 Here many voters stay home they lose faith in the system.
5 Theoretically the voters have a choice in a system like ours.
6 Their vote will not make a difference. When candidates must raise huge sums.
7 Wealthy candidates spend twenty or thirty million. Of their own money.
8 Big tobacco supports friendly senators, the gun lobby supports friends of the gun.
9 Business invests heavily in elections it outspends labor ten to one.
10 Turnouts are large in other countries. When issues like divorce are at stake.
11 Large numbers voted in the first free election in former Soviet Russia.
12 Eighty-nine percent voted against the party candidate. Endorsed by the government.

23 LINKING PUNCTUATION

no cm
cm SC

Apply the rules for linking two or more statements in a larger combined sentence.

You face decisions about punctuation when you combine two or more statements in a larger sentence. For instance, you may use **no comma** to set off a second statement (an added clause) when you need it to make the main point. You may need a **comma** to set off a second statement when you add optional, take-it-or-leave-it information. You will need a **semicolon** to set off the second clause when it follows a formal or weighty logical link like *therefore* or *however*.

23a Comma for Coordinator

cm

Use the comma before links like *and* or *but*.

And and **but** are **coordinators** (short for *coordinating conjunctions*). They make two statements "work together." Use a comma when each statement (or clause) has its own subject and verb. Other coordinators are **so, for, yet, or,** and **nor.** Each of the two statements is true independently of the other.

COMMA: The thin look was in**, and** yogurt sales soared.

Jogging is fine**, but** walking is healthier.

Aerobics became monotonous**, so** many turned to yoga.

Warming up is important**, for** the body dislikes sudden stress.

Doctors warn against diet fads**, yet** miracle diets keep appearing.

Supplements need to be monitored**, or** they may cause problems.

There is no magic bullet**, nor** do we expect one.

Put the comma before—and not *after*—the **and** or **but**:

known, but approval

MISUSED COMMA: The medication was *known but, approval* had been delayed.

Links like *and* and *but* also have other uses. Use no comma when they simply link *two words or phrases*—not two clauses, each with subject and verb.

NO COMMA: Executives are protected by stock options **and golden parachutes.**

We called his number several times **but without success.**

The buyer heard the news **and withdrew the offer.**

✓ ***EDITOR'S TIP:*** A coordinator may link two statements that already include commas of their own. You may then use a **semicolon** instead of a comma at the major break:

SEMICOLON: Now in the Big Bend the river encounters mountains in a new and extraordinary **way; for** they lie, chain after chain of them, directly across its way.

—Paul Horgan

23b Comma for Subordinator?

cm
no cm

Use a comma only when the subordinator adds optional information.

Words like **if, unless, because,** and **whereas** are **subordinators** (short for *subordinating conjunctions*). They introduce material that tells us when, where, why, or how. An *if* or *because* changes a self-sufficient, independent clause to a **dependent** clause, which normally cannot stand by itself. "If interest rates go up" does not become a sentence until we answer the question: "If interest rates go up, *then what?*" In each of the following examples, a subordinator links a dependent clause to the main clause.

DEPENDENT: Home buyers profit **if interest rates go down.**

Rate changes affect everyone, **because they raise the cost of money.**

Punctuation with subordinators depends on how essential the added clause is to the overall meaning of the sentence. Does it make all the difference? Or is it only added optional information?

23b.1

no cm

No Comma for *if/when*

Use no comma when you add a statement that makes all the difference. Words like **if, when, unless, after, while,** or **where** usually bring essential conditions into a sentence. They make the difference: a rebate **only if** you act now; a car **only after** you graduate. We call such an added statement **restrictive;** it limits or restricts what the sentence says.

NO COMMA: Your credit card will be canceled **if** you send payments late.

The phone will be disconnected **unless** you pay.

Low introductory rates may go up **after** you sign up.

If you reverse the order and put the *condition first,* use a comma to show where the main sentence starts:

COMMA: **If** you send payments late, your credit card will be canceled.

After you sign up, low introductory rates may go up.

Sometimes a clause starting with **when** or **where** does not really specify time or place. Instead, it merely adds to something that has already been specified or explained. Use a comma:

COMMA: They were awaiting the **fall showings, when** the new fashions are introduced.

Corporations maintain offices in **Delaware, where** the laws favor the corporation.

23b.2

cm

Comma for *although/whereas*

Use a comma when the main sentence is true, no matter what you add. When you use subordinators like **although** and **whereas,** the main sentence is true *regardless* of what the added statement says. The same is true with links like **no matter how** and **no matter what.** Use a comma before the added nonessential, nonrestrictive clause:

COMMA: He kept charging to his card**, although** his account was overdrawn. (he kept charging *regardless*)

Interest on loans was low**, whereas** interest on card balances was high. (it was low *regardless*)

They kept the family farm**, no matter how** unprofitable it became. (they kept farming *regardless*)

Because follows a comma if the reason it introduces is added optional explanation. But sometimes the added reason is the whole point of the sentence—NO COMMA.

COMMA: Many new immigrants were **Asian, because** racial quotas were lifted.

NO COMMA: Many immigrants **came because** the old country had offered them no future.

PUNCTUATION ESSENTIALS

Comma/No Comma with Subordinator

Subordinators (subordinating conjunctions) signal relationships like the following. The ones in the first group usually introduce essential, restrictive information.

No Comma

TIME: when, whenever, while, before, after, since, until, as soon as, as long as

PLACE: where, wherever

CONDITION: if, unless, provided

INTENTION: so that, in order that

REASON: because, since

The words in the second group usually introduce nonessential, nonrestrictive information.

Comma

COMPARISON: as, as though, as if

CONTRAST: though, although, whereas, no matter how, even though

✓ ***EDITOR'S TIP:*** Note a special use of **however** as a subordinator starting a nonessential, nonrestrictive clause. Use it with a comma:

COMMA: Traffic fines have to be paid, **however** unreasonable they may seem. (they have to be paid *regardless*)

23c Comma for *who/which/that?*

cm
no cm

Set off nonessential, nonrestrictive relative clauses.

Who (whom, whose), which, and **that** bring in added material. They tell us which one or what kind: the runner **who tripped**; drugs **that kill pain.** They fill in background material: Madonna, **whose road trips earn millions.** *Who, which,* and *that* are **relative pronouns**, and the clauses they bring into a sentence are **relative clauses.** They may appear at different positions in the main clause:

> People **who know how to talk** can buy on credit.
>
> —Creole proverb
>
> Cajuns spoke **Creole, which was a local French dialect.**

To punctuate relative clauses, you need to ask: Comma or no comma?

23c.1 Restrictive *who/that*

Do not set off restrictive relative clauses. They are restrictive when we need to know which one or what kind. ("A mole is **a spy who infiltrates the enemy's bureaucracy.**") Such relative clauses narrow the possibilities. They single out one thing or person or group:

NO COMMA: **Ex-convicts who carry guns** should go to jail. (only those)

In an emergency, call **the lawyer whose name appears on this card.** (this particular one)

The **number that he gave us** was no longer in service. (that specific number)

✓ ***EDITOR'S TIP:*** The pronoun *that* almost always introduces a restrictive clause. Shortened relative clauses with a pronoun like *that* or *whom* left out are always restrictive:

NO COMMA: The reviews [that] **we sent** were lost in the mail .

The lawyer [whom] **the firm retained** charged large fees.

23c.2 Nonrestrictive *who/which* *Set off nonrestrictive relative clauses.* A nonrestrictive clause does not limit the scope of the main clause; it does not single out one from a group or one group among many. It adds an explanation or reminder. Or it answers a question like "What else about them?" We already know which one or what kind. We now merely learn more about something already identified: Beethoven, **who was deaf;** aspirin, **which kills pain.**

Nonrestrictive clauses are nonessential. We do not need them to pinpoint one item or idea among several.

COMMA: The bill targeted **illegal aliens, who lack proper documentation.** (all do)

Sharks differ from **whales, which surface to breathe.** (applies to all)

We drove down **Pennsylvania Avenue, which leads past the White House.** (we've already focused on the street)

Use *two commas* when the nonrestrictive clause interrupts the main clause:

TWO COMMAS: Computers**, which perform amazing feats,** do break down.

YOUR TURN 62 Punctuating Dependent Clauses

Which of the following combined sentences need a comma? Put *C* for comma or *No* for no comma after the number of the sentence.

America's Musical Pioneers

1 **Before** jazz and rap became popular __________ American music had already conquered the world.

2 Stephen Foster composed "Oh! Susanna!" and other hit songs __________ **that** spread around the globe.

3 **When** a contemporary was traveling in India __________ he heard people sing "Oh! Susanna!"

4 They were singing in Hindi __________ **which** was the native language in the city of Delhi.

YOUR TURN 62 *(continued)*

5 Foster was a musician ________ **who** was paid poorly for his music.

6 He remained poor ________ **while** other popular composers prospered.

7 Foster worked at the time of the minstrel shows ________ **which** combined African and European musical traditions.

8 Popular music thrived in vaudeville shows ________ **until** radio and television took over.

9 People deserted the vaudeville theaters ________ **because** they could have a front row seat in their own living rooms.

10 The movies were offering top talent ________ **whereas** the local stages could offer only third-string performers.

23d Semicolon with *however*

SC

Use the semicolon with links like *however* and *therefore*.

Logical links like **however** and **therefore** are **connecting adverbs** and require a semicolon. Other logical links that work like *however* are **moreover, furthermore, consequently, indeed, in fact, besides,** and **nevertheless.** The words in this group also go by other names, including **adverbial conjunctions** or **conjunctive adverbs.** They are movable links: They may appear later in the second statement. Put the semicolon where the two statements join nevertheless.

SEMICOLON: The contract had expired; **therefore** the nurses went on strike.

The contract had expired; the nurses **therefore** went on strike.

The judge issued an injunction; **nevertheless** the teachers walked out.

The judge issued an injunction; the teachers walked out **nevertheless**.

PUNCTUATION ESSENTIALS

Logical Links and the Semicolon

Commonly used logical links signal the following relationships. Use them with a semicolon when they link two closely related statements.

OBJECTION:	however, still, nevertheless, nonetheless, on the other hand
LOGICAL RESULT:	therefore, consequently, accordingly, hence, thus
ADDED SUPPORT:	moreover, furthermore, similarly, besides, likewise, also
OPTION:	otherwise, instead
EMPHASIS:	indeed, in fact, as a matter of fact
TIME:	meanwhile, subsequently

✓ ***EDITOR'S TIP:*** Traditional rules require an additional comma—or additional commas—to mark off the *however* or *therefore* from the second statement. These added commas are no longer used in the **open punctuation** of current newsmagazines and are being phased out in current guidelines for effective writing.

ADDED COMMA:	The phone company had been broken up; **however,** years later the pieces were merging again.
ADDED COMMAS:	The merger was touted as improving efficiency; thousands of workers**, therefore,** lost their jobs.

23e No Comma for Noun Clause

no cm

Use no comma before a noun clause.

Use no punctuation when the place of a noun is taken by a clause-within-a-clause. Clauses replacing a noun are called **noun clauses.** They start with words like **that, why, how, where, who,** and **which:** tell me **that you understand**; explain **why it failed;** ask them **where they live.** Other words that might start a noun clause are **whoever** and **whatever:** take **whatever is available.**

NOUN:	The mayor announced **her plans.**
NOUN CLAUSE:	The mayor announced **that she would run for re-election.**
NOUN:	The paper never revealed **the source.**
NOUN CLAUSE:	The paper never revealed **who had leaked the news.**

Take out commas used mistakenly to set off noun clauses:

	found that excessive force
WRONG COMMA:	The police review board *found, that excessive force* had been used.

YOUR TURN 63 **Punctuating Combined Sentences**

What should be the punctuation at the space left in each combined sentence? After the number of the sentence, write *C* for comma, *SC* for semicolon, *NC* for no comma. (If your instructor requires added optional commas, rewrite the sentences including the added punctuation.)

Our Embattled Schools

1 Much public debate focuses on education ________ which is Topic One for many parents.

2 Schools are becoming crowded ________ therefore year-round classes are again being discussed.

3 Educators debate ________ where magnet schools should be tried.

4 Magnet schools attract gifted students _________ these may be missed in ordinary classrooms however.

5 Some political leaders promote voucher plans _________ and others oppose them.

6 Vouchers give parents money _________ that could pay for tuition at private schools.

7 Opponents claim _________ that tax money could then pay for religious instruction.

8 Teaching reading becomes a political issue _________ there is strong support for phonics.

9 Phonics asks students to sound out letters _________ but then phonics becomes fonix.

10 If parents are serious about education _________ they honor teaching and learning.

24 INTERNAL COMMAS

cm
no cm

Know where to use commas within a single sentence.

The comma is the multitasking mark that regulates traffic within a single sentence. A dozen basic comma rules cover most of the situations where you have to choose between a comma and no comma.

24a Commas for Modifiers

cm
no cm

Know when to set off modifiers in a sentence.

Modifiers come into a bare-bones sentence to add information or fill in detail. Many such modifiers are **prepositional phrases**, starting with words like *on, at, by, of, from, as, with, without, during, before, after, behind, across,* and *around.* These phrases usually blend into the sentence without a break.

NO COMMAS: Many immigrants perished **during the trek across the deserts and mountains of the West.**

The trail **from St. Louis to the Northwest** became known **as the Oregon Trail.**

Many other modifiers building up detail in a sentence are **verbals.** They are forms of verbs that do not serve as the complete verb but serve some other purpose in a sentence. Look for *-ing* forms coming into a sentence as modifiers (the oxen **pulling the wagons**; the riders **scouting the trail**). Look for forms ending in *-ed* or corresponding forms like *broken* or *known* (the traveling party **advertised in the handbill**; the leader **chosen by the group**). Look for a *to-* form, alone or as part of a phrase (the distances **to be covered**). To punctuate such modifiers, the basic question is: How important is the added material to the main point of the sentence? If it's added comment or optional information, use a comma or commas. If it's needed to make the main point, use no punctuation.

COMMAS: The Mormons**, persecuted for their beliefs,** kept moving west.
(the main point is that they kept moving west)

NO COMMAS: Members **challenging the leadership** were severely criticized.
(the main point is that it was those members who were criticized)

24a.1
cm
no cm

Essential/Nonessential *Use commas to set off optional, nonessential information.* The modifiers in the following sentences serve to single out, rule out, or narrow down. They are needed to show to what the statement applies. They are **restrictive**—no comma.

NO COMMAS: The restaurant excluded guests **without shoes.**
(other guests were welcome)

We saved containers **suitable for recycling.**
(we discarded the others)

The counselor **running the camp** talked like a drill sergeant.
(only that particular one)

Modifiers are *non*restrictive when they merely tell us more about something we have already identified. Commas set off the added information—not needed to tell us which one or what kind.

COMMAS: Her friend Myra, **replacing the camp counselor,** used a new system.
(we already have her name)

Recycled paper, **made from newspapers and books,** helps save the forests.
(we already know the kind of paper)

An **appositive** is a second noun placed next to the first as an added label. Most appositives are not needed to single out one thing among others (it's already been labeled and identified). They are usually added comment and therefore nonrestrictive. Set them off with commas. However, use no comma when the added detail is needed to tell two things apart:

COMMAS: Pizza, **the original finger food,** became the national dish of the young.

NO COMMA: They had trouble telling apart **Washington the city** and **Washington the state.**

✓ ***EDITOR'S TIP:*** Use **dashes** to set off a modifier that already contains one or more commas. The dashes then signal the major breaks:

DASHES: Her sister**—a stubborn, hard-driving competitor—** won many prizes.

24a.2
cm
no cm

Introductory Modifiers *Know when to set off an introductory modifier.* After a long modifier, show where the main sentence starts. Use a comma after **prepositional phrases** of three words or more:

COMMA: **Like many immigrants,** their grandmother came as an indentured servant.

In colonial etiquette books, women were instructed in the art of passivity.

Set off introductory **verbals** or verbal phrases regardless of length. Look for *-ing* forms coming as modifiers before the subject (**present participles**). Look for forms ending in *-ed* or corresponding forms like *broken* or *known* (**past participles**). Look for an introductory *to*-form, alone or as part of a phrase (**infinitives**):

COMMA: **Smiling awkwardly,** the new arrivals looked at the camera.

Warned of the ice, the ship took a southern route.

Known for its shallows, the river challenged even experienced pilots.

To read more about early Americans, click on Colonial America.

Set off verbal phrases that go with the sentence as a whole. Such sentence modifiers (**absolute constructions**) do not modify any one part of a sentence but go with the whole sentence. They may appear at either the beginning or later or at the end of the sentence. Some comment on the sentence as a whole; some provide explanation or background for the main statement:

COMMA: **To tell the truth,** I never heard the name.

The biographer did well, **considering the lack of documents.**

Their guides having failed them, the travelers turned back.

24a.3
cm
no cm

Transitional Tags *Commas are optional with expressions linking two sentences.* Tags like **after all, of course, unfortunately, on the other hand, on the whole, as a rule,** and **certainly** help us go on from one sentence to the next. Depending on how much you would make the transitional tag stand out when reading aloud, set it off from the rest of the sentence. The commas here are now often omitted in the **open punctuation** of much writing about current affairs.

OPTIONAL: **After all,** Chicago was a working class city.

New York had**, of course,** once been a Dutch town.

Los Angeles**, on the other hand,** had been part of Mexico.

Newspapers played up the incident**, of course.**

Tags that are set off require two commas if they do not come first or last in the sentence:

COMMAS: Institutions do not**, as a rule,** welcome dissent.

Use commas when transitional tags add *explanation or examples* to the same sentence. Use a comma *before* but not *after* **such as** and **especially.** Use a comma before *and* after tags like **for example, for instance, namely,** and **that is.** (The second comma is optional except for *that is.*)

ONE COMMA: Industry giants fight over programming languages, **such as Java.**

Companies discover new marketing tools, **especially websites.**

TWO COMMAS: Internet buying is growing rapidly**, for example, shopping for used or rare books.**

Two areas of Internet sales have been extremely profitable**, namely, stock market transactions and pornography**.

Internet sales promote disintermediation**, that is, cutting out the middleman.**

YOUR TURN 64 Putting In Needed Commas

For each of the following sentences, write down the words that should be followed by a comma and add the comma.

EXAMPLE: On the main island of Britain the Welsh hearing English constantly are now mostly bilingual.

ANSWER: **Britain, Welsh, constantly,**

Millions of Americans Are Bilingual

1 Throughout American history millions of Americans have been bilingual.

2 In many American homes parents speak Spanish to children answering in English.

3 To give their children a headstart other immigrant parents speak only English in the home.

YOUR TURN 64 *(continued)*

4 Some rural Americans in Louisiana a former French colony still speak Cajun French.

5 Coming to kindergarten immigrant children listen to teachers speaking English a foreign language for them.

6 Without special assistance students knowing no English fall behind in math or geography.

7 To help Chinese-speaking children some schools offer classes taught in Chinese.

8 Students with limited English proficiency still learning English can keep up with the basics.

9 Opposed by many educators the English-only movement fights bilingual education.

10 Bilingual Americans speaking more than one language are divided on the issue.

24b Commas for Series

cm

Use commas with three or more items of the same kind.

A **series** is a set of three or more parts of the same kind: **red, white, and blue; single, married, or divorced; good seats, top talent, and free parking.** Link the items in a set of three by commas, with the last comma followed by an *and* or an *or* that ties the whole set together.

SERIES: New sports became popular: **soccer, jogging, and lacrosse.**

The fans **threw bottles, taunted officers, and rocked cars.**

Only 18 percent of this country's 56 million families are conventionally "nuclear," with **bread-winning fathers, homemaking mothers, and resident children.**

—Jane Howard

The basic **A, B, and C** pattern can be stretched to four elements or more:

SERIES: The stand sold **nuts, raisins, apples, and every other kind** of organic lunch.

The repertory of the humpback whales includes **groans, chirps, clicks, bugles, and roars.**

Groups of words in a series may already contain commas. To prevent misreading, use **semicolons** to show the major breaks:

SEMICOLONS: Successive waves of African American music have swept over our popular culture: **the blues, from the South; reggae, from Jamaica: and rap, from the urban centers.**

✓ ***EDITOR'S TIP:*** In informal or journalistic writing, the last comma in a series is often left out. However, many teachers and editors still require the last comma. Use it to be safe:

LAST COMMA: Computer programs can now check student papers for **spelling errors, awkward sentences, and sexist phrases.**

YOUR TURN 65 Punctuating Items in a Series

What words in the following sentences should be followed by series punctuation or other needed marks? After the number of the sentence, write each such word, followed by the needed punctuation.

EXAMPLE: Lurid crimes sex scandals and sensational lawsuits start a feeding frenzy among the nation's journalists.

ANSWER: **crimes, scandals,**

The Rise of Tabloid Journalism

1 In the tabloids homelessness the national debt and global economic disaster do not exist.

2 The sex lives of movie stars TV personalities and politicians get top billing.

3 The inside story of celebrities filing for divorce checking into an alcoholism clinic or battling a drug problem is revealed.

4 Gruesome details about celebrities struggling with Alzheimer's breast cancer or obesity are explored.

5 According to media critics different kinds of journalism now cater to the same public appetite for gossip scandal and character assassination.

6 The *New York Times* a so-called newspaper of record your favorite hometown paper billing itself as a family newspaper and a supermarket throwaway feed the appetite for scandal and titillation.

24c With Dates/Addresses

cm

Use commas when giving data with several parts.

Dates, addresses, page references, and measurements often come in several parts. Mark them off by a comma (**New York, New York**). The last item is followed by a comma if the sentence continues. Separate date and year only if the month comes first (**October 3, 1999** but **3 October 1999**.)

DATES: The date was **Tuesday, September 29, 1998.**

On March 12, 1992, several water pumps stopped working at the nuclear plant.

ADDRESS: Forward mail to **127 Trimbull Street, Hurdville, Alabama,** starting the first of the month.

REFERENCE: The quotation is from **Chapter 5, page 43, line 7,** of the second volume.

Remember especially the comma that separates *city and state:*

CITY/STATE: The accident occurred at a nuclear power plant near **Harrisburg, Pennsylvania.**

At the **Lordstown, Ohio, and South Gate, California,** plants, laser equipped robots measure car bodies to make sure they meet exact specifications.

Use commas to separate the parts of *measurements* employing more than one unit of measurement. Here the last item is usually not separated from the rest of the sentence:

MEASURE: It is rare for a halfback to be only **five foot, nine inches** tall.

Five pounds, three ounces is an unusual weight for this fish.

24d With Coordinate Adjectives

cm
no cm

Use commas with coordinate adjectives.

Coordinate adjectives work together to tell us which one or what kind. They are interchangeable adjectives. Use a comma between them when you can reverse their order: a **brutal, bruising** sport (or a **bruising, brutal** sport); **slanted, sensational** reporting (**sensational, slanted** reporting would be the same thing). Use the comma only when an *and* could take the place of the comma. Both labels are equal parts of the same picture: a **long, highly critical** report (it was both long *and* highly critical).

COMMA: The **snoopy, brash** new magazine pilloried the most **annoying, appalling** people in New York and the nation.

The crowd expected a **hypocritical, cliché-ridden** speech. (they expected it to be both, not necessarily in that order)

Remember that not every pair of adjectives follows this pattern. Do not use the comma when you cannot change the order of two adjectives:

NO COMMA: The **smooth new** manager calmed the **angry male** customer. ("new smooth manager" and "male angry customer" wouldn't work)

✓ ***EDITOR'S TIP:*** Often an adjective and a noun combine to make up a label for a type of person or object: a **public servant**, a **short story**, the **black market.** An adjective that comes before the combined label modifies the combination as a whole—no comma.

NO COMMA: The book could be called a short novel or a **long short story.**

The governor was a **privacy-loving public servant.**

24e Repetition/Contrast

cm

Use a comma between repeated or contrasted elements.

Use commas between expressions that repeat the same idea:

REPETITION: **Innovate, innovate!** This is the law of Silicon Valley.

RESTATEMENT: We were there in the nine days before **Christmas, the *Navidad.***

Use the comma in sentences that line up several examples or implications of the same idea *in parallel form*:

PARALLEL: Undergraduate education must prepare the student **not to walk away from choices, not to leave them to the experts.**

—Adele Simmons

Use the comma also in sentences that line up *opposing ideas* in parallel form:

PARALLEL: The purpose of a college is **education, not training.**

Students should learn **to ask the right questions, not just to give the right answers.**

24f Parenthetic Commas

cm / no cm

Use commas to set off slight breaks or brief interruptions.

Some parts of a sentence briefly interrupt the normal flow of thought. They suspend the normal sentence traffic for a while, the way an officer might briefly halt motor traffic to let a pedestrian cross. Use commas to signal such brief comments you add to or insert into a sentence. Use **two commas** when you interrupt the sentence.

COMMENT: The loan was denied**, it seems.**

She opened the door for them**, a serious mistake.**

The trophy**, her first,** stood on the mantelpiece.

You will need these interrupting commas especially when you transcribe dialogue. Use them for the tags that start a comment or that address the listener:

TAG OPENING: **No,** she is not here.

TAG QUESTION: She is your friend**, isn't she**?

DIRECT ADDRESS: Your friends**, Marilyn,** are worried about you.

Use the interrupting commas when you hear a slight break in a sentence because of a change from usual word order:

NORMAL ORDER: **For her parents' generation,** work was a religion.

UNUSUAL ORDER: Work**, for her parents' generation,** was a religion.

YOUR TURN 66 Using Internal Commas

Which words in the following sentences should be followed by a comma? After the number of the sentence, write the word and a comma after it.

Women of the West

1 Surrounded by bearded Western males early women of the West often had little use for conventional femininity.

2 They might have trekked from St. Louis Missouri to Portland Oregon or to Los Angeles California.

3 Pioneering women entered traditional male reserves such as business and politics.

4 Driving a sixteen-yoke team of oxen Arizona Mary made a fortune.

5 Tillie Baldwin a bronco-busting rodeo star created new stunts and new fashions for the rodeo.

6 Martha Jane Canary known as Calamity Jane left behind feminine frills to ride for the Pony Express and scout for the U.S. Army.

7 Rose of Cimarron another outlaw is pictured wearing an old-fashioned gown but carrying a gun.

8 Carry Nation hatchet in hand launched her campaign of saloon smashing hymn singing and liquor spilling.

9 Among women in politics Mary E. Lease became a leader in the People's Party telling farmers to raise less corn and more hell.

10 Leaving behind conventional restrictions some women discovered smoking drinking and gambling.

11 Some of them fought for women's right to vote in the Wyoming territory smoked in public and rode horseback astride.

12 An editor in Boise Idaho denounced weak wasp-waisted putty-faced daughters of fashion.

25 UNNEEDED COMMAS

no cm

Use commas only where required by conventional comma rules.

Do not sprinkle your sentences with commas at places where you think you might hear a pause if the sentence were read aloud. Remove unnecessary or unconventional commas in the following places especially:

- When the subject of a sentence is loaded down with added material, do not put a comma *between subject and verb* just because your readers might need to catch their breath:

information campaigns and parental warnings do

UNNEEDED: Unfortunately *information campaigns and parental warnings, do* not always prevent the young from experimenting with drugs. (no comma between double subject—compound subject—and verb)

with unanswered questions cannot

Forms *with unanswered questions, cannot* be processed. (no comma after prepositional phrase with essential information)

- Do not set off *restrictive information*—needed to tell us which one (or which ones) or to narrow our choices:

Students with unreturned library books will

UNNEEDED: *Students, with unreturned library books, will* not receive their grades. (applies only to those)

Christians who see the Bible as literal truth were

Christians, who see the Bible as literal truth, were becoming a potent political force. (not all do)

- Put a needed comma before a coordinator like *and* or *but* (not after it)—and do not use a comma when the *and* links two words or phrases instead of two complete statements (or clauses):

had been strong, but U.S. teams

MISPLACED: Canadian hockey teams *had been strong but, U.S.teams* were becoming powerhouses.

Banner and the

UNNEEDED: Hockey fans often listen to the Star-Spangled *Banner, and the* Canadian anthem.

PUNCTUATION ESSENTIALS

Removing Unnecessary Commas

Take out the unnecessary commas in the following situations.

BETWEEN SUBJECT AND VERB:
The needle on the dial, swung erratically.

BETWEEN ADJECTIVE AND NOUN:
Action movies put a premium on crude, brutal, violence.

BEFORE PREPOSITIONAL PHRASE:
He had built his first computer, in a garage in California.

WITH RESTRICTIVE MODIFIER:
The hunt was on for migrants, entering the country illegally.

WITH RESTRICTIVE CLAUSE:
American diplomats, who speak Chinese, are rare.

WITH COORDINATOR JOINING ONLY WORDS OR PHRASES:
The Vikings reached Greenland, and the coast of North America.

AFTER (INSTEAD OF BEFORE) COORDINATOR:
They threatened to sue but, they never did.

WITH COORDINATOR JOINING TWO DEPENDENT CLAUSES:
Mortgages become cheap when interest rates drop, and when money is plentiful.

BEFORE NOUN CLAUSE:
We already know, what the future holds for the poor of the world.

AFTER *SUCH AS*:
The new plan called for more teaching of basics, such as, English and algebra.

AFTER LAST ITEM IN A SERIES:
Tourists, panhandlers, and pickpockets, mingled in the city square.

✓ ***EDITOR'S TIP:*** Other elements added to a sentence may require a comma in situations similar to those above.

26 SPECIAL MARKS

Know when to use colons, dashes, parentheses, and other special marks.

26a Using Colons

:/
no :/

Use the colon to add a list or explanation to a complete sentence.

The colon says "as follows." Use it to introduce a **list or explanation.** The colon signals that further explanation or detail is coming:

LIST: The term *Asian* covers many diverse **cultures: Chinese, Vietnamese, Filipino, Pakistani.**

EXPLANATION: Candidates short on ideas discovered a potent **new medium: attack ads.**

Make sure the colon follows a complete sentence. In the following example, the introductory statement (*common mistakes are*) would not make a complete a sentence. The added detail should become part of the sentence without a colon.

are being undercapitalized and

NO COLON: Common mistakes of new small businesses *are: being undercapitalized and* becoming overextended.

✓ ***EDITOR'S TIP:*** The colon may follow an introductory tag that is not a complete sentence if it introduces an **extended list,** set off as a separate column or chart:

EXTENDED LIST:

The park rules forbade:

1 walking on the grass
2 sleeping in the park
3 bringing in your dog
4 riding bicycles
5 kissing in public

PUNCTUATION ESSENTIALS

Using the Colon

Special uses of the colon include the following:

START A QUOTATION:	**Gloria Steinem said:** "Adults still need unconditional love."
FOLLOW A GREETING:	**Dear Senator Feinstein:**
ADD A SUBTITLE:	***American Voices: Culture and Community***
GIVE PUBLICATION DATA:	**New York: Simon,** 1998.
GIVE PAGE NUMBERS:	*Vogue* **July 1998: 211.**

26b Using Dashes

—/ no —/

Use dashes to signal a major break.

With most keyboards, use two hyphens (with no space on either side) to make a dash.

26b.1 Dramatic Dash

Use the dash (or two dashes) to set off words for dramatic effect. The dash then calls special attention to what follows:

> Schools began to stress a new kind of literacy—**computer literacy.**
>
> A force more powerful than logic—**namely, habit**—rules our writing system.

26b.2 Interrupting Dashes

Use dashes when you interrupt a sentence for needed examples or explanations:

> Simplified spellings—**thru, alright, dialog**—always find supporters.
>
> Our numerals—**1, 2, 3, and so on**—make one single sign stand for the whole word.
>
> Some symbols—**asterisks and apostrophes**—do not stand for sounds at all.

The material you insert may be words or phrases but also sometimes a *whole sentence:*

Some languages—**Hebrew and Arabic are examples**—are written from right to left.

26b.3 **Connecting Dash** *After introductory examples, use a dash when you go on to the point:*

Tribespeople from Laos, refugees from Guatemala, Jews from the former Soviet Union, medical students from Pakistan—**all share in the American Dream.**

✓ ***EDITOR'S TIP:*** When transcribing the stop-and-go patterns of speech, you may use a dash when breaking off a *half-finished thought:*

> Computerized translation machines will soon—**maybe they are already here.**

26c Using Parentheses

( )/ no ( )/

Use parentheses to play down inserted material.

Put parentheses around something you mention in passing. (You put them around explanations or examples that some people might welcome but that are not essential.) We call such added comments *asides*—they should not get in the way of the main point:

ADDED COMMENT: Pictographic writing **(writing based on pictures)** does not use letters for separate sounds.

A single symbol **(resembling a bird, perhaps)** stands for a whole word or a syllable.

Chinese symbols **(more complicated than our letters)** stand for words, not sounds.

Parentheses often signal optional backup, including *dates, addresses, page numbers*, and the like.

PAGE NUMBERS: The statistics on affirmative action **(page 42)** are eye-opening.

DATES: The birth date of King Tut **(about 1370 B.C.)** and the dates for his reign as Pharaoh of Egypt **(1361–1352 B.C.)** tell the story of a boy king.

! ***LITERACY ALERT:*** If you start a parenthesis, make sure you close it again at the end of the insert.

(on Pennsylvania Avenue) is

ADDRESS: The White House *(on Pennsylvania Avenue is* America's most famous address.

26d Slashes

Use slashes for special purposes.

Official records and documents may use slashes as dividers in series of numbers: **Series 2A/469.** When you do not set off lines of poetry but instead run them in in your text, use slashes to show line breaks:

SLASH: One of Shakespeare's best-known poems begins: "Let me not to the marriage of true minds / Admit impediments."

27 MARKING QUOTATIONS

Identify clearly all quoted material.

How do you show that you are bringing what others have said into your own text? Study the ways we use quotation marks and other marks when introducing and marking quotations. Look at how

PUNCTUATION ESSENTIALS — Punctuating Quotations

STANDARD QUOTATION:
The columnist wrote, "The important thing is to be in the buzz."

FORMAL OR WEIGHTY QUOTATION:
The rules were explicit: "No guns allowed on school property."

QUOTED PHRASE:
She said that the law added "legislative oomph" to the anti-spam movement.

SPLIT QUOTATION:
"Consumer outrage," the editorial said, "has prompted the new legislation."

QUOTE-WITHIN-QUOTE:
According to the biographer, "Whitman always dreamed of the 'true America.'"

QUOTED QUESTION:
Her standard question was: "Who stands to lose, and who stands to gain?"

QUESTIONED QUOTE:
Did the article actually say, "Ten billion pieces of spam a year are clogging the Internet"?

OMISSION:
The law says: "All businesses employing two or more employees . . . require a license."

INSERTION:
The entry read: "The third day of the climb [June 18] was a disaster."

INDIRECT QUOTATION:
A French law says that prying into a public official's private life is punishable by a year in jail.

we place quotation marks in relation to other punctuation. Know how to show deletions, additions, or any other changes that you made in the original text.

27a Direct/Indirect

Know how to introduce and punctuate direct quotations.

Use **quotation marks** to enclose all material you quote directly, word for word. In **direct quotation**, you reproduce exactly what someone else wrote or said:

DIRECT QUOTE: According to the report, **"Spam mail often hawks sex sites, pyramid schemes, and miracle drugs."**

When you use **indirect quotation**, you put someone else's ideas into your own words. Indirect quotation enables you to get at the gist of a statement or pull out the key points of a passage. In indirect quotation, you do *not* use quotation marks. You rely on an introductory source statement or **credit tag** to answer the reader who is likely to ask: "Who said?"

INDIRECT QUOTE: According to the report, **spam mail often peddles pornography, promotes pyramid schemes, or touts miracle drugs.**

The report claimed **that spam mail often peddles pornography, promotes pyramid schemes, or touts miracle drugs.**

! ***LITERACY ALERT:*** *Remove* quotation marks when you convert the original quotation to an indirectly quoted version:

MISUSED QUOTE: The tourist asked *whether "Michelangelo's original David was still on display in the piazza?"*

INDIRECT QUOTE: The tourist asked **whether Michelangelo's original David was still on display in the piazza.**

27a.1 **Identifying Quotations** *Know how to use quotation marks and other marks when punctuating direct quotations.* Use a **comma** to separate the quotation from the credit tag—the statement that identifies the source.

COMMA: The writer said, **"At various times, Christian leaders have taught that makeup was sinful."**

"Diet articles deal with food as if it were a foreign agent," the report said.

Use a **colon** instead of the comma for a more formal or emphatic introduction:

COLON: Mark Twain said: **"One person's comma is another person's colon."**

Use *no comma* with **partial quotations.** Use no comma when you quote only part of a sentence, or when a very short quoted sentence becomes part of a larger statement:

QUOTED PHRASE: Justice Brandeis called the **"right to be left alone"** the most valued right of civilized people.

One engineer called the company's drug-testing program **"a paranoid overreaction."**

SHORT QUOTE: **"Know what you can work at"** was the Victorian answer to **"Know yourself."**

Use *no comma* when the credit tag follows a question or exclamation:

NO COMMA: **"Did the paparazzi kill Princess Diana?"** the headline asked.

"To rest is to rust!" the poster said.

Check punctuation for **interrupted quotations.** Use commas before and after if the credit tag splits one complete sentence:

COMMAS: **"Both marijuana and alcohol,"** Dr. Jones reports, **"slow reaction times on a whole spectrum of tasks."**

Use a period (or semicolon) after the credit tag if it splits *two complete sentences*. Avoid a comma splice:

said. "Forming

COMMA SPLICE: "Our language is changing," the article *said*, "*forming* close ties is now called bonding."

27a.2 Single Quotation Marks *Show when the person you quote is in turn quoting someone else.* Use **single quotation marks** for the quotation-within-the-quotation.

QUOTE-WITHIN-QUOTE: In the words of his biographer, "Millions agreed with Ibsen when he said: **'It's time to move some of the boundaries.'**"

The report concluded: "The **'No Vacancy'** sign still often greets minority families looking for a place to live."

27a.3 Block Quotations *Set off long quotations as block quotations.* If your quotation is going to run to more than four lines, set if off as a block—*without quotation marks*. Indent it about an inch or *ten spaces*. Do not use additional paragraph indentation for the first line of your block quotation. (If you set off *several* paragraphs, use the additional paragraph indentation for the later paragraphs.)

BLOCK QUOTATION:

Disintermediation—cutting out the middleman—has become the new buzzword. People go to the ATM machine rather than to a teller to get their money. They order furniture on the net without going to a furniture store. As a business columnist said,

> Media watchers have been pointing to the way the Internet allows users to bypass the people mediating between producer and consumer—salespeople, realtors, and also journalists. When Congress puts a report on a sex scandal on the Web, it cuts out the media middlemen and lets interested members of the public point and click straight to the dirt.

Set off **lines of poetry** as block quotations, but center them on the page.

BLOCK QUOTATION:

> In the words of the poet Guiterman:
>
> The grizzly bear whose potent hug
> Was feared by all is now a rug.

27b End Marks

/ " End quotations correctly.

When you close a quotation, know where to place the final quotation marks. Keep commas *inside*, semicolons *outside* a quotation:

COMMA: As he said to the rescuers, **"I'm all right,"** he collapsed.

SEMICOLON: The sign said: **"No access to the sea";** however, we decided to push ahead.

Keep end punctuation *inside* the quotation except in special situations. Make sure a period comes before a final quotation mark:

PERIOD: The letter said: "You may already have **won $1,234,500."**

A question mark or exclamation mark usually also comes before the closing quotation mark. However, keep it *outside* the quotation if you are asking a question about the quotation. Keep it outside if you are using an exclamation mark to show surprise or indignation about the quotation:

QUOTED QUESTION: The poet kept saying: **"Where are they now?"**

QUESTIONED QUOTE: Who said, **"To err is human, to forgive divine"?**

QUOTED SHOUT: The officer shouted: **"Clear the road!"**

SHOUTED QUOTE: He actually said: **"You don't count"!**

Do not normally duplicate a terminal mark at the end of a quotation. Use only one question mark when you ask a question about a question:

QUERIED QUESTION: Did anyone ask, **"What can I do to help?"**

> **!** *LITERACY ALERT:* Remember to use quotation marks to end your quotation. Make sure you *close* a lengthy or involved quotation:
>
> END OF QUOTE: An article on several aborted satellite launchings in recent weeks started by saying: "Worldwide, people are becoming more dependent on satellites for pagers, mobile phones, military security, **and more."**

27c Insertion/Omission

[ ]/ el

Signal any changes you make in quoted material.

Identify comments or clarification that you insert into a quotation. Put them in **square brackets:**

INSERTION: The entry read: "Left Camp B Tuesday, February 7 **[actually February 6].** Are trying to reach Camp C before we run out of supplies."

In the words of the judge, "The members of the tribe **[the Paiute]** have clearly been denied their treaty rights."

Some writers insert **[sic]** into a quotation to show that a misspelling or inaccuracy was in the original text. This use of *sic*—meaning "this is how it was, and I am not responsible"—is often condescending. Try to do without it.

If you cut or delete something from a quotation, show that you have left out unnecessary or irrelevant material. Indicate the omission by three periods, called an **ellipsis.** Handbooks used to call for three *spaced* periods, but most software today has a single keystroke for the three periods showing omission.

OMISSION: The report concluded on a pessimistic note: "The cause of the crash . . . may never really be known."

If the omission comes after a complete statement in the original text, use a sentence period and then add the ellipsis (for a total of four periods).

OMISSION: "To be a bird is to be alive more intensely than any other living creature. . . . They live in a world that is always present, mostly full of joy." So wrote N. J. Berrill, Professor of Zoology at McGill University.

✓ ***EDITOR'S TIP:*** In special kinds of *scholarly writing* (like articles in scholarly journals or doctoral dissertations), the writer may be asked to show that ellipsis points were not already part of the quoted text. Square brackets then signal that the ellipsis points were added to the text to show an omission.

SIGNALED OMISSION: In the words of a professor zoology at McGill University, "To be a bird is to be alive more intensely than any other living creature. [. . .] They live in a world that is always present, [. . .].

27d Words Set Off

ital / " "

Set off words not used as part of your ordinary working vocabulary.

Use italics to set off words that are not part of your ordinary use of language. (Italics may be shown by underlining in a typed manuscript.) Sometimes quotation marks are used for words that may be new or difficult for the reader.

- Use italics when discussing **words as words**—for instance, talking about their history or multiple meanings:

WORD AS WORD: The word ***comet*** comes from the Greek ***aster kometes,*** meaning long-haired star.

Our word ***assassin***, from the Arabic ***hashshashin***, originally meant "hashish smoker."

- Use either italics or quotation marks for unusual or difficult **technical terms:**

TECHNICAL: She explained the **"Skinner box,"** a device used by behaviorist psychologists.

- Use italics to identify **foreign words.** Italicize words borrowed from foreign languages and not yet fully assimilated. Dictionary makers use italics or a special symbol for entries that they decide will still be foreign to many readers. For instance, they may italicize the Russian ***samizdat***, for literature published behind the back of Big Brother.

FOREIGN: For a Bolivian ***campesino***, the pay for a bird for the illegal parrot trade is not bad.

Young Latin American men are very touchy these days about ***machismo***, best translated as "an emphasis on masculinity."

—Linda Wolfe

Many **legal and scientific** terms borrowed from Latin or Greek are still Latin or Greek to the layperson and are italicized:

LEGAL: A writ of ***certiorari*** is used by a superior court to obtain judicial records from an inferior court or a quasi-judicial agency.

SCIENTIFIC: The California live oak—***Quercus agrifolia***—began to evolve more than ten million years ago.

✓ ***EDITOR'S TIP:*** Use quotation marks to show that an expression is not your own. These **distancing** quotation marks are often used for one-upmanship. They are often condescending—use them sparingly.

IRONIC: At a New York restaurant, lone diners share companionship over pasta at a special "friendship table."

Avoid **apologetic** quotation marks for slang or offensive language. If you quote objectionable language for purposes of discussion, show who used it:

have been filled by

APOLOGETIC: Many highly skilled positions *have been "infiltrated" by* women.

ATTRIBUTED: The manager said that many highly skilled positions had been **"infiltrated"** by women.

27e Titles and Names

ital / “ ”

Know how to set off titles and names.

Use **italics**—and in some situations quotation marks—to set off titles of publications, names of creative works, and names of ships or other conveyances.

27e.1 Titles of Publications *Distinguish between whole publications and their parts.* Put quotation marks around the titles of articles, poems, songs, and other items that are only *part* of a publication. Italicize (or underline) the *whole* publication.

PART	WHOLE
"A Study of Repeat Offenders"	in *Criminology Review*
"Mending Wall"	in *The Collected Poems of Robert Frost*
"A Mighty Fortress"	in the *Lutheran Hymn Book*

PUBLICATION: The index to the ***New York Times*** devoted barely three column inches to the heading "**Sex**" forty years ago.

In the chapter titled **"Pestilence"** in her ***History of Medieval Europe***, Grumberg blames the black rat for the spread of the plague.

Do *not* use italics when naming the Bible or its parts and other sacred writings: **Talmud, Koran.**

SCRIPTURE: She opened the **Bible** and read from the **Book of Job.**

27e.2 Art and Entertainment *Italicize the titles of works of art or entertainment.* Italicize (or underline) the titles of plays, major musical works including operas and ballets, movies, television and radio programs, and such works of art as paintings and sculpture:

ENTERTAINMENT: The musical ***Miss Saigon*** updated the story of Puccini's opera ***Madame Butterfly.***

ART: Every summer, an army of tourists troops past the ***Mona Lisa.***

27e.3 **Ships and Aircraft** *Italicize the names of ships and other craft.* For instance, italicize the names of space vehicles, planes, or trains: the space station ***Mir,*** the ***Challenger*** disaster, the liner ***Queen Elizabeth 2.***

VESSELS: The ***Titanic*** became the best-known ship of all time.

TRAINS: The ***California Zephyr*** and other great trains now live only in legend.

YOUR TURN 67 Quote/Unquote

Rewrite the italicized part of each sentence, adding punctuation as necessary for quotations.

Royal Kin Pregnant with Sextuplets

1 Tabloids take us to what science fiction writers call *a "parallel universe*

2 Who can resist a headline that *says Space Aliens Land in Nevada*

3 "Mom Swaps Twins *for Cookies said one headline*

4 A Turkish scientist claims he found a humanlike creature with green skin *in "a glass coffin that dates back to the Ice Age*

5 As one editor said about the many UFO *sightings: "Why don't they identify themselves*

6 The answer might be: "After a trip of a hundred light years, they *are exhausted*

7 After reading the tabloids, one critic *said Who needs monsters from outer space*

8 "Ghoulish *husband one article said turns spouse into ghoulash*

9 One mother *said she dyed her twins red and green so she could tell them apart*

10 In the words of one *editor With tabloids, you're in another world!*

28 SPELLING WORK

sp

Keep spelling problems from damaging your credibility.

Nothing makes your reader question your ability more quickly than simple everyday words misspelled. No matter how intelligent or hard-working you are, a misspelled *definite* or *receive* or *athlete* will make you look bad. Your electronic **spellcheck** will catch most of the spelling errors that would hurt your credibility. However, a computer program may not help you tell apart words that sound alike (**to**, **two**, or **too**?). It may not help you when spelling depends on how a word is used in a sentence. It will not help you when you are writing a memo or personal note by hand.

28a Spelling Demons

sp

Watch out for predictable spelling errors.

A few dozen spelling demons cause most of the spelling errors in student writing. For damage control, work on the *unforgivables*—common predictable words that stand out from the page. Give the right forms a chance to sink in. Type them over or trace them over. Spell the letters out loud. Put them on small cards that you can flip over as you ride the bus or have a Tab in the cafeteria.

28a.1 Memory Aids *Remember memory aids.* The human mind is wired to learn through tie-ins or associations. Remember memory aids or handles like the following:

SPELLING PROBLEM	MEMORY AID
separate	a sep**ar**ate **par**ade
definite	a defi**nit**e defi**nit**ion
surprise	a **sur**prising **sur**plus
perform	a **per**fect **per**formance
similar	a particu**lar** simi**lar**ity
independent	an indepen**dent** **dent**ist
achieve	their **chie**f a**chie**vement
environment	**iron** in the env**iron**ment
government	gove**rn**ments gove**rn**
too	**too** many **to**o**ls**

28a.2 Confusing Soundalikes *Sort out confusing doubles.*

Your spellcheck is not likely to catch wrong choices between correctly spelled words. Watch for high-priority items like **to/too** or **there/their/they're:**

to/too	**to** Detroit, **to** America, **to** the end (direction)
	to rest is **to** rust, the order **to** withdraw (action)
	too late and **too** little (over the limit)
	that **too** (that also)
TEST PATTERN:	It's not **too** late **to** send a copy **to** them **too**.
there/their/they're	here and **there**, **there's** no **there there** (place)
	their views, **their** dues (belonging to them)
	they're ready, **they're** gone (they are)
TEST PATTERN:	**There's** a chance **they're** ready to try **their** luck **there**.

SPELLING ESSENTIALS — Distinguishing Homonyms (Soundalikes)

Look out for soundalikes or near soundalikes:

accept/except	we **accept** (take *in*) money for dues; we **except** (take *out*) seniors (when you make an acceptance speech, you take something *on*; when you make an exception, you take something *out*)
affect/effect	absences **affect** grades (partial influence); the treatment had no **effect** (complete result)
allowed/aloud	smoking is not all**owed** (permitted); we read silently or **aloud**
Capitol/capital	the Capit**ol** (building) is in the capit**al** (the whole city)
cite/site/sight	**cite**d for reckless driving (given a citation), the **site** of the new school (it's situated there), the miracle of **sight**

(continued)

Distinguishing Homonyms (Soundalikes) *(continued)*

conscious/conscience	patients are con**scious** or uncon**scious**; defendants have a good con**science** or a guilty con**science**
council/counsel	counc**il**ors make up the city counc**il** (meeting as a group); camp coun**sel**ors coun**sel** young people (giving advice)
desert/dessert	**des**erts appear on maps (in **des**erted areas); **des**erving people may get their just **des**erts; **dess**erts appear on menus
lose/loose	win or **lose**; too tight or too **loose**
personal/personnel	a perso**nal** (private) matter; a perso**nnel** (staff) matter
presents/presence	we pre**sent** pre**sents** (gifts); we notice pre**sence** or ab**sence**
principal/principle	the princi**pal's** office, the princi**pal** (main) reason, princi**pal** and interest; a matter of princi**ple**, against my princi**ples** (basic rules or convictions)
quite/quiet	qu**ite** (entirely) true; seeking peace and qu**iet**
than/then	stranger th**an** fiction (comparison); now and th**en** (time)
whether/weather	**wh**ether or not (choice); foul **wea**ther (climate)

YOUR TURN 68 Choosing between Soundalikes

Which choice fits the context? Write it after the number of the sentence.

1 The documents arrived **to/too** late.
2 The decision **affected/effected** thousands of workers.
3 The subsidiary continued to **lose/loose** money.
4 The board **accepted/excepted** the chair's resignation.
5 The consultant talked about business **principals/principles**.

6 The new rules applied to all **personal/personnel**.

7 Large organizations do not have a **conscious/conscience**.

8 The company was **then/than** still family-owned.

9 They were paying interest but not reducing the **principal/principle**.

10 The shareholders expressed **their/there** dissatisfaction.

11 They located in Georgia because of lower taxes **their/there**.

12 The equipment was **quiet/quite** old.

13 No one knew **whether/weather** the suppliers could meet the deadline.

14 The meeting took place later **then/than** we expected.

15 Two members of the city **counsel/council** had resigned.

28a.3 Silent Letters *Catch silent letters or letters not heard in informal speech.* With some words, the gap between spelling and pronunciation is unusually wide. Your spellcheck should catch the following:

accident**ally**	basic**ally**	Feb**r**uary	for**eign**
can**d**idate	conde**mn**	de**bt**	dou**bt**
incident**ally**	lib**r**ary	mo**rt**gage	quan**t**ity
sover**eign**			

Check endings that blur in pronunciation: **-ate/-ite, -able/-ible, -ant/-ent.** Go over the following list to see which words might give you trouble:

a accept**able**, accept**ance**, advis**able**, attend**ance**, attend**ant,** brilli**ant**, perform**ance**

e consist**ent**, excell**ence**, excell**ent**, exist**ence**, independ**ent**, persist**ent**, tend**ency**

i irresist**ible**, plaus**ible**, poss**ible**, suscept**ible**

! *LITERACY ALERT:* Never write *of* for **have** in combinations like **could have been** and **might have been.**

should have **might have**
We *should of* known that they *might of* failed.

28a.4 Odd Pairs *Watch out for different spellings of the same root.* Some words are confusing because they appear in different versions. The root -**cede** is spelled with a single *e* in re**cede** (like a flood), pre**cede** (causing a precedent), con**cede** (making a concession), se**cede** (from the union), and inter**cede** (stepping in). However, ex**ceed** and pro**ceed** have a double *e*, as do the pro**ceed**s of a sale. Then, the single *e* appears again in proc**ed**ure.

Watch out for other odd pairs: conscien**ce** but conscien**tious**, dissen**t** but dissen**sion**, gen**ius** but ingen**ious**, pron**ounce** but pron**unci**ation, curi**ous** but curi**osity**.

till/until	**till** dark but un**til** dark
four/forty	**four** and **four**teen but **for**ty thieves
nine/ninth	**nine** and n**ine**ty but the *Ninth Symphony*

Spelling may depend on how you use a word in a sentence:

advise/advice	we adv**ise** somebody (verb), but we give adv**ice** (noun)
choose/chose	we ch**oose** now (present), but we ch**ose** then (past)
lead/led	they **lead** now (present), but they l**ed** then (past)

Changes from singular to plural may trip up the writer: one **man**/several **men**, one **woman**/several **women**, one fresh**man**/several fresh**men**, one Irish**man**/several Irish**men**. Most words like **piano** simply add -*s* for the plural (**pianos**). But other words, like **potato**, add -*es* instead (**potatoes**). Most words like **roof** simply add -*s* for the plural (**roofs**). But other words, including **life** and **wolf**, change the ending to -*ves* (**lives, wolves**).

-os	pian**os**, radi**os**, studi**os**, rode**os**, sopran**os**
-oes	her**oes**, potat**oes**, tomat**oes**, vet**oes**
-fs	roo**fs**, chie**fs**, che**fs**, ree**fs**, belie**fs**
-ves	li**ves**, wi**ves**, cal**ves**, wol**ves**, kni**ves**, loa**ves**

For some words, dictionaries list both spellings as acceptable:

BOTH RIGHT: zer**os** and zer**oes,** tornad**os** and tornad**oes,** buffal**os** and buffal**oes**

scar**fs** and scar**ves,** hoo**fs** and hoo**ves,** el**fs** and el**ves**

! *LITERACY ALERT:* Add the *-ed* (or *-d*) in **used to, supposed to,** and (being) **prejudiced.** (When we have **a prejudice** against a group, we **are prejudiced** against them.)

used to
He *use to* sell cars.

supposed to
She was *suppose to* meet us.

prejudiced.
They were *prejudice.*

YOUR TURN 69 Making the Right Spelling Choices

What form of the missing word would fit the context? Write the missing form after the number of the sentence.

1	use	China ________ to experience large-scale famines.
2	woman	We recognized the voices of several of the ________.
3	freshman	________ were expected to live on campus.
4	prejudice	The townspeople were ________ against the newcomers.
5	pronounce	The French teacher kept correcting their ________.
6	advise	The lawyer had given the client bad ________.
7	hero	The new movies presented vigilantes as ________.

YOUR TURN 69 *(continued)*

8	veto	Repeated _________ by the governor were commonplace.
9	proceed	The college had elaborate _________ for handling complaints.
10	woman	The convention delegates chose a _________.

28a.5 Special Problems *(it's/its)* *Watch for one-of-a-kind items.*

Spell **a lot** and **no one** as two words. Spell **nowadays** as one. (Often, **a lot** will sound too informal—use *much* or *many* instead.) Both **all right** and **alright** are now all right, but make it two words if an editor or teacher insists on the older spelling.

! ***LITERACY ALERT:*** Take care of the *it's* problem. **It's** is short for *it is* or *it has*. It's a contraction—the apostrophe shows something's been left out. Use *it's* only when you definitely mean *it is:* **it's** now too late; do it because **it's** right. Or use *it's* when you mean *it has*: **it's** been snowing, **it's** happened twice before. To avoid the *it's* trap, try to do without *it's* altogether. (More than half of the time it's wrong.)

Your best strategy is not to use *it's* at all. Use *it is* or *it has* if that's what you mean. Use *its* (*without* the apostrophe) to show where something belongs. **Its** is a **possessive** pronoun—showing ownership or similar close relationship: the company and **its** real estate; the church and **its** followers; the firm and **its** clients.

CONTRACTION:	check to see if **it's** (it is) loaded
	return the form if **it's** (it is) unsigned
POSSESSIVE:	the party and **its** leadership
	the agency and **its** representatives
	the corporation and **its** stock
	the school and **its** policies

28b Spelling Rules

Remember a few basic spelling rules.

Let each basic spelling rule help you with a whole set of spelling problems.

28b.1 ***ie/cei*** *Put the i before the e except after c.* The combinations **ie** and **ei** often stand for the same long *ee* sound. (**Believe** rhymes with **receive.**) With a few important exceptions, put *i* before *e* except after *c.*

ie	They bel**ie**ved in bel**ie**fs of true bel**ie**vers.
cei	We re**cei**ved the re**cei**pt for the new **cei**ling.
ie	bel**ie**ve, ach**ie**ve, ch**ie**f, gr**ie**f, n**ie**ce, rel**ie**ve, p**ie**ce (a part)
cei	re**cei**ve, con**cei**ve, con**cei**ted, per**cei**ve, re**cei**pt

EXCEPTIONS: either, neither, leisure, seize, weird; financier, species

28b.2 **Doubled Final Letter** *Know when to double a final consonant before a vowel.* Know when to double a single final consonant—like *n, p, d,* or *r*—before the endings *-ed, -ing, -er,* or *-est.* All these endings start with a vowel.

DOUBLING:

plan	pla**nn**ed, pla**nn**ing, pla**nn**er
begin	begi**nn**ing, begi**nn**er
stop	sto**pp**ed, sto**pp**ing
red	re**dd**er, re**dd**est

Doubling takes place only when two conditions are met:

- The sound before the final letter has to be a **short vowel,** as in *plan* or *stop*. It must not be a long or double vowel, as in *boat, fool,* *aim, read,* or *feed,* or a long vowel signaled by the silent *-e* in *bite, hope,* and *bare.*

drop-dro**pp**ing BUT droop-drooping, bet-be**tt**ing BUT beat-beating
hop-ho**pp**ing BUT hope-hoping, wrap-wra**pp**ing BUT rape-raping
wri**tt**en BUT write-writing, bi**tt**en BUT bite-biting

- The syllable with the doubled consonant has to be **stressed,** as in admit-ad**mitt**ed, regret-re**grett**ed, forget-for**gett**ing, occur-oc**curr**ed-oc**curr**ing-oc**curr**ence. There is no doubling in pairs like **ed**it-editing, pro**hib**it-prohibiting, **ben**efit-benefited.

	SINGLE LETTER	DOUBLED LETTER
refer	**ref**erence	re**ferr**ed, re**ferr**ing
prefer	**pref**erence	pre**ferr**ed, pre**ferr**ing

✓ ***EDITOR'S TIP:*** Former exceptions, like **trav**elled, **wor**shipped, and **pro**grammed, now usually follow the rule, with no doubling: **traveled, worshiped, programed.**

28b.3 Omitted Final Letter

Know when to drop a final silent -e. Drop a silent *-e* at the end of a word if you add an ending that starts with a vowel, like *-ing* or *-able* (bore-bor**ing**, hate-hat**ing**, love-lov**ing**-lov**able**). Keep the *-e* before an ending that begins with a consonant, like *-ful* or *-ly* (bore/bore**dom**, love/love**ly**).

The following are exceptions:

DROPPED *e:* argue-argument, due-duly, true-truly, whole-wholly, judge-judgment, acknowledge-acknowledgment

KEPT *e:* mile-mileage, dye-dyeing (tinting or coloring, as against die-dying)

A final *-e* may signal the difference in the final sound of *rag* and *rage,* or of *plastic* and *notice.* Keep such a final *-e* not only before a consonant but also before endings starting with *a* or *o:*

ge advantage-advanta**ge**ous, change-chan**ge**able, courage-coura**ge**ous, outrage-outra**ge**ous

ce notice-noti**ce**able, peace-pea**ce**able

28b.4 ***y/ie*** *Know when to change a final* y *to* ie. Change the final *y* in a word like *city* or *study* when you add an ending. Especially, change it to *ie* before the *-s* ending (one city/several cit**ies**; sixty minutes/the sixt**ies**; several study/one stud**ies**). Change the *y* to *i* before other endings (like *-ed*). However, keep the *y* before *-ing* (dr**ied** but dr**ying**, bur**ial** but bur**ying**).

ie family-famil**ies**, fly-fl**ies**, study-stud**ies**, try-tr**ies**, quantity-quantit**ies**, copy-cop**ied**, dry-dr**ier**

i beauty-beaut**iful**, bury-bur**ial**, busy-bus**iness**, lively-livel**ihood**, noisy-nois**ily**

y bur**ying**, cop**ying**, stud**ying**, tr**ying**, worr**ying**

When it follows another vowel, the *y* usually stays: dela**ys**, jo**ys**, pla**yed**, valle**ys**. Exceptions: day-d**ai**ly, gay-g**ai**ly, lay-l**ai**d, pay-p**ai**d, say-s**ai**d.

YOUR TURN 70 **Tracking Changing Words**

Combine the following words with the suggested endings:

accompany_ed, advantage_ous, argue_ing, benefit_ed, carry_s, come_ing, confide_ing, differ_ing, excite_able, friendly_ness, lively_hood, occur_ing, prefer_ed

28c Variant Spellings

Check alternative spellings in your dictionary.

Some American students were educated in Britain, Canada, India, Pakistan, or other countries that were long in the British orbit. If you are one of these students, shift to the streamlined American spelling for words like the following:

BRITISH	AMERICAN
colour, glamour, humour	col**or,** glam**or,** hum**or**
organise, realise, civilise	organi**ze,** reali**ze,** civili**ze**
organisation, civilisation	organi**zation,** civili**zation**
centre, theatre	cent**er,** theat**er**
encyclopaedia, anaesthetic	encyclop**e**dia, an**e**sthetic
travelled, travelling, cancelled	travel**ed,** travel**ing,** cancel**ed**
offence, defence	offen**se,** defen**se**
connexion, reflexion	conne**ction,** refle**ction**

Here are a few one-of-a-kind items:

cheque, foetus, smoulder	che**ck,** f**e**tus, sm**o**lder

YOUR TURN 71 Your Personal Spelling Check

Use the following as your personal **spelling check.** Have someone dictate these sentences to you. Then run them through your spellcheck to see where you slipped. (Or trade your sentences with another student for peer checking.) Work on the words that give you trouble.

1 Her presence was definitely a surprise.
2 Companies try to eliminate the competition.
3 Foreign governments owe debts.
4 Amateurs benefited like other athletes.
5 The absence of controls was disastrous.
6 She was a prominent professor of psychology.
7 The independent candidate loved the environment.
8 Keep business decisions confidential.
9 We preferred studying in the library.
10 She probably thought criticism indispensable.
11 Her opponent accused her of hypocrisy.
12 The dissatisfied sponsor hated the performance.
13 It was a strictly practical approach.

14 A repetition of the tragedy is inevitable.

15 The subtle difference was irrelevant.

16 We doubted the privileges were necessary.

17 Undoubtedly the quantity will increase in February.

18 The committee checked every conceivable option.

19 The marriage succeeded exceptionally well.

20 Manufacturers developed a new device.

29 MANUSCRIPT MECHANICS

Know special features of our writing system.

Follow basic conventions for features with special uses: capital letters, hyphens, apostrophes, numerals, and abbreviations.

29a Using Capitals

cap
lc

Capitalize names and words derived from names.

Capitalize the pronoun *I* and the first word of a sentence. Capitalize **proper names**—the names of people, places, countries, languages, periods, institutions, ships and other craft, books, and works of art: **Abraham Lincoln, Lithuania, Arabic, the FBI, *Moby Dick*.** Capitalize titles that go with a name: **Justice Marshall.** Capitalize the names of days and months (**Tuesday, October**), but use lower-case for the seasons (**summer**). Capitalize major words in titles: ***Gone with the Wind.***

SPELLING ESSENTIALS

Using Capitals

Review major uses of capitals:

NAMES:	Eleanor Roosevelt, Albert Einstein, Sappho, Cesar Chavez, Godzilla
NAMES WITH TITLES:	Senator Feinstein, Madame Curie, Professor Madrid, Chief Crazy Horse, Captain Ahab, the Reverend Jesse Jackson
PLACES:	the Everglades, Grand Rapids, New York City, North Dakota, Brazil, Africa, Australia, the Arctic
DAYS AND MONTHS:	Monday, Saturday, January, March, September (BUT spring, summer, autumn, winter)
NATIONAL ORIGIN:	Swiss watches, French Canadian, Polish American, Japanese cars, the Vietnamese community

LANGUAGES:	English-only, Spanish-speaking, Yiddish, Portuguese
INSTITUTIONS:	Internal Revenue Service, University of Michigan, Oakland Tech, Foothill College, Valley High School, the Brighton School for the Blind, the Salvation Army, the CIA
RELIGIONS:	Muslim, Buddhist, Southern Baptist, Methodist, Christian, Roman Catholic, Greek Orthodox
PARTIES:	Democrats, Republicans, the Green Party (BUT democratic institutions, a republican form of government)
PERIODS AND EVENTS:	the Middle Ages, the Gilded Age, Reconstruction, World War II
VESSELS AND CRAFT:	the *Titanic*, the *Challenger*, the *Voyager*
CREATIVE WORKS:	*Gone with the Wind, Star Wars, Animal Farm*, the *Ninth Symphony*, the *Mona Lisa*, "On the Duty of Civil Disobedience"
COLLEGE CLASSES:	Economics 1A, Advanced Calculus, Introduction to Electrical Engineering, Computer Programing 12A, Humanities 2 (BUT a history major, a humanities program, social science professors, engineering students)

✓ ***EDITOR'S TIP:*** Some titles of persons or labels of institutions come to stand alone and are as good as a name: the **Pope**, the **Queen** (of England). U.S. political terms may go either way—capitalized or lower-case: the **President** or *president*, the **Constitution** or *constitution*, the **Federal** or *federal* government. Believers capitalize pronouns referring to the deity: And **God** will not abandon **His** people. When it stands for scripture, **Bible** may be capitalized but may also be lower-case (it's always lower-case when used figuratively for a trusted guide: the *bible* of computer programers).

Follow basic guidelines for choosing between capitals and lower-case:

29a.1 Party Labels *Capitalize the labels of movements and institutions.* Capitalize movements and ideas named after people (the **Lutheran** tradition). Change lower-case general labels for ideas (*democratic* forms of government) to capitalized when they name specific parties, religions, or institutions (the **Democratic** party).

MOVEMENTS: **Marxist** intellectuals, **Freudian** psychiatrists, the **Darwinian** theory of evolution, **Buddhist** congregations

IDEAS: Believers in truly **democratic** institutions distrust both **Democrats** and **Republicans.**

29a.2 Names of Regions Distinguish between general directions (lower-case) and names of specific regions (capitalized):

GENERAL DIRECTION	SPECIFIC REGION
we traveled due *south*	he loved **Southerners** and the **South**
go *west*, they were told	we moved to the **Midwest**

29a.3 Capitalizing Titles *Capitalize major words in titles of publications, including the titles of your own papers.* Capitalize the first and last words of the title. Capitalize the remaining words except articles (*the, a, an*), prepositions regardless of length (*in, at, by, against, around, without*), and coordinators (*and, or, but*). Remember to italicize—or underline—titles of complete publications.

TITLES: ***Writing for the World Wide Web***
Composing Cyberspace

29a.4 Titles of Your Papers *Type your title like ordinary text except for the use of capital letters.* Capitalize the words in your own titles as you would the words in titles of publications (DO NOT USE ALL CAPITALS). Do *not* italicize (or underline) the title of your paper. Do not put it in quotation marks unless it is a quotation.

Use a question mark if it is a question, but do not use a period even if your title is a complete sentence.

PLAIN:	America's Unwanted
QUOTATION:	"Don't Ask, Don't Tell"
QUESTION:	A Nation of Immigrants?
SENTENCE:	The Minimum Wage Is Not a Living Wage

YOUR TURN 72 Using Capital Letters

For each sentence, capitalize all words that should be capitalized and write them after the number of the sentence.

1 Scholars in germany traced the common roots of european languages including english, french, latin, greek, and russian.

2 The conference brought together catholic priests, baptist ministers, jewish rabbis, and mormon elders.

3 The worship of the virgin mary started in europe and spread to new world areas like mexico.

4 Both democrats and republicans began to court african american voters in the south.

5 The fighting irish became the nickname of the team from notre dame university in indiana.

6 The copernican astronomy, newtonian physics, darwinian evolution, marxist economics, and freudian psychiatry are milestones in the history of ideas.

29b Using Hyphens

hy

Use the easy-to-miss hyphen for many combined words.

The hyphen signals that a group of words is in-between: It's between separate words and a new combination. A pair of words may start as two words (**baby boom**), pick up a hyphen (**baby-sitter**), and finally become one word (**crybaby**).

SEPARATE WORDS:	commander in chief, labor union, high command, high school, vice versa, off year, best man
HYPHENATED:	vice-president, brother-in-law, computer-aided, trade-off, cancer-causing
ONE WORD:	stepmother, bridesmaid, coauthor, checklist, highlight, headquarters, blackout

SPELLING ESSENTIALS

Where to Use Hyphens

Know common uses of the hyphen:

NEW BLENDS:	cost-effective, gender-neutral, trade-off, gang-related
ETHNIC LABELS:	Anglo-Saxon, Irish-American, Asian-American, Mexican-American (now often Irish American, Asian American, Mexican American)
NUMBER PAIRS:	ten-speed, six-pack, one-sided, three-cornered, one-way, two-dimensional, first-class, second-rate
-ing PAIRS:	law-abiding, Spanish-speaking, cancer-causing, award-winning, money-losing
-ed PAIRS:	dark-haired, Washington-based, air-conditioned, career-oriented, middle-aged, single-handed
DUAL ADJECTIVES:	fuel-efficient, cost-effective, oil-rich, water-repellent, image-conscious, toll-free, foreign-born, college-bound
WITH *off, in:*	off-season, drive-in, off-duty, take-off, cave-in
KINSHIP WORDS:	daughter-in-law, father-in-law, in-laws, great-grandchild
DOUBLE NUMBERS:	twenty-four, thirty-nine
COMPASS POINTS:	south-southeast, north-northwest
SPECIAL LABELS:	two-by-four, cash-and-carry, fly-by-night

29b.1 hy

Prefix and Hyphen *Use a hyphen with selected prefixes.*

Prefixes are attached at the beginning of words. Use a hyphen with **self-**, **ex-** (in the sense of former), and **all-**. Use a hyphen with prefixes like **pro-** and **anti-** when they come before a capitalized label (**pro-Israel**). You may also use a hyphen when a prefix might cause a confusing meeting of identical sounds: **co-operate** (but now more often **cooperate**).

self-, ex-, all-:	self-conscious, self-explanatory, self-confidence, ex-husband, ex-convict, all-purpose, all-important
BEFORE CAPS:	pro-Arab, anti-American, non-Catholic
IDENTICAL SOUNDS:	anti-intellectual, semi-independent; re-entry (but also reentry), re-examine (but also reexamine)
NO HYPHEN:	noncontroversial, nonaligned

29b.2 hy

Group Modifiers *Hyphenate a combination used as a group modifier.*

What kind of accident? A **hit-and-run** accident. What kind of plan? A **pay-as-you-go plan.** The hyphenated combination takes the place of an adjective modifying a noun: (a *conservative* position) a **right-of-center** position; (a *moderate* policy) a **middle-of-the-road** policy.

NO HYPHEN	HYPHEN
time to wake up	a **wake-up** call
doing it yourself	a **do-it-yourself** project
cutting and pasting	a **cut-and-paste** job

✓ ***EDITOR'S TIP:*** Hyphenate fractions when they are used as modifiers: How full? **Two-thirds** full, **three-quarters** empty. Practice varies for other uses: **Two thirds** (or **two-thirds**) stayed home.

29b.3 hy

Dividing Words *Use the hyphen when dividing words at the end of a line.*

Typists used to divide long words at the end of a line to produce a more regular right margin. Dictionaries still divide words into syllables to show where you could put a hyphen when dividing the word: **pro cras ti na tion, ful fill ment, per mit ted.** Today, readers are used to the irregular margins of text typed at the computer—with no division of words except at the hyphen of already hyphenated words (**self-righteous; hard-to-find** originals). If you want a neat regular right margin, you can **justify** your text—with the computer stretching or squeezing each line of typing to make it fill the exact space available.

If you divide words in a typewritten text, do not divide if you would leave only one or two letters behind on a line or shift only one or two letters to the next.

NO DIVISION: again, binary, voter, alike, navy

YOUR TURN 73 Adding Needed Hyphens

After the number of each sentence, write all combinations that need to be hyphenated, adding the needed hyphens.

1 Risk taking researchers in state of the art companies were developing cutting edge medications.

2 Anti American and anti Israel demonstrators listened to pro Arab speeches.

3 The ex Senator working for the Washington based group called the proposal self serving, one sided, and two dimensional.

4 The new style management replaced the old money losing operation with a more cost effective three step procedure.

5 Cost cutting competitors were marketing IBM compatible user friendly PCs.

29c Apostrophe for Possessives

poss
no ap

Use the apostrophe for possessives.

Use the apostrophe to show ownership or belonging. The **possessive** form of nouns shows who owns something or where something belongs. Whose fee? The **broker's** fee. Whose files? The **agent's** files. Form the **singular** possessive (something belongs to one person) by adding the apostrophe and then *s* to the plain form:

WHOSE? a **friend's** car, one **person's** opinion, the **manager's** parking space, our **mayor's** office, the **mind's** eye, the **student's** name, the **dean's** list

Besides ownership or belonging, the possessive signals other relationships that tell us whose: the **governor's enemies**, the **jury's verdict**, the **rock star's accident**, an **impostor's exposure**, our **committee's activities.**

! *LITERACY ALERT:* Do not overcompensate by putting an apostrophe where it does not belong. In the following sentence, *players* answers the question who? and not whose? It is the subject of the sentence, not a possessive:

	players
WHO?	The *player's* were talking about a strike.
WHOSE?	The **player's suspension** had expired.

29c.1 **Plural Possessives** *Distinguish between singular and plural possessives.* Know the two different forms: one **applicant's** dossier (apostrophe first), several **applicants'** dossiers (apostrophe last). If the plural noun ends in *-s*, add only the apostrophe. Do not add a second *s:* a quarrel between **lovers**—a **lovers'** quarrel; the revolt by the **slaves**—the **slaves'** revolt.

SINGULAR	PLURAL
the **twin's** bicycle	the **twins'** birthdays
a **parent's** duties	both **parents'** duties

However, use the *-'s* ending (apostrophe first) for possessives of **irregular plurals.** Add the apostrophe plus *s* when a plural noun such as **children, women, men,** or **people** does not already end with the plural *-s:*

PLURAL: **children's** toys, **women's** rights, **men's** wear, **people's** prejudices

! *LITERACY ALERT:* Watch for spelling changes as you move from the singular to the plural possessive: one **family's** debts/both **families'** debts, one **woman's** career/several **women's** careers.

29c.2 **Time and Value** *Use the apostrophe in familiar expressions specifying time or value.* Use the apostrophe in the **evening's** program, **today's** newspaper, **yesterday's** issue, **tomorrow's** edition, this **year's** results, a **moment's** notice, a **dollar's** worth. Distinguish between singular and plural:

SINGULAR	PLURAL
one **week's** pay, a **month's** salary	three **weeks'** pay, two **months'** salary
a **day's** work, an **hour's** drive	two **days'** e-mail, three **hours'** drive
a **dollar's** worth	two **dollars'** worth, fifty **cents'** worth

29c.3 **Indefinite Pronouns** *Use the apostrophe with the possessive forms of indefinite pronouns.* **Indefinite pronouns** do not point to a specific person (they include or exclude a larger group of people). Use the apostrophe in **everybody's** surprise, **anyone's** guess, at **someone's** suggestion, **nobody's** fault, with **no one's** help, **one's** best friends (also: at **someone else's** house). However, do not use the apostrophe with the **possessive pronouns** *its, hers, ours, yours, theirs.*

NO APOSTROPHE: both **its** ears, it was **hers,** this is **yours**

See **28a** for *its/it's.*

29c.4 **Groups of Words** *Know how to use the apostrophe with groups of words.* Treat **compound words** that stand for a single entity the way you would single words. Put the apostrophe plus *-s* or the apostrophe alone at the end of the last word in the group:

SINGULAR: the **commander-in-chief's** orders, a **father-in-law's** hopes

PLURAL: her **brothers-in-law's** store, my **in-laws'** support

Follow the same rule when using the possessive of words that jointly name a group or a team: **Simon and Schuster's** spring list, **Laurel and Hardy's** comedies, **Ben and Irene's** marriage. But use two separate possessives for members of a team when differences or separate identities seem important:

SEPARATE: **Laurel's and Hardy's** origins had been very different.

Ben's and Irene's views of marriage were very similar.

> ✓ ***EDITOR'S TIP:*** Should you add another *-s* for the possessive of names already ending with *-s?* Practice is divided: **Dolores'** presentation or **Dolores's** presentation; **Charles Dickens'** novels or **Charles Dickens's** novels. Choose the simpler or the more traditional form, but be consistent—deal with all such names the same way. However, usually there is no added *-s* after Greek or Hebrew names: **Socrates'** dialogues, for **Jesus'** sake.

29c.5 Plurals of Symbols

Know exceptional uses of the apostrophe for plurals that are not possessives. The apostrophe used to appear before the plural *-s* in plurals for letters of the alphabet, numbers, symbols, abbreviations, and words discussed as words: only three **A's** and four **B's**; dial three **1's** and four **6's**; average **I.Q.'s**; too many **maybe's.** Current style sheets recommend omitting the apostrophe for these uses except for letters discussed as letters. Note that the letters but not the plural *-s* are italicized: two ***e'*s** meet in *reenforce.*

NO APOSTROPHE: the **80s;** the **1920s;** a number with several **2s** and **3s;** cloned **PCs; ifs** and **buts**

YOUR TURN 74 Apostrophes for Possessives

Rewrite the following sentences, using apostrophes as needed for possessives.

1 Both parents consent was required for a sons or daughters participation in this clubs activities.

2 A months salary for this companys top management equaled several years earnings for Colombias peasants.

3 The womens studies group invited several of South Americas most outstanding poets.

4 This new judges ruling outlined the mans and the womans responsibility for the childrens well-being.

5 Several patients records were studied by an insurance companys lawyers after these clients complaints.

29d Apostrophe for Contractions

ap
no ap

Use the apostrophe in informal contractions.

Apostrophes used in **contractions** show that something has been left out: three **o'clock**; yes, **ma'am**; class of **'99.** Use the apostrophe in the contractions or shortened forms of informal speech and writing. Remember that **they're** is short for *they are*. Remember that **can't** is short for *cannot*. An occasional **can't** or **won't** can give your writing an informal or casual touch. However, avoid contractions in formal reports, research papers, and letters of application.

FORMAL	INFORMAL
cannot, will not, should not	**can't, won't, shouldn't**
you are right, they are late	**you're** right, **they're** late
I will be back, they will call	**I'll** be back, **they'll** call
let us ask, time is up	**let's** ask, **time's** up

! ***LITERACY ALERT:*** Avoid common misspellings. Make sure not to misspell **don't** and **doesn't**. These are shortened forms of *do not* and *does not*. Use **who's** only to mean *who is* (**who's** guilty?). **Whose** means *of whom, belonging to whom* (**whose** turn is it?). Use **they're** (and not **there** or **their**) when you mean *they are*.

do not	We **don't** usually respond to unsolicited mail.
does not	The new modem **doesn't** work.
who is/has	No one knows **who's** responsible.
whose	We wondered **whose** responsibility it was.
they're (they are)	**they're** late, **they're** dissatisfied
their (of them)	**their** belongings, they and **their** friends
there (as in *here and there)*	no one was **there, there** is no excuse

Use **it's** only when it's really an abbreviation: **it's** (it is) raining; **it's** (it has) been difficult. Otherwise use **its**—the possessive pronoun that shows where something belongs: a nation and **its** leaders (tells us whose leaders); the bird beat **its** wings (tells us whose wings); the ruble lost half of **its** value (tells us whose value).

See **28a** for more on *its/it's*.

29e Using Numbers

num

Use numerals for exact figures; spell out round numbers.

Use numerals for exact figures that someone might use in crunching numbers. Also use figures for numbers with decimal points or fractions (**4.8** million, **3¾** hours).

EDITOR'S GUIDELINES

Using Numbers

Use numerals in pinpointing dates, times, and locations:

ACTUAL COUNTS:	Attendance was **78,590** fans.
DETAILED SUMS:	Tickets were **$17.50.**
MEASUREMENTS:	We drove **17.2** miles at an average speed of **37** miles an hour.
PERCENTAGE POINTS:	Ticket sales were up **17** percent.
DATES:	September **1, 2000; 1780** B.C.
STREET NUMBERS:	**2389** Constitution Avenue, Suite **#7**
PAGE NUMBERS:	Chapter **3**, pages **22–24**
TIME:	The plane leaves at **8:40** a.m.

In statistical reports, research reports, or charts, you may be using numerals throughout. In ordinary writing, use spelled-out figures for simple numbers from one to ten. Spell out **round numbers** requiring no more than two words (almost **two hundred** years, **eight thousand** dollars). When spelled out, numbers from 21 to 99 are hyphenated (**twenty-five** dollars a seat).

SIMPLE NUMBERS:	between **seven** and **nine** years old
ROUND NUMBERS:	about **sixty-five** reservations; more than **two thousand** copies
ROUNDED-OFF TIME:	at **seven** o'clock; half past **ten**

Study the use of numerals and spelled-out figures in the following examples:

> Sportswriters tracking coverage by **four** or **five** networks deal with mind-numbing figures.
>
> A network that covered football for **38** years but lost its contract for several years spent **$4 billion** to get the broadcast rights back.
>
> **Two** or **three** years ago, the minimum wage for an NFL football player was **$158,000.**
>
> A **37**-year-old kicker who averaged **45.4** yards in seven punts was paid **$375,000.**
>
> Only about t**hree thousand** players share in the bonanza.
>
> A team may have to cut a tentative roster from **64** to **59** players.

✓ ***EDITOR'S TIP:*** Avoid starting a sentence with a numeral.

WRONG:	*13* people were injured in the accident.
BETTER:	**Thirteen** people were injured in the accident.
	According to the police, **13** people were injured in the accident.

29f Using Abbreviations

ab

Use widely employed abbreviations, but avoid shortcuts.

Abbreviations save time and space, but some look like excessive shortcuts, and others appear only in limited technical contexts.

29f.1 Widely Used Initials *Use widely recognized initials (without periods).* Use **NASA** (for National Aeronautics and Space Administration) or **PC** (for personal computer).

INITIALS: FBI, CIA, DNA, AIDS, SAT scores, PTA, IBM, AFL-CIO, CNN

If your readers may not recognize an abbreviation, explain it when you first use it:

The **NRC (Nuclear Regulatory Commission)** filed a report on the incident.

29f.2 Titles and Degrees *Use acceptable abbreviations for titles and degrees.* Use **Mr., Mrs.** or **Ms., Dr.,** and **St.** (Saint) before names, and use **Jr.** (junior) and **Sr.** (senior) after names. Use standard abbreviations for degrees like **BA, MA, PhD,** or **MD** (also written with periods: B.A., M.A., Ph.D., M.D.). Use **Prof.** only before the full name.

TITLES: Ms. Alicia Travis; Dr. Theresa Santos or Theresa Santos, MD; John K. Menninger, Sr.; St. Augustine; Prof. Pat C. Kaminsky but Professor Kaminsky

29f.3 Time and Number *Use familiar abbreviations for time and number.* After or before numerals, use **BC** or **AD** for calendar years, **a.m.** and **p.m.** for hours, and **no.** for numbers:

TIME: 5 BC to AD 65 (also 5 B.C. to A.D. 65); between 8:30 a.m. and 3 p.m. (also 8:30 A.M. to 3 P.M.)

NUMBER: volume 7, no. 2

29f.4 **Addresses and Locations** *Except when addressing correspondence, spell out addresses and locations.* In your papers, spell out abbreviations like *NY* and *CA* (exceptions: **Washington, DC** and *US* in combinations like **US Army**).

	United States, Mariposa Avenue Los Angeles.
LOCATIONS:	In the *U.S.*, they lived on *Mariposa Ave.* in *L.A.*

29f.5 **Measurements** *Spell out most measurements.* Use *lb.* (pound), *oz.* (ounce), *ft.* (foot), and *in.* (inch) in documents like invoices and blueprints, but spell them out in ordinary writing. Spell out % (**percent**), but use the dollar sign for exact amounts: **$283.67.** Abbreviate unwieldy measures like **mph** (miles per hour) when they are used with figures: **95 mph, 1200 rpm.**

✓ ***EDITOR'S TIP:*** Use the & or *and*-sign (the **ampersand**) and abbreviations like **Inc.** and **Bros.** only when organizations use them in their official titles:

> **Morgan Bros.** moved the advertising account from **Amselm & Amselm** to **FutureTrends Inc.**

29g Using Italics

ital

Know when to use italics (italicized print).

Use **roman** (straight letters) for ordinary text and **italics** (slanted letters) for special purposes. For handwriting or text typed on a typewriter, you may have to use underlining (underscoring) to show that italicized letters should be used in a printed version.

29g.1 **Italics for Emphasis** *Italicize (or underline) to make to make words stand out.* Save these emphatic italics and other attention-getters—exclamation marks, dashes—for special situations.

EMPHATIC: The law favored ***unmarried*** couples.

The governor had ***read*** the letter but not signed it.

29g.2 **Words as Words** *Italicize (underline) words you discuss as words and words still considered foreign.* Dictionaries use special symbols (or italics) to signal that an imported word is not yet fully assimilated.

WORDS AS WORDS: Dictionaries explain the origin of ***gulag, shalom,*** and ***paparazzi.***

FOREIGN: News bulletins from the Middle East talked about ***jihad*** and ***intifada.***

29g.3 **Titles of Publications** *Italicize (underline) titles of whole publications.* Italicize (underline) the names of books, newspapers, and magazines.

PERIODICALS: A good bookstore stocks hundreds of periodicals, from the ***American Scholar*** and the ***Atlantic Monthly*** magazine to ***Body Builders Today*** and ***Beauty and Bikers.***

✓ ***EDITOR'S TIP:*** Do *not* italicize material—an article, a poem, a short story—that is part of a larger publication. Italicize the *whole;* enclose the *part* in quotation marks.

WHOLE AND PART: Shirley Jackson's short story **"The Lottery"** provoked an outpouring of outraged mail when it first appeared in the ***New Yorker.***

See **36** for underlining (underscoring) of titles in bibliographical listings—Works Cited for MLA (**36b**), References for APA (**36c**).

29g.4 **Creative Works** *Italicize (underline) works of art, music, and entertainment.* For instance, italicize (underline) the names of paintings, operas, musicals, major musical compositions (*The Ninth Symphony*), ballets, plays, radio programs, movies, and television shows.

PROGRAMS: Listener-supported public television gave audiences ***Sesame Street, Masterpiece Theater,*** and ***Nova.***

ART: Advertisers discovered that Leonardo's ***Mona Lisa,*** Michelangelo's ***David,*** and Picasso's ***Guernica*** were icons known to millions.

29g.5 Crafts and Vessels *Italicize (underline) individually named ships, trains, aircraft, and other crafts and vessels.*

VESSELS: The ill-fated ***Titanic*** became the most famous ship of all time.

YOUR TURN 75 Words Set Off

After the number of each sentence, write words or phrases with needed italicizing or quotation marks.

1 Carrying brochures titled Immortal Florence, tourists wait in line for hours to see Botticelli's Primavera.

2 The chapter titled Toward War in Grogan's History of the Civil Conflict devotes several pages to the incident at Harper's Ferry.

3 The Mayflower, the Titanic, and the Challenger are among vessels known to everyone.

4 Brokoff's book Commissar is a history of the nomenclatura, the privileged elite of the Soviet Union.

5 An essay called Glory of the Baroque in Mendel's History of Western Music calls Bach's St. Matthew Passion unsurpassed.

PART FOUR

WRITING ENGLISH AS A SECOND LANGUAGE

If English was not your first language, use the full range of opportunities to improve your use of it. Millions of Americans have always been bilingual—using more than one language. They have often spoken one language with family, friends, and neighbors and another in school, on the job, or in the office. Depending on where you live, you may hear not only English but also Spanish, Russian, Chinese, or Vietnamese. Many students in American colleges speak and write English as a second language. Some are learning to use it as a third language. Increasingly students encounter instructors from a second-language background. Becoming fluent and confident in a second language is a very major undertaking but is also an incredibly rewarding and educational experience.

How good is your English? Where do you fit on the spectrum that goes from limited proficiency to nearly perfect English? Some students are still working to build up their vocabulary and make better use of sentence resources. Others speak and write almost like a native.

TIPS FOR BILINGUAL WRITERS

Working on Your English

How can you become more confident in using the resources of your second language?

1 ***Immerse yourself in the language.*** Plunge in—swim in the language the way fish swim in the sea. Listen to talk radio and talk television. Pick movies with much talk—like romantic comedies with few car chases or shootouts. Do as much Internet surfing as you can. Subscribe to *Newsweek* or *The Nation* or *Ms.* magazine.

2 ***Learn how to build up new language habits.*** If you see and hear something over and over again, it sinks in. If you hear it only once or twice, you may not remember it at all. Go over sample sentences or new expressions. Repeat them to yourself. Read sentences over silently, and read them out loud. Tape public affairs programs on PBS, and replay the tapes while commuting to work or to college.

3 ***Become a word watcher.*** Read the clues as you watch language in action. For instance, pick up the meaning of new words and expressions from the **context**—from what goes with them. You can often tell the meaning of words from how they are used, from what comes before and after. Suppose your mechanic keeps saying: "Your xxxxx is leaking gasoline. Your xxxxx may cause a fire. Your xxxxx is not pumping fuel properly. You need to have your xxxxx repaired." The word you are picking up is *fuel pump*—a gadget that pumps the gasoline that serves as fuel for your engine.

4 ***Learn basic rules—and variations from the basic rules.*** The first stage in language learning is to learn the basic rules. For instance, how do most of the words in the language show the difference between one and more than one? How do they show the difference between present and past? The second stage in language learning is to learn more and more of the major variations on the basic patterns and the exceptions to the basic rules. What words and expressions do *not* use the *-s* ending to show plural (as in *dollars*) or the *-ed* ending to show past (as in *delayed*)?

5 ***Branch out beyond your language community.*** If you are more comfortable with your first language, you may tend to stay with others who speak it. They understand your thoughts and your jokes. However, remember you need as much exposure to the second language as possible. Make friends with people who speak English only. Talk to strangers at bus stops, in the cafeteria, at the gym, or at the checkout line in the supermarket. Practice your English whenever you can.

30 ENGLISH AS A SECOND CULTURE

esl

Become more aware of how you think and write.

What cultural influences have shaped your personality as a writer? People from different cultures do not all think and write alike. Young people do not just learn facts or study subject matter. They also learn differing ways to think about elders, about learning, or about the past. For instance, cultural traditions and educational systems differ in how they teach young people to relate to authority. If you had a bumper sticker on your car, would it say "Respect Authority"? Or would it say "Question Authority"? Are you likely to think of older people as wise experienced guides? Or are you more likely to think of them as out of touch, "over the hill"?

As a student in a writing class, you may have to think about cultural differences that affect how you express yourself in writing. Different cultural traditions shape the way we form opinions and present these opinions to others. We learn how to think of ourselves and others. We learn different patterns of self-esteem and self-doubt. A Korean-born English teacher of English as a Second Language often demonstrates the two different cultural personalities that still affect her writing and teaching. Her two different versions of "Who I Am" might go something like this. What makes them different?

TRADITIONAL:

I was born in Korea. I learned English only after I came to this country. I still make many mistakes. It took me many years to become a teacher, and people may consider it strange that I teach English. Joining the American mainstream is a long difficult journey. I still have a long way to go, but I am doing my best.

CURRENT AMERICAN:

I was born in Korea. Although I knew no English when I arrived here, I am now a teacher of English at an American college. I feel I am in a special position to understand the challenges facing teachers of English as a second language. Immigrants have a special contribution to make to American education, because they have experienced the challenge of mainstreaming students at first hand.

YOUR TURN 76 **Who Am I?**

Prepare *a journal entry* exploring different roles you play. Do you have different identities or personalities—depending on the situation? Do you talk and act differently depending on whether you are relating to your own family and friends or to the larger mainstream culture? Give some striking examples.

30a Learning a Second Culture

Study the way cultural patterns carry over into your writing.

When newcomers learn American English as a second language, they at the same time learn American ways as a second culture. Each in their own way and in varying degrees, they begin to become Americanized. Some of the personality traits they adopt or adapt are also writing traits. They are patterns of personal and verbal behavior that carry over into writing. Here are qualities valued more in American culture and in American college writing than in some other cultures:

ASSERTION At some point you are likely to be told: "Speak up!" "Take a stand!" "Make your voice heard!" Some people who are too shy or too meek are told to take assertiveness training. You have a right to state your own opinion, to vote for a candidate of your own choice, and to worship at a time and place of your own choosing. In your writing, learn to take a stand—state and defend what you think and feel.

PARTICIPATION At some point you are likely to be told: "Join in!" "Make a contribution!" "Ask questions!" Try not to sit in the back row. Do not let others dominate the conversation. Join in the dialogue. Study how opinions take shape in the give-and-take of class discussion. Study how decisions are made in the give-and-take of committee meetings. In your writing, show that you have listened to others—and that you have learned to talk back to them.

THE PERSONAL CONNECTION Learn to put your own achievements in a good light. This does not mean bragging or showing off. It means giving yourself credit where credit is due. In a self-evaluation for a cooperative project, specify the time and effort you put into the work. Explain how you brought a fresh perspective to the task or helped resolve personality conflicts. In a discussion of a controversial topic, show why your firsthand personal experience makes you more of an authority on the topic than others.

EVEN-HANDEDNESS In an American context, self-confidence and assertiveness are valued. However, they do not give you the right to drown out or put down others. In some cultures, the male or the rich person or the elderly person tends to have bragging rights. If you come from such a background, you may at times be told: "Let the other person talk!" Try not to come across as self-righteous—sure that you alone have the truth. Feel free to disagree with people, but show them respect.

YOUR TURN 77 **Making Your Voice Heard**

Help your class imitate a **talk show** format. (Volunteer to be the host or a facilitator!) Participate in the discussion of a current topic like the following. Keep track of how actively you participate in the discussion. (Your classmates may want to rank you on a scale from nonassertive to assertive.)

English-only for government offices
porn on the Internet
legislation against stalkers
restricting immigration
abolishing ethnic studies
angry white males
false accusations of rape
same-sex marriages
athletic scholarships for women

30b From Narrative to Opinion

Shift gears from the narrative to the expository mode.

Story telling is an age-old form of human communication. In many cultures, people asked for an opinion may say: "Let me tell you a story." The story then is going to be a story with a point. It makes a comment on the issue at stake, although the listener may have to think about the connection. At other times, the person asked for an opinion might say, "Let me remind you of a proverb." The proverb might be a saying like "When you drink the water, think of the source." Again, the listener or reader can think about the proverb and see how it applies to the present situation.

When writing in your current college setting, you may have to shift from such a **narrative** or story-telling mode to a more **exposi-**

tory style. In the western tradition of argument and debate, people asked for an opinion are likely to start with something assertive and explicit. They take a stand, and they follow through with reasons or examples. They are used to saying something like "It's my opinion that . . ."; "I am convinced that . . ."; "It seems to me that. . . ." They may bring in a brief story or anecdote *later* to help support their main point. But their basic style is likely to be: "This is what I think, and here are the reasons why."

When you find yourself writing in a story-telling mode, imagine a reader who is saying: "What is the point? Why are you telling me this?" When you record a personal experience, imagine a reader who is saying: "So what did you learn from the experience?" Imagine a reader saying: "Why is this in here at this point? What are you trying to prove?"

YOUR TURN 78 The Point of the Story

Write a *journal entry* using a brief story to help support a point. Use the following story or another brief story. Start with the point you are trying to make—spell it out, explain it, apply it to a current situation. Then use the story for backup. Then, if you can, add an example or support from your own personal experience to establish the personal connection.

> The Greek writer Nikos Kazantsakis tells a brief story that is one of my favorites: "There was a smell of fig trees in the air. A little old woman who was walking past stopped next to me. She lifted up some leaves covering a basket she was carrying. She picked out two of the figs in the basket and offered them to me. 'Do you know me from somewhere, granny?' I asked. She looked at me, surprised. 'No, my lad. Do I have to know you to give you something? You are a human being. So am I. Isn't that enough?'"

30c Key Ideas Up Front

Formulate key points and present them up front.

Some cultural traditions encourage a leisurely or roundabout style of argument. People take their time and finally lead up to the desired point. The ancient Greek philosopher Socrates loved to lead his students slowly down the path to the right conclusion. However, for a survival skill in the American college setting, you learn to sum up your point up front. Use a brief introduction to lead up to it—or sometimes just plunge in. As you work on a draft, keep asking yourself: What's the point? What's the message?

Practice putting a key point or **topic sentence** at the beginning of a paragraph. Ask: What point am I trying to nail down in this particular paragraph? For instance, you may have read mind-boggling figures on how the four or five major networks scramble to cover professional football. Come right out and say so:

TOPIC SENTENCE:

The networks covering major league sports pay mind-boggling sums for the right to broadcast the games. In one recent year, ESPN paid $4.8 billion for the Sunday night football game alone, up 140 percent from the previous contract. (This is for just one game a week—out of four or more covered by the media.) For one part of the football season, CBS paid $4 billion. Fox paid $4.4 billion for another part. ABC paid another $4.4 billion for another slice of the pie. These sums are paid out in a society where school boards in affluent communities fire the music teacher and the art teacher for lack of funds.

Practice spelling out a central idea or **thesis** early in your paper. Ask: What is the message of my paper as a whole? As your paper takes shape, keep asking yourself: How does this all add up? What is my tentative thesis, and how do I have to adjust it in the light of new arguments and new evidence? After checking things out and weighing the pro and con, what do I really think? Practice leading up to the central idea or thesis of your paper after a brief introduction that brings the issue to life:

THESIS:

The religion editor of a small-town newspaper recently wrote about high school students in a public high school who were kept from saying a prayer from the podium at commencement. She said they were denied their right to exercise religious freedom. In many parts of the country, school prayer has become a hot-button issue for school boards and political candidates.

Religion is again a major force in American politics and cultural life, often lining up citizens of a community on one side or the other. . . .

On a Sunday night, television evangelists reach huge audiences. . . .

New nondenominational congregations promote a new spirituality in huge auditoriums. . . .

In the African American community, organizations like the Black Muslims or the Promise Keepers try to counter the corrosive effect of poverty and drugs. . . .

YOUR TURN 79 What's the Point?

What topic sentence is missing in each of the following paragraphs? Compare your answers with those written by your classmates. (Who sums up the point best?)

1 ______________________________________. On the large riverboats that traveled up and down the Mississippi, fire was a common occurrence. Sparks would fly from the tall chimneys and set fire to the bales of cotton or boxes of cargo piled on deck. A boat would hit a snag or a sandbar in the river and sink. A tree snag could tear the bottom of a steamboat. The worst danger was an exploding boiler. Boilers were made of iron, and if the fires were too high they could explode. Too much steam could blow them to pieces.

2 ______________________________________. Farmers used to have their children work for them in the fields, and only slowly over the centuries did farmers start to use hired help. Family members cared for the sick before nurses were paid to take care of them. Canning fruit and vegetables and making clothes for the family were part of the housewives' unpaid chores. Today we pay babysitters instead of having family members provide child care. Young Americans are taught to drive, swim, or ski by paid instructors rather than by older brothers and sisters.

3 ______________________________________. In the early days of America, only men who owned substantial property were allowed to vote. Gradually the right to vote was extended to all adult males. Freed former slaves and their descendants struggled for many years for full voting rights. American women had to wait till 1920, when the Nineteenth Amendment finally granted them the right to vote in every state. More young people were given a chance to participate in the political process when the voting age was lowered from twenty-one to eighteen.

4 ______________________________________. We frequently see letters to the editors of a newspaper complaining about the cramped conditions in a local zoo. Owners of small menageries are criticized for keeping animals caged under atrocious conditions. Animal trainers in circuses are accused of abusing the animals they train. Animal rights organizations publish manifestoes demanding the liberation of zoo animals. Large zoos feel the pressure to expand in order to create more natural habitats for their animals.

5 ______________________________. Some developers are installing flickering gaslights outside higher-priced homes. They use such early American symbols as hitching posts, old lanterns, and town-criers' bells. Expensively printed brochures are illustrated with pictures of spinning wheels and muskets from the days of the American colonies. Antique stores prosper. Grey-haired hostesses in period costumes greet guests in restaurants adorned with pictures of horse-drawn carriages.

30d Joining the Dialogue

Learn to argue in a *yes-but* format.

Educated readers pride themselves on keeping communication channels open. They ask people to engage in dialogue. One way to keep the channels open is to argue in a **yes-but** style. We then try to find areas of agreement. We try to honor honest disagreement. We use phrases like the following:

YES-BUT: I agree fully with what was said but would like to add a point. . . .

I know this is a widely shared view, but I have had somewhat different experiences. . . .

I have often heard this view expressed, yet it seems to me an important point is often overlooked. . . .

Depending on your cultural background, you may have to make a special effort to respect other views. You then try not to dismiss or brush off dissenting opinions. You resist the temptation to make people who disagree with you look ignorant or ridiculous. (You totally resist the temptation to make fun of their English, their looks, or their family background. No *ad hominem*—no personal attacks!)

On a subject like affirmative action or welfare reform, you recognize that you are dealing with a complex issue. People of goodwill may have reached very different conclusions. On a topic like mandatory helmets for all bicycle riders or complete smoking bans in airports and public places, you try to show your respect both for those who want to honor traditions of personal choice and those who believe in the need to fight aggressively against threats to public health.

YOUR TURN 80 Playing the Devil's Advocate

When you play devil's advocate, you make people think about the arguments on the opposing side. Pick a topic on which you have a strong personal opinion. Then write *a journal entry* presenting what you see as strong arguments or strong evidence on the other side. Here are some sample topics:

1 If I wanted to argue for (or against) romance in the workplace, this is what I would be up against: ____________________

2 If I wanted to argue for (or against) teenage curfews or other curbs on the activities of juveniles, these are arguments I would have to confront: ____________________

3 If I wanted to argue for (or against) new restrictions on immigration, these are arguments I would have to deal with:

____

4 If I wanted to argue for (or against) an electrified fence along the Mexican border, these are the arguments I would have to take on:

____

5 If I wanted to argue for (or against) English-only in government offices and official business, this is what I would have to contend with: ____________________

31 ENGLISH AS A SECOND LANGUAGE

esl

Expand your sentence resources while watching out for first-language interference.

Your basic tool as a speaker and writer is the English sentence. If you are using English as a second language, you have a double assignment:

- *First of all, keep working at extending your repertory.* Build up your range. Strengthen your command of the *underlying patterns* that give shape to the rich variety of English sentences. For instance, keep watching how the language deals with different relationships in time or what the conventions are for addressing people.
- *At the same time, minimize first-language interference.* Keep an eye especially on things English does *differently* from other languages. When speaking your first language, were you used to different ways of showing the distinction between one and many or between the present and the past? You need to work on areas where the habits and patterns of your first language may interfere—where they may get in the way of your using English like a native.

YOUR TURN 81 Learning a Second Language

How can you tell that the student who wrote the following poem is learning English as a second language? Select several lines and explain what changes would be needed to make them standard English. (Your class may want to collaborate in creating a standard English version of the poem.)

A Lost Photograph

I was six year old.
I remember I take picture with my father.
I was standing near my father.
In my hair I had to tie a bow.
I was wearing two necklace.
I had long earring.
My father was wearing uniform army.
My face prouded.
Now my father passed away.
I moved many time.
I lost my old picture.
I always remember have good time with my father.
In my life I never have again.

31a Nouns and Number

esl Use plural signals: one, or more than one?

Words that label people, ideas, or things are **nouns**. Most such label words—*car, student, instructor*—point to things we can count. These **count nouns** show a difference in number by a change in the word itself. Many nouns signal the change from one to several by adding the *-s* ending: one **hour** (singular) but two **hours** (plural); one **friend** but several good **friends**. After words like *campus* and *tax*, you need the *-es* ending: several new **campuses**, a range of new **taxes**.

> ***EDITING PRIORITIES:*** During final proofreading of your papers, make sure you have used the *-s* ending for the plurals of nouns:
>
> PLURAL *-s:* He grew up with **a single parent**, not **both parents.**
>
> The family owned **a bicycle** and **several motorcycles**.
>
> Citizens offered first **one reward** and then **several rewards**.
>
> **Instruction** in diving included **instructions** for avoiding sharks.
>
> This current **investigation** differs from earlier **investigations**.
>
> PLURAL *-es:* Voters should be wary of quick **fixes.**

Only a few English words use an unusual plural—without the *-s* ending. Remember: one **woman** but several **women** (pronounced *wimmin*); one **tooth** but all his **teeth**; one **crisis** but several **crises**. A few English words have no plural signal: (deer) **deer,** (mouse) **mice,** (louse) **lice**; also **people** (when meaning persons—not a whole nation).

UNUSUAL: **One woman** works there, and **several other women** have applied.

One man used to handle the job, but now **two men** share the work.

She has **one child**, and he has **three children**.

He favored his **right foot** instead of using **both feet**.

UNMARKED: Many **people** believe in self-improvement.

When *this* and *that* come before a noun, they also change from singular to plural. The **pointing pronoun** *this* becomes *these.* The other pointing pronoun **that** becomes *those:* **this term** but **these terms; this** new **regulation** but **these** new **regulations; that building** but **those buildings.**

Some English nouns do *not* have separate plural forms. Such **bulk nouns** stand for things that don't usually come as individual items:

SINGULAR ONLY: Group members talked about their **unhappiness.** (no *unhappinesses*)

The Greeks thought **chaos** came before the **cosmos.** (no *chaoses*)

However, a bulk noun like *hair* (a person's whole head of hair) may in special situations be used as a plural:

> The victim's **hair** was light blond, and **the hairs** found on the clothing of the accused matched hers.

✓ ***EDITOR'S TIP:*** In special situations, even count nouns are used without a plural signal. Study the hyphenated combinations in the following examples:

UNMARKED PLURALS: a **two-parent** family, a **three-year** lease, a **six-foot** wall, a **two-day** meeting, a **five-point** spread

YOUR TURN 82 Changing Singular to Plural

Change all nouns in the following sentences from one (singular) to more than one (plural). Read the changed sentences over several times, paying special attention to the plural forms.

EXAMPLE: A top athlete signed a contract for a huge sum.

ANSWER: Top **athletes** signed **contracts** for huge **sums.**

1 An immigrant from a Scandinavian country founded a town in a northern state.

2 A vote from a member of a minority helped decide a recent election.

3 A Mormon congregation built a tabernacle in a large city.

4 An investigation revealed an irregularity in a negotiation for a contract.

YOUR TURN 82 *(continued)*

5 A researcher reported on a promising new medication for a mental illness.

6 A child moving to a different city will find a friend at the new school.

7 A scandal may keep a crisis in a foreign country off the front page.

8 A man and a woman may react differently to the same speech.

9 An automated system will often forward a message to the intended user.

10 A freshman might be unable to enroll in a required class.

31b Nouns and Articles

esl

Know when and how to put articles before nouns.

Articles are brief signal words that tell us: "A noun is ahead—a word that we use to label people, ideas, or things." Often the noun follows immediately: **the airport, a helicopter, the pilot.** Often other material comes between the article and the noun: **the** new **airport, a** corporate **plane, a** female **pilot.** Not all languages have articles, so learning how to use them is a high priority for many students of English as a second language.

Like Spanish or Italian, English has two kinds of articles used as signal words or noun markers. We use **a** or **an**—the **indefinite** article—when we are not yet singling out one from many. We are not pointing to one definite example:

INDEFINITE: We should plant **a tree**.
(We haven't decided what kind.)

The car needs **a** new **engine**.
(We have not yet picked one.)

There's never **a police officer** when you need one.
(At this point *any* officer would do.)

He had **an exam** every day this week.
(Each was one of several.)

We use **the**—the **definite** article—when we mean: "This particular one." We have singled out one from the many. When we say, "**The officer** approached," we are referring to one we had previously noticed or mentioned—that particular one. Perhaps we mean the officer in a police car that drove up behind us. Perhaps we mean the officer on duty at the desk. In all of the following examples, we mean "this particular one":

DEFINITE: There was no way to save **the tree**.
(the particular one)

The officer asked for my license.

The engine had been rebuilt.

The exam was all true-and-false.

31b.1 Definite or Indefinite *Watch your choice of articles.*

As a rule of thumb, ask yourself: Am I thinking of a *general* type of person or thing? Or am I thinking of a *specific* person, object, or place?

GENERAL: The community needs **a school** and **a hospital.**
(this is the general idea—not yet pinned down to specific examples)

SPECIFIC: He left **the school** and went to **the hospital.**
(this school and that particular hospital)

Study the shift from general to specific in sets like the following:

> **A bystander** tried to break up the fight (could be *anybody* at this point). After some pushing and shoving, **the individual** identified himself as a plain-clothes officer (we are talking about the person previously mentioned).

31b.2 Missing Article *Fill in missing articles.*

Put in the missing **a** or **the** in sentences like the following: "They took him to the hospital *in ambulance*" (should be **in an ambulance**). Missing articles are a common sign of first-language interference—carrying over patterns from languages that do not use articles the way English does. Missing articles are needed in all the following sentences:

in the Peace Corps
Sharon served *in Peace Corps* in Africa.

to the supervisor
Manuel talked *to supervisor* about the change.

in a dorm.
First-year students live *in dorm.*

in the United States.
Millions of refugees have started new lives *in United States.*

When you talk in general about more than one (plural), the indefinite article disappears. However, the definite article would stay—it would still show that you are thinking about specific examples:

GENERAL (no article):

Our communities need **schools** and **clinics**—not **gun stores** and **liquor stores.**

SPECIFIC (articles):

Taxpayers starve **the schools** and **the clinics,** while the **liquor stores** prosper.

31b.3 Unneeded Article *Take out unnecessary articles.*

Bulk nouns like *food, furniture, water, garbage, rice,* or *advice* are different from count nouns, which allow us to count individual items. Bulk nouns or lump nouns stand for things that we can weigh or measure in bulk or think of as a whole. We don't usually say *a concrete* or *an advice* because we don't usually break these words up into individual items. (We would say "a kind of concrete" or "a piece of advice.") Bulk nouns therefore usually appear without an indefinite article: We pour **concrete**; we reject **advice**. We buy **furniture**; plants need **water** (no article). Words for general qualities, like *boredom, patience, happiness*, work the same way: Money doesn't buy **happiness** (no article).

Even with bulk nouns, you will use **the** when you zero in on a definite example:

GENERAL: **Rice** is a staple in many Asian countries.

SPECIFIC: **The rice** we had for dinner was from Burma.

GENERAL: We were looking for an apartment without **furniture.**

SPECIFIC: **The furniture** they rented was ultramodern.

GENERAL: **Patience** was not his outstanding trait.

SPECIFIC: **The patience** they showed was admirable.

GENERAL: We stopped only for **fuel** and water.

SPECIFIC: **The** spent **fuel** of nuclear reactors is a huge headache.

✓ ***EDITOR'S TIP:*** Names of individual persons, places, or countries (proper names) do not use an article: in Africa, from Germany, for Argentina. But watch for exceptions like **the** United States, **the** United Kingdom, **the** Dominican Republic, **the** Netherlands, and place names like **the** Everglades, **the** Great Lakes, **the** South. Rivers, oceans, and canals usually have the article: **the** Mississippi, **the** Thames, **the** Ganges, **the** Atlantic, **the** Caribbean, **the** Panama Canal.

31b.4 Idiomatic Articles

Know when to use or omit the article in common expressions. When a customary way of saying something does not seem to fit any general rule, we call it an **idiomatic** expression. Track idiomatic expressions like the following.

ARTICLE: in the office, in the hospital, in the library, in the army, at the track, after the accident, at the bus station, on the air

NO ARTICLE: at work, in school, in college, by accident, on time, by train, at sea, on credit, on duty

Track contrasting pairs where the article makes a difference in meaning:

This bus is not **in service.** (not being used)
She spent two years **in the service.** (in the military)

Seals move slowly **on land.** (as opposed to in the water)
Few farmers remain **on the land.** (cultivating agricultural land)

Few family farms remain. (stresses how few there are)
A few small-scale farmers remain. (stresses that some are left)

✓ ***EDITOR'S TIP:*** Some uses of articles are different in British English. For instance, in England you might hear *in hospital* rather than *in the hospital*.

YOUR TURN 83 Selecting Articles

After the number of each sentence, fill in the right choice: *the, a* (or *an*), or *no* (for no article).

1 When we arrived home from the dance, Pat paid for _____ limousine.
2 The governor returned the bill to _____ legislature.
3 They had four children but did not have _____ boy.
4 You can reach all major cities in France by _____ train.
5 Women recruits encountered _____ harassment.
6 The announcer used racial slurs on _____ air.
7 Many co-workers play _____ tennis regularly.
8 We have not settled on a candidate, but we need _____ capable person.
9 The flag became a symbol of _____ Old South.
10 _____ earthquake of 1906 destroyed much of San Francisco.

31c Verbs and Time

esl

Select the right forms of verbs to show time.

In many sentences, **verbs** tell us what people *do*. Verbs fill us in on who does what:

The student **applies** for admission.

Schools **admit** students.

Administrators **evaluate** records.

However, verbs also help answer the question: Who does what *when?* Verbs can show a change in the timeframe by a change in the word itself:

Counselors **advise** students (now).

Counselors **advised** students (then).

Students **send** in transcripts (now).

Students **sent** in transcripts (before).

The law **is** in effect (now).

The law **was** in effect (in the past).

Often another added verb helps the main verb tell us when. We call such added verbs **helping verbs**, or auxiliaries.

We got your call (in the past).

We **will contact** you (in the future).

We noticed the error (some time ago).

We **have adjusted** the bill (more recently).

Together, changed word forms and added helping verbs help us cover many relationships in time (called **tenses**). In final editing of your writing, do a verb check.

PRIORITIES FOR BILINGUAL WRITERS

How Verbs Show Time

In final proofreading of your papers, pay special attention to the forms of English verbs:

PRESENT (action happening now or today, or all the time):

Today, only new students **sign up**.

A long line **forms** in the morning.

Many students now **register** by phone.

PAST (action already finished):

Yesterday, I **filled** out the forms.

After they **arrived**, the college **raised** the tuition.

Last year, I **made** several new friends.

PERFECT (finished recently or still important):

My cousin **has finished** most requirements for the degree.

Their friends **have** always **supported** them.

Fee increases **have changed** the plans of several friends.

PAST PERFECT (already finished before something else took place):

The day before, I **had missed** my appointment.

Before they arrived, they **had waited** months for their visas.

When she enrolled again, the college **had changed** the requirements.

FUTURE (action that is scheduled or expected but has not yet happened):

The lab **will close** early this afternoon.

Grades **will be sent out** next week.

31c.1 **-s for Third Person Singular** *Use the -s form as needed for present action.* Almost all English verbs have two different forms for the present tense: **agree** and **agrees**, **arrive** and **arrives**, **do** and **does**. We use the plain or unmarked form of the verb after *I* and *you:* I **speak** normally. You **shout**. We also use the plain form after plurals—when talking about several, people, objects, or ideas: Australians **speak** English. Angry people **shout**.

However, we shift to the *-s* form when talking about someone else. We use it when talking about one thing or idea at a time. We say that the *-s* form of the verb is needed for **third person singular**—talking not about me or you but a single third party or a single thing, with action now.

-*S* FORM:

My Australian friend **speaks** funny English. He **pronounces** words differently. His accent **makes** him sound like Crocodile Dundee. Everyone **realizes** he is from down under, but he **doesn't** mind. He **knows** everybody **thinks** he **comes** from the outback and **misses** the song of the cookaburra bird.

Words like *everybody* or *anybody* are treated as singulars. They stand for many people, but we seem to be thinking of them one at a time: Everybody **makes** mistakes (each one of them). Nobody **likes** taxes. Anyone **knows** that.

✓ ***EDITOR'S TIP:*** If the English language had been designed by a computer programer, it would have one signal for singular (always the same) and a different signal for plural. However, because English dates from a pre-computer age, the *-s* ending serves *two* different functions. It serves as a plural signal for nouns (She received several telephone **calls**). However, it serves as a singular signal for verbs (He **calls** here regularly).

YOUR TURN 84 Checking the *-s* Ending

The following passage is from a peer review. Check it for use of the *-s* ending. Where is it used right for third person singular, present time (one third party or thing, with action now)? Where is the *-s* ending missing? Write down all verbs in this passage. Add the needed *-s* ending where it is missing.

An employer often encourage an applicant by a glowing job description. In this paper, the student writer describes his mixed feelings about his experience at work. At first he complain about his job but then realize the value of the experience. He knows that only a lucky employee like the job. The employer often think of workers in terms of labor costs. Sometimes the employer shows little sympathy when an employee need time off because of family or health problems. Like other employees, this writer imagine the ideal job—a job he likes and think of with pride. He seems to have a definite goal, but he knows a long road stretch in front of him.

31c.2 ***-d/-ed* for Past and after *have*** *Check for omitted -d or -ed endings.* Do not leave off the *-d* or *-ed* ending for past tense. Do not omit it after the helping verb *have (has, had)*.

seceded

OMITTED *-d/-ed:* The South *secede* from the Union.

had agitated

Abolitionists *had agitate* against slavery.

have reevaluated

Historians *have reevaluate* the rivalry between North and South.

Not all English verbs use the added ending to show changes in time. There may be a change in the word itself. Track unusual (**irregular**) verbs like the following.

take	It **takes** time (it always does). We **took** her advice (in the past). We **have** always **taken** her advice seriously (and still do).
choose	The voters **choose** presidents (every four years). The voter **chose** Clinton (twice in a row). Three times before, they **had chosen** a Republican (this was before Clinton).
lead	America again **leads** in space exploration (as of now). For years the Russians **led** in the space race (this was some time ago). The space race **has led** to some spectacular disasters (and we may not have seen the last of these).

See **10d** for a checklist of irregular verbs.

31c.3 Plain Form with *do* *Use the plain form of a verb with the helping verb* do. Do not use the *-d* or *-ed* ending after *do, does,* or *did.* Forms of *do* (*does, did*) help us ask questions or make negative statements: **Do** you **mind**? The switch **does** not **work**. The reporter **did** not **verify** the story. We use the plain (or unmarked) form of the main verb when using a form of *do* as an auxiliary (or helping) verb.

did not exercise.
PAST: My roommate *did not exercised.*

YOUR TURN 85 Selecting Verb Forms

Your instructor may ask you to rewrite the passage about the Australian friend—changing it first to a passage about *several* Australian friends, and changing it again to a passage about an Australian friend you had in the *past.*

31d Verbs and Helping Verbs

esl

Study the full range of combinations for English verbs.

Students of a language like English or French are amazed to discover the full range of possible forms and combinations for verbs.

EXTENDING THE RANGE **Generating English Verbs**

How many different combinations could you generate if your verb generator were programed for a few simple rules of English grammar? You first put a word like *will* or *can* (if any). You then put a form of *have* (if any). You then put a form of *be*—such as *am, is, are, was, were,* or *been* (if any). Then you put the right form of the main verb.

Here is a sampling of what your verb generator might print out:

CAN	*HAVE*	*BE* +	MAIN VERB =	COMPLETE VERB
can			investigate	**can investigate**
	has		investigated	**has investigated**
should	have		investigated	**should have investigated**
		was	investigated	**was investigated**
might		be	investigated	**might be investigated**
		is	investigating	**is investigating**
could	have	been	investigated	**could have been investigated**
	has	been	investigating	**has been investigating**
may	have	been	investigating	**may have been investigating**

What special forms should you watch for in addition to the forms for past (*investigated*), perfect (*have investigated*), and future (*will investigate*)?

31d.1 Plain Form after *can/will* *Use the plain form after words like* can *and* will. The plain form of the verb follows the common helping verbs (or auxiliaries) *will* or *would, can* or *could, may* or *might, shall* or *should*. The helping verb *will* is followed by the plain or unmarked form of a verb to show future: We **will help** you (this is a definite promise). Other helping verbs that work the same way in a sentence show various degrees of possibility:

We are sure we **can help** you. (a strong possibility)

We **would help** you if we **could get** permission.
(this sounds more uncertain)

We **should help** you. (but don't count on it)

Change the main verb if *have* becomes part of the combination:

This **might have helped**.

We **could have gotten** permission.

31d.2 Passive Verb with *-d/-ed*

Use the form with -d *or* -ed *for passive verbs.* An active sentence tells us who does what: The staff **discharged** the patient early. A **passive** sentence turns the normal Who-does-what sequence around. It tells us who had what done. The spotlight is on the target or the result:

SHORT PASSIVE: The patient **was discharged** early.

COMPLETE PASSIVE: The patient **was discharged** early **by a cost-conscious staff**.

The verbs that signal "this was done" use a form of *be* as a helping verb. *Be* is a special verb that preserves separate forms after *I* and *you:* I **am** firm. You **are** stubborn. He **is** wrong-headed. Unlike other English verbs, it also shows singular or plural in the past (except after *you*): One **was** selected. The others **were** disqualified. When a form of *be* starts a passive verb, you may have to verify that the main verb ends in *-d* or *-ed:*

PASSIVE VERBS: The office *was search* [was searched] by government agents.

Many records *had been remove.* [had been removed.] Files *had been shred.* [had been shredded.]

For irregular verbs, use the same form for the passive that you would use after *have*:

Three judges **will choose** from the final four. They **have** not yet **chosen** the winner. The runner-up **will be chosen** first.

They **take** no prisoners. No prisoners **had been taken.**

31d.3 Progressive Verb with *-ing*

Use the -ing *form for action in progress.* Special **progressive** forms of verbs show that an action is in progress or something is still happening. Progressive forms of verbs start with a form of *be (am, are, is, was, were, has been*, and so on). They combine it with the special *-ing* form of the main verb.

The world's forests **are disappearing.**

Protesters **are making** plans to disrupt logging operations.

During the Redwood Summer, activists **were living** in trees.

This summer, they **will** again **be trying** to protect the groves.

Environmentalists **have been reexamining** their tactics.

Old-growth forests **are** still **being cut** down.

Verify that you have used the *-ing* form rather than the plain form when something is continuing or still going on:

PROGRESSIVE: The companies ~~*are move*~~ **are moving** their mills to Mexico.

The NIS ~~*is reinforce*~~ **is reinforcing** the border patrols.

YOUR TURN 86 The Range of Verbs

Show the range of several English verbs in brief sentences including the following possibilities:

-ed or other form for simple past

-ed or other form after *have* for perfect

-ed or other form after *be* for passive

plain form after *do* for negative or question

-ing after *be* for progressive

SAMPLE SETS:

1 We **asked** for advice. We have **asked** for advice. We were **asked** for advice. Did you **ask** for advice? We were **asking** for advice.

2 They **took** our advice. They have **taken** our advice. Our advice was **taken**. Do not **take** their advice. We are **taking** your advice.

31e Idiomatic Verbs/Prepositions

esl

Aim at the natural, idiomatic way of saying things.

During an intermediate stage in learning a language, we find words for most of what we want to say. However, our sentences may seem labored—they show that some of it is still hard work. A native speaker could say the same thing more easily, more naturally. An

idiom is a natural, familiar way of saying something. Here are different idiomatic expressions using the word *mind.* Can you explain the different meanings to someone using English as a second language?

> What's **on your mind?**
>
> What did you **have in mind?**
>
> He **changed his mind.**
>
> **Keep** us **in mind.**
>
> They haven't **made up their minds.**

31e.1 Idiomatic Verbs *Find a better verb.* In the following sentence, look at the verb—the word that brings action into the sentence or sets things in motion: "More Americans *are paying devotion* to obscure religious cults." Readers will get the meaning, but something is not quite right. We pay attention, but we **show** devotion. Maybe we should say that more people **are committing** themselves to cults. Or they **owe allegiance** to cults. Edit sentences like the following for unidiomatic verbs:

> **held**
> My cousin *occupied* the same position in her company.
> (We **hold** a position, **engage in** an occupation, or **follow** a trade)
>
> **submitted**
> The applicant *subjected* his résumé.
> (We **submit** applications, **file** reports, or **register** a complaint)

31e.2 Idiomatic Prepositions *Choose a more idiomatic preposition.* Many prepositions show time: **before** the show, **after** the performance, **during** the break, **within** a week. Other prepositions show location or place: **in** the folder, **at** the entrance, **under** the table, **over** the counter, **beside** the door, **below** our projections. Still other prepositions show how something is done: **by** hand, **with** effort, **without** a net, **through** connections. English prepositions trip up the learner because they do not have just one simple meaning. They don't have a one-to-one meaning that could be quickly punched into a computer. Here are three different meanings of the preposition *by:*

TIME (no later than):	**by** Wednesday
PLACE (very close to):	**by** the lake
METHOD (using the hands):	**by** hand

Study contrasts like the following:

We were **surprised by** his decision.

He expressed **surprise at** our success.

Two jurors **disagreed with** the majority.

One judge **dissented from** the majority opinion.

She seldom **agreed with** her instructors.
(was of the same opinion)

The members **agreed on** a course of action.
(worked out a common plan)

Everyone **agreed to** the arrangement
(was willing to accept)

TIPS FOR BILINGUAL WRITERS

Using Idiomatic Prepositions

Study the prepositions in the following idiomatic expressions. Watch for similar combinations in your reading and listening:

We were **fascinated by** their explanations.

The FBI was **interested in** his background.

Some people are **allergic to** berries.

Management was **prejudiced against** older workers.

The design was changed to **prevent** the airbags **from** inflating accidentally.

He reluctantly **parted with** his convertible.

Their lawyers did not **comply with** the request.

All components **conformed to** exact specifications.

We **compared** this year's **with** last year's results.

He **compared** the new structure **to** a prison.

The company was **short of** cash.

The new CEO was **deficient in** imagination.

YOUR TURN 87 Choosing the Right Link

What is the missing preposition? Complete each of the following:

objecting _____ a proposal; taking care _____ children; deprived _____ nutritious food; persevering _____ a task; refrain _____ name-calling; indifferent _____ the heat; inferior _____ the competition; inconsistent _____ sound practice; accused _____ a crime; had abstained _____ voting; dissenting _____ an opinion; superior _____ the other choices; cleared _____ all charges; not compatible _____ a roommate; charged _____ murder

31e.3 Idiomatic Verbals

Choose the right verbal. After verbs like *start, stop,* or *refuse,* we often expect to learn "started *what?*" Often a **verbal** will give the answer: started **to compete**; stopped **competing**. The verbal may be a special verb form starting with *to* or another ending with *-ing*. When do you use the one, and when the other? After verbs like *start, love,* or *hate,* either form would be natural English:

started **to solve** the equation	loved **to cook** for us
started **solving** the equation	loved **cooking** for us
hated **to leave** the area	continued **to harass** them
hated **leaving** the area	continued **harassing** them

However, with the following verbs, the *to* form is the idiomatic choice:

ought **to reconsider**	managed **to alienate** everybody
refused **to pay** the bill	proceeded **to decode** the message
expected **to succeed**	encouraged us **to continue**

With the following verbs, the *-ing* form is the idiomatic choice:

postponed **paying** the bill	recommended **starting** over
stopped **complaining**	enjoyed **watching**
discontinued **making** the product	delayed **reopening** the street

In editing your writing, look for mismatched verbals:

recommended filing
MISMATCHED: They *recommended to file* the forms early.

YOUR TURN 88 A Paper for Peer Editing

The bilingual author of the following student paper has come a long way toward using English effectively for her own purposes. For instance, how effective is the image comparing harmful stereotypes to a dragon to be slain? How does the student author use the concept of "double jeopardy"? How effectively does she draw on personal experience?

Can you help the author edit her paper for idiomatic English? Study the highlighted words or phrases. For each, what would be a more idiomatic choice? Do you agree with the changes made at the beginning as examples of the editing needed?

Slaying the Dragon

The dragon that every woman, especially Asian women, must slay is the stereotype that women are subordinate to men.

Asians in general are stereotyped as self-sufficient, brainy "nerds" that do homework all day long and have no social lives. Classified [as] into the quiet types that are taught not to [make waves] cause waves in society, typical Asians [are seen as living up] submit as a perfect picture to the "yes, sir–no, sir" image of being inferior with other races.

In a similar view, the woman of today still has to deal with the stereotype that women are only second to men in society. This is most often seen in the workplace as men attain more promotions and

YOUR TURN 88 *(continued)*

advancements while the women are trapped in a "glass ceiling" to the corporate ladder.

To be stereotyped as one or the other is difficult, but to be stereotyped as both is even worse. It is a double jeopardy that every Asian woman must face and fight in the liberal, yet still male-dominating American society. Personally, I find it confusing to distinguish the reason why I am usually discriminated against. Is it because I am Asian, female, or both?

Two summers ago, I was employed in an insurance company as a telemarketing representative. There were at least twenty-five student applicants with only six positions offered. With my luck, the company decided to hire me on a temporary basis.

I shared an office with two other telemarketing representatives, who all happened to be female and Caucasian. We adopted quite well to our new workloads and new friendships. The other three newly hired telemarketing representatives (TR) were also women, two Caucasian and the other Mexican, called Sandra.

As the summer progressed, we met most of our employers and the different department heads. They seemed genuinely friendly, but I could not help but notice that none of them were minorities. In fact in our department of thirty employees, there were only three minorities: an Asian temp, Sandra, and myself. It was odd especially for an office in a city where minorities make up at least 60 percent of the population. I did not bother with making an issue of it since I enjoyed my work.

Gradually, the head of telemarketing asked a few of the TR's to stay overtime at least once every other week. We would go to dinner after work with our other co-workers. Once, the subject of wages was brought up, and carelessly comparing our pay, we found our male co-workers were apparently being paid more for the same work. The difference was $1.80 from the pay of one of the male temps to my salary. And although no one else noticed but Sandra and I, both our wages were a few nickels lower than the pay of the rest of the women. With all this in mind, we started analyzing what else were the defects of the company.

We noticed that most department heads and higher-room employees were male, while the telemarketing department was predominately female. There was one female Asian manager and one male African-American manager. The company obviously stereotyped women by giving them positions in telemarketing representatives and the usual secretarial jobs (making coffee for the men, filing documents, etc.) and dominated the much higher paying and status jobs with male employees. We were all bothered by this, but only a few of us were willing to take action.

We also remembered an incident when photographers were taking pictures for a publicity campaign for the company brochure. Naturally, our multicultural group picture was included to show the "family atmosphere" of the firm. Sandra and I felt that we were only hired because the company needed some "color" for occasions like publicity brochures.

YOUR TURN 88 *(continued)*

Even though we are in the 90s, the stereotypes against women and Asians have not changed. Women such as a local Asian news anchor—a woman that people depend on to bring news into their homes—have not slain the dragon that has been around from the beginning of time, flaring fire into Asian women's paths to success. Most people see her first as an "Asian woman who was offered a break, and a TV journalist second," according to a friend who is a sophomore in journalism at the college.

To know the problem is the first step to solving it. But for Asian women like myself, the reason against the stereotype will always be an unanswered question: Is it because I am Asian, a woman, or both?

31f Checking Sentence Structure

esl Check for unusual sentence structure.

Some variations from normal English sentence structure result from first-language interference. You may have to rewrite sentences that do not follow normal English word order.

31f.1 Verb First *Normally make the verb follow your subject.* The most common English sentence is a "who does what" sentence. It goes from the subject to the verb—it first focuses on something and then puts it in motion. Some other languages use "what does who" or "who what does" patterns instead. In English, the **verb-first** sentence appears only in a few traditional expressions: **Said the judge**: "That's enough."

The student argued
VERB FIRST: *Argued the student* with the teacher.

31f.2 **Subjectless Verb** *Normally supply a subject for your verbs.* In some languages, the who in "who does what" may be left out. The result is a **subjectless verb.** In English, this usually happens only in jottings in a diary or in informal notes. This abbreviated style was also used in old-fashioned telegrams, where customers were charged by the word.

	We arrived	**We hiked**	**We built**
TELEGRAM STYLE:	*Arrived* at noon.	*Hiked* to campsite.	*Built* a fire.

31f.3 **Duplicated Subject** *Take out a pronoun that duplicates your subject.* In some languages, the who in "who does what" is taken up again just before the verb. The result is a **duplicated subject**: The *agent she* studied the documents. In English, this duplication occurs only in nonstandard dialects.

illegals is called

DUPLICATED: *The guide* smuggling in illegals *he is called* a coyote.

Greece applied

My cousin from Greece *she* applied for a visa.

YOUR TURN 89 **Se Habla Español**

The following sentences are adapted from a short story about Americans who have come to New York from Puerto Rico. Like other second-language speakers, the people in the story weave words from their first language into their conversation. Can you tell what the Spanish words mean? Have you observed a similar **code-switching**—the mixing in of words from a first language—by a group of people using English as a second language? Write a paper about the meanings and uses of words that have come into their English from the other language.

1 My father and uncle had been chicken farmers and grocers—gallineros and bodegueros—but the jobs in Nueva York were mostly for unskilled jibaros.

2 We were going to be americanos—not our parents but just we, los hijos.

3 It was muy tarde to go back to the island.

YOUR TURN 89 *(continued)*

4 They did not want us to hang around with bandoleros—no public school amigos for us.

5 La Avenida Tercera was a strip of ladrones, highwaymen posing as merchants.

6 She waited for the clientes to disperse to go cash their checks at Cohn's farmacia.

7 Illness was another diablo in his life.

8 He wanted to be told that muy pronto he would be walking again.

PART FIVE

WRITING THE RESEARCH PAPER

Informal research goes into most writing you do in college. An educated person does not pretend to know everything—but has learned how to find out. As a college student, you are learning how to sift information from a range of sources—experts, insiders, researchers, official agencies, personal testimonials—in trying to answer questions like the following:

- What exactly does the Second Amendment say about the right to bear arms? What exactly does the First Amendment say about an "establishment of religion"? (And what does that phrase mean?)
- Is it true that in spite of roads clogged with millions of cars air quality has improved in key areas both in this country and in Europe as the result of strong anti-pollution initiatives?
- Is medicine close to a breakthrough in curing cancer?

- Is there a consensus among scientists on the dangers of the ozone layer?
- Are there hard statistics on what workfare has done to move people off welfare?

In a formal research project, you conduct a systematic search for the best current information and thinking on your subject. In many college courses, you will write formal research papers based on a thorough study of background materials and authoritative sources. Policies regarding length of papers and time devoted to them vary from school to school and class to class. You may be asked to devote your time to one major research project, or you may have a chance to work on one or more shorter papers as a trial run.

32 STARTING YOUR RESEARCH PROJECT

Get your bearings and define your topic.

What makes a research paper different? In a well-researched paper, you bring together the best current information and thinking on your topic. You want to know more than the average newspaper reader, so you check out what insiders or experts know. You may have read about a current social or scientific issue but have not followed it up in depth. For instance, you may know about efforts to bring back the wolves or to prevent global warming. Or you may have read about efforts to change IQ tests to make them cover more of the true range of human intelligence. You start researching your topic when you ask:

- Why is this an issue?
- Who are the authorities on this topic?
- Where do the experts agree, and where do they disagree?
- Who else would have inside information or firsthand experience?
- What conclusions would be reached by a fair-minded observer?

32a Defining the Research Paper

Know the requirements for research-based writing.

A research paper means a major investment in time and effort. To make your investment pay off, keep in mind key requirements for a successful paper:

- *Go beyond hearsay to authoritative sources.* Start asking the basic question: "How do I know this?" Who makes this claim? Who found this out? What backs this up? You will need to go beyond statements like "Science tells us . . ." or "History teaches. . . ." Instead, you ask: What scientist tells us this—based on what research? Which historian makes this claim—based on what evidence? Who is your source, and what makes it reliable?
- *Explore the full range of available material.* In the era of the information highway, material on almost any topic is out there somewhere. Use the search strategies recommended by teachers and librarians and outlined in this book. You may start by surfing the Internet, discovering a whole range of opinions and perspectives

on your topic. However, some of what you find there may be in shortened and quasi-anonymous form. Push on to more complete and more permanent sources. For example, discover scholarly or scientific journals that are **refereed**—the articles have been sent out for approval to referees who are authorities on the subject. Look for timely books by insiders or experts. Check the testimony of eyewitnesses.

- *Make full use of library resources.* Discover the resources and the limitations of your college library. Wander about the library, familiarizing yourself with the layout of reading rooms and special collections. If you have access to magazine shelves or to the book stacks, spend time browsing, the way compulsive readers and books lovers do. Find out about special services—interlibrary loans, articles stored on film (such as microfilm), or articles photocopied for you from professional publications. Learn to work your way around obstacles. For example, someone else has already checked out an important book. (Try your public library?) Your library does not subscribe to a scholarly journal for lack of funds. (Get a printout of an article through an interlibrary service?)
- *Pull together what you have learned.* When you **synthesize** the results of your research, you bring together what you have found out. As you make progress on your project, start asking: "How does this add up?" Not all the data and ideas you accumulate will point in the same direction. Is it possible to arrive at a consensus of informed opinion? For instance, are we winning the fight against AIDS? How effective will current medications prove in stemming the epidemic? How effective have efforts been to educate the young or women to the seriousness of the threat? Can you find a common thread in the testimony of researchers, physicians, and patients? You will be looking for areas of agreement, weighing the evidence and trying to reach a balanced conclusion.
- *Document your sources.* Show where you found your evidence. **Documentation** means charting a retrieval path for all material you have fed into your paper. You give credit to the people whose ideas, research findings, or statistics helped you reach your conclusions. You furnish information that will guide the interested reader to the right book or article or Internet source. As needed, you will specify authorship, complete title, place, date, version of a publication, or exact page. Accurate documentation satisfies readers who say: "Take me to your sources, so I can check for myself. Let me see whether you have quoted the authors correctly and made fair use of their data."

- *Learn to work in a collaborative environment.* Research in college, as in the outside world, is a combination of personal initiative and group cooperation. Share your discoveries and your frustrations with others. Learn from them, and let them learn from you. Learn from feedback from your fellow students and from your instructor. Turn to librarians for help. If your instructor provides special handouts or e-mail messages, scan such material carefully. What requirements seem especially important? What predictable problems should you avoid? Here is a sample message an instructor sent to students:

INSTRUCTOR'S E-MAIL MESSAGE:

Dear Writing Two Students:

So far we have stressed being creative in looking for answers, for as I've said, knowing how to find data is as important as what you find.

Now we need to work on evaluating data. We need to know where information comes from—who is accountable or responsible for it. For instance, it makes a difference if lung cancer research comes from researchers funded by a tobacco company or from researchers at the Mayo Clinic or university medical center.

Guard against over-dependency on the WWWeb, for many of the academic resources you'll need may either not be on the WWWeb or be there only in abbreviated or adapted versions or summaries. When you can, go to the complete original source. And don't limit yourself to the first few sources you find. The success of your research paper will rest on the expertise you develop on your issue. The more you know, the stronger your conclusions.

Next week, we'll work on identifying authors and looking at their credentials.

32b Avoiding Plagiarism

Never pass off someone else's work as your own.

In a carefully documented paper, you protect yourself against any possible charges of **plagiarism.** Never copy or adapt another writer's work without acknowledgment. When you plagiarize, you take material from your sources and pass it off as your own. You quote someone else's words without quotation marks. Deliberately or inadvertently, you present information and ideas as your own that are someone else's intellectual property.

RESEARCH ESSENTIALS

Insurance against Plagiarism

A full-disclosure policy like the following will prevent any suspicion of plagiarism:

- ***Use quotation marks for everything you copy.*** When taking notes, use quotation marks for everything you copy verbatim—word for word. Never copy chunks of material without noting exactly what is direct quotation.
- ***Include a source tag with everything you feed into your notes.*** Keep track of the exact source for everything from your reading and exploration. Do not clip material from newspapers and do not photocopy material without recording the source.
- ***Keep a detailed research log.*** Track your progress. Keep a log or research record that shows how your paper took shape—in case anyone ever questions whether it is indeed your own work.
- ***Save all interim materials.*** Save all notes, scratch outlines, early drafts, and feedback from the instructor and fellow students.
- ***Talk about your research process.*** Talk freely with your peers and your instructor about promising leads, lucky finds, and dead alleys. Make sure your coworkers and your instructor know that your paper was the result of honest effort.

Some plagiarism is careless or unintentional. Intentionally dishonest plagiarism is a different problem. Suppose a student has struggled to produce acceptable work and then suddenly turns in a superior paper. What happened? Did a roommate or friend step in? Did the student download a canned paper? Did a term paper factory mail a ready-made paper? Those who sell canned papers sometimes claim that what they do is legal. However, they are not the ones who risk ruining their academic careers.

OPTIONS FOR WRITING 17 Starting a Research Log

Many instructors require you to keep a **research log**. In weekly or biweekly entries, you may start by writing about your interest in the topic. What previous reading, coursework, or personal connection makes it seem worthwhile? Later, you may start writing about promising leads. You may report on your experiences with library services.

Study the following sample entry by a fellow student. How might the tips given here help you with a research project of your own?

RESEARCH LOG ENTRY:

I found that much has been published on my chosen topic—research into alternative kinds of intelligence. The controversy over defining and testing intelligence has a special interest for me, since like many high school students I hated SAT tests. It was long assumed that intelligence was a single faculty that could be measured like the cholesterol count of a person trying to lose weight. However, now researchers claim that there are different ways of being smart. Some of us are smart about people but poor with numbers and vice-versa.

I am not having too much trouble finding books. I checked out *The Bell Curve* by Herrnstein and Murray and *Emotional Intelligence* by Goleman. I thought it was crucial to check out *The Bell Curve*, since there are many articles arguing with its claim that intelligence can be measured by conventional tests and is hereditary according to race. *Emotional Intelligence* gives a clear explanation of what emotional intelligence is and how it is left out by traditional tests. It was easy to find periodicals with information about emotional intelligence but difficult to narrow my search. I have found general articles, but it is tough to find specific applications to areas like teaching or hiring. I really liked an article from *Time* entitled "Teaching Feelings 101." The author talked about a school in New Haven, Connecticut, that is stressing emotional intelligence as just as important as mathematics and science.

32c Defining Your Topic

Focus on a question worth asking and worth exploring.

Give real thought to your choice of topic. Make sure it asks a question that means enough to you to keep you going through a major project, with its ups and downs. If you are given a specific topic, try hard to find a personal angle or to discover why others have considered it important. Listen to advice like the following:

- *Focus on a limited topic that you can explore in depth.* Narrow down broad subjects like "Crisis in Education" or "Our Endangered Planet." If you care about our endangered wildlife, you may want to focus on the big birds: What are the survival chances of the condor, the eagle, and the crane? Or you may want to focus on a test case—the wolf, the coyote, or the grizzly—in the struggle to protect the predators against their hereditary natural enemy (human beings).

- *Consider starting from a foothold of previous knowledge.* Maybe you love the outdoors and have followed the fight to save forests and green spaces from developers, mining interests, and timber corporations. You have followed efforts in Congress to buy up remaining pockets of old-growth forests ahead of the chainsaws. You know friends who have gone to the redwoods to live in treehouses to defy the encroaching timber interests. You have read pamphlets urging lumberjacks to make common cause against companies clear-cutting the forests and moving the sawmills to Mexico. If you can draw on this much previous reading and personal testimony, you will have a headstart.
- *Consider a topic that has a strong personal connection.* Current advances and setbacks in breast cancer research have a profound personal meaning for those who have watched the struggle with cancer from close by. Similarly, current political campaigns promoting an English-only America have a special meaning for recent immigrants and other bilingual Americans.
- *Think twice about choosing a highly specialized subject.* In specialized courses in the sciences or in technology, you will be asked to write about subjects that require technical knowledge or special training. However, if you decide to explain gene splicing to a general audience, make sure you have enough technical knowledge or background to understand the arguments. Make sure you can explain them to the general reader.

32c.1 The Short Investigative Paper

You may be asked to prepare a short informal research paper of perhaps 8–10 pages, requiring maybe no more than 8–10 sources. You may be asked to include at least one or two nonprint sources, including an oral source or informal interview. Here are some possible topics for you to consider and to discuss with your classmates:

1 BIG BROTHER IN THE WORKPLACE Possible areas to explore: the trend toward employee surveillance—monitoring of phone calls and e-mail—electronic tracking of employee performance.

2 CAMPAIGN FINANCE Possible areas to explore: financing of a recent national or local election—hard figures on spending—information about sources of the money—legislation and proposals for change.

3 THE QUEST FOR LONG LIFE Possible areas to explore: new approaches to prolonging the life span—new insights into the dynamics of aging—new medications—changes in lifestyle.

4 TRACKING CRIME RATES Possible areas to explore: falling crime rates—fact or media event?—causes and effects—initiatives in key cities (New York, Los Angeles).

5 THE WORKFARE EXPERIMENT Possible areas to explore: key initiatives and key legislation—track record of government and of business—estimates of numbers involved—projections of success or failure.

6 THE MOVEMENT FOR SCHOOL PRAYER Possible areas to explore: separation of church and state—proponents and opponents—options and alternatives.

32c.2 **The Full-Length Research Paper** Assignments for full-length research papers will generally spell out a minimum number of pages and minimum number of sources. The following is a sampling of issues in major areas of interest to the general reader. On which of these would you have background information or a personal interest that could give you a headstart? On one or two of these, would you be well qualified to brief your classmates?

Ecology and Life Sciences
regulating the whaling industry
the attack on animal research
reintroducing the predators in national parks
saving the redwoods
America's last wild rivers
the mission of Greenpeace

Psychology
recognizing alternative kinds of intelligence
women and science aptitude
violence-prone personalities
biochemistry and mental illness

Cultural Issues

the English-only movement
second thoughts about bilingual education
pros and cons of all-women or all-black colleges
the myth of the model minority
foreign countries resisting Americanization
recognizing gay couples as domestic partners

Issues in Communications

censorship and the Internet
censorship of rock lyrics
defunding Public Broadcasting
violence in the movies
the growth of religious programing

Women's Issues

the impact of Title IX on college sports
the need for child care
the cult of thinking thin in American culture
feminism and pink-collar occupations
the glass ceiling for women executives

Rewriting History

slave revolts
Mexican identity: indigenous tradition vs. Spanish heritage
the story of the relocation camps
reviving anti-immigration sentiment

32c.3 Topics across the Curriculum In a writing program stressing preparation for writing in different academic disciplines, you may be encouraged to look for a topic in a specialized field or in an area related to your intended major field of study. You and your audience will be expected to pay detailed attention to the findings of experts and become more familiar with the specialized terminology of the field. Topics like the following will require you to identify different points of view or reconcile different perspectives:

Psychology

Beyond the IQ: Alternative Kinds of Intelligence
Cultural Bias in Standardized Tests

History

Border States: Divided Loyalties during the American Civil War

Controverted History: Jefferson and Hemings

Life Sciences

Genetic Engineering and Agriculture

Law

Custody Fights: Going to Court

Intellectual Property and the Law

Education

Biology and Censorship: Teaching Evolution

Religious Studies

Women and the Early Christian Church

Revisionist Views of Junipero Serra and the Spanish Missionaries

Physical Education

Gender Parity in Collegiate Sports

YOUR TURN 90 Filing a Planning Report

Prepare a preliminary planning report discussing a possible topic. Among the above topics, choose one on which you feel qualified to brief your classmates. What are key questions the topic raises? What essential background information or context can you fill in? What is the unfinished agenda? Would you write on the topic? Why or why not?

33 SEARCHING FOR SOURCES

Learn how to tap into the full range of sources.

Guidelines for research-based writing will often give you detailed advice on how to conduct your search. Where should you start? What is the best way to get your bearings—to get a sense of what is out there? How do you sift your material—focusing on what is truly useful and reliable? Learn to look for promising leads. Be prepared to change direction as necessary as you learn more about your subject. Explore the full range of available resources. Remember that for a researcher false starts and delays are often part of the job. Be stubborn—keep looking for material that will prove helpful and instructive.

33a First Search on the Computer

Quick-search the Internet for background and data on current topics.

For current issues and controversies, the Internet may be good place to start your research. Surfing the net, you can discover quickly what the issues are and what the latest thinking is on your subject. On many current topics, simply typing in a key word or phrase like *Internet censorship* will generate an avalanche of possible sites for you to visit.

- Major newspapers and general-interest magazines, as well as some more specialized magazines, are online. Newspapers from the *New York Times* to *USA Today* and magazines from *Time* to *Atlantic Monthly* are read by users on their computer screens. **Online editions** like those of the *New York Times* have a search tool that will call up articles on a current topic if they appeared in recent weeks. The online edition may lack some visual materials (graphs and maps, for instance), but it may also add special updates.
- You can check essential background facts in **online encyclopedias** and other reference books available online or on CD-ROM—some for free, some for a fee.

33a.1 Going to Websites *Check out the websites of organizations or institutions known for their strong interest in an issue.* Many organizations, publishers, and even individual authors have **websites** giving information, promoting a point of view, or offering services. Most websites have **hyperlinks**: When you click on terms that appear in blue and are underlined, they will take you to more detailed information or further instructions. Most websites are **interactive**, inviting questions and comments.

For background on current gun control initiatives, one student researcher went to sites like the following:

WEBSITES VISITED:

www.nra.org

This is the official homepage of the National Rifle Association. It guides the researcher to speeches by prominent NRA officials (like Charlton Heston), videos, and archives providing facts, statistics, and information about gun-related legislation.

www.agca.com

This the website for the Anti-Gun Coalition of America. This site provides information on people, organizations, and businesses that favor strong anti-gun legislation. It provides helpful links to other sites.

www.gunownersca.com

While the NRA has moved toward possible compromise on issues like gun safety and safety training, the Gun Owners group is known as one of the more uncompromising pro-gun groups, sometimes called the Marine Corps of the pro-gun movement. Following up the Gun Owners logo may lead the researcher to "fact sheets" and other publications by the Gun Owners Foundation Online.

33a.2 Discovering Online Sources *Discover the range of online sources.* For background on current events or trends in American culture, the student researcher has instant access to a full range of **online sources.** Newspapers and newsmagazines from *The Washington Times on the Web* to *Time Online* provide access not only to the current daily or weekly issue but often also to back issues in the **archives**. Often online editions will have added features such as special columns or opportunity to interact with editors or other readers.

Here are some typical addresses. The retrieval code (the **URL**, for uniform resource locator) for online material often appears in angled brackets.

NEWSPAPER ONLINE:

New York Times on the Web <http://www.nytimes.com>

NEWSMAGAZINE ONLINE:

Time Online <http://www.pathfinder.com/time>

MAGAZINE OF OPINION ONLINE:

Atlantic Unbound <http://www.TheAtlantic.com>

REFERENCE WORK ONLINE:

Britannica Online <http://www.eb.com>

Study the way the following sample item identifies an article from an online source. The two dates for each item show first the date it was posted and then the day it was accessed.

Richard Brookhiser. "Let Us Pray." Time Online 19 Dec. 1994. 29 Apr. 1999 <http://www.pathfinder.com/time/magazine/archive/1994/941219/941219.essay.html>.

See **3c** for more on the range of online sources.

33a.3 Using Search Engines

Learn to locate material on the net. In rapidly evolving cyberspace, competitors are developing imaginative and more effective ways of indexing electronic resources, promising faster and more efficient ways to help you find your way on the information highway. Most users of the net have their own favorite search engine, whether the most universally used Yahoo! or another widely used search engine like Excite.

Librarians will encourage you to explore **alternative search engines** beyond those most commercially successful. Are you looking for recent material by an author known for his authoritative comments on current issue—such as Howard Rheingold discussing virtual reality? Your instructor or a librarian might recommend AltaVista as the search engine most likely to produce recent publications, reviews, or biographical background. Other frequently recommended search engines have included Infoseek, Lycos, or WebCrawler.

You may want to track the same key subject using several major search engines and comparing the results. In addition, librarians will encourage you to search **specialized databases** like Biosis for the life sciences, Psychlit for psychology, or Legal Resources Index for law.

See **3c** and **33c** on using the Boolean system in tracking electronic sources.

Here are some precautions to observe as you use material from electronic sources:

- *Print out hard copy when you can.* Remember that a site on the net may have moved or closed by the time you try to revisit it. Teachers and editors often recommend that you download Internet material just in case it might be gone when you try to return to it on the net. Remember that the material may be available only for a limited time—so that others may not be able to access it later.
- *User beware.* Quality and reliability of Internet material vary greatly. Unlike traditional print publishing and mainstream media, much online publication lacks the middle layer of editors, copy editors, or prepublication reviewers who sift the flow of raw communication and decide what is fit to print or put on the air. The material you find on the net may be abridged—shortened or adapted without a clear indication of what was left out.
- *Try to track authorship.* The exact source of information may not be clear—who is responsible? who is accountable?
- *Move beyond the net.* You will often have to go beyond the net for material published more than ten or fifteen years ago. You will have to go beyond the net for detailed technical information in specialized journals with limited circulation. You will have to go off the net for most material from books, although chapters from books or full-length books will increasingly be available online.

In the following entry from a research log, a student talks about making full use of the Internet and going beyond:

RESEARCH LOG ENTRY:

I always find myself on the Internet and I am constantly using search engines like Yahoo to look up a particular topic. Many times I have entered a word such as *music* and have had explicit or X-rated sites appear included in my list to choose from. I decided to concentrate on programs designed to keep children away from such sites. I called my topic "cybercensorship." By looking for titles under "Internet censorship" and "cyberspace censorship" I found a tremendous amount of information. There were many articles with titles like "A Bad Day in Cyberspace" and "The

Murky World of Internet Porn." However, not all my best sources were on the net, like an article called "The Cyber Vice Squad." The author said, "Sex-related material is a tiny fraction of what's available on the Internet . . . but it's a really conspicuous fraction." I was apprehensive that on a relatively new topic such as Internet censorship I would not find books studying it in depth, but I found good background information in Jan Constantine's *The Internet and Society* and Debbie Richter's *Understanding the Internet.*

33b Newspapers and Periodicals

Explore the full range of periodical publications.

In a country proud of its free press, newsstands display an incredible range of daily, weekly, or monthly publications. They offer local and out-of-town newspapers, newsmagazines, journals of opinion, popular-science magazines, or cyberspace publications. Professional organizations and universities publish periodicals digesting research in areas like science, social science, and the humanities. Although censors at times drive a publication off the shelves, Americans have unprecedented access to publications covering current developments in politics, business, science, culture, popular culture, or education.

Get to know one or more publications in each of the following categories:

LOCAL NEWSPAPERS Local newspapers often take over national and international news from an outside news organization. However, they also give you a firsthand look at local politics, local crime, pro-growth and anti-growth issues, and the grass-roots concerns of community life. Cities that used to have two or three major newspapers now have only one, with a limited range of editorial opinion. Media critics warn that news judgment and editorial opinion are increasingly subject to review or control by advertising managers.

NEWSPAPERS OF RECORD *New York Times, Washington Post, Wall Street Journal, Chicago Tribune, Los Angeles Times, Christian Science Monitor*

Opinion makers respect the influence of newspapers that reach a national audience and pride themselves on high editorial standards. Editorial opinion ranges from moderately liberal sympathies at the *New York Times* to the conservative, business-oriented *Wall Street Journal.* A student researching current trends in America's prisons found *New York Times* articles citing expert opinion on surging inmate populations in local jails, on construction of both state and federal prisons as a growth industry, and on sexual abuse of women prisoners in the nation's jails.

✓ **EDITOR'S TIP:** The *New York Times Index* provides a guide to major news events of the past. If you know the approximate period of a sex scandal or sensational murder trial, you can track background material in this index. The *Wall Street Journal Index* is another guide to yesterday's news.

WEEKLY NEWSMAGAZINES *Time, Newsweek, U.S. News & World Report*

Ranging from right of center to archconservative, the mainstream newsmagazines, owned by big corporations, are shifting toward a jazzed-up sound-bite format while putting their spin on the week's news. However, their staple fare continues to be an easily digestible blend of fact, selected popular opinion, and authoritative testimony on "hot button" issues like sex in the military or campaign finance. They provide a vehicle for pundits like George Will, Roger Rosenblatt, and Margaret Carlson, commenting on topics like sex, morality, multiculturalism, or affirmative action.

MAGAZINES OF OPINION *Harper's, Atlantic Monthly, National Review, New Republic, Mother Jones, Nation, Commonweal, Commentary, Utne Reader*

Magazines of opinion range from the ultraconservative *National Review* to the *Nation,* long a lone voice of socialist opinion in the American press. The *New Republic,* with strong ties to Israel and the anti-Communist American left, presents a range of often contentious liberal and conservative opinion. The long-established *Harper's* and *Atlantic Monthly* print extensive analyses of long-range trends—embattled schools, divorce, welfare reform. Publications like *Mother Jones* and the *Utne Reader* provide a forum for independent voices—ecologists, people in the alternative media—who are underrepresented in the mainstream press.

GENERAL-INTEREST SCIENCE AND CULTURE *Psychology Today, Scientific American, National Geographic, Discover*

Devoted to the continuing education of the general reader, these journals counteract the "dumbing down" effect of sound bites and scandalmongering journalism. They often employ writers who make challenging material intelligible and fascinating. They assume an audience able to follow explanations of how the human brain constructs colors from visual input or how carbon dating enables anthropologists to date million-year-old human fossils.

SPECIAL-AUDIENCE MAGAZINES *Forbes, Business Week, Ms., Ebony, Art News, Educational Leadership, Corrections Today*

Many special-focus publications have a definite agenda or commitment. They range from publications aimed at a large cross-section of the business community to limited-audience publications like *Alcoholism and Drug Abuse Weekly*. In an issue of *Business Week*, you may find articles on sports as a billion-dollar business or on a maverick entrepreneur like Ross Perot, with the magic touch for returning a faltering enterprise to profitability. *Ms.* magazine, co-founded by Gloria Steinem, has long been the leading voice of the American women's movement, printing articles by leading feminist authors and critics.

A student looking for material looking at our prisons from a civil rights or human rights perspective located promising sources like the following:

PROMISING LEADS:

Kevin L. Jackson, "Differences in the Background and Criminal Justice Characteristics of Young Black, White, and Hispanic Male Federal Prison Inmates, " Journal of Black Studies

"A Nation of Inmates," Progressive

"Section 1983 Civil Liability of Prison Officials for Denying and Delaying Medication and Drugs to Prison Inmates," Issues in Law & Medicine

AUTHORITATIVE PROFESSIONAL JOURNALS *New England Journal of Medicine, Nature, Chronicle of Higher Education, National Law Journal*

Presiding over the country's most prestigious medical journal, the editors of the *New England Journal of Medicine* have in recent years published expert testimony on issues like medical marijuana or the lack of scientific evidence to support huge damage awards in breast-implant litigation. In *Nature*, one of the most prestigious international journals for the science community, you may find a report updating current knowledge on the animal origins of the AIDS virus. The *Chronicle of Higher Education* reports in depth on trends in school funding, teacher training, tenure, tax money for private schools, or censorship cases.

A student looking for material on our skyrocketing prison population found authoritative data and comment in sources like the following:

PROMISING LEADS:

Thomas B. Marvell, "Age Structure Trends and Prison Populations," Journal of Criminal Justice

David E. Rovelle, "Prison Suits Reduced by Filing Limits: Prison Population Rises Faster than Inmate Petitions," National Law Journal

Kelly McMurry, "Nation's Prison Population Rose in 1996," Trial

SPECIALIZED TECHNICAL AND SCIENTIFIC JOURNALS *The Journal of the American Medical Association* (JAMA), *Social Science Research, American Demographics,* and many others

The authors of articles in scholarly journals are often university-based specialists. They typically base their findings on in-depth study, detailed surveys, or carefully planned and carefully tracked experiments. For instance, a 1997 article on homelessness in *Social Science Research* by two geography professors from the University of Southern California studies "Shifting Margins of Housing Status in Los Angeles." It gives detailed national and local statistics on both the "literally homeless" and those without a home of their own who are doubled up with family or friends. It examines key factors like affordability, or housing costs as part of income, in an era of shrinking public assistance.

A student looking for scholarly material on the changing American family found sources like the following:

PROMISING LEADS:

Peter Francese, "The 100 Millionth Household," American Demographics

Byron M. Lyndholm, "The Future of the Family in Industrial Societies," Population and Development Review

Gail M. Johnston, "The Transformation of American Families: Employment Dislocation and the Growth of Female-Headed Families," Journal of the Population Association of America

Specialists subscribe to publications that keep them up to date on current developments in their special area of interest. For readers with a special interest in books and libraries, *American Libraries* magazine may print articles on attempts to censor young adult literature or install filtering software blocking "adult only" sites. For computer specialists, *Wired*—available online and in a print version—evaluates cutting-edge hardware and software and tracks trends in digital home entertainment or states' efforts to squash spam.

Your library may provide you with a guide to scholarly or academic sources that looks like the following:

GOING TO THE SOURCES

Scholarly and Research Journals

EXAMPLES:

American Historical Review
Journal of American History
National Law Journal
Journal of Educational Research
Journal of Aesthetics
Social Psychology Quarterly
Theatre Research International
Plasma Physics

VALUES AND USES:

Reports of original research; in-depth analysis of issues related to the discipline; academic-level book reviews; articles may be approved for publication by expert referees or by peer review; often on the basis of blind submissions (referees do not know identity or affiliation of the author)

LANGUAGE:

Academic; can be very technical; uses the language of the discipline

AUTHORS:

Researchers, academics, professors, scholars, experts

DOCUMENTATION:

Notes and bibliographies; often very extensive documentation

PUBLISHED BY:

Universities, scholarly presses, and academic or research organizations

GRAPHICS:

Graphs, charts, formulas, depending on the discipline; no glossy ads

ACCESS:

Through the library's general periodical index but mainly through specialized indexes like *PsychLit, Art Index, Sociological Abstracts, Religion Index,* or *Communication Abstracts*

YOUR TURN 91 Checking Out a Publication

Read an issue of a periodical other than a newspaper or newsmagazine cover to cover. Prepare a **review-critique**. What is the intended audience? What is the nature and scope of key articles? Study the following sample review by a fellow student. What points stand out? To judge from this review, would you make a good reader for this publication? Why or why not?

RESEARCH LOG ENTRY:

Psychology Today

Psychology Today is a science magazine aimed at a general American audience. I was fascinated by how the authors linked psychology to everyday events. Every article in the end came back to science. The first article I read, "Radioactive Shrinks" by Peter Doskoch, discussed radio talk shows and their doubtful psychological validity. He interviewed radio therapists—Dr. Joy Browne, Dr. Helen Friedman, and Dr. Laura Schlessinger—to try to distinguish their shows from trashy love advice. Dr. Laura, the best known therapist on the air, has 20 million listeners who support her "moral health" attitude. At the end of his article, Doskoch includes what these three therapists say about their shows: "Psychology has a lot to offer people. We are giving them new ways to look at their problems." He closes the article with "That's a mission we [*Psychology Today*] can stand behind. After all, it's our mission, too."

A column entitled "Two Years Later, A Quieter Mind," written by Annie Murphy, talks about Kay Redfield Jamison and her book, *An Unquiet Mind*, in which she discusses her battle with manic depression. This book was a surprising success and was on the New York Times bestseller list for two years (selling more than 400,000 copies). In an interview with Murphy, Redfield complained that people treat her differently when they find out that she has a mental illness. Since the book, she had begun writing *Night Falls Fast*, which is about the devastation and pain and suffering of suicide, and in which she draws on bringing in neurological and psychological research. Jamison says, "It's been a relief to turn back to science. You get into this business of talking about your own experiences and you forget why you went into science."

Psychology Today informs readers about science, but it is not a science magazine for specialists. It is accessible to the general reader. I learned so much that I subscribed to the magazine for my own personal education and enjoyment.

YOUR TURN 92 **Tracking an Issue**

Trace **press coverage** of a current issue during a recent time period. Study extent of coverage, emphasis or slant of articles, recurrent themes, and the spin given to the news. Are there significant differences between treatment of the same issue in different publications—or kinds of publications?

Keep track of all source information: author, exact title of item or article, nature of item (editorial, column, news report), full name of publication, specific and inclusive page numbers, special section or edition. If you include material from the Internet, check out the nature of the item: complete article? abridgment? selection? summary? Copy the Internet address (or URL).

33c Searching the Indexes

Find and sift material in current or recent periodicals.

How do you find articles related to your topic? Your first stop will normally be the general computerized periodical index of your library. You go to this master index and feed in key words related to your search. You may look for at least some material aimed at the general reader, which can help you understand important terms and concepts. However, you will also want to push on to more technical or scholarly sources, which will be enable you to look at key issues in depth. For truly specialized insider's or expert's material, you may have to go beyond the library's centralized index to specialized databases available online or on CD-ROM.

When searching for articles, you are likely to use some variation of the **Boolean system.** It enables you to narrow your key word or phrase to the right point. It does so in two ways:

- An unrestricted key word like WHALING might generate several thousand entries. A key phrase like WHALING INDUSTRY would already narrow the field. With the Boolean system, you then use the **link words** *and, or,* and *not* in order to zero in on your specific concern. For instance, you decide to try

  whaling industry *and* regulations

  You may still receive a sizable list of sources to consult, but they will all be focused more directly on a key question: efforts to regulate, restrict, or ban whaling in order to save the whales from extinction. The link word *not* can screen out entries when your key word has different meanings in two large separate areas. If you want to check current research on immunity to disease, you might try "immunity *not* law *or* legal." This way you would screen out articles about witnesses granted immunity from prosecution in a court of law.

- The way you would actually type in your key words for the whaling paper might be one of the following:

  whaling industry and regulat*
  whal* and regulat*

This way the computer would search not only for titles and descriptions with the exact word *regulations* but also with related words like *regulation* and *regulating*. You type only the root of your key word, followed by an asterisk. If you type *intelligen**, the computer will search for all versions of the word with different endings, such as *intelligent, intelligence, intelligences.*

Remember that a huge subject heading like INTELLIGENCE may cause an avalanche of entries impossible to sort out. A more specific topic like MULTIPLE INTELLIGENCE may bring up a manageable range of articles more clearly focused on your actual topic. Since everyone writing on this topic might not use the exact term *multiple intelligence,* you may also want to try combinations like *intelligen* and educat** or *intelligen* and test**.

From the beginning, look for a notation showing whether a listed article is from a publication actually in your library. The indexes most useful for you will be listings that include brief **summaries** of the articles. **Subject headings** give you additional key words to use in searching for other material. The following two articles seemed especially promising to a student researcher taking stock of current theories about different kinds of human intelligence—going beyond the logical, analytical intelligence measured by the traditional IQ.

COMPUTER LISTINGS:

Record 5 of 22

AUTHOR	Sternberg, Robert J.
TITLE	What should we ask about intelligence? (intelligence measurement) by Robert J. Sternberg.
APPEARS IN	American Scholar 1996, v65, n2, Spring, p205(13)

SUMMARY	Conventional intelligence tests are outmoded and only measure analytical intelligence, which is only one type of knowledge. Revolutionary theories of intelligence conclude that there a multiple types of intelligences. One theory postulates there is analytical intelligence, creative intelligence, and practical intelligence. Research and actual experience show that students who excel on intelligence tests and standard academic tests such as the GRE do not necessarily have the creative skills and practical knowledge needed to succeed in higher academia.
SUBJECT	Intelligence tests — Research. Intellect — Varieties. Intelligence levels — Measurement. Knowledge, Theory of — Research.

Record 11 of 22

AUTHOR	Cappon, Daniel.
TITLE	A new approach to intuition: IQ2. (Intuition Quotient Test) (includes the IQ2 test for assessing intuition) by Daniel Cappon.
APPEARS IN	Omni 1994, v16, nl2, Sept, p34(8)
SUMMARY	Dr. Cappon believes that intuition has an equal role in human intelligence as its counterpart, analysis. He has created the IQ2 test as a scientific measurement for intuition. Cappon's research is aimed at demystifying intuition and restoring its reputation.
SUBJECT	Intuition — Analysis. Intellect — Analysis. Intelligence levels — Measurement.

Remember the limitations of the most commonly used computerized indexes:

- As needed, branch out beyond the main periodical index to more **specialized indexes**. For example, turn to *PsychLit* for topics covered in psychological journals. A librarian may be able to alert you to a specialized index especially useful for your topic.
- For material published prior to the era of electronic indexes, go back to the printed multivolume **periodical indexes** on the shelves of your library.
- If you can, use a database that includes **abstracts** of articles. An abstract goes beyond a minimal summary. It may outline purpose, approach, and procedure, as well as key findings. It may

summarize key steps in the argument or key evidence. This way you may get enough of a preview of an article to help you decide if it is worth checking out. Examples of resources you might consult are *Sociological Abstracts* and *Historical Abstracts*.

Here is an entry from a research log with pointers on what to expect when you look for material in periodical sources:

RESEARCH LOG ENTRY:

I am getting better at finding material. During a library tour, I learned how to use *PsychLit*, a database focusing on psychology topics. Typing in a keyword or subject and the year or years generates a list of possible sources. During my research so far, my main problem has been that I would find a listing for an article but couldn't find the actual document in the library. The most recent issues of many periodicals were on the shelves in the periodical room, and back issues from previous years were in bound volumes in the library stacks. But many of the issues in between were missing because according to the librarian recent issues of the periodical were at the bindery being bound into the collected volumes. Also, sometimes an article or book that had been checked out by another student had been returned but not yet sorted and put back on the shelves. On the plus side, I found that many major newspapers and magazines are now available online. Often the whole issue is available online without some of the visuals or graphics but sometimes with added other materials.

YOUR TURN 93 Checking a Periodical Index

Check out a specialized periodical index in a field of special interest to you. Study coverage, format, and use of abbreviations. Report on your experience, citing and discussing sample entries.

33d Searching for Books

Consult books by writers who are authorities on your subject.

In searching for strong materials, you will often be looking for a book that is an in-depth study. Its author may have invested years of research. Much effort may have gone into reading previous treatments of the subject (the relevant expert **literature** on the subject), charting areas of agreement and disagreement, and checking out recent findings.

33d.1 Secondary and Primary Sources *Value primary over secondary sources.* Often an important book will take you beyond secondhand accounts. The author or authors may have gone to **primary sources**—not trusting someone else's account of letters or legislation or someone's will. They may have searched out the original letters or found legal documents in archives. They may have conducted taped interviews, searching out insiders or eyewitnesses.

Suppose you are exploring the multicultural origins of traditional jazz in New Orleans, with its mix of African, traditional European, and local French-Creole influences. You may want to keep handy a reference book like *The New Grove Dictionary of Jazz*, edited by Barry Kernfeld (Macmillan, 1988). This is a source you may come to trust when checking names, dates, and other basic facts. You may find several books that are general treatments of the New Orleans jazz scene—books like William Carter's *Preservation Hall* (W. W. Norton, 1991). Other books may explore special areas of your subject—books like William J. Schafer's *Brass Bands and New Orleans Jazz* (Louisiana State University Press, 1977) or Robert Palmer's *Deep Blues* (Viking, 1981). You may check out biographies of jazz greats—books like Dorothy Tait and Ann Fairbarn's *Call Him George* (Peter Davies, 1961). You may find autobiographies like Sidney Bechet's *Treat It Gentle* (Da Capo, 1978).

Authors have their own agenda or commitment or emphasis. Some books will show that the author had a score to settle or an ax to grind. Comparing your different sources will enable you to make allowance for an author's bias. You will be able to check different treatments of the same events or to compare similar statistics. You will be able to draw your own conclusions.

YOUR TURN 94 Learning from Reviews

Study the range of reviews of a recent book dealing with an issue of special interest to you. Can you identify different perspectives of reviewers? Do they share basic criteria or interests? Do they disagree on important points? Prepare a report presenting your findings.

33d.2 Indexes and Catalogs *Search for books by author's name, book title, or subject area.* In most libraries, computerized indexes have replaced traditional card catalogs, which used to have rows of small drawers with index cards. However, looking for a book is very similar—whether you use a computer listing or go manually through the traditional printed cards.

When you know of a promising book, you can look for it under the **author's name.** Suppose you are writing a term paper about emerging global competition between huge trading blocks or common markets. You can look under *Thurow* if you have heard of Lester Thurow's *Head to Head: The Coming Economic Battle among Japan, Europe, and America.* If you are not sure of the author's name, you can look for the **book title:** *Head to Head.* If you are not yet aware of Thurow's book, you might find it when looking for books focused on global competition under the right **subject heading.** You might try headings like *Global Economy, Global Competition, International Economic Relations, U.S.—Economic Policy, Japan—Economic Policy, European Union—International Trade,* or *Trade Wars—U.S. and Japan.*

The catalog entries that follow illustrate the information about books that the entries provide. The **call number** will direct you or the librarian to the right section and the right shelf in the library. **ISBN numbers** are an international standardized numbering system used to identify and order books. The entry will tell you how substantial a book is (how many pages?). It may tell you if the book includes a **bibliography** or list of sources the author has consulted. (Often such a list can guide you to other promising sources.)

Here are the three kinds of entries for books found by a student writing about women in college sports:

AUTHOR ENTRY:

Call #:	LB 2343.32 F54 1991
Author:	Figler, Stephen K.
Title:	Going the distance: the college athlete's guide to excellence on the field and in the classroom / by Stephen K. Figler. Princeton, N.J.: Peterson's Guides, 1991. xi, 208 p.: illus; 23 cm.
Notes:	Includes bibliography: p. 203-208.
Subjects:	College student orientation - United States College athletes - United States.

TITLE ENTRY:

The American sporting experience

GV
583 Riess, Steven A.
R53 The American sporting experience / Steven A. Riess.
New York: Leisure Press, 1984.
400 p.; 23 cm.

Bibliography: p. 398-400
ISBN 0-88011-210-7
1. Sports - United States - History - Addresses, essays, lectures. I. Title

GV583.R53 796.0973
84-7188

SUBJECT ENTRY:

GV
709 SEX DISCRIMINATION IN SPORTS
N44

Nelson, Mariah Burton

Are we winning yet?: how women are changing sports and how sports are changing women, by Mariah Burton Nelson.

1st ed. New York: Random House, 1991
238 p.

Bibliography: pp. 215-224, and index

33d.3 Bibliographies and Reviews *Pick up hints about books from informal and formal sources.* You will often learn about an important book by talking to your instructor, another faculty member, a librarian, or a fellow student. For instance, if you are writing about an aspect of the Holocaust, someone will sooner or later alert you to a Harvard researcher's book that generated tremendous interest in the United States and Europe. Goldhagen's *Hitler's Henchmen* reopened the question of what role the German people as a whole played in the campaign of extermination against European Jews. The resulting discussion directed attention to other important books by historians researching the question of shared guilt.

For many subjects, you can find a printed or computerized **bibliography**—a listing of important books and of articles in periodicals. Bibliographical listings often follow an entry in an encyclopedia or a chapter in a textbook. Each of the three books found by the student writing about women in college athletics included a bibliography that listed additional readings worth checking out.

Especially useful are **annotated bibliographies**, which give a capsule account of each source. The following entry is from *An Annotated Bibliography of California Fiction* by Newton D. Baird and Robert Greenwood. Note that it lists two reviews that were written when the book was originally published.

ENTRY FROM ANNOTATED BIBLIOGRAPHY:

1371 [Kerouac, John.]

ON THE ROAD. By Jack Kerouac. New York: Viking Press, 1957. 310 pp.

Two romantic anarchists, Sal Paradise and Dean Moriarty, pursue a vaguely defined notion of purpose on the roads up and down the North American continent, in stolen cars, in buses, airplanes, and by hitch-hiking. California, in part.

Commonweal 66:595 S 13 '57
San Francisco Chronicle p. 18 S 1 '57

To help you judge the value of promising books, check **book reviews**—a feature of many general-interest periodicals and professional publications. Periodicals like the *New Republic, New Yorker,* and *New York Review of Books* print extended reviews likely to include background on the author, comments on the author's previous work, and references to previous treatments of the same subject. *Book Review Digest* excerpts reviews written shortly after publication of a book.

A student exploring events leading up to the Civil War might enter the following note in the research log after reading a review of a new book.

RESEARCH LOG ENTRY (book review):

Scott L. Malcomson, "The Color Line," review of Russell Banks's novel *Cloudsplitter* (Harper Flamingo) in *The New Yorker*, 8 Apr. 1998, pp. 102-04.

Owen Brown tells his life story. He was a son of John Brown, the firebrand abolitionist, who in 1859, raided the federal arsenal at Harper's Ferry in the slave state of Virginia. John Brown, with twenty-one white and black followers, hoped to ignite a general slave revolt that would end slavery. The son participated in the raid and was one of five survivors when federal troops retook the arsenal two days later. (The father was later hanged.) The son describes his father's preaching about abolition to local whites and running escaped slaves north to Canada and freedom. The review stresses John Brown's crossing over from the nonviolent mainstream abolitionist movement to "guerrilla warfare" and armed insurrection, foreshadowing the bloody civil war that erupted two years later. John Brown's failed mission becomes a symbol of the inability of white America to cross "the color line."

33e Using Nonprint Sources

Consider adding live authentic material from nonprint sources.

Consider turning to nonprint sources when exclusive reliance on print would make your paper too impersonal. In a paper on crime rates, add authentic firsthand material from interviews with a local police chief, social workers, or volunteers who have worked in local jails. For a science topic, draw on one of the spectacular science programs on public television. If you are interested in Irish history, a play by an Irish playwright can dramatize the age-old antagonism between Catholic and Protestant or the attempt to revive the ancient Irish language.

A student was investigating the survival of regional dialects and other variations from the standard language of school and the media. Listening to a radio interview helped her understand the pride that speakers of a local or regional variety of a national language often feel in their linguistic heritage.

RESEARCH LOG ENTRY (radio interview):

I heard an interview on National Public Radio with three Scottish writers whose books have sparked controversy with their bold and raw use of language. Especially with James Kelman's prize-winning novel, *How Late It Was, How Late*, the number of expletives became the focus of many of the interviewer's questions, rather than the actual contents of the book. Kelman explained that he wrote the way his characters would speak, without stopping to count the number of times a certain word was said. He uses the language that the characters would have in their heads or in their mouths. The word *dialect* was mentioned, and the Scottish authors tried to explain the negative undertones that they felt came with the word. They thought it implied an inferiority to a standard language. Duncan McLean remembers being taught in school that the language he spoke "was somehow inferior and had to be got rid of," and he was told many times that words he was using simply "did not exist." There are classrooms in Scotland still today where children are not allowed to use the word "aye" instead of "yes," for example. In any case, it adds to the appeal of a book if a character says, "Auld Jean-Claude's ready tae git doon tae some serious swedgin," rather than "Jean-Claude's ready to fight."

Source: PBS 8 Jan. 1998

33f Fact-Checking in Reference Books

Turn to reference books for background information.

You refer to reference books when you need them. You may turn to them to get your bearings—to get a preliminary overview of a subject. Or you may want to check specific points—getting reliable information from recognized authorities.

General encyclopedias, as their advertising promises, provide "a world of knowledge." They give you a rundown of generally accepted historical facts, the best current scientific knowledge, and an insider's introduction to culture and the arts. They can keep you from overlooking important background information and from leaping to conclusions.

- The most prestigious general encyclopedia is the 32-volume *Encyclopaedia Britannica*. It is divided into articles with in-depth coverage (the Macropedia) and shorter reference articles (the Micropedia). The *Britannica* has long been known for its high standards of scholarship and for drawing on big-name contributors (including at one time Albert Einstein and Sigmund Freud).
- The *Encyclopedia Americana*, another traditional multivolume encyclopedia, has often been recommended to students of science and technology. *Collier's Encyclopedia* is often advertised as being designed with the needs of students in mind. The *Columbia Encyclopedia* has often been considered the handiest of the compact (one-volume) encyclopedias.

Major encyclopedias, including the *Britannica*, are now available on CD-ROM as well as online. Insiders consider the *Microsoft Encarta* the most clearly state-of-the-art of the multimedia online encyclopedias. It is available on CD-ROM and in an abridged online version. Suppose you are working on a paper dealing with a question about the Civil War, or War between the States. Perhaps you are exploring the attempted compromises between North and South over the issue of slavery, or you are checking into how extensive opposition to slavery really was in the North.

You might start by calling up the article on "Civil War" in the online *Encarta*—to make sure of basic historical facts. For instance, which Southern states at first seceded from the Union to form the Confederacy? Which joined later? As you read, you can click on the **links** (usually appearing in blue and underlined) highlighting special topics. These will lead you to more detailed information. For instance, what were the provisions of the Missouri Compromise? (You would click on this underlined topic.) How did the Dred Scott case test its constitutionality? How did the Supreme Court rule in this case, and why? You might want to note background facts like the following for use in your paper:

BACKGROUND FACTS:

Civil War Stats

Four million Americans were slaves at the beginning of the war in 1861. Total deaths in the war were more than 600,000, with another 500,000 wounded or maimed. More Americans were killed than in all other wars combined. During the period of

Reconstruction (1865-1877), voting rights and property rights were secured by black Americans, but segregation and disenfranchisement (loss of the right to vote) resulted as Southern whites slowly regained political power.

Source: Microsoft Encarta

Major areas of study have their own **specialized reference works.** These may include manuals, handbooks, encyclopedias, dictionaries, or almanacs. Specialists from aeronautics engineers to jazz aficionados usually have an established reference source that is their bible and that they turn to in order to check facts or settle a debated point. Specialized reference works can summarize for you generally accepted knowledge in a field, clarify important technical terms, and bring you up to date on current developments. They can introduce you to much that specialists and insiders know and that as a newcomer you may need to learn. Here is a sampling of reference works you might consult:

Biography

- *Who's Who in America*, a biographical dictionary with capsule biographies of outstanding living men and women
- *The Dictionary of American Biography* (DAB)
- *Who's Who of American Women*
- *Notable American Women*
- *American Men and Women of Science*
- *Contemporary Authors*
- *Biography Index*, a guide to biographical material in books and magazines

Science, Technology, and Environment

- *McGraw-Hill Encyclopedia of Science and Technology* (updated by the *McGraw-Hill Yearbook of Science and Technology*)
- *Encyclopedia of Computer Science and Technology*
- *McGraw-Hill Encyclopedia of Environmental Science*
- *Encyclopedia of Earth Sciences*
- *Encyclopedia of Bioethics*

Social Science and Humanities

- *International Encyclopedia of the Social Sciences*
- *Encyclopedia of Psychology*

- *Dictionary of American History*
- Langer's *Encyclopedia of World History*
- *New Grove Dictionary of Music and Musicians*
- *Larousse Encyclopedia of Music*
- *McGraw-Hill Encyclopedia of World Art*
- *Encyclopedia of Religion*
- *Encyclopedia of Education*

Cultural Studies

- *Women's Studies Encyclopedia*
- *Multicultural Encyclopedia*
- *Encyclopedia of African American Civil Rights*
- *Handbook of Hispanic Culture in the United States*
- *Handbook of North American Indians*
- *Asian and Asian American Studies*
- *Encyclopedia of World Cultures*
- *Encyclopedia of Homosexuality*

Public Affairs

- *Vital Speeches of the Day*
- *Facts on File*

✓ ***EDITOR'S TIP:*** Do not make your research paper *a digest of information* from a reference book. Research is more than summarizing preassembled material. Check out different authorities—with their own points of view. Go beyond generally agreed-upon facts to new challenges and perspectives.

YOUR TURN 95 **Using Reference Tools**

Examine an often consulted reference work in an area of special interest to you. Prepare a report on its extent of coverage, format, and usefulness. Describe one or two sample entries. Does the work seem intended mainly for the specialist? How helpful is it for the outsider or for the general educated reader? Provide helpful advice to prospective users.

33g Starting Your Source List

Keep a record of promising sources.

While checking for possible sources, you will be identifying the most promising ones. (You may discard many others that do not seem useful.) Many researchers keep an eye out for the names of authorities they recognize. They turn to journals or publishers with an established reputation. They also look for titles that promise a well-focused treatment or a fresh perspective.

Early in your search, start preparing **source entries** or source cards for material you consider using in your paper. Collect these entries in your preliminary source record. This working bibliography will serve a double purpose. You include all the information you need to access the source—or to return to it if you have already examined it. However, you also include all the information you will need for a full accounting of your sources at the end of your finished paper.

> ✓ ***EDITOR'S TIP:*** Verify all of your source information carefully. Double-check dates, page numbers, and electronic addresses.

SOURCE ENTRIES FOR ONLINE SOURCES Record the full name of the author (or authors). Include any subtitle with the title. Include the date the item was posted, and add the date you accessed the source. Copy the full retrieval path or electronic address.

SOURCE ENTRY:

People for Ethical Treatment of Animals. "Let's Visit Animal Research Laboratories." 16 Sept. 1995. 28 Nov. 1998 <http://www.envirolink.org/arrs/peta/labvisit/office.html>.

SOURCE ENTRIES FOR ARTICLES Record the full name of the author (or authors). Include any subtitle with the title of the article. Give the name of the publication. Keep track of dates of publication. Include the complete page numbers for the whole article. For newspapers, you may have to note the section of the paper along with the page numbers (*A5-7*) and also special editions (*Western ed., Late Ed., Peninsula Ed.)*. For scholarly journals, you may have to include the number of the volume—usually the collected issues for a year, to be bound together as a single volume. You may want to include a brief note reminding you why an article seemed especially useful.

SOURCE ENTRY:

Periodical Room	Kaminer, Georgia. "The Belle of Amherst: The Enigma of Emily Dickinson." Studies in American Culture 13 (1998), 132-45.

The author traces the changes in Dickinson's reputation from her early image as a New England eccentric through her rediscovery by twentieth-century critics to her current recognition as America's greatest poet.

SOURCE ENTRIES FOR BOOKS Record authors' full names and any subtitle. Include publishing data: place, publisher, and year (usually the year the work was copyrighted). Include names of editors and translators (using the abbreviations *ed.* and *trans.*). Give the number of a new or revised edition (for instance, *3rd ed.* or *rev. ed.*). When using a selection that is *part* of a book, identify both the whole book and the individual article, story, or poem. Include the complete page numbers for the individual selection.

Include call numbers or access information, like "Social Science Reading Room" or "Menges Law Library."

SOURCE ENTRIES:

HQ 1426 H347	Helgeson, Sally. The Female Advantage: Women's Ways in Leadership. New York: Doubleday, 1990.
Humanities reading room	Guilaine, Jean, ed. Prehistory. Trans. Stephen Bunson. New York: Facts on File, 1991.
Multicultural Center library	Tan, Amy. "Alien Relative." Charlie Chan Is Dead: An Anthology of Contemporary Asian American Fiction. Ed. Jessica Hagedorn. New York: Penguin, 1993. 450-61.

34 USING YOUR SOURCES

Put the results of your search to good use.

From the wealth of information and opinion available to you, learn to pull out material that is clearly relevant—related to your topic. Experienced researchers have an eye for what is promising and potentially useful. They are alert for key pieces of evidence or for data that can help settle a debatable question. They spot revealing inside information. They take note when a usually cautious expert takes a stand on an important issue.

✓ ***EDITOR'S TIP:*** As you accumulate material, err on the side of completeness. When you are not sure a piece of information or a quotation will be useful, include it tentatively in your notes anyway. It's much easier to discard something later than to have to retrace your steps to relocate something that turned out to be needed after all.

34a Focusing Your Search

Know what to look for during your exploratory reading.

During your exploratory reading, you are prospecting for promising material—material that will provide input for your first draft. Look for material that makes you say: "This will help me clear up a key question. . . . This provides essential background. . . . This gives me evidence for a debatable point. . . . This is an objection I will have to address." Depending on your topic, materials like the following will be useful:

SCIENTIFIC OR TECHNICAL INFORMATION *Look for material that will help you explain technical matters to a layperson.* For instance, most readers have heard of Prozac or some other miracle medication. To establish your credibility as a researcher, you would have to check it out. What is it—what is its chemical composition? Where did it come from—what is its clinical history? What are major claims and counterclaims?

HISTORICAL BACKGROUND *Look for material that helps put a current issue in historical perspective.* Current issues have their roots in past events; they have a history. For instance, defining feminism or the women's movement, you are likely to examine its roots in the struggle to give women the right to vote. The suffragist struggle—to extend suffrage or the right to vote to women—forced many to confront their assumptions about the role of women in society.

EXPERT OPINION *Listen to the testimony of experts.* On a debated subject, what is the expert testimony of those who have studied the issue? For instance, how does code-switching work—how do people move from one language, or from one variety or dialect of English, to another? The language scholar J. Douglas Allen-Taylor said:

> Most African Americans speak standard English in a business or school setting, or when they are around white people they do not know, and then slip into some form of Black English among the home folks. The transition is so fluid and unthinking that many African Americans may not even know it's happening, just as Mexicans can flow back and forth between Spanish and English within the same conversation.

OFFICIAL DOCUMENTS *Check the actual text of documents, laws, or initiatives.* Opposing sides in arguments may both mention the Constitution, the First Amendment, or the Second Amendment. What exactly does the document say? What were the intentions and reservations of the people who crafted them? On issues involving immigration policy or the war on drugs, what is the law? How has it been challenged or upheld? On election-year issues, what is the exact language of initiatives or propositions?

INSIDER'S TESTIMONY *Listen to insiders who know what goes on behind the scenes.* Investigators interested in the inner workings of government agencies or corporations may listen to former high-level employees. If you are writing about trends in electronic surveillance, you are likely to seize on the inside story of a surveillance specialist talking about miniaturized TV cameras built into eyeglasses and supersensitive microphones picking up conversations in the middle of Central Park.

TEST CASES *Check out the real-life stories of affected individuals.* Issues may remain lifeless unless you can relate them to the experiences of real people. On issues like child care, you may want to take notes on case histories of single mothers or double-wage-earner couples.

STRIKING STATISTICS *Look for statistics showing that your examples are not isolated cases.* Detailed statistics from a trustworthy source can show the seriousness of a problem. They can document progress toward solving it. Remember that readers are wary of being manipulated by figures. Who compiled your statistics? For what purpose? Are they detailed enough to give a rounded picture? Here are some of the statistics a student writer collected on efforts to bring back the wolves into the American wilderness and national parks:

KEY STATISTICS:

Wildlife biologists in Canada estimate that there are between 45,000 and 60,000 wolves in Canada. Perhaps 10,000 wolves live in Alaska and another 2,000 in other northern states, for a total of perhaps 72,000 grey wolves in North America.

The Sierra Club claims that its polls show 72.4 percent of the population in the states affected favoring plans to release additional wolves into the wild.

The federal government spent about $1 million for an airlift by helicopter of 15 grey wolves from Alberta to Yellowstone Park, while additional similar missions were being discussed, with a projected cost of $13 million over five years.

34b Taking Notes

Develop your own system of tracking usable material.

Experienced note takers develop their own system for accumulating notes, selecting and adapting usable material. They highlight important points as they read, download or photocopy key pages, and scribble notes in the margin. They copy key passages and summarize others, getting them ready to be fed into a first draft. Here is a sampling of the kinds of notes that you will find useful:

SUMMARY OF KEY INFORMATION:

Falling Crime Rate

Jack Maple, lieutenant of the New York Transit Police, had watched the numbers rise steadily. Crime was going up and no one knew how to stop the trend. Maple had "a vision": He drew a map tracing the city's subway lines and turned it into a crude mapping system for charting crime-ridden neighborhoods. His system helped police departments deploy more officers in areas where crime was heaviest. Maple's mapping system helped change police methods from waiting for crimes to happen to pre-emptive strategies for discouraging crime.

Eric Jenner, "Computer-Based Crime-Fighting, From the Ground Up," New York Times 12 Dec. 1997: 18

DIRECT QUOTATION FOR KEY IDEAS:

Falling Crime Rate

The mayor and his supporters claim much of the credit for New York's City's drop in crime. They subscribe to the "broken-window" theory of crime: If small infractions are overlooked, a general spirit of lawlessness slowly takes over. "The zero-tolerance policy encourages police to focus on quality-of-life violations—public drinking, lewd behavior, loud music—as a means to discourage more serious crimes. The idea is that when left untreated small disorders breed large ones."

Richard Lacayo, "Good Cop, Bad Cop," Time 1 Sept. 1997: 42

DETAILED AUTHORITATIVE STATISTICS:

Growing Prison Populations

Total number of prison inmates tripled from 319,600 in 1980 to 999,800 in 1994, while the U.S. population increased only 15%. Number of inmates in local jails increased 165% from 182,300 in 1980 to 483,700 in 1994. About 1 million people lived in prisons and 3.7 million were on probation or parole. In 1993, 68% of state prisoner were under the age of 35. In 1991, 600,000 juveniles were under some type of correctional supervision. Of these, 80% were on parole and 17% (more than 100,000) were in prison. In many prisons, minorities are the majority. In 1993, 51% of the inmates were black and 14% were Hispanic. Women made up 6% of the prison population; 6% of the women were pregnant. About three-fourths of the prisoners, both men and women, have children under the age of 18.

Paula Mergenhagen, "The Prison Population Bomb," American Demographics Feb. 1996: 36-42

34c Organizing Your Notes

While taking notes, keep an eye out for patterns that emerge.

How will you organize your notes? From the beginning of your search, you will keep your eye on what goes with what. Which of your notes show the same kind of thing—pointing in the same direction? Which show a countertrend or an important exception? Where do your authorities agree? Where do they disagree, and why? Study the following set of notes for a paper on how we see changing crime rates reflected in the mirror of the press. How do these notes add up? What conclusions do they suggest? How would you structure a paper or a section of a paper using these notes?

SAMPLE NOTES:

Dropping Crime Rate

Areas including New York, Los Angeles, and Washington, D.C., have experienced more than a 20 percent drop in the number of murders over the last year. Other violent crimes such as armed robbery, rape, and assault declined over 10 percent. These figures continue a six-year trend, but the drastic drop this year was more than experts had predicted. Partial explanations include a thriving economy, a smaller numbers of youths in high-risk age groups, and better police methods. "All the usual explanations do not really account for why we are seeing such sharp drops now on top of several years of decreased crimes."

Robert Suro, "Major Cities Show Drop in Homicides," Washington Post 31 Dec. 97: A1

Dropping Crime Rate

Typical headlines tout drop in crime.

Fox Butterfield, "Property-Crime Rate Plunges in U.S." New York Times 12 Oct. 97: A1

Dropping Crime Rate

Rosy estimates of declining crime ignore reports of police corruption and incompetence. In Washington, D.C., over 300 police officers have "tainted backgrounds," and the police academy has a "no-fail" policy. Many officers have incredibly low numbers for making arrests and stay away completely from high-crime neighborhoods. Many crimes go unreported.

Carl Rowan, "D.C. Confidential," The New Republic 19 Jan. 98: 20

Dropping Crime Rate

The way to stop youths from committing violent crimes is to apply swift and certain punishment, without leniency. In Boston, after the highest murder rate ever in 1990, criminal justice took on a new face, as the Boston police began to work with the ATF (Alcohol, Tobacco, and Firearms Agency) to combat gang violence. Murder and violent crimes dropped significantly over the next two or three years. "Possible offenders won't commit violent crimes if police convince them that the violence will not be tolerated."

Gordon Witkin, "Swift and Certain Punishment," U.S. News & World Report 12 Dec. 97: 1-2

Dropping Crime Rate

Homicides are at a 20-year low. In 1995, the murder rate was so high that the FBI was called in to help fight crime. Increased police staffing and new policing methods in neighborhoods have been credited with bringing about the drop in crime. Very positive article—helping to restore tarnished reputation of L.A. and L.A. Police Department (LAPD) after Rodney King riots and role of "rogue cop" Fuhrman in O. J. Simpson trial?

Matt Lait, "Homicides at 20-Year Low," The Los Angeles Times 29 Dec. 97: A1, A6

34d Organizing Your Paper

Use a working outline to organize your paper.

In a successful research paper, you pull together a mass of material. How does it all add up? You sort out your notes, put together what belongs together, and lay out the material so that it will make sense to your readers. As your paper begins to take shape, you keep asking yourself:

- Does my paper have a clear plan?
- Can I explain what comes first and why?
- Can I explain what comes next and why?
- Can I funnel the results into a statement summing up what I found?
- Will this statement hold up as my unifying thesis?

34d.1 Your Working Outline *Use a working outline to get your material under control.* By definition, a **working outline** is not poured in concrete. It gives you something to work with—to develop, to adjust. You may start with a scratch outline that is just a few jottings sketching an overall strategy. You gradually add missing parts of the puzzle, and you discard entries that turn out to be side issues. You move things around so that first things come first. Gradually, you work out an organizing strategy that will give shape to your paper as a whole. Here are examples of organizing strategies that, alone or in combination, may help you lay out your material:

THEN AND NOW A major section of your paper, or your paper as a whole, might be built around a contrast of then and now. You may be studying the transformation of city neighborhoods that is taking place as coffee outlets, bookstores, and video rental stores operated by large chains replace the smaller independent businesses operated by local owners. What was the neighborhood like before? What is happening now?

PROBLEM TO SOLUTION You document the existence of a problem—for instance, pill-happy consumers disregarding possible side effects, taking too many hormone tablets or diet supplements without reading the fine print. You identify the major causes fueling the trend. Then you look at proposed remedies, quoting the advocates of the different solutions. Quoting experts or insiders, you try to show the consequences of different causes of action. You choose and defend the best answer.

STAGES IN A PROCESS Working on your topic may lead you to think of major stages in a historical process. For instance, causes that mobilize much support include saving the whales, protecting the forests, or challenging animal research. Such causes have a history. They go through phases. For example, they may move from initial enthusiasm to obstacles and second thoughts and finally on toward success or defeat. In a paper intended as a status report, you may first document the origins of the movement or crusade, then examine obstacles and setbacks, then look at landmark decisions or victories, and then look at projections for the future.

The following might be your first scratch outline for a paper on the movement to save the whales:

SCRATCH OUTLINE:

—the endangered whale

—efforts at regulation and international treaties

—non-cooperating nations (Norway, Japan)

—whaling rights of indigenous people of the Arctic

—current numbers?

Further into your project, the following might be your working outline. A more detailed program or itinerary for your paper is taking shape:

WORKING OUTLINE:

Saving the Whales

I The romance of nineteenth-century whaling ships
(voyages to distant oceans, the struggle with nature)

II The whales endangered by predatory industrialized whaling
(modern whaling ships as floating factories depleting the oceans)

III Ecologists raising public consciousness
(campaign to save the whales)

IV Regulations setting quotas and controlling exploitation
(international efforts and treaties)

V Resistance from whaling nations and indigenous peoples

VI Successes and remaining problems
(rebounding of some formerly endangered kinds of whales)

34d.2 Your Trial Thesis *Push toward a tentative thesis.*

Charting your course and pushing toward a thesis normally go hand in hand. Sometimes you will start with tentative assumptions that turn out to be wrong or need to be drastically revised. Often you will start with a **working hypothesis**—an idea that your research will test. For instance, you may have set out to test your general impression that the movement to save the whales has been a success. You may then have to adjust this working assumption in the light of what you find. You may discover that the movement to save the whales has had mixed results. It has been a qualified success. A trial thesis like the following could sum up your findings.

TRIAL THESIS:

In spite of opposition and setbacks, the movement to save the whales has become one of the few success stories among the efforts to save the endangered wildlife of our planet.

Suppose you are studying different ways of looking at the reports of falling crime rates in major cities. Political leaders take credit; critics are distrustful of political hype; some claim that disillusionment or apathy among citizens causes much crime to go unreported. How would you sum up your findings in your trial thesis? Your thesis and your working outline might look like this:

WORKING OUTLINE:

Spinning the Crime News

TRIAL THESIS: Different interested parties put their own spin on claims of falling crime rates in major cities.

I headlines highlight falling crime rates

II cities tout positive news about falling crime rates
  New York
  Los Angeles
  Washington, D.C.

III dissenting voices question official figures
  police corruption and non-performance in D.C.
  neighborhood voices on unreported crimes

IV conservatives take credit for deterring crime
  candidates' speeches about "cracking down"
  emphasis on harsh sentencing laws

V high-crime cities need to refurbish their image
  good news for the tourism industry
  good news for boosters trying to attract business and industry

34d.3 Your Formal Outline

Prepare a formal outline when it is required for your project or your area of study. Use a detailed outline first of all as a writing tool: It can make visible the structure of your thinking, projecting your own thinking as if on a screen. You can then attend to gaps, missing connections, or awkward backtrackings. At the same time, especially for ambitious projects, a **formal outline** serves as a help to your readers. It charts an itinerary for them, preparing them for major waystations and turns in the road.

Study the traditional format of the formal outline in the following example. Notice the sequence of main heads (roman numerals), subheads (capital letters), and sub-subheads (arabic numerals). In the unlikely event that you need a fourth level, use lower-case letters (a., b., and so forth) for the sub-subsubheads. Notice the use of similar wording for related entries, helping the reader see the connections ("Struggle for . . ."; "Struggle for . . ."; "Struggle for . . .").

FORMAL OUTLINE:

The Range of Feminist Thought

THESIS: Like other mature political movements, feminism is not a one-track movement but unites women with different agendas.

I. Equal-Rights Feminism—emphasis on legislation
   A. Struggle for voting rights: suffragist movement
   B. Struggle for property rights
      1. Inheritance rights
      2. Community property
   C. Struggle for divorce legislation to protect rights of women

II. Equity Feminism—emphasis on economic advancement
   A. Beyond "pink-collar" occupations: secretaries, waitresses, nurses
   B. Advances in the professions
      1. Women doctors
      2. Women judges and lawyers
      3. Women on university faculties
   C. Struggle against tokenism and glass ceiling for women executives

III. Victim Feminism—emphasis on violence against women
   A. Fighting demeaning stereotypes
   B. Protecting battered women
   C. Working on rape prevention

IV. Cultural Feminism—emphasis on women's role in human culture
   A. Earth mothers and mother goddesses in early religions
   B. Counteracting the patriarchal culture of power and war
   C. Honoring women as nurturers and creators

YOUR TURN 96

Study the following working outline. Can you explain how the writer sorted out the material? Does the order or sequence of major points make sense? Would you recommend reordering or regrouping some of the categories? What trial thesis might the writer formulate to sum up what she has found?

WORKING OUTLINE:

Women in Medicine

I Women in medical school
  then: nearly 100% male
  now: near gender parity

II Nurturing quality of women in health care
  more time spent with patients
  more empathetic and better listeners

III Use of "female" qualities as excuse for sexual harassment
  failure of acceptance by older colleagues (Francis Conley case)
  sexual harassment in medical school
  sexual harassment by patients

IV Pay gap between male and female physicians
  fewer women in higher-paying specialties like surgery or neuroscience
  more women as family practitioners

V Women getting better health care
  more women physicians taking care of women
  more research being done on women

VI What women would like to do about their roles in medicine
  creation of new women's health specialty

35 DRAFTING AND REVISING

Take your paper through successive stages of drafting and revising.

As you write an early draft, the challenge you face is to *integrate* a large body of material. You synthesize—you pull together data and opinions from a range of sources in order to make them part of a coherent whole. As you work on different parts of your draft, keep asking yourself: "How does this fit in? How is it part of the larger picture? How does it fit into my overall plan?"

35a Feeding Notes into Your Draft

Study ways of using your notes in your first draft.

As you write your first draft, you feed the material from your notes into your paper at the right points. The essential skill is to choose and fit in the material that will develop the points in your outline. You work in the material from your notes in such a way that the seams do not show. Suppose that in your notes you have included a quotation from an economist who explains the current and growing trend toward temporary employment:

OUTSOURCING—Pressuring unions

"Temporary workers and outsourcing make up the bulk of today's contingent workforce—millions of Americans whose labor can be used and discarded at a moment's notice and at a fraction of the cost of maintaining a permanent workforce. Their very existence acts to drive wages down for the remaining full-time workers. Employers are increasingly using the threat of temp hiring and outsourcing to win wage and benefit concessions from unions—a trend that is likely to accelerate in the years ahead."

Rifkin, <u>End of Work</u>, p. 194.

How are you going to use this material in your paper? Here are some possibilities:

EXTENDED DIRECT QUOTATION When a author takes a stand on an important issue or explains a key concept, you may decide to let the quoted author have his or her say. You quote several sentences word for word, so that your readers can take in exactly what the person said. When the direct quotation runs to more than three of four lines, you type it as a **block quotation**:

> In his widely read End of Work, Rifkin explains the mechanisms that work to reduce the number of full-time permanent employees and to turn a steadily growing number of workers into economic nomads:
>
> > Temporary workers and outsourcing make up the bulk of today's contingent workforce—millions of Americans whose labor can be used and discarded at a moment's notice and at a fraction of the cost of maintaining a permanent workforce. Their very existence acts to drive wages down for the remaining full-time workers. Employers are increasingly using the threat of temp hiring and outsourcing to win wage and benefit concessions from unions—a trend that is likely to accelerate in the years ahead. (194)

PARAPHRASE When you are trying to explain an important idea or process, you may decide to **paraphrase.** You put the material into your own words. This way you can highlight and clarify key points.

> In his widely read End of Work, Rifkin explains the mechanisms that work to reduce the number of full-time permanent employees and to turn a steadily growing number of workers into economic nomads. Temporary jobs and jobs farmed out by outsourcing account for most of our current nonpermanent, available-for-hire labor force. It is made up of workers who can be hired for short stints and then abruptly fired again, with total labor costs only a small percentage of those for full-time workers. Merely by being available to employers as an option, they tend to lower wages for everyone else. By threatening to hire temporaries or to outsource jobs, employers can pressure unions into accepting wage cuts and reduced benefits. This trend is likely to speed up in future years (194).

PARTIAL QUOTATION This is the most flexible and effective way to work an author's material into your paper. Quoted phrases and parts of sentences become part of the flow of your own text.

> In his widely read End of Work, Rifkin explains the mechanisms that work to reduce the number of full-time permanent employees and to turn a steadily growing number of workers into economic nomads. Temporary jobs and jobs farmed out by outsourcing account for most of today's **"contingent workforce"**—made up of nonpermanent, available-for-hire employees. Their **"labor can be used and discarded at a moment's notice and at a fraction of the cost of maintaining a permanent workforce."** Merely by being available to employers as an option, they tend to lower wages for everyone else. Increasingly employers are **"using the threat of temp hiring and outsourcing to win wage and benefit concessions from unions"**—pressuring unions into accepting wage cuts and reduced health and pension benefits. This trend is likely to speed up in future years (194).

BRIEF QUOTATION IN LARGER CONTEXT You may be pulling out a key idea to combine or contrast with other related material. The quoted author's idea becomes part of a larger picture:

> Economists discuss economic trends as the work of large impersonal forces. In the language of economists, **"Temporary workers and outsourcing make up the bulk of today's contingent workforce—millions of Americans whose labor can be used and discarded at a moment's notice and at a fraction of the cost of maintaining a permanent workforce"** (Rifkin 194). However, for millions of "downsized" and "outsourced" workers, the changes in the workforce are a frustrating daily reality. In the words of one of their number, the **"obsession with boosting creativity has created widely disparate numbers of working Americans."** One **"is prosperous, whipping around chanting slogans"** that extol new management philosophies. Another **"works each day fearful that it will be the last; and another has fallen through the cracks into dislocation and a dreadful wage depression with little prospect of improvement"** (Swardson 33).

35b Writing a Strong First Draft

Avoid predictable problems to write a strong first draft.

Teachers and editors tell writers to push ahead with their first draft. Keep typing, they say, and leave rough spots to be smoothed over later. Even so, regardless of your opportunities to rewrite, remember from the start guidelines like the following:

- *Do not rely too much on one single source.* Are you feeding in data and ideas from the same source for most of a page (or even several pages in a row)? Your source may indeed be an outstanding authority on diet pills or on juvenile crime. However, *show* that this source is indeed a leading authority—by bringing in other sources that share the same ideas or agree with them at least in part.
- *Do not use many long undigested quotations.* Use extended exact quotations—set off as **block quotations**—for special purposes. For instance, use them to document an author's exact stand on a controversial issue. (Let the original author have his or her say.) Use them when you want to reproduce exact detailed technical information. (Don't risk getting essential details wrong.) However, big chunks of direct quotation may break up the flow of your paper. Your readers may lose sight of the overall argument or of the larger picture. Break up chunky extended quotes—mix quotation, explanation, and commentary.
- *Do not expect a single example to prove a point.* Try packing a single paragraph with several examples of the same trend or detailed statistics from several sources. The following paragraph keeps adding related examples to show that in discussions of sensitive issues we are influenced not merely by *what* is said but also by *how* it is said. We are influenced not just by the news but by the spin given to the news:

  The words used in discussing a sensitive issue often imply a choosing of sides, sometimes subtly and sometimes more obviously. When discussing proposals for resegregating of the sexes in the military, conservative media voices described the results of integrating the sexes in terms suggesting belittling and ridicule. Mark Thomas, a journalist writing for *Time* magazine, talked about sexual relations by members of the armed forces as "boys" and "girls" engaging in "hanky-panky." In unsegregated buildings, soldiers were "cruising for sex" (104-05). An article by Dawn MacKeen in *Salon* magazine talked about training that was "more like a sex ring than a military education," with bases "becoming sexual proving grounds" (17). On the other hand, a proposed return to sex-segregated training was often discussed in terms suggesting strong approval or respect. Dana Priest in the *Washington Post* talked about avoiding "an erosion of discipline and cohesion" (A1). The article in *Time* talked about eliminating sexual distractions and building "true esprit de corps."

35c Revising Your Draft

Revise early drafts in response to feedback.

Learn to be your own critic. As you reread your draft, ask yourself: What went well? Where were you struggling? What needs work? Note passages that make you say: "This is already in good shape—but let me add some explanation for the outsider." Or, "Let me tone this down—so I won't alienate some of my readers." Look especially for places where you say to yourself: "This I didn't really explain. This I didn't really support. This I didn't really document. This really doesn't belong here."

✓ ***EDITOR'S TIP:*** If at all possible, allow time between an early draft and revision. If you reread a finished draft right away, you may read what you think you said rather than what is there in cold print.

35c.1 Responding to Peer Reviews *Look for constructive criticism in peer reviews.* When you react to peer reviews, you will welcome comments that compliment you on your hard work and a job well done. You will try not to get angry at readers who seem to complain about little things while missing major points. However, you will learn most from readers who understand what you are trying to do—but who can also point to specific problems that need attention.

Your instructor may use a format like the following for peer reviews of your research paper:

PEER REVIEW

Research Paper Review Checklist

Author ____________________ **Reviewer** ____________________

1 ***Purpose:*** What did the writer focus on, or what did the writer set out to do?

2 ***Thesis:*** What is the writer's thesis? Where is it stated? How would you restate it in your own words? Does it set up a program or pattern for the paper to follow?

3 ***Organization:*** What is the overall plan? What are the major sections or stages of the paper? Are they easy or hard to follow? Are there missing links or awkward backtrackings?

4 ***Sources:*** How well does the paper use sources? Is there enough support for the author's findings or conclusions? Where is the evidence strong or convincing? Where is evidence weak or missing?

5 ***Style:*** Is the writing clear and effective? Are there murky, hard-to-follow passages? Are there passages where the style is too chummy or condescending? Are there passages where technical concepts need better explanation?

6 ***Documentation:*** Was documentation clear and adequate? Does it follow the conventions of the chosen documentation style? Are there any special problems?

7 ***Audience:*** Are you a good audience for this paper? Did you learn something from it? Did it change your mind? Did you enjoy reading the paper?

35c.2 Responding to Instructor Feedback *Look for pointers on how to build on the strengths and shore up the weaknesses of an early draft.* Every research project is different and presents a new challenge. However, instructors and editors often make comments like the following on an early version of a paper:

- *Bring the issue to life.* Does your introduction sound like a rehash of the assignment? Try using a striking **starter quote.** Or use provocative **new statistics** that put the issue in a new light.

FIRST DRAFT:

Today's Jails

In our modern society there are an estimated one and a half million people in jail. It is very difficult to discern the who's, how's, and why's of the people in them. Through the use of newspapers, scholarly journals, and people with firsthand experience we can begin to understand today's jails and their occupants. . . .

REVISION:

Americans behind Bars

"I have visited some of the best and worst prisons and have never seen signs of coddling, but I have seen the terrible results of the boredom and frustration of empty hours and pointless existence," says the editor of *Prison Photos Gallery*, published by the U.S. Department of Justice. Every year, more people are sent to jail than the entire combined populations of our thirteen least populous states (Burger 3-4). Who are the people who pass through the gates of our overcrowded prisons, swelling their population to an estimated one and a half million people?

- *Make the basic outline of your paper stand out.* Is there a **preview** or overview early in your paper? Are there strong links or **transitions** at the turning points? Signal more clearly when you are moving on to a new key stage in your overall plan.

FIRST DRAFT:

Family Values

In the past thirty or forty years the American family has changed drastically. "One child in four is now born to unmarried parents. The number of couples who live together outside of marriage has increased sevenfold since the 1970s. Divorce has been epidemic for some twenty-five years. And families with children are feeling particularly burdened these days" (Morano 53). What has caused this change from family-oriented households to today's fragmented or endangered families? *One of many answers, according to a journalist for Fortune magazine, is that "families are no longer a big plus for a corporation; they are a big problem." In fact, "if you want to have children, proceed at your own risk. You must be very talented, or on very solid ground, to overcome the damage a family can do to your career" ("Is Your Family" 1).*

Today many top executives are forced to put in an 80-hour workweek. The time commitment and the indispensable additional networking leave businessmen and businesswomen drained and stressed, with a serious impact on the development of their neglected children. . . .

In the 1970s, divorce changed from one of the forbidden subjects to an "accepted solution to marital problems." . . .

Olivia Vlahos in a recent article describes families on the "lower echelons" of society as virtually non-existent. . . .

COMMENT: You start with a good strong quote that dramatizes the issue and that leads into your key question about the current situation. But then you slide into your first major section without giving us a hint of your overall plan. And later you move on to other important areas without a clear signal that you are moving on to another major part of the general picture. (Note that your title gives no real hint of your intention or agenda.)

REVISION:

Our Endangered Family Values

In the past thirty or forty years the American family has changed drastically. "One child in four is now born to unmarried parents. The number of couples who live together outside of marriage has increased sevenfold since the 1970s. Divorce has been epidemic for some twenty-five years. And families with children are feeling particularly burdened these days" (Morano 53). What has caused this change from family-oriented households to today's fragmented or endangered families? **Among the many answers, several stand out: the pressures of competing in the marketplace that subject many couples to a high degree of stress; the temptation to end marital problems by divorce; and the breakdown of the family on the lowest rungs of society.**

For all the talk about family values, today's corporations do not offer a hospitable climate for family-oriented employees. According to a journalist for Fortune magazine, "Families are no longer a big plus for a corporation; they are a big problem." In fact, "if you want to have children, proceed at your own risk. You must be very talented, or on very solid ground, to overcome the damage a family can do to your career" ("Is Your Family" 1). . . .

Often, economic pressures do not merely have a negative impact on family life but destroy the family altogether. In the 1970s, divorce changed from one of the forbidden subjects to an "accepted solution to marital problems." . . .

While dysfunctional families and broken homes are commonplace among the affluent, many sociologists and journalists seem to take them for granted among the nation's poor. Olivia Vlahos in a recent article describes families on the "lower echelons" of society as virtually non-existent. . . .

- *Check for sweeping generalizations and hasty conclusions.* Try to draw carefully *limited* conclusions from *ample* evidence. Try to stay close to what your evidence shows.

FIRST DRAFT:

Olivia Vlahos in a recent article describes families on the "lower echelons" of society as virtually non-existent. "Many children with parents in jail or hopelessly drug-addicted must bring themselves up on the streets. Some take refuge in gangs of their peers and deal drugs" (4). It is easy to see that in lower-income families and welfare cases family values are not always a hot topic. When the daily routine consists of a backbreaking, low-paying job and concern about where the next meal will come from, the family slips through the cracks. Children are for the most part neglected and uneducated, allowing them to form their own values on the street. *Parents are the only ones to blame.*

> COMMENT: In a research paper, you can't use *sweeping generalizations and accusations* like this. (Parents "are the only ones" to blame? What about drug dealers? employers abandoning poor neighborhoods? authorities unable to cope with gangs? media bombarding excluded kids with images of ostentatious wealth?) Ideally, some interviews or printed personal testimony from "lower-echelon" parents would help here.

- *If necessary, revise your overall strategy.* Much revision is like fine-tuning, but sometimes a major reshuffling is necessary. If necessary, be prepared to move major chunks of material around for a more effective presentation. For instance, does a paper assembling encouraging data about the fight against multiple sclerosis in the end let down the reader with warnings against premature optimism? Perhaps you can counterbalance these necessary cautions by not making them the last word in your paper. Perhaps you can shift them to a place *before* a final section that would look at the most recent breakthroughs and confident projections for a better future.

- *Strengthen weak links.* Do you go on from one major point to the next with a weak *also* or *another?* ("We must *also* consider . . ."; "*another* important point is . . .") Put in stronger **transitions** that show the logical connection. (Why are you going on to the next point here? What is the connection?)

FIRST DRAFT:

There are *many points of entry* into homelessness, including poverty and the lack of affordable housing. . . .

Another point to consider is medical needs. . . .

Also, a growing number of homeless are mothers with children. . . .

A Campus Ministry Director sends students to shelters and soup kitchens to help out. . . .

REVISION:

Contrary to familiar stereotypes, poverty is the root cause of homelessness. . . .

A second closely related reason for homelessness is the inability to deal with medical problems. When families are living hand-to-mouth, the risk of a sudden illness or medical emergency sending them into the streets is high. . . .

A third major cause of homelessness is the rending of the social safety net. Welfare benefits have shrunk with inflation and have often been cut outright. As one welfare mother admitted to a group of county officials, "You see before you a welfare cheat. Each month I ask myself whether I should let my children go hungry or be a criminal. I am constantly forced to earn money off the books and lie about my income to feed my kids." . . .

Although the problem of homelessness seems immense and too big to handle, communities are providing grass root efforts to cope with its effects. Brother Matthew Hearst, a Campus Ministry director, places students at shelters and soup kitchens as voluntary helpers. . . .

- *Clarify terms that might confuse your reader.* For instance, you may be referring to "stepfamilies" and "binuclear families." Will your readers know what these are? Add capsule definitions and maybe brief examples:

REVISION:

There are actually several subcategories under the heading of the traditional nuclear family. There are first-marriage families, with both spouses in their first marriage. **Then there are remarried couples or binuclear families, with one or both of the spouses in their second or subsequent marriage. Often these are at the same time stepfamilies. Some or all of the children were born before the current marriage, so that children have a stepfather or a stepmother and often half-brothers or half-sisters.**

- *Aim for a stronger punchline.* Is your paper winding up with well-meaning thoughts that everyone has heard before? ("We must find ways to provide job training and employment opportunities as an alternative to jail.") Are you aware of any concrete proposals or successful initiatives? Point to something specific to make your readers think or to make them take heart. Or look for a strong final quotation by someone who makes your main point better than you or most of us could.

FIRST DRAFT:

. . . The family has drastically changed from the days of home-cooked meals and everyone there at the dinner table. It is time to put the emphasis back on family values. *Parents must learn the importance of morals and putting the family first.*

REVISION:

. . . The family has drastically changed from the days of home-cooked meals and everyone there at the dinner table. **Nevertheless, today many look for a way to turn things around—to make every effort to work things out. Proposed laws and tax initiatives focus on how to keep families together—subsidizing child care or providing child care at work, for instance. In the words of one child care worker, "Politicians are catching on to the new trend—caring."**

36 DOCUMENTING YOUR SOURCES

Give detailed, accurate information about your sources.

Documentation discloses the sources of your material. Careful and complete documentation charts a retrieval path for the data, information, or ideas you have worked into your paper. Ideally, a documented paper enables your readers to check your sources and to verify the use you have made of them. Always imagine a reader who asks: "Where did you find this? What is your source?" To answer these questions, you guide your reader to the right article or book or Internet source. You give the exact location or page. You provide full publishing data—identifying authors, titles, places and dates, or specific issues of a publication. For electronic sources, you will often have to provide the lengthy strings of abbreviations needed to access material on the net.

36a Following a Documentation Style

Follow the documentation style of your academic discipline or field of study.

Guidelines for documentation tell you in detail how to encode your publishing data. Don't look for a single standardized format—the **documentation style** changes from one area of research to another. You may be asked to follow one set of instructions for a paper in an English class and another for a term paper in economics or sociology. However, you will be asked to track much the same information, and the way you present it will often be similar.

The documentation styles most widely required in introductory college classes employ a two-track system. First, you include minimal information in parentheses in the text of your paper. These brief notes are called **parenthetic documentation**. They typically pin down page numbers or dates of publication. Here are two common versions:

> Carol Herbst, research scientist at the Lacault Institute, says that global warming may actually be followed by a disastrous drop in temperature later (34). Her theory has . . .

A research scientist at the Lacault Institute says that global warming may actually be followed by a disastrous drop in temperature later (Herbst 34). Her theory has . . .

In either case, the author's name will guide your reader to the detailed publishing information that will appear in a final alphabetical source list. This list will be labeled **Works Cited** or **References.** The listing is today no longer labeled the *bibliography*—literally the "book list"—because it often includes nonprint sources. Here is a quick preview of how entries in your final listing of sources would look. Each set gives an example for a newspaper or magazine article, for a book, and for an Internet source.

WORKS CITED MLA STYLE (for research papers in English or history):

Suro, Robert. "Major Cities Show Drop in Homicides." Washington Post 31 Dec. 1997: A1+.

Hawking, Stephen. Black Holes and Baby Universes and Other Essays. New York: Bantam, 1993.

Lewis, Nicole. "The Need for Help Goes On." Washington Post 23 Jan. 1998: DO5. 30 Jan. 1998 <http://www.washingtonpost.com/wp-srv/WPlate/1998-01/23/0711-012398-idx.html>.

REFERENCES APA STYLE (for research papers in the social sciences):

Hout, M., & Lucas, S. R. (1996, August 16). Narrowing the income gap between rich and poor. The Chronicle of Higher Education, 42, (49) B1.

Steinem, G. (1992). Revolution from within: A book of self-esteem. Boston: Little, Brown.

Lewis, P. H. (1996, January 15). The Internet's very nature defies censorship by government or individual. The New York Times. [Online]. Available: http://www.nytimes.com/library/cyber/week/0115block.html [1998, March 15].

Both of these widely used documentation styles have done away with the **footnotes** that used to give publishing information page by page. Detailed publishing data are now given only at the end. However, such bibliographical footnotes are still used in a style outlined in the *Chicago Manual of Style* (CMS). In both the MLA and APA styles, numbered **endnotes** used as explanatory notes may appear before the final alphabetical listing of sources used.

✓ ***EDITOR'S TIP:*** Styles for documenting electronic sources are still evolving. Different guides may give you slightly different information and show slightly different models for the retrieval information or **URL** (for Uniform Resource Locator). For updated guidelines for a major academic area, you may want to access one of the following:

- guide to APA documentation for electronic sources: http://www.uvm.edu/~xli/reference/apa.html
- guide to Council of Biology Editors (CBE) documentation: http://www.cbe.org/cbe
- guide to Institute of Electrical and Electronic Engineers (IEEE) documentation—for areas including computer science: http://www.ieee.org

36b doc Documenting Your Sources—MLA Style

Follow the MLA style for research papers in the humanities.

You will usually be asked to document research papers in the humanities—English, history, philosophy—in the MLA style. The MLA (Modern Language Association) is for teachers of writing and literature what the AMA (American Medical Association) is for physicians. As a professional organization, the MLA sets standards that are widely observed. The MLA guidelines for documenting research are outlined in the *MLA Style Manual* (Second Edition, 1998) and in the MLA *Handbook for Writers of Research Papers* (Fifth Edition, 1999).

36b.1 Parenthetic Documentation (MLA)

Provide page references and other needed data in parentheses in your text. For many of your readers, authorship and respect for authors and intellectual property will be especially important. Most of the time, you should therefore identify author and publication when first *introducing* a quotation. You then later need only a simple page reference in parentheses. However, look at sample references for special situations.

1 STANDARD PAGE REFERENCE You identify the author and the publication in your text. You then give the page number in parentheses. Put it *after* a final quotation mark but *before* a final period.

> Allan Sloan, a columnist for Newsweek, said, "This has created more than $4 trillion of new paper wealth for stockholders" (50).

2 AUTHOR AND PAGE If you have *not* named the author in your text, include the author's name with the page reference. (No comma between name and page number.)

> A columnist for Money magazine says, "When Sanjiv Sidhu brought his software company public . . . 25 of his employees became millionaires" (Reeves 170).

3 TITLE AND PAGE If you are quoting from *several works* by the same author, include the title of each work with the page reference. If it's a long title, use a shortened form.

> Jeremy Rifkin published The End of Work: The Decline of the Global Labor Force and the Dawn of the Post-Market Era in 1995. He has often written about "obsolete patterns of work" (End of Work 17); he predicts that "by the year 2020, less than 2 percent of the entire global workforce will still be engaged in factory work" ("Civil Society" 11).

4 AUTHOR AND TITLE WITH PAGE When quoting from several works by an author you have not yet named, include the author's name and also the title of the publication with your page reference. Put a comma between author and title.

> In France, immigrants from Muslim North Africa are "increasingly resisting assimilation and integration" (Belvedere, Rise of Islam 187).

5 MORE THAN ONE AUTHOR When several authors have coauthored an article or a book, include their names with your page reference if you have not already named them in your text. For more than three authors, give the name of the first author and then put et al. (no italics)—Latin for "and others."

> Tests are increasingly becoming the target of censorship (Beckers and Santos 134). In California, an ambitious new testing program was abandoned when community groups claimed that the test questions "constituted an invasion of the students' privacy" (Verbrook et al. 79).

6 BLOCK QUOTATION At the end of a block quotation, start the parentheses after the final punctuation. For instance, put the page reference *outside* the final period. (Remember to indent the whole block quotation about one inch or ten typewriter spaces—double the normal paragraph indentation.)

> In *Myths about Aging*, Moeller tries to counteract familiar stereotypes. He points to the large numbers of mentally alert and intellectually active older people:
>
> > Older people seem mentally slow or disoriented when we deprive them of intellectual stimulus and active involvement with other people. Provided they remain active and are not isolated or cast off, the majority of older people remain mentally alert. Few of them show signs of mental deterioration or senility. (114)

7 SECONDHAND QUOTATION Show when you are quoting not from the original source but at second hand. (Your Works Cited will then list the secondhand source.) Whenever you can, however, quote directly from an original source.

> When Marie Curie talked about the challenge of combining her "lofty career" in science with raising a family, she said: "It is my whole life that is at stake" (qtd. in Quinn 78).

8 MULTIVOLUME WORK Use an Arabic numeral followed by a colon to specify the volume you have used. The following page reference directs readers to the third book that a British historian published as part of his classic *History of England:*

> Writing about the period between the two great wars, the British historian Trevelyan said that the isolationist movement in America and the pacifist movement in Britain between them "handed the world over to its fate" (3:301).

9 INTRODUCTORY MATERIAL Use roman numerals (instead of regular arabic page numbers) when you find them used in a book for a preface or other introductory material:

> In her introduction to Dancing on the Edge of the World, Ursula K. Le Guin says, "I try to limit myself to topics on which, without claiming expertise or wisdom, an effort to think honestly and feelingly might do some good" (vii).

10 NONPRINT MATERIALS In the electronic age, researchers more and more draw on nonprint sources. When you quote from an interview, media source, or exhibit, highlight in your text the name of the interviewer, interviewee, director, scriptwriter, or producer whose name will appear in your final listing of sources. If you are going to list the source by its title, highlight the title or include it in parentheses.

> An exhibit at the Wiesenthal Museum in Los Angeles provided a photographic record of what the organizers called the "stunning multiethnic range of American immigration" (Nation of Strangers).

11 LITERARY CLASSIC Use arabic numerals separated by periods for such divisions of literary works as act and scene in a Shakespeare play. However, some authors prefer the more traditional use of capital and lower-case roman numerals (Hamlet III.ii.73-76).

> The ghost in Shakespeare's Hamlet is seen by sober observers who pride themselves on being punctual: "You come most carefully upon your hour" (1.1.6).

12 BIBLE QUOTATION Use arabic numerals for chapter and verse (Luke 2.1), although some authors prefer the traditional style (Luke ii.1).

36b.2 **Works Cited (MLA)** *Provide complete information about your sources at the end.* On a separate page at the end of your paper, start your final alphabetical listing of the sources you have used. Give complete publishing data—specifying who, what, where, and when. For the MLA style, put **Works Cited** as the heading of this final list. You may want to paste up the following checklist next to your computer when preparing a paper MLA style.

DOCUMENTATION ESSENTIALS — Works Cited—MLA Style

The following features set the MLA style apart from other documentation styles:

1 first line of entry flush left, next line or lines indented
2 author's last name first (Wolf, Naomi)
3 full first names when used by authors—not just initials
4 quotation marks for article or other *part* of a publication ("The Raven")
5 underlining (or italics) for *complete* publication (Writing on Line)
6 normal use of capitals as in other titles (The Grapes of Wrath)
7 no articles (*The, A,* or *An*) before names of publications (New York Times)
8 months abbreviated if more than four letters (Jan., Mar., Sept.)
9 names of publishers shortened (Prentice for Prentice-Hall Inc.)
10 complete page numbers for articles (do *not* use *p.* or *pp.*)
11 Internet address in angled brackets (<. . . . .>)

Guide to Sample Entries—MLA Style

A. ENTRIES FOR PERIODICALS—Newspapers, magazines, journals

1 STANDARD NEWSPAPER ARTICLE
2 TITLE AND SUBTITLE
3 NEWS ITEM
4 EDITORIAL
5 STANDARD MAGAZINE ARTICLE
6 COAUTHORED ARTICLE
7 SAME AUTHOR
8 VOLUME NUMBERS
9 VOLUME AND ISSUE
10 BOOK REVIEW
11 TITLE WITHIN A TITLE

B. ENTRIES FOR BOOKS

12 STANDARD ENTRY FOR A BOOK
13 SUBTITLED BOOK
14 COAUTHORED BOOK
15 SAME AUTHOR
16 EDITED BOOK
17 TRANSLATED BOOK
18 NEW EDITION
19 BOOK IN A SERIES
20 SPECIAL LINE OF BOOKS
21 WORK IN SEVERAL VOLUMES
22 INTRODUCTORY MATERIAL
23 PART OF A COLLECTION
24 ENCYCLOPEDIA ENTRY
25 INSTITUTIONAL PUBLICATION
26 PAMPHLET OR BROCHURE
27 REISSUED BOOK
28 PUBLISHED CORRESPONDENCE
29 BIBLE OR LITERARY CLASSIC
30 TITLE WITHIN A TITLE

C. ENTRIES FOR ELECTRONIC SOURCES—Online, CD-ROM, e-mail

31 NEWS SERVICE ONLINE
32 NEWSPAPER ONLINE
33 NEWS DIGEST ONLINE
34 ONLINE PUBLICATION ONLY
35 BOTH ONLINE AND PRINT PUBLICATION
36 REFERENCE BOOK ONLINE
37 CD-ROM
38 E-MAIL

D. NONPRINT SOURCES—Interviews, letters, talks, media sources

39 PERSONAL INTERVIEW
40 PUBLISHED INTERVIEW
41 PERSONAL LETTER
42 TALK OR LECTURE
43 PRINTED SPEECH
44 TELEVISION OR RADIO PROGRAM

A. ENTRIES FOR PERIODICALS—Newspapers, magazines, journals

1 STANDARD NEWSPAPER ARTICLE Include date and complete page numbers. As needed, identify the section of the paper or a special late or regional edition. (The + sign shows that an article is concluded later in the issue, on a later page or pages.)

Petersen, Melody. "Tough Laws Get Credit for Drop in New Jersey Violent Crime Rate." New York Times 26 July 1997: A25-26.

Richter, Paul. "Armed Forces Training Is Too Soft, Panel Finds." Los Angeles Times 17 Dec. 1997, late ed.: A1+.

2 TITLE AND SUBTITLE Add a subtitle after a colon:

Mancuso, Phyllis B. "War in Cyberspace: The Duel between Microsoft and AOL." Midland News 3 Jan. 2000: C5-7.

3 NEWS ITEM List an unsigned news item—with no reporter or author identified—alphabetically under the first word of the title:

"Fired Editor of AMA Journal Takes New Post." San Francisco Chronicle, peninsula ed., 25 Feb. 1999: A6.

4 EDITORIAL List a signed editorial under the author's name. List an unsigned editorial under the first word of the title (other than *the* or *a/an*). Identify each as an editorial.

Kramer, Janet. "Focus on Magnet Schools." Editorial. Oakland News 12 Mar. 2000: C3.

"Our Overburdened Courts." Editorial. Tacoma News Tribune 9 Jan. 1999: B6.

5 STANDARD MAGAZINE ARTICLE Give date (or month) and complete page numbers:

Holstein, William J. "Rewiring the Brain." U.S. News & World Report 1 Mar. 1999: 52-53.

Bergman, Carol A. "The Road to Reform: Activists Need Fresh Strategies to Win." Nation 20 Sep. 1999: 46-48.

Baum, Rudy. "Animal Rights Groups Press Their Agenda." Chemical and Engineering News May 1991: 47.

6 COAUTHORED ARTICLE If several people worked together on an article, identify the first author with last name first. Then type the other authors' names in regular order. The abbreviation et al. ("and others") is optional for three or more authors:

Ramos, Sara, and Eileen Bertolt. "Latina Magazine Finds Its Niche." Journalism News July-Aug. 1999: 5-6.

Alexander, Karen, Johnny Dodd, and Jamie Reno. "Zero Conduct." People 13 Oct. 1997: 50-53.

Olasky, Marvin, et al. "When Race Matters, and When It Doesn't. " American Enterprise Nov./Dec. 1998: 48-52.

7 SAME AUTHOR For an additional article by the same author, use three hyphens instead of repeating the name:

Butterfield. Fox. "Drop in Homicide Rate Linked to Crack's Decline." New York Times 27 Oct. 1997. A12+.

- - -. "Homicides Plunge 11% in US. FBI Report Says." New York Times 2 June 1997. A12+.

8 VOLUME NUMBERS Many professional or technical journals do not use new page numbers starting with page 1 in each new issue. Instead, they have consecutive, continuing page numbers for the current volume (usually all the issues for the current year). The second issue for the current year might start with page 178, the third with page 269, and so on. To help readers locate an article, give the volume number, followed by the year, and then followed by page numbers.

Cartmill, Manuel. "Animal Rights: A Reply to Howard." Journal of Mammalogy 75 (1994): 1080-96.

Cotton, Paul. "Animals and Science Benefit From 'Replace, Reduce, Refine' Effort." The Journal of the American Medical Association 270 (1993): 2905-07.

9 VOLUME AND ISSUE If each new issue of a scholarly or scientific journal starts with page 1, include the number of the issue. Put a period after the volume number, and then type the number of the issue.

Francese, Peter. "The 100 Millionth Household." American Demographics 18.3 (1996): 15-16.

Chiles, James R. "Casting a High-Tech Net for Space Trash." Smithsonian 29.10 (1999): 48-55.

10 BOOK REVIEW Start an unsigned review with the abbreviation *rev.* for "review." For a signed review, include the reviewer's name and also any title for the review.

Rev. of The Penguin Book of Women Poets, ed. Carol Cosman, Joan Keefe, and Kathleen Weaver. Arts and Books Forum May 1990:17-19.

Deak, Istvan. "The Beginning of the End." Rev. of Nazi Germany and the Jews, by Saul Friedländer. New Republic 11 and 18 Aug. 1997: 42-45.

11 TITLE WITHIN A TITLE When the title of an article includes the title of another article, shift to single quotation marks for the title-within-a-title:

Lundgren, Norma. "A Reply to Johannson's 'Hospitals Can Make You Sick.'" American Health June 1999: 78-79.

B. ENTRIES FOR BOOKS

12 STANDARD ENTRY FOR A BOOK Give the last name of the author first. Underline (italicize) the title. Then give the publishing data: place, publisher, and year. Shorten publishers' names: *Harcourt* (for Harcourt Brace, Inc.); *Oxford UP* (for Oxford University Press).

Hughes, Robert. Culture of Complaint. New York: Warner, 1993.

Shafer, William J. Brass Bands and New Orleans Jazz. Baton Rouge: Louisiana State UP, 1977.

13 SUBTITLED BOOK Add the subtitle after a colon:

Holeton, Richard. Composing Cyberspace: Identity, Community, and Knowledge in the Electronic Age. Boston: McGraw-Hill, 1998.

14 COAUTHORED BOOK For a book with several authors, put the last name first for the first author listed. Then give the other authors' names in regular order. For a book with more than three authors, use the first author's name and then type et al. for "and others" (no underlining or italics).

Berry, Jason, Jonathan Foose, and Tad Jones. Up from the Cradle of Jazz. Athens: U of Georgia P, 1986.

Fischer, Claude S., et al. Inequality by Design: Cracking the Bell Curve Myth. Princeton: Princeton UP, 1996.

15 SAME AUTHOR For an additional work by the same author, use three hyphens instead of repeating the name:

Rose, Mike. Lives on the Boundary. New York: Penguin, 1990.

- - -. Possible Lives: The Promise of Education in America. New York: Penguin, 1996.

16 EDITED BOOK For a book assembled by an editor, include the abbreviation *ed.* Use *eds.* if there are several editors. If the editor has worked on output by a single author, start with the original author's name.

Hall, Nina, ed. Exploring Chaos: A Guide to the New Science of Disorder. New York: Norton, 1994.

laGuardia, Dolores, and Hans P. Guth, eds. American Voices: Culture and Community. 4th ed. Mountain View, CA: Mayfield, 2000.

Dickinson, Emily. The Complete Poems of Emily Dickinson. Ed. Thomas H. Johnson. Boston: Little, Brown, 1978.

17 TRANSLATED BOOK Include the translator's name after *Trans.:*

Freire, Paulo. Pedagogy of the Oppressed. Trans. Myra Bergman Ramos. New York: Seabury, 1970.

Bonner, Elena. Mothers and Daughters. Trans. Antonina W. Bouis. New York: Vintage-Random, 1993.

18 NEW EDITION If a book has been updated or revised, show that you are using a later edition of the earlier work:

Zettl, Herbert. Television Production Handbook. 7th ed. Belmont, CA: Wadsworth/Thomson Learning, 2000.

19 BOOK IN A SERIES After the title of the book, show that it is part of a series of books focused on a special area of study or research.

Rose, Mike. Writer's Block: The Cognitive Dimension. Studies in Writing and Rhetoric. Carbondale: Southern Illinois UP, 1984.

20 SPECIAL LINE OF BOOKS Include the name of a special imprint or line of books. For instance, the Vintage Books are a special line of books published by Random House (you would type *Vintage-Random*).

Wilson, August. The Piano Lesson. New York: Plume-Penguin, 1990.

21 WORK IN SEVERAL VOLUMES A history of the Civil War may take up several volumes, with the separate books sometimes published over a number of years. Specify the volume if you have used only one; if more than one, list the whole multivolume work. Here are some possibilities:

Woolf, Virginia. The Diary of Virginia Woolf. Ed. Anne Olivier Bell. New York: Harcourt, 1977. Vol. 1.

Churchill, Winston S. The Age of Revolution. New York: Dodd, 1957. Vol. 3 of A History of the English-Speaking Peoples. 4 vols. 1956-58.

Trevelyan, G. M. History of England. 3rd ed. 3 vols. Garden City: Anchor-Doubleday, 1952.

22 INTRODUCTORY MATERIAL If you quote from introductory material by someone other than the author, start with the contributor's name and use the right label: Introduction. Preface. Foreword (or sometimes: Afterword). Include page numbers for the introductory material. (Sometimes these are given as lower-case roman numerals. In the second sample entry, the roman numerals stand for 21–57.)

Bellow, Saul. Foreword. The Closing of the American Mind. By Allan Bloom. New York: Simon, 1987. 11-18.

DeMott, Robert. Introduction. The Grapes of Wrath. By John Steinbeck. Ed. Robert DeMott. New York: Viking, 1989. xxi-lvii.

23 PART OF A COLLECTION When you list an article from a collection of essays by different authors, list the individual selection first. (Do the same for a poem or story that is part of an anthology of literature.) Then identify the collection. Include the editor's name (after *Ed.*) or the editors' names (after *Eds.*). Then give the publishing data for the collection.

Boyte, Harry C. "The Politics of Innocence." Beyond PC: Toward a Politics of Understanding. Ed. Patricia Aufderheide. St. Paul, MN: Graywolf, 1992. 177-79.

When you list several articles from the same collection, you may choose to list the whole collection as a separate entry in your Works Cited. You then also list the individual selections. **Cross-reference** them to the whole collection, giving simply the editor's name but also showing the complete page numbers. This way you don't have to repeat the full publishing data each time. Items like the following would appear in appropriate alphabetical order in your Works Cited:

Aufderheide, Patricia, ed. Beyond PC: Toward a Politics of Understanding. St. Paul, MN: Graywolf, 1992.

Boyte, Harry C. "The Politics of Innocence." Aufderheide 177-79.

D'Souza, Dinesh. "The Visigoths in Tweed." Aufderheide 11-22.

24 ENCYCLOPEDIA ENTRY For entries appearing in alphabetical order in the best-known encyclopedias, you don't need the publisher's name or page number. However, because of frequent updates or revisions, you may have to specify the edition.

"Aging." Encyclopaedia Britannica: Macropaedia. 1993 ed.

25 INSTITUTIONAL PUBLICATION Studies and reports often list an organization, commission, or institution as the author.

Commission for Urban Education. Giving Inner-City Students Their Chance. Los Angeles: Munras, 1999.

26 PAMPHLET OR BROCHURE Informal locally published material may not identify authors or give full publishing information. Give as much information as you can. Use *n.d.* for "no date of publication."

Foothills Walking Club. Saving the Green Spaces. Fremont, CA. n.d.

27 REISSUED BOOK If an older book is being reissued unchanged, include the date of the original publication. If new material has been added (for instance, a new introduction), include that information.

Wharton, Edith. The House of Mirth. 1905. Introd. Cynthia Griffin Wolf. New York: Penguin, 1986.

28 PUBLISHED CORRESPONDENCE When you quote from a specific letter, show who wrote it, to whom, and when.

Hemingway, Ernest. "To Lillian Ross." 28 July 1948. Ernest Hemingway: Selected Letters, 1917-1961. Ed. Carlos Baker. New York: Scribner's, 1981. 646-49.

29 BIBLE OR LITERARY CLASSIC Specify which of the many different Bible translations or editions of a Shakespeare play you have used. Put the editor's name first if you want to highlight the editor's contribution.

> The Holy Bible. Revised Standard Version. 2nd ed. Nashville: Nelson, 1971.
>
> Hubler, Edward, ed. The Tragedy of Hamlet. By William Shakespeare. New York: NAL, 1963.

30 TITLE WITHIN A TITLE An underlined (italicized) book title may include the name of another book. Shift back to roman (not underlined) for the title-within-a-title:

> McNulty, Irene. An Unauthorized Guide to Joyce's Ulysses. Chicago: Wishbone, 1997.

C. ENTRIES FOR ELECTRONIC SOURCES—Online, CD-ROM, e-mail

Guidelines for documenting electronic sources are in flux. They are being updated as new technology evolves and as users find new ways to make it serve their purposes. You are likely to find some variations in style in current guides. The following guidelines are based on the section on electronic sources in the *MLA Style Manual* (Second Edition, 1998). Some of the examples that follow are taken from that manual.

For most of your entries, start with as much of the usual publishing information as is available—including authors, titles, and dates. This way a reader may be able to locate the material even if a net address has changed or the material is no longer available online.

- Include the **access date**—the date you accessed the source or site. The date of access will often follow the date the material was published or posted. (The access date can tell your reader how recently the material was available.)
- For material from the net, include the **Internet address**—the **URL** (uniform resource locator). Put it between angled brackets. Typically, the electronic address will start with the access mode, usually **<http:// . . . >**. (Other access modes include *telnet* and *ftp*.) The address will then go on to the relevant path and specific

file names (often beginning with **www.** for the World Wide Web). If you can, have the whole URL on the same line. If not, have a break only after a period or slash. Double-check to make sure that dots, slashes, colons, capitals, and spacing are exactly right. URLs are like phone numbers—one small error makes them useless. (Do not add hyphens or final periods.)

- For material from other electronic sources, specify the **medium**, such as CD-ROM, diskette, or magnetic tape.

Here are sample entries:

31 NEWS SERVICE ONLINE Include both publication date and access date:

"Murders Down in New York, Los Angeles." CNN Online. 29 Dec. 1997. 7 Jan. 1998 <http://cnn.com/us/9712/29/urban.homicides/html>.

32 NEWSPAPER ONLINE Include authors and original page numbers if available:

"Guiliani Vows an Even Shinier Polish on Big Apple." Washington Post Online. 2 Jan. 1998. A19+. 7 Jan. 1998 <http://search.washingtonpost.com/wpsrv/Wplate/1998-01/02/1211-010298-idx.html>.

Coates, Steve. "A Dead Language Comes to Life on the Internet." New York Times on the Web 28 Oct. 1996. 20 Apr. 1997 <http://www.nytimes.com/web/doscroot/library/cyber/week/1028Latin.html>.

33 NEWS DIGEST ONLINE Include reporters' names if available:

Aldinger, Charles. "U.S. Panel Urges Separate Military Barracks." Time 16 Dec. 1997. 9 Feb. 1998 <http://pathfinder.com/news/latest/RB/1997Dec16/150.html>.

34 ONLINE PUBLICATION ONLY Increasingly you will find material published only online, with no corresponding print publication:

People for Ethical Treatment of Animals. "Let's Visit Animal Research Laboratories." 16 Sept. 1995. 28 Nov. 1997 <http://www.envirolink.org/arrs/peta/labvisit/office.html>.

35 BOTH ONLINE AND PRINT PUBLICATION Increasingly you will find books available both in print versions and online:

Barsky, Robert F. *Noam Chomsky: A Life of Dissent*. Cambridge: MIT P, 1997. 8 May 1997 <http://mitpress.mit.edu/e-books/chomsky/>.

36 REFERENCE BOOK ONLINE If you can, give version number and date:

Britannica Online. Vers. 97.1.1. Mar. 1997. Encyclopaedia Britannica. 7 Apr. 1997. <http://www.eb.com/>.

37 CD-ROM For material on CD-ROM, add the producer of the CD-ROM and production date if available. Since databases on CD-ROM are often updated, give the date of the version you used if available.

Morring, Frank, Jr. "Russian Hardware Allows Earlier Space Station Experiments." *Aviation Week and Space Technology* 16 (May 1994): 57. *InfoTrac: General Periodicals Index*. CD-ROM. Information Access. Aug. 94.

38 E-MAIL Give dates for e-mail to you or to others:

Fanscesco, Theresa. E-mail to the author. 3 Mar. 2000.

Bruno, Philip. "Re: Uninsured." E-mail to Susan McNeil. 12 Aug. 1999.

D. NONPRINT SOURCES—Interviews, letters, talks, media sources

39 PERSONAL INTERVIEW Keep track of dates for interviews and other oral sources.

Canderas, Sylvia. Personal interview. 29 Oct. 1999.

Bandover, Phil. Telephone interview. 12 June 1998.

40 PUBLISHED INTERVIEW Give the names of persons interviewed and persons doing the interviewing. Label the material as an interview.

> Asimov, Isaac. Interview. Scientists Talk about Science. By Anne Harrison and Webster Freid. Los Angeles: Acme, 1987. 94-101.

41 PERSONAL LETTER For a letter to you, name the letter writer and label the material as a letter. Give the date.

> Lau, Victoria. Letter to the author. 7 Apr. 1999.

42 TALK OR LECTURE Identify the speaker and give an appropriate label (Lecture, Keynote speech) along with such data as the occasion, the sponsor, the location, and the date. If you know the title of the talk, include it in quotation marks.

> Kernan, Dorothy. Keynote speech. Opening General Sess. New World Forum, Dallas. 8 June 1995.

> Vindavi, Jean. "Trash Journalism and a Misinformed Public." Valley Lecture Series, Santa Clara. 7 Nov. 1999.

43 PRINTED SPEECH If you are quoting from a printed version of a speech, add full publishing data to the information about place, sponsor, and date. Use *rpt.* for "reprinted."

> Malkowski, Vladimir. "Dissent and the End of the Soviet Empire." Public Affairs Forum, Albuqerque. 23 Aug. 1998. Rpt. West Coast Review Spring 1999: 76-82.

44 TELEVISION OR RADIO PROGRAM Underline (italicize) the title of a program. For an episode in a series, put the title of the specific episode in quotation marks, followed by the name of the series (with no italics or quotation marks). Identify the network or station, and include the location and date. Pull a name out in front to highlight a person's contribution.

> The Poisoned Planet. Narr. Jean Laidlaw. Writ. and prod. Pat Verstrom. WXRV, Seattle. 12 Feb. 1996.

> Marlowe, Carl. "The Early Stravinsky." The Great Composers. KPFA, Berkeley. 9 Mar. 1999.

36b.3 Preparing Final Manuscript (MLA) *Follow instructions concerning style and format.* Take time to study any special instructions for preparation of final manuscript.

- Unless otherwise instructed, use **double-spacing** throughout, including block quotations and list of Works Cited.
- Identify your sources in your running text, using credit tags giving names, credentials, and titles as appropriate. Use **parenthetic documentation** in your text (primarily page numbers for MLA, dates for APA).
- Start a separate page for your final bibliography—**Works Cited** page MLA style; **References** page APA style.
- Use **running heads** at the top of every page (your name and page number MLA style; short title and page number APA style).
- Do without a separate title page unless one is required by your instructor.

You may want to include **endnotes,** appearing on a separate page before the final alphabetical listing of sources. Use the heading "Notes." Writers use such notes to provide additional backup, more detailed explanation of technical matters, or interesting sidelights. A raised Arabic numeral (**superscript**) in your text directs your reader to the numbered note giving the added information. For instance, in the following paper on the rich in America, the student writer might have considered adding a note about income at the opposite end of the scale:[2]

> 2. A recent study calculated total yearly income for a worker putting in 40 hours a week at the legal minimum wage as little over $10,000.

36b.4 Sample Research Paper (MLA)

Study the following sample research paper documented in the MLA style. Answer questions like the following:

- Has the writer focused the paper on a central question? (What is the core issue, and how important is it?)
- Is there a central thesis, and if so what is it?
- For you, what are key points the writer tried to bring out?
- Does the paper have a workable overall plan? (Was it easy or hard to follow?) Did you at any point lose the thread of the argument?
- What is the range of sources? Does the writer show them to be relevant and credible?
- Which quotations or other evidence did you find most instructive or persuasive? Which least?
- Does the writer use varied ways of introducing and working in quoted material? Does the presentation of material anywhere get monotonous or mechanical?
- Does the Works Cited list include unusual entries?
- Are you part of the ideal audience for this paper? Why or why not?

Vardell 1

Pat Vardell

English 2

28 April 1999

The Newly Rich in America

Old money in America was based on natural resources such as land, minerals, and oil. Many of the ultra-rich Americans about forty years ago were rich either through inheritance from wealthy family members or from their success in striking oil. Today, most of the rich in society are people who have capitalized on the massive increase in new technologies. In 1982, Forbes magazine's listing of the 400 richest in America included 85 people with inherited wealth; in a recent year, there were only 39 in this category. In 1982, 40 of the richest people owed their wealth to mining, gas, or oil. Today only 15 do. During the same time period, the number of the country's richest who owed their wealth to computers or software grew dramatically from 4 to 26.

eye-openin[g] statistics

Leonard Riggo, the founder of Barnes & Noble, is quoted in Money magazine as saying, "The wealth is deeper and more expansive than in the past--not four hundred or a thousand rich, but tens of thousands" (Reeves 170). The numbers of the rich are increasing because of more entrepreneurs cashing in on new technologies, growing demand for top entertainers, and more investment-savvy people. Business publications and newsmagazines print admiring articles about the newly rich. Only a few dissenting voices remind us that many of our immigrant ancestors "came here with nothing," that many Americans do not share in today's prosperity, and that "hunger lasts the whole year round" (Lewis, DO5)

insider's quotation

source identified in parens.

COMMENTARY 1 Starting the Search

The student writer's interest in the topic grew out of previous reading and talks with friends. As a future business major, Pat had read articles about shifting patterns of wealth in America. Was it true that inheritance of the family's wealth, as with well-known Americans from JFK to George Bush, was no longer the main road to riches? Pat started to track news items on topics like the following:

- A retired computer consultant had developed a system of computer trading that earned him $17,000 in paper profits during a three-month period.
- In the nineties, many newspaper and magazine articles focused on skyrocketing executive pay. A CEO of one of the nation's largest banks had received total annual compensation in excess of twenty-five million dollars.
- Million-dollar executive salaries were becoming commonplace in space-age industries. A chief executive of a large computer firm dismissed after less than a year took home total compensation in excess of seven million dollars.

In preparation for a research project, Pat did some of the following:

- Pat started to read discussions of the "phenomenal returns" from the stock market boom of the nineties.
- Pat started to collect newspaper and magazine articles about executive compensation consultants advising corporations and their shareholders.
- Pat started to look at comparative statistics for other major industrial countries (Japan, Germany), where executive pay levels do not approach the record levels attained in the United States.
- Pat started to track reports of million-dollar contracts and signing bonuses negotiated by star athletes and media stars.

Vardell 2

For Americans riding high in the New Economy, America is in the "golden age of capitalism." Allan Sloan, columnist for Newsweek, says, "The biggest trend in the U.S. economy for the past 20 years has been the decline of manufacturing and a corresponding shift to high technology, finance, and entertainment." The transformation of the American economy from business producing things to business thinking up new things has made getting rich much faster. Sloan states, "It took Andrew Carnegie three decades to become a centimillionaire by making steel. It took Jeff Bezos three years starting Amazon.com"--an Internet book site (52).

standard quotation with page number

With the rapid increase in technology, more new-style entrepreneurs are sprouting in order to capitalize on it. For example, Silicon Valley and other high-tech areas have seen an enormous number of companies bloom in the last decade. The "cyber-rich" are in the right business at the right time and they have become zillionaires, thanks to much help from Wall Street. For example, Bill Gates, founder of Microsoft, is America's richest. As Sloan said in his Newsweek column, "With $38 billion, he's three times as rich as John D. Rockefeller was" (49). The co-founder, Paul Allen, is also a multibillionaire. Many other people in the company became millionaires, too.

Richard Reeves, columnist for Money magazine, says, "When Sanjiv Sidhu brought his software company public . . . 25 of his employees became millionaires" (170). The growing interest of the stock market and the explosive IPO market (Initial Public Offering) has made many new companies decide to go public. The IPO market has made many companies' employees instant

COMMENTARY 2 Going to Sources

During the course of the search, the student writer tracked down an array of sources, ranging from news items in daily newspapers to the analysis of current trends in book-length studies. The authors represent a range of political perspectives. As you keep reading, you will see the writer feeding in materials from sources including the following:

- current *newspaper* articles reporting on mega-dollar contracts of executives and celebrities as part of the current news
- largely uncritical articles in mainstream *newsmagazines* like *Time* and *Newsweek* reporting skyrocketing executive compensation
- articles in the respected conservative British *journal of opinion* the *Economist,* weighing the broader implications of current developments
- articles or *book-length* sources by a respected sociologist like Andrew Hacker and an economist like Lester Thurow, both looking at long-range trends transforming our society
- editorials or articles by widely read *liberal journalists* like Barbara Ehrenreich or Molly Ivins, raising questions about the values of our society allowing huge disparity of wealth

Vardell 3

millionaires. Venture capitalists have helped beginning companies to become successful. Hugh Dahlke, founder of Data Research, said in an interview that venture capitalists have helped him in raising money and support for his company. He said, "I have no plans of becoming public yet, but the venture capitalists have given me a strong foothold in my company's niche."

oral source

Top executives in space-age companies often receive a combination of salary, bonuses, and stock options that puts them in the multimillion dollar bracket. Graef "Bud" Crystal, a former compensation consultant, was quoted in an article on executive pay as calling the current level of compensation in cutting-edge companies "astounding- -stupefying." Crystal said:

block quotation—quoted at second hand

> It's not as if every company has performed beautifully. Lots of companies are under-performing and their executives are being paid too much. It amazes me that there is no great outrage among investors. (qtd. in Louis, E1)

The executives in the companies are at the top of their profession in most cases, where multimillion-dollar earnings are commonplace. The same is true of top names in the world of entertainment. Athletes, movie directors, star performers, or any type of celebrity are making more money than ever in society today. Michael Weinstein, editorial columnist for the New York Times Magazine, writes that celebrities like Michael Jordan, Danielle Steel, or Steven Spielberg "earn super-incomes because the market for sports and entertainment has, with the growth of telecommunication, spread worldwide" (45).

integrated partial quote

COMMENTARY 3 Integrating Quoted Material

Study the way the writer wove material from the sources into the finished text. Most of the quoted material follows **credit tags** identifying the source by name and establishing briefly the credentials of the quoted author. Direct quotations range from short quoted phrases through partial quotations (parts of a sentence) to a few selected block quotations.

ATTRIBUTED DIRECT QUOTATION:

Allan Sloan, columnist for <u>Newsweek</u>, says, "The biggest trend in the U.S. economy for the past 20 years . . ."

Graef "Bud" Crystal, a former compensation consultant, was quoted in an article on executive pay as calling the current level of compensation in cutting-edge companies "astounding." . . .

Richard Reeves, columnist for <u>Money</u> magazine, says, "When Sanjiv Sidhu brought his software company public . . ."

He quotes Robert Frank as saying, "The value of a production depends . . ."

According to Frank, "After becoming a free-agent, he signed . . ."

ATTRIBUTED INDIRECT QUOTATION OR PARAPHRASE—**Including summary of data:**

In 1982, <u>Forbes</u> magazine's listing of the 400 richest in America included 85 people with inherited wealth; in a recent year, there were only 39 in this category. . . .

Hugh Dahlke, founder of Data Research, said in an interview that venture capitalists . . .

The economists Robert Frank of Cornell and Philip Cook of Duke showed that huge audiences translate into huge compensation. . . .

MATERIAL UNATTRIBUTED IN THE TEXT—**source included in parentheses:**

. . . An internal memo told complaining staff members that King's show was the most widely watched program on CNN **(Carneras B2).**

Vardell 4

The economic theory that explains why entertainers are making more money than ever is the "winner-take-all" theory of society. The economists Robert Frank of Cornell and Philip Cook of Duke showed that huge audiences translate into huge compensation for top talent. Robert Samuelson, columnist for Newsweek, says that huge earnings represent "big bets being made on people who are expected to produce." He quotes Robert Frank as saying, "The value of a production depends primarily on the efforts of only a handful of top players." One reason the winner-take-all market thrives is that free agency has liberated athletes to shop for the best possible contract. For example, a 24-year-old NBA basketball star signed a few years ago with the Los Angeles Lakers. According to Frank, "After becoming a free-agent, he signed a contract that was 6 years for $120 million with the Lakers." Also, football, baseball, and basketball players have profited even more from huge TV revenues for their sports and the rise of ticket prices (43). The winner-take-all philosophy extends to star performers in the media. In 1998, CNN doubled the salary of talk-show host Larry King by signing him to a five-year $7 million contract while at the same time laying off 70 employees in a cost-cutting move. An internal memo told complaining staff members that King's show was the most widely watched program on CNN (Carneras B2).

credentials of experts

summarized information

The use of celebrities and athletes for endorsements in marketing has opened up dizzying sources of additional revenue for them and at the same time heightened their public appeal. O. J. Simpson, ex-football star and star performer in commercials for the

COMMENTARY 4 Correlating Sources

Study the way the student writer uses material from the sources to develop paragraphs that each support one key point. The following sample paragraph draws on *one single source*. It starts with a statement of the key point, goes on to an explanation of the major cause or major process, and concludes with a striking pair of examples.

MATERIAL FROM ONE SINGLE SOURCE:

For Americans riding high in the New Economy, **America is in the "golden age of capitalism."** Allan Sloan, columnist for Newsweek, says, "The biggest trend in the U.S. economy for the past 20 years has been the decline of manufacturing and a corresponding **shift to high technology,** finance, and entertainment." The transformation of the American economy from business producing things to **business thinking up new things** has made getting rich much faster. Sloan states, "It took Andrew Carnegie three decades to become a centimillionaire by making steel. It **took Jeff Bezos three years starting Amazon.com"**--an Internet book site (52).

Several paragraphs toward the end of Pat's paper show well how an effective writer brings together supporting material from *several different sources* to support the same key point. In the following example, quotations from several very different sources point in the same direction:

CORRELATING SEVERAL SOURCES:

At the same time, **there are dissenting voices.** Foreign observers marvel at the disparities of wealth in a country founded on the belief that all are created equal. In an article originally published **in the French Le Nouvel Observateur, Jean-Paul Dubois** describes a millionaire entrepreneur and an unemployed man living on disability checks with six dependents as "living on different planets" (43). **David Siulvich, writing in the British journal Economist, says,** "The gap is growing rapidly between the rich and non-rich," keeping people who are not rich increasingly from participating fully in society (78). **Michael Hout and Samuel R. Lucas, writing in the Chronicle of Higher Education, claim** that in 1995, U.S. executives were paid $224 for every dollar earned by a worker, representing a much greater gap than in other industrialized countries (B1).

Vardell 5

Hertz rental car company, bought a Rolls Royce, a Bentley, and a Ferrari as well as a mansion that cost $5 million. He had reportedly accumulated a fortune of $12 million to spend on a team of highly paid defense lawyers when he was accused of killing his ex-wife and her escort in a sensational knife murder (Nix 13).

For people who are neither CEOs of high-tech companies nor superstar athletes, the stock market of the 90s created unprecedented opportunities for sudden wealth. A bull market created waves of new money and made many individual investors millionaires. During a span of two years in the 90s, market averages doubled. Allan Sloan, columnist for Newsweek, said, "This has created more than $4 trillion of new paper wealth for stockholders " (50). A 900 percent rice in the Dow since August of 1982 lured in millions of new investors. Also, companies' IRA (Individual Retirement Account) programs heightened people's interest in stocks. For years, the economy seemed to be producing only good news.

Over the last few decades, the rich have been growing in number and getting richer. People's financial assets are drastically growing, but the wealth is in the hands of the few. Michael Sivy, journalist for U.S. News & World Report, states, "In 1975 about 20 percent of the nation's net worth was held by the top 1 percent of households; today 36 percent is" (13). A pair of articles in the New York Times Magazine gave statistics about the income distribution in American households in 1979 and in 1993. The income bracket of $500,000 to $1 million had grown from 0.1 percent in 1979 to 0.2 percent in 1993, showing a 100 percent increase. The income

Vardell 6

bracket of more than $ 1 million had multiplied five-fold (Hacker 65; Weinstein 102).

correlated data from three sources

The faces of the superrich have changed dramatically in the last couple of decades. This is due in large part to the country's transformation from a traditional manufacturing society to a postindustrial society with high-tech technology as the driving force. Bullish economists predict that advanced technology will keep on rapidly expanding and will be the rocket booster making more people rich in the future.

major transition

At the same time, there are dissenting voices. Foreign observers marvel at the disparities of wealth in a country founded on the belief that all are created equal. In an article originally published in the French Le Nouvel Observateur, Jean-Paul Dubois describes a millionaire entrepreneur and an unemployed man living on disability checks with six dependents as "living on different planets" (43). David Siulvich, writing in the British journal Economist, says, "The gap is growing rapidly between the rich and non-rich," keeping people who are not rich increasingly from participating fully in society (78). Michael Hout and Samuel R. Lucas, writing in the Chronicle of Higher Education, claim that in 1995, U.S. executives were paid $224 for every dollar earned by a worker, representing a much greater gap than in other industrialized countries (B1).

summarized data

Critics of current social policy say that the widening gap between rich and poor will undermine the consensus on which a democratic society is built. As early as 1990, Barbara Ehrenreich, looking back over "a decade of greed," criticized a new

Vardell 7

"overclass" for creating a "culture of profligacy" (231). She has written about women trapped in "pink-collar" jobs, sharing with them for instance the lives of restaurant employees barely able to pay the rent. The American Catholic Bishops stated in late 1995:

quoted phrases

> The U.S. economy seems to be leading to three nations living side by side, one growing more prosperous and powerful, one squeezed by stagnant incomes and rising economic pressures, and one left behind in increasing poverty, dependency, and hopelessness. (qtd. in Fischer 3)

key quote set off

Some economists warn that societies in the past have not tolerated maximum private profit unless it serves the common good. In Head to Head, Lester C. Thurow, of MIT's Sloan School of Management, warns businesses against becoming exclusively fixated on their "private obligation to maximize profits and shareholder wealth." He claims they also have the "social obligation of being a vehicle for maximizing national growth and a higher standard of living for everyone." If it is to survive, capitalism needs a "heart transplant" (286).

extended use of a single source

Vardell 8

Works Cited

Carneras, Theresa. "The King of Talk Shows." Entertainment News 13 June 1998: B2.

Dahlke, Hugh. Interview. 7 Feb. 1999.

Dubois, Jean-Paul. "Living on Different Planets." World Press Review 43.7 (1996): 43.

Ehrenreich, Barbara. The Worst Years of Our Lives: Irreverent Notes from a Decade of Greed. New York: Pantheon-Random, 1990.

Fischer, Claude S., et al. Inequality by Design: Cracking the Bell Curve Myth. Princeton: Princeton UP, 1996.

Hacker, Andrew. "Who They Are." New York Times Magazine 19 Nov. 1995: 65-67.

Hout, Michael, and Samuel R. Lucas. "Narrowing the Income Gap between Rich and Poor." Chronicle of Higher Education 42.49 (1996): B1.

Kivlich, David. "Economy Booming."" Economist July 1996: 54-56.

Lewis, Arthur M. "It's Raining Options: Executives Reap Rich Rewards as Firms Bestow More Stock than Cash." San Francisco Chronicle 1 June 1998: E1+.

Lewis, Nicole. "The Need for Help Goes On." Washington Post 23 Jan. 1998: DO5. 30 Mar. 1998 <http://www.washingtonpost.com/wp-srv/WPlate/1998-01/23/ 0711-012398-idx.html>.

Machan, Dyan. "The Last Article You Will Ever Have to Read on Executive Pay? No Way!" Forbes 20 May 1996: 176.

Nix, Shann. "O. J. Mania: American Tragedy." San Francisco Examiner Magazine 30 Oct. 1994: 12-15.

Vardell 9

Reeves, Richard. "The New Wealth." Money Oct. 1997: 169-78.

Samuelson, Robert. "The More and Less Deserving Rich." Newsweek 25 Apr. 1994: 43.

Sivy, Michael. "In the Money." U.S. News & World Report 16 Mar. 1996: 13.

Sivluich, David. The Gap in Income." Economist July 1996: 56.

Sloan, Allan, et al. "The New Rich." Newsweek 4 Aug. 1997: 48-55.

Snyder, Bryan. "A Maximum Wage." Dollars and Sense July/Aug. 1995: 30-31+.

Thurow, Lester C. Head to Head: The Coming Economic Battle among Japan, Europe, and America. New York: Warner Books, 1993.

Weinstein, Michael. "Why They Deserve It." New York Times Magazine 19 Nov. 1995: 102-04.

36c doc Documenting Your Sources—APA Style

Follow the APA style for research papers in the social sciences.

Authors writing for publications in the social sciences follow the APA style of documentation. This style is outlined in the *Publication Manual of the American Psychological Association* (Fourth Edition, 1994.) You will be following the APA style when writing papers for courses in psychology, linguistics, or education. Like the MLA style, the APA style asks you to give brief source information in parentheses in the text of your paper. Then you provide complete data in an alphabetical listing of **References** at the end. For your running heads, you use the shortened title of your paper instead of your name. A major distinctive feature of the APA style is emphasis on date of publication.

36c.1 Parenthetic Citation (APA) *Use the author-and-date method when following the APA style.* Use the **author-and-date** method both in the text of your paper and in your list of references. You first use it when you briefly identify sources in the text of your paper. Put the author's name and year or date of publication in parentheses: (Lucas, 1998). Do not include the author's name between the parentheses if you have already mentioned it in your text (1998). Often, the APA style gives a source and the publication date without a page reference. (Interested readers are expected to check out the relevant research literature and study its findings.) However, include page numbers with all direct quotations.

In the following sample citations, study the use of commas, of the abbreviations *p.* or *pp.* for "page" or "pages," or the *and*-symbol &—the ampersand, used instead of *and.*

1 AUTHOR AND DATE ONLY Standard citation:

> Medical schools in the past have not taught students how to relate to others or show compassion for their patients (Buonaconti, 1998).

2 DATE ONLY Author's name in your own text:

> As defined by Grayfield, <u>anorexia nervosa</u> is a condition of extreme weight loss that results when young women compulsively starve themselves (1993).

3 PAGE REFERENCE For direct quotation or specific reference:

> Censorship today is often not of the "crude racist variety" but covers up its true intentions with charges of "bad language" (Bledsoe, 1999, p. 27).

4 WORK BY SEVERAL AUTHORS Name only the first coauthor. Use et al. (for "and others") for the remaining name or names. Identify all authors in your list of References at the end of your paper.

> The harmful effects of diets deficient in essential nutrients have been well documented (Veroux et al., 1994).

5 SAME AUTHOR For several publications published by the same author in the same year, use *a, b, c,* and so on, in order of publication:

> Ferguson's studies have consistently challenged the tobacco industry's attempts to discredit scientific research (1997, 1998a, 1998b).

6 REFERENCE TO SEVERAL SOURCES List in alphabetical order, divided by semicolons:

> New statistics document the continuing increase in the use of part-time and temporary college instructors (Benscot, 1998; Graf & Swanson, 1998).

7 UNKNOWN OR UNLISTED AUTHOR Identify the source by its shortened title:

> Jury selection has become the subject of study for self-styled "experts" ("Psyching Out," 1999).

8 INSTITUTIONAL AUTHORSHIP In general, use acronyms or abbreviations only in the second or later citation:

> Pressure to approve untested medications prematurely can have disastrous results (National Institute of Mental Health [NIMH], 1997).

> Researchers are tracking the long-term effects of medications for the treatment of emotional disorders (NIMH, 1997).

9 CITATION AT SECOND HAND Show that you did not consult the original source. In your list of References, include only the publication where you found the material.

> Disappointing figures on the results of bilingual education programs were compiled in a study by Feldman and Ramos (as cited in Lewellen, 1997).

10 PERSONAL COMMUNICATIONS Identify letters, memos, e-mail, or telephone interviews as personal communications. Include the date. Since the reader cannot check or verify them, do not include personal communications in your list of References.

> Officers often claim that local newspapers give a negative slant to police work (Richard Nguyen, personal communication, January 7, 2000).

36c.2 **References (APA)** *Follow the instructions for the final alphabetical listing in the APA style.* Use the heading **References** for your final alphabetical listing of your sources. Use the **author-and-date** sequence, putting the date of publication in parentheses after the name of the author. Special features include the use of gender-neutral initials for first names and middle names. Since authors using the APA style are often dealing with ongoing research, you may see special notations like (in press). This takes the place of the publication date and shows that a study is in the process of being published. A notation like the following after a title shows that research results are still being evaluated and perhaps processed for possible publication: Unpublished raw data.

DOCUMENTATION ESSENTIALS

References—APA Style

The following features set the APA style apart from other documentation styles:

1 indented first line of entry, next line or lines flush left
2 last name first, with initials for first and middle names
3 date in parentheses after author (author-and-date style)
4 names of months not abbreviated
5 no quotation marks for article or other part of publication
6 lower-case within title of article (or other *part* of a publication)
7 underlining (or italics) for complete publication
8 underlining extends to punctuation mark
9 square brackets for special part of publication
10 abbreviations *p.* or *pp.* before page numbers
11 online material signaled by notation [ONLINE]
12 Internet address underlined, introduced by "AVAILABLE:"

Guide to Sample Entries—APA Style

A. ENTRIES FOR PERIODICALS—Newspapers, magazines, journals

1 STANDARD NEWSPAPER ARTICLE
2 TITLE AND SUBTITLE
3 NEWS ITEM
4 EDITORIAL
5 LETTER TO THE EDITOR
6 STANDARD MAGAZINE ARTICLE
7 COAUTHORED ARTICLE
8 SAME AUTHOR
9 VOLUME NUMBER
10 VOLUME AND ISSUE
11 REVIEW
12 LIMITED CIRCULATION ITEM

B. ENTRIES FOR BOOKS (and other whole publications)

13 STANDARD ENTRY FOR A BOOK
14 SUBTITLED BOOK
15 COAUTHORED BOOK
16 SAME AUTHOR
17 EDITED BOOK
18 TRANSLATED BOOK
19 NEW EDITION
20 STUDY IN A SERIES
21 SPECIAL LINE OF BOOKS
22 WORK IN SEVERAL VOLUMES
23 INTRODUCTORY MATERIAL
24 PART OF A COLLECTION
25 ENCYCLOPEDIA ENTRY
26 INSTITUTIONAL OR GOVERNMENT PUBLICATION
27 PAMPHLET OR BROCHURE
28 UNPUBLISHED MATERIAL
29 TITLE WITHIN A TITLE

C. ENTRIES FOR ELECTRONIC SOURCES—Online, CD-ROM

30 ONLINE PUBLICATION
31 ARTICLE IN ONLINE JOURNAL
32 DATABASE ON CD-ROM
33 DOCUMENT READ ON CD-ROM
34 VIRTUAL BOOK
35 COMPUTER SOFTWARE

D. NONPRINT SOURCES—Talks and media sources

36 UNPUBLISHED TALK OR LECTURE
37 TELEVISION OR RADIO PROGRAM
38 RECORDING
39 ART WORK

A. ENTRIES FOR PERIODICALS—Newspapers, magazines, journals

1 STANDARD NEWSPAPER ARTICLE

Include the date and complete page numbers. Specify section or special edition as needed. Keep *the* in names of publications:

Kotlowitz, A. (1994, February 13). Their crimes don't make them adults. The New York Times Magazine, pp. 40-41.

Armstrong, S. (1994, March 7). Colorado tries more carrot and less stick in punishing juvenile crime. Christian Science Monitor, pp. 1, 4.

Nordheimer, J. (1994, August 2). Murder trial begins for teen-ager. The New York Times, late ed., p. B5.

2 TITLE AND SUBTITLE Add the subtitle after a colon:

Kahn, K. (1998, June 4). Disorder in the Supreme Court: Former clerk exposes political infighting. San Francisco Chronicle, p. E5.

3 NEWS ITEM List an unsigned news item or article—with no reporter or author identified—under the first word of the title (not counting the articles *The, A,* or *An*):

Tougher treatment urged for juveniles. (1994, August 2). The New York Times, late ed., p. A16.

4 EDITORIAL List an unsigned editorial under the first word of the title. List a signed editorial under the author's name. In brackets, identify the piece as an editorial.

Youth and crime. (1995, January 10). [Editorial]. The Christian Science Monitor, p. 18.

Gomez, A. (1998, February 25). The return of Big Brother [Editorial]. The Fremont Guardian, p. 11.

5 LETTER TO THE EDITOR In brackets, identify the piece as a letter.

Chau, V. (2000, March 7). Phone companies slam consumers [Letter to the editor]. Oakland Tribune, p. C3.

6 STANDARD MAGAZINE ARTICLE. Include the date at the beginning and complete page numbers at the end.

Bello, W. (1998, January 12/19). The end of the Asian miracle. The Nation, pp. 16-21.

Wiggins, R. (1996, October). How the Internet works. Internet World, pp. 54-60.

7 COAUTHORED ARTICLE List all coauthors, last names first. Use the & sign for "and."

Houghtalin, M., & Mays, G. L. (1991). Criminal dispositions of New Mexico juveniles transferred to adult court. Crime and Delinquency, 37, 393-407.

8 SAME AUTHOR For an additional article by the same author, repeat the name and list the articles according to date. If the same author published two or more works the same year, use lower-case letters to set them apart: (1999a) (1999b).

Butterfield, F. (1997a, June 2). Homicides plunge 11% in U.S. FBI report says. New York Times, pp. Al, 12.

Butterfield, F. (1997b, October 27). Drop in homicide rate linked to crack's decline. New York Times, pp. A12, 17.

9 VOLUME NUMBER Many technical or scholarly journals have continuous page numbers for the several issues of the same volume—usually the issues for one year. Give the year of the volume after the author's name. Put the volume number (underlined) before the complete page numbers.

Cartmill, M. (1994). Animal rights: A reply to Howard. Journal of Mammalogy, 75, 1080-1096.

10 VOLUME AND ISSUE If a technical or scholarly journal has separate page numbering for each new issue, put the number of the issue in parentheses (not underlined) after the volume number:

Dornbusch, S. N. (1994). Additional perspectives on homeless families. American Behavioral Scientist, 37(3), 44-49.

11 REVIEW Start with the reviewer's name and the date of the review. If the review has it own title, include the title. In square brackets, first specify the medium—for instance book, film, television program, video program—and then give the title of the item being reviewed.

Deak, I. (1997, August 11 &18). The beginning of the end [Review of the book Nazi Germany and the Jews]. The New Republic, pp. 42-45.

Kraus, S. J. (1992). Visions of psychology: A videotext of classic studies [Review of the video program Discovering Psychology]. Contemporary Psychology, 37, 1146-1147.

Danato, H. (1999, February 2). [Review of the book Gloria Steinem: Her passions, politics, and mystique]. West Coast Review, pp. 69-70.

12 LIMITED CIRCULATION ITEM For desktop publications like newsletters or zines, give an address if it might help readers track the publication:

Zapato, F. (1999, June 8). The zany world of zines. Wrong Track News, p. 2. (Available from Wrong Track Press, 2787 Garner Road, Rockville, MD 20852)

B. ENTRIES FOR BOOKS (and other whole publications)

13 STANDARD ENTRY FOR A BOOK Give the last name of the author first, followed by initials for first names. Put the date of publication in parentheses. Use lower-case in titles except for names or other normally capitalized words. Then give the publishing data: place of publication and publisher. Spell out publishers' names—for instance, Harcourt Brace or University of Louisiana Press.

Goleman, D. P. (1997). Emotional intelligence. New York: Bantam Books.

Lanham, R. A. (1993). The electronic word. Chicago: The University of Chicago Press.

14 SUBTITLED BOOK Add the subtitle after a colon:

Turkle, S. (1995). Life on the screen: Identity in the age of the Internet. New York: Simon & Schuster.

15 COAUTHORED BOOK For a book with several authors, put the last name first for each of the authors. Use the *and*-symbol &.

> Sternberg, R. J., & Wagner, R. K. (1986). Practical intelligence. New York: Cambridge University Press.

> Boyer, P. S., Clark, C. E., Hawley, S. M., Kett, J. F., Salisbury, N., Sitkoff, H., & Woloch, N. (1995). The enduring vision: A history of the American people. Lexington: D. C. Heath.

16 SAME AUTHOR For an additional work by the same author, repeat the name. Arrange works in order of publication. If the same author published two or more works the same year, use lower-case letters to set them apart: (1999a) (1999b).

> Rose, M. (1990). Lives on the boundary. New York: Penguin Books.

> Rose, M. (1996). Possible lives: The promise of education in America. New York: Penguin Books.

17 EDITED BOOK For a book assembled by an editor, include the abbreviation *Ed.* in parentheses. Use *Eds.* if several editors have worked on the book. If the editor has edited the work of a single author, put that author's name first and list the editor in parentheses after the title.

> Hall, N. (Ed.). (1994). Exploring chaos: A guide to the new science of disorder. New York: W. W. Norton.

> Popkewitz, T. S., & Tabachnick, B. R. (Eds.). (1981). The study of schooling: Field based methodologies in educational research and evaluation. New York: Praeger.

> Einstein, A. (1999). Essays on science and religion (L. Protov, Ed.). Los Angeles: Academia Press.

18 TRANSLATED BOOK Include the translator's name, followed by the abbreviation *Trans.*:

> Freire, P. (1970). Pedagogy of the oppressed (M. B. Ramos, Trans.). New York: Seabury Press.

19 NEW EDITION If a book has been updated or revised, show that you are using a later edition of the earlier work.

> Zettl, H. (2000). Television production handbook (7th ed.). Belmont, CA: Wadsworth/Thomson Learning.

20 STUDY IN A SERIES A research report is often published as a monograph—a publication presenting the results of a study or experiment. If the study is published as part of a series, include volume numbers and serial numbers where they apply.

Harris, P. L., & Kavanaugh, R. D. (1993). Young children's understanding of pretense. Monographs of the Society for Research in Child Development, 58 (1, Serial No. 231).

21 SPECIAL LINE OF BOOKS Include the name of a special imprint or line of books. For instance, the Vintage Books are a special line of books published by Random House (you would type *Vintage-Random*).

Schwartz, I. M. (1989). (In)justice for juveniles: Rethinking the best interests of the child. Lexington, MA: Lexington-Heath.

22 WORK IN SEVERAL VOLUMES Specify the volume if you have used only one; if more than one, list the whole multivolume work:

Gravensberg, S., & Martin, K. (1998). Handbook of early psychology: Vol. 2. New York: Lafitte.

Trevelyan, G. M. (1952) History of England (3rd ed., Vols. 1-3). Garden City, NY: Anchor-Doubleday.

23 INTRODUCTORY MATERIAL If you quote from introductory or other added material, start with the contributor's name and use the right label: Introduction. Preface. Foreword (or sometimes: Afterword). Include page numbers for the introductory material. (Sometimes these are given as lower-case roman numerals.)

Aufderheide, P. (1992). [Preface]. In P. Aufderheide (Ed.), Beyond PC: Toward a politics of understanding (pp. 1-4). St. Paul, MN: Graywolf Press.

Bayh, B. (1989). [Foreword]. In I. M. Schwartz, (In)justice for juveniles: Rethinking the best interests of the child (pp. xi-xiii). Lexington, MA: Lexington-Heath.

24 PART OF A COLLECTION When you list a selection from a collection of work by different authors, list the individual selection first. Then identify the collection.

Boyte, H. C. (1992). The politics of innocence. In P. Aufderheide (Ed.), Beyond PC: Toward a politics of understanding (pp. 177-179). St. Paul, MN: Graywolf Press.

25 ENCYCLOPEDIA ENTRY Give full publishing information.

> Bergmann, P. G. (1993). Relativity. In The new encyclopedia Britannica (Vol. 26, pp. 501-508). Chicago: Encyclopaedia Britannica.

26 INSTITUTIONAL OR GOVERNMENT PUBLICATION Studies and reports often list an organization, institution, or agency as the author. Include identification numbers for reports issued by organizations or official agencies. Source information on such documents often includes acronyms like DHHS for Department of Health and Human Services or NTIS for National Technical Information Service.

> National Institute of Mental Health. (1990). Clinical training in serious mental illness (DHHS Publication No. ADM 90-1679). Washington, DC: U.S. Government Printing Office.

27 PAMPHLET OR BROCHURE Identify the nature of informal or locally published print materials. Include an address to help readers obtain a copy.

> Calavaras Family Center. (2000). Living with the hyperactive child. [Brochure]. Fremont, CA.

> Farm Workers Alliance. (1999). A living wage. [Brochure]. (Available from Farm Workers Alliance, 3789 Salinas Road, San Jose, CA 95112)

28 UNPUBLISHED MATERIAL Use an appropriate label when you have consulted a manuscript that has not been printed: Unpublished manuscript. Unpublished doctoral dissertation. If you found the dissertation through the brief summary published in *Dissertation Abstracts* (now *Dissertation Abstracts International*), include the volume number and identification number. If you have read the material on microfilm, include the appropriate source information.

> Farnwell, N. (1989). Models of conflict resolution in labor disputes. Unpublished doctoral dissertation, University of Missouri, Columbia.

> Legrange, D. L. (1993). Psychological profiles in hiring middle managers. Dissertation Abstracts International, 54(01), 531B. (University Microfilms No. AAD93-15887)

29 TITLE WITHIN A TITLE An underlined (italicized) book title may include the name of another book. Shift back to roman (not underlined) for the title-within-a-title:

Patras, S. (1999). Filming The Grapes of Wrath. Los Angeles: Connoisseur Books.

C. ENTRIES FOR ELECTRONIC SOURCES—Online, CD-ROM

Guidelines for documenting electronic sources are being updated as new technology and new uses for it evolve. For most entries, start with any of the usual publishing information available to you—including author, date (in parentheses), and title.

- After the title, include the **document type** or electronic medium in square brackets, for instance [Online] or [CD-ROM].
- For material from the net, include the **Internet address** or URL (for "uniform resource locator"). Put it after the notation *Available:* (with the colon). Typically, the electronic address will start with the access mode, usually http:// . . . (Other access modes include *telnet, gopher,* and *ftp.*) The address will then go on to the relevant path and specific file names (often beginning with www. for the World Wide Web). Try to have the whole URL on the same line, or else try to have a break only after a period or slash. Double-check to make sure that dots, slashes, colons, capitals, and spacing are exactly right. (Do not add hyphens or final periods.)
- After the net address, give the **access date**—the date you accessed or visited the source or site. Put it in square brackets, for instance [1999, September 23]. The following sample entries are adapted from recent guidelines for using electronic sources:

30 ONLINE PUBLICATION Much publication now takes place on the Internet without a prior print version.

Land, T. (1996, March 31). Web extension to American Psychological Association style (WEAPAS) [Online] (Rev. 1.2.4). Available: http://www.beadslands.com/weapas [1997, April 24].

31 ARTICLE IN ONLINE JOURNAL Articles in online periodicals may not include conventional page numbering.

Moulthrop, S. (1995, August 21). You say you want a revolution? Hypertext and the laws of media. Postmodern Culture, 1(3) [Bitnet Document]. Available: http://jefferson.village.virginia.edu/pmc/contents.all.html [1995, October 3].

32 DATABASE ON CD-ROM

The world factbook 1994 [CD-ROM]. (1994). Washington, DC: Central Intelligence Agency [Producer and distributor].

33 DOCUMENT READ ON CD-ROM

Morring, F., Jr. (1994, May 16). Russian hardware allows earlier station experiments [CD-ROM]. Aviation Week & Space Technology, 140, 57. Abstract from: InfoTrac General Periodicals Index-A; Abstract 15482317.

34 VIRTUAL BOOK Increasingly, whole books will be available online.

Thoreau, H. D. (1854). Walden [Online]. Available: http://www.inform. umd.edu:8080/EdRes/ReadingRoom/HistoryPhilosophy/OnWaldenPond [1997, February 7].

35 COMPUTER SOFTWARE Specify the version for repeatedly updated products.

Verbena, F. K. (1999). The interactive math tester (Version 3.2) [Computer Software]. Scottsdale, NJ: PsychServ.

D. NONPRINT SOURCES—Talks and media sources

The APA style generally makes no provision for listing private communications, such as unpublished letters, telephone conversations, or e-mail. These are not a matter of public record, and a reader would have no way of consulting or verifying them. Identify such sources only as part of your parenthetic documentation, for instance (e-mail to the author, 27 January 2000).

36 UNPUBLISHED TALK OR LECTURE Identify the speaker or speakers. Include the month if available. Describe the occasion.

Krakauer, V. (1999, December). The attack on bilingual education. Paper presented at the meeting of the West Coast Linguistic Society, San Diego, CA.

Hormel, V. S., & Lermontov, R. (1998, June). First-language interference in children of Vietnamese immigrants. In R. S. Mendoza (Chair), New directions in ESL pedagogy. Symposium conducted at the Mid-State TESOL Conference, Sacramento, CA.

37 TELEVISION OR RADIO PROGRAM Identify major contributors, such as the director and producer.

Grabowski, L. (Producer), & Sanchez, A. (Director). (1999, November 17). Testing the glass ceiling. New York and Washington, DC: Public Broadcasting Service.

38 RECORDING Specify the medium, such as [CD] or [Cassette]. As appropriate, identify songwriter, copyright date, performer, and performance date.

Jackson, M. (1991). Take my hand, precious lord. On Mahalia Jackson: Gospels, Spirituals, and Hymns [CD]. New York: Sony Music Entertainment.

Handy, W. C. (1928). Back Country Blues [Recorded by Monroe, L.]. On Going to the Roots [Cassette]. New York: Classic Records.

39 ART WORK

DeSanto, L. (2000). Alienation [Art work]. San Jose, CA: Institute of Mexican American Art.

36c.3 Preparing Final Manuscript (APA)

Observe distinctive features of the APA style. Double-space all materials. Use the title or usually a shortened title instead of your name as the **running heads:** *Slave Revolts* instead of *Slave Revolts in the Caribbean.* Start a new page for your **References.** Follow any special instructions from your instructor concerning use of a title page or inclusion of a formal outline. Your instructor may require you to include an **abstract** on a separate page at the beginning (with the heading *Abstract*). An abstract is a brief summary of the paper (perhaps 150–250 words), showing its focus and major findings.

36c.4 **Sample Research Paper (APA)** *Study the following sample research paper documented in the APA style.* Answer questions like the following:

- Has the writer focused the paper on a central question? (What is the core issue, and how important is it?)
- Is there a central thesis, and if so what is it?
- For you, what are key points the writer tried to bring out?
- Does the paper have a workable overall plan? (Was it easy or hard to follow?) Did you at any point lose the thread of the argument?
- What is the range of sources? Does the writer show them to be relevant and credible?
- Which quotations or other evidence did you find most instructive or persuasive? Which least?
- Does the writer use varied ways of introducing and working in quoted material? Does the presentation of material anywhere get monotonous or mechanical?
- Does the References list include any unusual entries?
- Are you part of the ideal audience for this paper? Why or why not?

Multiple Intelligences 1

Running head: MULTIPLE INTELLIGENCES: ENHANCING LEARNING

Multiple Intelligences: Enhancing Learning

Alice Birgen

English 2

Professor Gertold

February 6, 1999

Multiple Intelligences: Enhancing Learning

Academic intelligence is the kind of intelligence that most refer to when discussing how smart a person is. Although academic intelligence does matter, it is not the only thing that brings success in life. Students may be able to memorize facts and statistics to earn good grades, but how is memorizing statistics and information going to help them succeed in the world? This kind of question is the basis for multiple-intelligence research.

central question

The theory of multiple intelligences helps researchers develop an understanding of people and their behaviors. Studies of teaching methods have given researchers some suggestions for the best way to help children learn. Gardner, cognitive researcher at Harvard, created his own ideal school based on his theory of the seven categories of intelligence. Gardner was one of the first to challenge the "standard notion of intelligence as a single capacity, with which an individual is born, and which proves difficult, if not impossible to alter" (1983, p. 12). The goal of educators is to improve schools so that they will develop students' abilities to the fullest. The theory of multiple intelligences can improve schools and change the way we look at students and their potentials.

key quotation

date and page in parens.

A student named Alice, a 4.0 average student with 800s on her test scores, started number one in her class but dropped to the bottom 20 percent of her class. Her example is often cited to prove that the customary way of testing intelligence does not go far enough. What questions should be asked when we measure intelligence? Sternberg, a professor of psychology at Yale University, writes in his article "What Should We Ask About

credentials of experts

Multiple Intelligences 3

Intelligence?" that "the revolutionaries do not believe that conventional tests adequately sample the universe of tasks needed to assess intelligence" (1996, p. 208). Researchers comment, "Revolutionaries see the so-called intelligence quotient--the IQ--as neither a quotient nor an indicator of intelligence" (1996, p. 208). Khalfa, the author of What Is Intelligence? writes, "An important practical question is the validity of attempts at measuring degrees of intelligence on a single scale, such as IQ tests" (1994, p. 7). Intelligence is an ability or set of abilities that permits an individual to solve problems. Sternberg and Wagner quote Wigdor and Garner as concluding that "more than 'academic' intelligence is necessary for successful performance in the real-world settings" (1986, p. 52).

correlated quotes from several sources

Jordan, the author of "Multiple Intelligences: Seven Keys to Opening Closed Minds, " reports:

block quote for key quotation

> Gardner argues that the previous definition of intelligence had been limited to the ability to solve problems in isolation, while his research was revealing that human capacity extends to another kind of problem solving, that can be identified within specific domains of brain function that he defines as the seven intelligences. (1996, p. 29)

Gardner's theory of multiple intelligences includes seven abilities that may be grouped under larger headings like analytical intelligence, creative intelligence, and practical intelligence. The IQ test generally tests the analytical aspect of intelligence, which Gardner subdivides into the linguistic intelligence and logical-

preview of major topics

mathematical intelligence. According to Gardner, the more overlooked categories of intelligence are the more creative and practical types of intelligence. These include musical intelligence, bodily-kinesthetic intelligence, spatial intelligence, interpersonal intelligence, and intrapersonal intelligence.

Linguistic intelligence and logical-mathematical intelligence are the two types of intelligence Gardner believes "get the most attention in American schools" (Smagorinsky, 1995, p. 20). Gardner describes linguistic intelligence as the intelligence used in reading a novel, writing a poem or an article, or generating an extemporaneous talk. It is described by Hoerr, in "Introducing the Theory of Multiple Intelligences," as the "sensitivity to the meaning and order of words" (1996, p. 9).

author and date in parens

Logical-mathematical intelligence is used in solving mathematical problems, evaluating logical arguments, or completing the traditional syllogism. ("All human beings are mortal. Socrates is a human being. Therefore, Socrates is mortal.") It is the ability to recognize patterns and order and to handle chains of reasoning. These two types of intelligence are most commonly evaluated in standardized testing. Many people would recognize them as the reading, writing, and math portions of tests.

While Gardner includes the linguistic and mathematical-logical intelligences which are mainly valued in modern American schools, he also includes the more creative and less exclusively intellectual kinds of intelligence, such as musical intelligence and bodily-kinesthetic intelligence. Sternberg, in an article in The American Scholar, describes musical intelligence as "the intelligence used in remembering a tune, singing a song, or composing a sonata" (1996, p. 209). Hoerr describes it as the "sensitivity to pitch, melody, rhythm, and tone" (1996, p. 9). Musical intelligence is the ability to produce and appreciate music. Dancers, figure skaters, musicians, music critics, and others who understand rhythm, melody, tone, and other aspects of musical expression are blessed with musical intelligence.

extended definition

Bodily-kinesthetic intelligence is the ability to use the body effectively to solve problems. Hoerr describes it as "the ability to use the body skillfully and handle objects adroitly" (1996, p. 9). Bodily-kinesthetic intelligence would be used in dancing ballet, performing gymnastics, or playing tennis. Smagorinsky explains in his article "Multiple Intelligence in the English Class: An Overview," how Gardner distinguishes between having athletic skills and having bodily-kinesthetic intelligence. Gardner believes "a player who can 'see' a playing field well and make the appropriate move has bodily-kinesthetic intelligence" (1995, p. 21). Gardner also believes massage therapists who are able to understand the body's needs and can apply appropriate pressure possess bodily kinesthetic intelligence (Smagorinsky, 1995).

key example

The most practical types of intelligence Gardner refers to as spatial intelligence, interpersonal intelligence, and intrapersonal intelligence. These are not tested through IQ tests yet are very important in daily activities. According to Hoerr, Gardner identifies spatial intelligence as "the ability to perceive the world accurately and to re-create or transform aspects of the world" (1996, p. 9). Spatial intelligence would be used in daily activities when trying to

partial quote

find one's way in unfamiliar territory or trying to fit something in a trunk. It is also being able to judge where a ball will land after being hit. Peter Smagorinsky, writing in the English Journal, comments, "Gardner believes spatial intelligence was fundamental to the survival of the sailors and was their most important means of problem solving" (1995, p. 20). Smagorinsky describes Gardner's favorite example, the sailor who spent much of his life at sea "navigating ships according to the sun's position (and at night, the position of the stars), recognizing weather patterns, sizing up waves, repairing and maintaining the ship's facility, getting sustenance from knowing how to fish and preserve foods attained through trade, and having the savvy to barter effectively once on land" (1995, p. 20). This is a good example of requiring a person to be practical and possess what Gardner refers to as spatial intelligence, rather than being "book smart."

classic example

quoted phrase

Smagorinsky comments, "With the explosion of the telecommunications and computer industry and the resultant emphasis on producing and comprehending images, spatial intelligence will undoubtedly become increasingly important in economic development in our society" (1995, p. 20).

The more personal forms of intelligence needed in real-life situations are interpersonal and intrapersonal intelligence. Interpersonal intelligence is the ability to read and respond to the needs of others. It refers to people who have the ability to figure out what others are saying by their expressions and the ability to communicate with others. Smagorinsky points to "good teachers, therapists, salespeople, politicians, and others who deal

paraphrase of key point

effectively with the public" as those who demonstrate interpersonal intelligence (1995, p. 21). Those who have the ability to understand people and relationships are considered to have interpersonal intelligence (Hoerr, 1996). Interpersonal intelligence is considered to be a great quality in people, yet it is an intelligence which the traditional IQ test does not test. Interpersonal intelligence is used in most jobs interacting with people and is very important in daily life.

Intrapersonal intelligence is also very important. Gardner includes it as one of his seven intelligences. Intrapersonal intelligence is the ability to look into oneself for self-knowledge and understanding (Smagorinsky, 1995). Smagorinsky considers "those who are highly reflective, those who seek and benefit from therapy, those who learn from their mistakes, those who practice yoga, and others who have the ability to come to a greater understanding of themselves" as those who have great intrapersonal intelligence (1995, p. 21). Intrapersonal intelligence is needed to understand one's emotional life as a way of understanding oneself. Other researchers have started to talk about emotional rather than merely intellectual intelligence (Goleman, 1995). Gibbs said in an article about research into emotional intelligence that in the past we have worshipped "the hardware of the brain and the software of the mind." However, we have neglected psychologists who talk about understanding our own feelings and regulating emotion "in a way that enhances living" (1995, p. 24).

Gardner's theory considers all aspects of life, as opposed to the restricted conventional intelligence tests that only consider the first two categories charted by Gardner's theory. Teele discusses

major transition

the implications of recognizing alternative intelligences for methods of teaching in his article "Redesigning the Educational System to Enable All Students to Succeed." Currently, "schools tests, class assignments and teaching methods usually focus on the linguistic and logical-mathematical intelligences and often miss the talents, gifts, and abilities of the many students who are stronger in the other five" (1996, p. 65). As a result, children go to school with gifts or talents, wanting to learn, but instead find failure and frustration. School becomes something to be endured (Hoerr, 1996). According to Hoerr, "Too many kids are reminded of their shortcomings and inadequacies, and their strengths are ignored in school" (1996, p. 36). Students are taught to learn specific answers to specific questions, answer problems in a designated way, and memorize lists of definitions to write down on a test. The students are not willing to explore new approaches to problem solving because they have been taught only to seek the "one correct answer" (Jordan, 1996). According to Sternberg's article in The American Scholar, "The reason conventional intelligence tests predict school achievement as well as they do is that schools, like conventional tests, tend to emphasize analytical skills far more than they emphasize creative and practical skills." Sternberg goes on to explain that "students who depart from a teacher's expectations or point of view find themselves graded down for having done so" (1996, p. 209). This type of teaching does not allow students to use their creative intelligence; rather, it limits them to the use of linguistic and logical-mathematical intelligence.

varied credit tags

Multiple Intelligences 9

The theory of multiple intelligences can help reach more students and give them the opportunity to demonstrate what they have learned. McClaskey quotes Hernstein and Murray, who say, "What really counts about intelligence are the ways in which people process the information they receive" (1995, p. 56). In the English Journal, a professional journal for teachers, McClaskey writes, "No longer can educators measure intelligence solely through strict memorization or even application; rather we must consider a fresher definition of intelligence as the ability to respond successfully to new situations and learn from experience" (1995, p. 57).

source information

Gardner believes all types of learners must be recognized in schools and in a society at large, or else many individuals will never realize their full potential (Jordan, 1996). He suggests that the ideal school would accommodate each individual's needs by insisting upon an assessment specialist providing regular updated intelligence evaluations of each student's strengths, weaknesses, and inclinations (Jordan, 1996). The multiple intelligence approach does not mean schools are backing away from teaching students how to read, write, and calculate; instead it means, for instance, encouraging students to write and create stories with meaning and using their more personal intelligences.

Coppock performed a classroom study to observe the composing process of students engaged in non-written literary interpretations. Coppock filmed students as they read a story and then worked out an interpretive "text" through a picture, dance, or other type of creative composition. The teacher supplied the

account of major research

Multiple Intelligences 10

students with an abundance of supplies such as paper, pencils, markers, or musical instruments and also allowed them to get their own supplies. "The process of creating these interpretive texts appeared to serve a dual purpose: the students' thoughts both shaped and were shaped by the texts they composed" (Smagorinsky, 1995, p. 22). The interviews with the students revealed that in composing their texts the students engaged in a variety of processes that teachers value in student writing. After observing the students the researchers concluded that "non-written texts are capable of providing the same potential for enabling the construction of meaning as written texts" (Smagorinsky, 1995, p. 25).

The theory of multiple intelligences is supported by Winfield, a computer teacher. He believes "people who are able to learn by different methods have success, when learning only by reading might have been a failure." He comments that he teaches students to learn "first by observing a procedure and then by applying it." He believes that "people should always be attempting to fit what they learn into their own full picture of what is important, relevant and useful." He says, "In this way, what they learn will have a personal meaning. . . . Learning from mistakes and applying what you have learned is the key to success" (personal communication, January 7, 1999).

omission from quotation

nonprint source

Although many may be unaware of schools basing their teaching on the multiple intelligence theory, there are schools that apply the theory to their teaching methods. Key School, opened in 1987, was the first school in the United States to be founded on

Gardner's theory of multiple intelligences. The seven intelligences were used as the starting point for reflective practice and professional development (Bolanos, 1996).

Changing schools to revolve around the theory of multiple intelligences cannot be done gradually. Rather, Smagorinsky informs the reader, "It must be part of a larger effort to reconceptualize teaching and learning." The introduction of multiple-intelligence activities must be accompanied by large changes in the values of the classroom and coordinated with what students believe to be appropriate and acceptable ways of thinking and communicating in English class (1995, p. 25). Trying to base schools on the theory of multiple intelligences brought up the question of how students could cover the required curriculum and yet not be constrained by it. To answer this question, suggestions were made intending to help teachers and students expand their current assessment tools to include Gardner's multiple intelligences theory.

Based on the theory of multiple intelligence, suggestions for homework assignments and take-home tests, for evaluations and quizzes, for problem solving, and for creating graphs and analyzing statistics as well as drawing and naming angles were made to enhance the logical-mathematical intelligence (Teele, 1996). Oral presentations, written assignments, and creative writing were suggested to enhance the linguistic intelligence.

To move on to the intelligences that are currently overlooked, researchers suggested musical intelligence and bodily-kinesthetic intelligence be assessed through musical compositions, productions, performances, listening assignments, movement, sports, interpretive drama, and building mock-ups for projects to scale (Teele, 1996). Suggested spatial activities were student projects, graphics, sketching, analyzing or creating cartoons, and mapping. The more personal intelligences, for example interpersonal intelligence, should be assessed through group evaluation, joint goal setting, peer evaluations, and one-on-one conferences. Intrapersonal intelligence should be enhanced through self-evaluations, reflective assignments, journals, logs, and diaries (Weber, 1996).

Gardner defines intelligence best as "the ability to solve problems that one encounters in real life situations, to generate new problems to solve, to make something or offer a service that is valued in one's culture" (McClaskey, 1995, p. 59). Gardner concludes, "If we recognize multiple intelligences, we can reach more students, and give those students the opportunity to demonstrate what they have understood" (1996, p. 3).

clincher quotations

Multiple Intelligences 13

References

Balanos, P. M. (1996, December). Multiple intelligences as a mental model: The key to renaissance middle school. NASSP Bulletin, pp. 36-42.

Gardner, H. (1983). Frames of mind: The theory of multiple intelligences. New York: HarperCollins.

Gardner, H. (1996, November). Probing more deeply into the theory of multiple intelligences. NASSP Bulletin, pp. 1-7.

Gibbs, N. (1995, August 7). The EQ factor. Time, pp. 23-27.

Goleman, D. P. (1997). Emotional intelligence. New York: Bantam.

Hoerr, T. R. (1996, November). Introducing the theory of multiple intelligences. NASSP Bulletin, pp. 8-10.

Jordan, S. (1996, November). Multiple intelligences: Seven keys to opening closed minds. NASSP Bulletin, pp. 29-36.

Khalfa, J. (1994). What is intelligence? New York: Cambridge University Press.

McClaskey, J. (1995, December). Assessing student learning through multiple intelligences. English Journal, pp. 55-59.

Smagorinsky, P. (1995, December). Multiple intelligence in the English class: An overview. English Journal, pp. 20-26.

Sternberg, R. J., & Wagner, R. K. (1986). Practical intelligence. New York: Cambridge University Press.

Sternberg, R. J. (1996, Spring). What should we ask about intelligence? American Scholar, pp. 205-218.

Teele, S. (1996, November). Redesigning the educational system to enable all students to succeed. NASSP Bulletin, pp. 65-75.

Weber, E. (1996, November). Creative communities in high school: An interactive learning and teaching approach. NASSP Bulletin, pp. 80-85.

36d Documentation Styles: CBE, AIP, Chicago

Follow the documentation style of other academic areas.

For research papers in the sciences, you may be asked to follow the style of the Council of Biology Editors (CBE), the American Institute of Physics (AIP), or the American Chemical Society (ACS). For papers in journalism, the arts, or history, you may be asked follow the guidelines of *The Chicago Manual of Style* (CMS).

Instead of requiring parenthetic documentation, guidelines may ask you for fuller publishing information in **footnotes** or now usually **endnotes.** Software now often handles the job of spacing footnotes properly at the bottom of a page. Usually these notes will be numbered consecutively. A raised numeral (called a **superscript**) in your text directs the reader to a note that appears at the bottom of a page or as part of a set of final notes. For instance, these instructions about traditional footnotes might be credited to a manual giving full instructions about different documentation styles across the curriculum.[1]

---

1. Christine A. Hult and Thomas N. Huckin, <u>The New Century Handbook</u> (Boston: Allyn and Bacon, 1999), pp. 296-298.

PART SIX

SPECIAL HELPS FOR WRITERS

Language is a rich human activity—with amazing resources and with traps for the unwary. Speakers and writers turn to handbooks, manuals of style, and dictionaries for guidance when they face confusing choices. They look for guidance when something they said (or the way they said it) attracts negative attention. When looking for advice in such situations, remember some basic points:

- Language is to a large extent a matter of convention. In much of our speaking and writing, we follow established conventions—customary ways of putting ideas into words and formating papers or letters. When we depart from convention, we are likely to attract attention—sometimes favorable, sometimes unfavorable.

- Language brings strong personal reactions into play. It is not a neutral signaling code, like our system of numbers. Speakers and writers learn to reckon with the strong personal preferences of listeners and readers who find certain expressions annoying, illogical, or pompous.
- Language is undergoing a slow but constant process of change. Has a new expression become part of ordinary everyday language—or will some readers still consider it newfangled or pretentious?

37 GLOSSARY OF USAGE

gl

Check out expressions often questioned or criticized.

This glossary is designed to give you fair warning concerning expressions that have been criticized as uneducated, informal, or illogical. As writers, we hope to be judged by how honestly and effectively we develop and convey our message. However, a basic fact of every writer's life is that people will also judge us by the language we use. Communication breaks down when instead of responding to an important point we are making a reader says, "Bad grammar" or "Poor English!"

Is it all right to say "*like* I said" instead of "*as* I said"? (And is it all right to spell all right *alright?*) Must we say "It is I" when we knock on a door and someone wants to know who is knocking? Conservatives consider many everyday expressions as plain wrong. Liberals answer that many traditional rules were artificial, outlawing expressions that have long been part of natural effective English and are widely used by educated people. This glossary will encourage you to steer a middle course. However, it will also encourage you to write natural effective English without constantly looking over your shoulder. If an expression is widely used by well-educated and successful Americans in speech and writing, it's all right.

- **aggravate** In writing, use it to mean "make worse" (or more grave). Avoid its informal use in the sense of "annoy" or "irritate":

  FORMAL: When you **irritate** him, you **aggravate** his condition.

- **ain't** Nonstandard for *am not, isn't, aren't,* or *hasn't.* (She *ain't* been seen since.)

- **allusion/illusion** An allusion is a brief mention that reminds us of a story or an event (the speaker's **allusion** to Watergate). An illusion is a deceptive appearance or false hope (The Vietnam war destroyed many **illusions**).

- a **lot** Always spell as two words. "*A lot of* money" is informal; try to do without it. And "*lots of* money" is slang:

  SAFE: She owed us **a large amount of** money.

- **alumnus/alumna** Some words from other languages have kept separate forms not only for singular and plural but also for gender: (one male) **alumnus,** (several male) **alumni;** (one female) **alumna,** (several female) **alumnae.**

- **amount, number** Use amount only when thinking about bulk or a sum (the total **amount** of the debt). Use number when thinking about countable items (the **number** of whooping cranes).

  COUNTABLE: A large **number** (not amount) of applications were turned down.

  The **number** (not amount) of small business bankruptcies was growing.

- **and/or** *And/or* is sometimes necessary in commercial or official documents in order to cover all possibilities (in case of accident and/or disability). Do without it in ordinary writing.

- ***and* or *but* beginning a sentence** A traditional rule banned *and* and *but* at the beginning of a sentence. But many writers occasionally start sentences with *and* or *but* merely to avoid weightier or more formal links like *moreover, however,* and *nevertheless*. Don't overdo the initial *and* or *but.*

  He was plagued by financial worries. **But** nothing could cramp his generous heart.

  —*Time* magazine

- **anyways, anywheres, anyplace** These are common expressions in folk speech. In writing, use **anyway** or **anywhere.**

- **as** *As* is nonstandard as a substitute for *that* or *whether* ("I don't know *as* I can come"). It is also nonstandard as a substitute for *who* ("Those *as* knew her avoided her").

- **attribute/contribute** **Attribute** means to trace to a cause or a source: The governor **attributed** her success to perseverance. **Contribute** means to give one's share, make a contribution.

- **awful/awfully** In writing, use *awful* only for something truly horrible (The plane went down with an **awful** loss of life). Do not use *awful* or *awfully* as an informal substitute for *very* or *extremely:*

  VERY INFORMAL: That was *awful* close. [very]

  The terms had been *awfully* attractive. [extremely]

- **bad/badly** Use the adjective **bad** after the linking verb *feel*, which shows a condition—the state someone is in: The resignation made everyone feel **bad.** Use the adverb **badly** to show *how* something is done: The transfer was handled **badly.**

- **being as, being that** Nonstandard as substitutes for *because* (*being that* I was ill).

- **between/among** A favorite quibble of people critical of other people's language. Use **between** when choosing between two (between the two of us). Use **among** when choosing **among** more than two (fierce competition among the new players). However, **between** is also right when more than two things can be considered in pairs of two:

  RIGHT: Bilateral trade agreements exist **between** many countries.

- **bursted, bust, busted** *Bursted* is a nonstandard form of *burst:* The tank **burst** (not *bursted*) and killed two of the workers. *Bust* for arrest (a cocaine *bust*) is slang.

- **but what** Use **that** instead of *but what* after words like *doubt:* We never doubted that (not *but what*) they would return.

- **but yet, but however** Expressions like *but yet* or *but however* are said to be redundant; they say *but* twice. Use only one of the logical links at a time: The full amount had been paid, **but** (not *but yet*) the computer kept sending a bill.

- **calculate, reckon, expect, guess** Do not use these words instead of *think* or *suppose*. In written English, **calculate** and **reckon** imply actual computing or number crunching. **Guess** implies real guesswork. In the sense of *think* or *suppose*, these verbs are informal or dialectal.

- **can/may** Formal written English uses **can** for ability—being able to. It uses **may** to show permission. The use of *can* to indicate permission is common in speech and writing but is still sometimes considered informal:

  INFORMAL: You **cannot** come in without identification.

  FORMAL: Visitors **may** (are permitted to) enter the compound only if they **can** (are able to) show a badge.

- **cannot help but** *Cannot help but* is often criticized as illogical or confused. Choose either **cannot help** or **cannot but:**

  BOTH RIGHT: I **cannot help wishing/cannot but wish** that I had never met you.

- **can't hardly, can't scarcely** Like double negatives, these expressions duplicate the negative idea. Use **can hardly** or **can scarcely.**

  can hardly
  WRONG: Countries like Russia *can't hardly* pay the interest on their debts.

- **censor/censure** To **censor** means to interfere with speech or writing to bend it to the censor's standards (or to ban it outright). Censorship is the result. To **censure** is to express disapproval in a very serious official manner (as in a vote of censure).

- **center around** Logical readers expect a discussion to **center on** an issue, not to *center around* it.

- **compare with/compare to** We compare two cars **with** each other to see how they both rate. We compare a car **to** a bug to show what the car is like.

- **couple of** In formal writing, **couple** refers to a closely bonded pair (the **couple** had been together for many years). Avoid the loose informal *a couple of* or *a couple* standing for two or more—several or a few (*a couple of* minutes, only *a couple* dollars).

- **credible, credulous, creditable** News stories may be **credible** or **incredible**—easy or hard to believe. The people who read them may be **credulous** or **incredulous**—easy or hard to fool. An action (like a good deed) that does someone credit is a **creditable** action

- **data is/data are** *Data* was originally a plural, meaning "facts" (**these data are** suspect). However, in today's world of technology and computers, *data* is used as a singular (**this data has** just become available). To be safe, use *data* as a plural in nontechnical writing.

- **different than** **Different from** used to be expected in formal English, but **different than,** widely used in speech, has become acceptable in writing.

  BOTH RIGHT: We tried a **different** method **than we had used** last year.

  We tried a **different** method **from the one we had used** last year.

- **disinterested, uninterested** In formal English, **disinterested** means "not swayed by personal, selfish interest"—unselfish, impartial. (They expected her to be a **disinterested** judge.) Avoid *disinterested* in the sense of uninterested or indifferent.

  uninterested
  MISLEADING: The judge seemed *disinterested* in our problems.

- ***due to* as preposition** Use **due to** as an adjective: His absence was **due to** ill health. (Also: His absence, **due to** ill health, upset our schedule.) In both examples, you could substitute another adjective: His absence was **traceable** to ill health. Avoid *due to* as a preposition meaning *because of:*

  because of
  PREPOSITION: Computer chips may fail *due to* poor quality control.

- **each other, one another** Conservative editors distinguish between **each other** (referring to two) and **one another** (referring to more than two):

  TWO: Her parents had known **each other** since childhood.

  MORE THAN TWO: Members of the immigrant community supported **one another.**

- **enthused, enthuse** Avoid these very informal shortcuts. Use **enthusiastic** and **turn enthusiastic.**

- **etc.** Avoid *etc.* It's short for Latin *et cetera*—"and so on." It says "there is more"—but it's an easy out when you don't really have an additional example or further data. Besides, *ect.* is a common misspelling. Also, *and etc.* is redundant—duplicating the idea of "and." Stay out of trouble by doing without *etc.* altogether.

- **flout/flaunt** We **flout**, or defy, conventions that hem us in. We **flaunt**, or show off, flashy new clothes or cars.

- **flunk** Slang for **fail.**

- **had ought, hadn't ought to** *Had ought to* is nonstandard; *hadn't ought to* is informal. Use **ought to have** and **ought not to have.**

  ought to have
  NONSTANDARD: The company *had ought to* notify us.

  ought not to have
  INFORMAL: You *hadn't ought to* ask him.

- **hopefully** *Hopefully* basically means "with hope, full of hope": The players looked at the display board **hopefully** (in hopes of winning). Many teachers and editors object to *hopefully* when used to mean "let us hope" or "it is to be hoped":

  We hope they
  INFORMAL: *Hopefully, they* will revise their figures.

- **if/whether** *If* is sometimes criticized when used to express uncertainty after such verbs as *ask, don't know, wonder,* or *doubt.* The more formal subordinator is **whether:** Economists doubt **whether** the law will do much good.

- **in/into** Formal writing requires **into** rather than *in* to show direction:

  into the country.
  INFORMAL: Millions of new immigrants came *in the country.*

- **infer/imply** A speaker **implies** something; the audience **infers** what is meant.

- **in terms of** A vague all-purpose expression frequent in jargon: "What have you seen lately *in terms of* new plays?"

  JARGON: What did she expect *in terms of* salary?

  BETTER: What salary did she expect?

- **irregardless** Use **regardless.**

- **less/fewer** Use *less* when talking about extent, amount, or degree: **less** friction, **less** money, **less** heat. Use *fewer* for things you can count: **fewer** hours, **fewer** customers, **fewer** complaints.

- **like/as** Use **like** as a preposition: fly **like a bird,** drift **like a cloud.** Avoid it as a subordinator starting a clause, with its own subject and verb: *like* a bird *flies, like* a cloud *had passed.* Use **as** or **as if** instead.

  as
  INFORMAL: We did everything exactly *like* the instructions said.

  as if
  They acted *like* they had never talked to a foreign visitor before.

- **literally** **Literally** means "in plain fact." (The earthquake **literally** leveled the village.) Do not use it figuratively.

  completely
  MISUSED: They *literally* blanketed the city with leaflets.
  (they did not use an actual blanket)

- **media is/media are** *Media,* like *data,* was originally a plural (the **media give** people what they want). In the media today, *media* is used as a singular (the **media is** often criticized by intellectuals). To be safe, use *media* as a plural in courses in the humanities (English, history, philosophy).

- **myself/himself** The *-self* pronouns are typically used as **reflexive pronouns**—they point back to something already mentioned: **The governor** signed the letter **himself. The other candidates** took **themselves** out of the running. Handbooks used to rule against the free-standing use of the *-self* pronouns as emphatic substitutes for the plain personal pronouns like *I/me* or *he/him.* However, this emphatic use of the pronouns has long been standard English:

  STANDARD: My uncle, my father, and **myself**
  Did give him that same royalty he wears.

  —Shakespeare, *Henry IV,* Part One

- **number of** *Number* is singular when it refers to a sum or total: The **number** of dead and injured **was** still **rising.** However, *a number of* is plural when it means "several": **A number of** complaints **were** received.

- **off of** Nonstandard for *off* or *from*: We took his name **off** (not *off of*) the list. They deducted 10 percent **from** (not *off of*) the price.

- **one/one's** "*One* should watch *their* language" is informal spoken English, mixing singular and plural. "**One** should watch **one's** language" is grammatically correct but sounds old-fashioned. "**One** should watch **his or her** language" is politically correct. "**People** should watch **their** language" or "**We** should watch **our** language" might work best.

- **plus** Use as a mathematical term ($2.50 **plus** tax) but not instead of *and* or *also:* The vote count had been slow, **and** (not *plus*) ballots had been lost.

- **possessive with verbal noun** A traditional rule required a possessive before a verbal noun (or gerund) in sentences like the following: We heard about **Clara's winning** a scholarship. Today the plain form is generally acceptable: Imagine **Clara winning** a scholarship!

- **predominate** A verb referring to something that is happening: Jeans and T-shirts **predominated** in the crowd. Often confused with the adjective that puts a label on something: The **predominant** sentiment was in favor of acquittal.

- **preposition ending a sentence** A much-taught rule used to ban the final preposition (as a word to end a sentence *with*). The rule was hard to enforce because the final preposition has long been part of educated English: He had always needed someone to lean **on.** We needed something to remember her **by.**

- **reason is because** Often criticized as redundant, since the *because* repeats the idea of giving a reason. Use **reason is that** to be safe: **The reason** the jury voted to acquit is **that** they doubted the main government witness.

- **split infinitive** A wedge splitting the *to*-form has become acceptable: unable **to fully understand** the instructions. However, the split infinitive can be awkward when the wedge is more than one word:

  to correct their children constantly and indiscriminately

  AWKWARD: For parents *to constantly and indiscriminately correct* their children is counterproductive.

- **superlative with two** A traditional rule discourages use of the superlative when only two things are being compared: the **better** of the two (instead of *the best of the two*)—and the **best** of three.

- **that/who** *That* in reference to people is educated written English. Handbooks used to require *who* in reference to people (**the scientist who** discovered penicillin). They allowed *that* only in reference to something nonhuman (**the drug that** saved a million lives). However, one of Shakespeare's most famous passages begins "Give me that **man / that** is not passion's slave."

- **where at** Omit the redundant *at* in *where at*. Use "**Where** is the police?" instead of "*Where's* the police *at?*"

38 EFFECTIVE BUSINESS COMMUNICATIONS

Use language effectively when taking care of business.

Effective business communications get attention, provide needed information, and get results. Some basic guidelines apply both in the private and the larger public sphere. They are worth keeping in mind when you are taking care of personal business—for instance, letters of application, requests, and complaints. They may prove useful in business transactions on the job—for instance, interoffice memos, evaluations, letters to prospective customers, responses to customer complaints, letters of recommendation, or reports to higher-ups.

BUSINESS COMMUNICATION ESSENTIALS

Basic Guidelines

The following rules of thumb will help you compose effective business communications:

1 ***State your business early in your communication.*** Your reader's first question is going to be: "What is this about?" Are you asking for information? Are you trying to correct a mistake? Are you requesting help or support? Are you trying to trace documents?

2 ***Give essential information.*** Help your readers locate a previous contact, transaction, or request in their files. Summarize or review briefly the previous history or the current situation. Include key dates, document numbers, or order numbers. Provide complete addresses, phone numbers, fax numbers, or e-mail addresses if they might be needed. (Double-check addresses and numbers for accuracy.)

3 ***Spell out what you expect or request.*** What action do you expect your readers to take? What do you ask or expect them to do?

4 ***Highlight separate points.*** If there are several options for your reader to consider, make them stand out clearly, perhaps in separate numbered paragraphs. If several steps or requirements are necessary to reach a desired outcome, mark each off clearly. (Make sure important ifs or buts will not be lost in hurried reading.)

(continued)

Basic Guidelines ***(continued)***

5 ***If you can, stress mutual benefits or convenience.*** What are the advantages for the people on the other side if they grant your request? What should make them feel good about attending to your needs?

6 ***Express personal interest or appreciation.*** Make your readers feel that their interest or work or contribution is valued. To secure your readers' cooperation, you may want to trace problems to misunderstandings or faulty communication before you assign blame.

38a Current Business Formats

Know basic conventions of business correspondence.

Business organizations and government agencies often have guidelines or style sheets describing an approved style. Individuals now often use their word-processing software to design their own attractively laid out letterheads. Here and in the message itself, appearance counts: It will be hard for the recipient to take your business seriously if you yourself don't prepare your message with care.

38a.1 Return Address *Provide complete return information.* Organizations give complete return information in their letterheads, often including department or division of the company, street address or Post Office box, floor or office number, and the like. Both organizations and individuals today often include phone number, fax number, and e-mail address. The date of your message may appear as *February 24, 2000* (with the comma) or *24 February 2000* (no comma).

RETURN ADDRESS AND DATE:

4282 Bryant Street #41
Santa Clara, CA 95050
e-mail: FDrusig@info.com

February 24, 2000

38a.2 **Inside Address and Greeting** *Use conventional greetings and courtesy titles.* When you can, address your letter to the right individual rather than an organization or agency. You may be able to find out who the right person is by calling the company or agency or by consulting a college or organization directory. Use *Mr.* or *Ms.*—but use *Mrs.* if the person addressed used *Mrs.* with her signature in previous correspondence. Use *Dr.* or *Prof.* in the address but spell out *Prof.* in your greeting: *Dear Professor Gutierrez.* (Also *Dear Reverend Watson* or *Dear President Locatelli.*)

Note that much modern business communication uses *no paragraph indent* in the actual message that is the body of the letter. In fact, in a straight **block format**, all elements of the letter, including the return address, are typed flush left. However the traditional indentation for paragraphs is also still widely used.

INSIDE ADDRESS AND GREETING:

4282 Bryant Street #41
Santa Clara, CA 95050
e-mail: FDrusig@info.com

February 24, 2000

Ms. Theresa Molino
Personnel Director
Outreach Inc.
289 Valdez Ave.
Tucson, AZ 85721

Dear Ms. Molino:

Thank you for your letter about your work with job seekers in today's competitive high-tech labor market. We have some additional questions about patterns of "outplacing" of laid-off managers in the current corporate environment. . . .

What if you cannot target a specific individual? The traditional "Dear Sir or Madam" sounds stilted today. Most people today are used to receiving e-mail with a subject heading but often no personal greeting. You may want to use a stripped-down modern style similar to the e-mail format:

INSIDE ADDRESS AND SUBJECT HEADING:

4282 Bryant Street #41
Santa Clara, CA 95050
e-mail: FDrusig@info.com

February 24, 2000

Personnel Director
Outreach Inc.
289 Valdez Ave.
Tucson, AZ 85721

SUBJECT: Patterns of Outplacing and Rehiring in High-Tech Corporations

We have heard about your work with job seekers in today's competitive high-tech labor market. We wonder if you would be willing to help us with a study of patterns of outplacing in the current corporate environment. . . .

38a.3 Conclusion and Notations

Conclude your letters on the right note. Traditionally, business letters close with "Sincerely yours" or "Yours Truly," followed by your handwritten signature above your typed name. When you have established a good relationship, you may want to shift from full names to more friendly first names both in your greeting and in signing your name. Just make sure using first names will not sound pushy or chummy. You may use "Best wishes" or All the best" if you want something more personal than "Sincerely yours."

Most people today do their own keyboarding, but use your initials and the typist's initials if you had a typist: *KM/crm.* If you are forwarding copies to others, list their names after *cc.* If you send files or other enclosures with your letter, list them after *encl.* If you need to add afterthoughts **(postscripts)**, add them after *P.S.*

✓ ***EDITOR'S TIP:*** In the computer age, a stripped-down modern no-nonsense style is beginning to dispense with such amenities as the "Sincerely yours" and the handwritten signature.

CLOSING AND NOTES:

Conducting this study and preparing the report have been rewarding experiences. Your taking time out from a busy schedule to compile the data we requested and to answer our queries has helped us immeasurably to complete our project on schedule. Please note the acknowledgment of your contribution in the preface to the enclosed interim draft of our project report.

Sincerely yours,

Fran Drusig

Fran Drusig
Research Associate

FD:mcr
encl.: Project Report
cc: Dean McIntyre

P.S. Please call me if any part of the enclosed report raises questions or seems incomplete.

38a.4 Businesslike Style *Avoid old-fashioned business jargon.* Business people, like lawyers and doctors, have been trying to streamline their use of language, bringing it closer to effective everyday English. Edit for expressions like the following:

OLD-FASHIONED	CURRENT
we are in receipt of	**we have received**
the above-mentioned report	**in the report mentioned earlier**
it has come to my attention that	**I have learned that**
at the present point in time	**now**
at an early date	**soon**
in the event that	**if**
at your earliest possible convenience	**as soon as possible**

38b Applying for Jobs

Write an effective letter of application.

A letter of application is easy to write if an employer badly needs someone with your qualifications and if at most one or two other candidates are in the running. In more competitive situations, your assignment is to make the prospective employer say: "This person has the background, the energy or enthusiasm, and the self-confidence to make a meaningful contribution in the job we are trying to fill." You need to show a convincing interest in the job and the employer; you need to highlight your qualifications without seeming to exaggerate; and you need to project self-confidence without sounding conceited or cocky.

An effective letter brings the dry facts in your résumé to life. Study the following example:

LETTER OF APPLICATION:

Pat Lasvinas
6786 Blauer Drive
Kenwood, OH 44601

2 March 2000

Ms. Christina Malik
Director of Personnel
New Age Accountancy
2239 East Erie Drive
Chicago, IL 60616

Dear Ms. Malik:

Having studied accounting for four years and having practical experience as an intern, I believe I could be the "experienced tactful auditor" you were looking for in your ad in the *Journal of Accountancy* (February issue).

As an accounting major, I especially liked Auditing Theory and Practice. In it, I could see specific application of principles encountered in my human relations and psychology classes. Social scientists' research findings were evident in our auditing discussions of autocratic, custodial, collegial, and supportive leadership styles.

Questions about leadership and motivation seemed to recur throughout the course: What really motivates executives? Why are auditors actually feared at many levels? How can those fears be overcome? How can an ego be salvaged? The professor's most frequent admonition was "Consider the human element." That element was the focus of my term report in auditing, "Auditors Must Consider Egos."

This report gave me an opportunity to apply principles of organization, human relations, and clarity as learned in Business Report Writing. It taught me how such techniques as using positive language and using hypothetical case histories could be used to get ideas across to managers or executives without offense.

Working with managers has been part of my responsibilities as a part-time assistant at Sycos-Honeywell, Inc., for the past four months. Working with auditors, cost accountants, and tax accountants, I came to appreciate seasonal necessities for working long and irregular hours, keeping information confidential, trying to be right the first time, listening carefully, and relating to others' concerns.

References on the enclosed sheet have said they would be glad to comment on my knowledge of accounting and my relationships with others. Whether you want to call or write, I welcome a chance to discuss the "tactful auditor" job with you.

Sincerely yours,

Pat Lasvinas

38c Writing Your Résumé

Write an effective résumé.

Preferably on one single page, give the prospective employer a rundown of your educational background and previous experience. In each of the following categories, put the current or most recent items first. Include the basic facts but go beyond the basic facts.

EDUCATION Highlight especially meaningful courses with brief notes on their emphasis or educational value.

EXTRACURRICULAR ACTIVITIES Include especially any experiences as mentor, as a residence adviser, as a student journalist, or in student government.

WORK EXPERIENCE Include any volunteer work.

INTERESTS Especially include any life experiences that broadened your outlook, developed your ability to work with others, or tested your ability to organize or direct.

REFERENCES Omit from the list teachers or former employers who seem surprised or reluctant when you ask them for support.

Study the following sample:

SAMPLE RÉSUMÉ:

RÉSUMÉ FOR PAT RECARDO
12227 Consuedo Avenue
San Jose, CA 95112
(408)555-0096
e-mail: PRecardo@info.com

EDUCATION:

2000	B.S. in Journalism and Technical Communication, San Jose State University
1998-2000	San Jose State University, San Jose, California journalism major with emphasis on technical writing, graphic design, computer languages, and website design
1996-98	Evergreen Community College, San Jose

WORK EXPERIENCE:

1999-2000	Internship at *Silicon Valley News* responsibility for monitoring articles in national publications
1998	Campaign volunteer for city council election
1997-98	Office assistant, Language Arts Department at Evergreen College handling telephone inquiries and scheduling appointments

PERSONAL EXPERIENCE:

1990-92	U.S. Army dependent attending Department of Defense Dependents schools in Würzburg, Germany

PERSONAL INTERESTS:

Hiking and conservation; membership in Sierra Club

REFERENCES: See attached list

INDEX

Notes to Readers: Boldfaced numbers direct you to the guide numbers in the handbook (see page tops). Guide numbers preceded by **(std)** direct you to Section 21 on standard English. Guide numbers preceded by **(esl)** direct you to Sections 30–31 on English as a second language. The notation **(gl)** directs you to the alphabetized Glossary of Usage (Section 37).

a lot, (gl) 517
Abbreviations, **29f:** 359–360
Absolute constructions, 246
Abstract vs. concrete words, **6f.2:** 172–173
Abstracts (of research papers), 499
Accusative form. *See* Objects
Acronyms. *See* Abbreviations
Active vs. passive voice, **18a:** 262–264
Ad hominem arguments, 125
Addresses (Internet). *See* URLs
Addresses (street)
  abbreviations of, **29f.4:** 360
  in business correspondence, **38a.1–2:** 526–528
  commas with, **24c:** 314
  numerals for, 357
Adjectives
  adverbs vs., 242, 244
  comparative/superlative forms, 192, 288, (gl) 524
  definition of, **7c.1:** 192, 242
  as sentence fragments, **9b.2:** 211
  with linking verbs, **14a.3:** 244
Adverbial conjunctions, 204. *See also* Connective adverbs
Adverbs
  adjectives vs., 242, 244
  connective, 199, **8d:** 204–205
  definition of, **7c.2:** 193, **14a:** 242–244
  informal, 243
  misplaced, **14c.2:** 247
  as sentence fragments, **9b.1:** 210–211
  with other modifiers, **14a.2:** 243
  without *-ly* ending, **14a.1:** 243
aggravate, (gl) 517
Agreement (of subject and verb), **11:** 224–232
  blind, **11a:** 225–226
  borderline singulars/plurals, **11e:** 228–232
  combined subject and, **11b:** 226–227
  definition of, 224
  logical, **11d:** 228
  loose, **11e.6:** 231
  postponed subject and, **11c:** 227
  pronouns and, **12d:** 235
ain't, (gl) 517
AIP style, 514
Aircraft/Ships (capitalizing names of), **27e.3:** 333, **29g5:** 362
allusion/illusion, (gl) 517
alumnus/alumna, (gl) 517
American Institute of Physics (documentation style of). *See* AIP style
American Psychological Association (documentation style of). *See* APA style
among/between, (gl) 519
amount/number, (gl) 518
Ampersands, 360
and beginning a sentence, (gl) 518
and/or, (gl) 518
Antecedents (of pronouns), **12:** 233–237. *See also* Pronouns
Antonyms, **6g.2:** 178
anyways/anywheres/anyplace, (gl) 518
APA style, **36c:** 487–513
  abstracts, 499
  guide to, 487
  manuscript preparation, **36c.3:** 499
  parenthetic documentation, **36c.1:** 487–489

APA style *continued*
References lists, 455, **36c.2:** 489–499. *See also* References lists
running heads, 499
sample research paper, 500–513
Apostrophes (for)
contractions, **29d:** 356–357
possessives, **29c**: 352–355
Appositives
commas with, 309
dangling modifiers and, 245
definition of, 211
as sentence fragments, **9b.3:** 211
standard uses of, (std) **21e:** 288–289
Argument, **4d–e:** 114–129
ad hominem, 125
cultural differences regarding, (esl) **30d:** 371–372
logical fallacies, **4e.3:** 124–126
presenting alternatives, **4d:** 114–120
principles behind, **4e.2:** 122–124
structure of, **4e**: 121–129
styles of, **4e.1:** 121–122
word choice in, 156
yes-but style of, (esl) **30d:** 371–372
Art work/Entertainment (capitalizing titles of), **27e.2:** 332, 347, **29g.4:** 361, 499
Articles
definite vs. indefinite, 376–377, (esl) **31b.1:** 377
ESL topics, (esl) **31b:** 376–380
idiomatic use of, (esl) **31b.4:** 379
missing, (esl) **31b.2:** 377–378
noun markers and, 184
nouns and, (esl) **31b:** 376–380
unneeded, (esl) **31b.3:** 378–379
as, (gl) 518
as/like, (gl) 522
-ation/-otion nouns, **18b.2:** 266
attribute/contribute, (gl) 518
Audience (of writing), **1b:** 9–12. *See also* Instructor feedback; Peer reviews
Auxiliary verbs, 186–187, 224, 239, 381. *See also* Helping verbs; Linking verbs
awful/awfully, (gl) 518

bad/badly, (gl) 519
Bandwagon, 126
be. See also Auxiliary verbs; Helping verbs; Linking verbs
forms of, (std) **21a.1:** 281–282
missing, (std) **21a.5:** 285–286
verbs with, (std) **21a.4:** 284–285
because/because of, **17d.1–2:** 259
being as/being that, (gl) 519
between/among, (gl) 519
Bibliographies (of books), 423, **33d.3:** 424–425
Bibliographies (of papers). *See* References lists; Works Cited lists
Bilingualism/Bidialectalism, 280, 363–364. *See also* English as a second language
Blind agreement, **11a:** 225–226
Block quotations, 80–81, **27a.3:** 327–328, 444, 446, 458
Book reviews, **33d.3:** 424–425
Books, **33d:** 421–425
bibliographies of, 423, **33d.3:** 424–425
call numbers of, 423
catalogs of, **33d.2:** 422–424
documenting, 431, 464–468, 493–497, 498
indexes to, **33d.2:** 422–424
ISBN numbers of, 423
primary vs. secondary sources, **33d.1:** 422
reviews of, **33d.3:** 424–425
Boolean system, 89, 418–419
Booster quotes, 84
Brackets, 82, **27c:** 329–330
Brainstorming, **1d.1:** 14–15
Bridge paragraphs, 56
British vs. American spelling/usage, 344, 379
Bulk nouns, 378
bursted/bust/busted, (gl) 519

Business communication, **35:** 525–533
conclusions/notations of, **38a.3:** 528–529
formats for, **38a:** 526–529
guidelines for, 525–526
inside addresses/greetings of, **38a.2:** 527–528
letters of application, **38b:** 530–531
postscripts of, 528
résumés, **38c:** 532–533
return addresses of, **38a.1:** 526–527
samples of, 527, 528, 529, 530–531
signatures of, 528
subject headings of, 527–528
written style of, **38a.4:** 529
but beginning a sentence, (gl) 518
but what, (gl) 519
but yet/but however, (gl) 519
Buzzwords, **6e:** 170–171

calculate/reckon/expect/guess, (gl) 519
Call numbers, 423
can/may, (gl) 519
cannot help but, (gl) 520
can't hardly/can't scarcely, (gl) 520
Capitalization (of), **29a:** 346–349
course names, 347
days and months, 346
names/personal titles, 346, 347
parties/movements/institutions, 347, **29a.1:** 348
places/regions, 346, **29a.2:** 348
titles of art work/entertainment, 347
titles of publications, 347, **29a.3:** 348
titles of student papers, **29a.4:** 348–349
Card catalogs, **33d.2:** 422–424
Catalogs (of books), **33d.2:** 422–424
Cause and effect, **4c:** 111–113
CBE style, 514
censor/censure, (gl) 520
center around, (gl) 520
Characters (in)
drama, 138
fiction, 132–134
Chat rooms, 93
Chicago Manual of Style (documentation style of), 455–456, 514
Class publications, 48
Classification, **4b:** 106–111
Clauses
definition of, 197
dependent, 201, **23b:** 299–301
independent, 197–198, 204
relative, 205–206, 213–214, **23c:** 302–303
restrictive vs. nonrestrictive, 201
Clichés, 36, **6e:** 170–171
Clincher quotes, 84
Clincher sentences, 51
Clustering, **1d.2:** 16–17
Colons, **26a:** 320–321, 326
Combined objects, 190–191
Combined subjects, 190–191, **11b:** 226–227
Comedy, 139
Comma splices. *See also* Sentences
correcting, **22c:** 296
definition of, **8a:** 197–198, 204
Commas (with)
absolute constructions, 310
addresses, **24c:** 314
appositives, 309
connecting adverbs, **23d:** 304–305
coordinate adjectives, **24d:** 314–315
coordinators, 199, **23a:** 298–299, **25:** 318–319
credit tags, 326
dates, **24c:** 314
dependent clauses, 201
direct quotations, **27a.1:** 326–327
independent clauses, 197–198, 204
infinitives, 310
introductory dependent clauses, **23b:** 299–301

Commas (with) *continued*
introductory modifiers, **24a:** 308–312
measurements, **24c:** 314
nonrestrictive modifiers, **24a:** 308–312
nonrestrictive vs. restrictive clauses, **23b–c:** 299–303, **24:** 308–312, **25:** 318–319
noun clauses, **23e:** 306, 319
open punctuation, 211, 305, 310
page numbers, **24c:** 314
parallel clauses, 296
parenthetic elements, **24f:** 316–317
past/present participles, 310
prepositional phrases, 308, 310
quotation marks, 328
relative clauses, **23c:** 302–303
repeated/contrasted elements, **24e:** 315–316
series, 296, **24b:** 312–313, 319
subordinators, **23b:** 299–301
transitions, **24a3:** 310–311
unnecessary, **25:** 318–319
verbals, 308, 310
Comparative/superlative forms (of adjectives), 192, (std) **21d:** 288, (gl) 524
compare with/compare to, (gl) 520
Comparison and contrast, **4a:** 100–106
parallel order method, 102
point-by-point method, 101–102
transitions used in, 103
Complex sentences. *See* Sentences, patterns of
Compound words, **29c.4:** 354–355
Computers. *See also* Internet
editing using, 43, 334, 335
effects on communication, 93
searching for source materials using, **33a:** 408–412
spelling check using, 334, 335
Conclusions (of papers), **1g.10:** 36
Conclusions/notations (of business letters), **38a.3:** 528–529
Concrete vs. abstract words, **6f.2:** 172–173
Conditional verb forms, 253
Conflict (in drama), 138–139
Conjunctions. *See* Connective adverbs; Coordinators; Subordinators
Conjunctive adverbs. *See* Connective adverbs
Connective adverbs
definition of, **8d:** 204–205
examples of, 199
commas with, **23d:** 304–305
Connectives, 199, **15c:** 249–250
Connotations, **6a.3:** 155–157
Context, 153
Contractions
formality of writing and, 160
forming, 340, **29d:** 356–357
misspellings of, 356
contribute/attribute, (gl) 518
Coordinate adjectives, **24d:** 314–315
Coordinating conjunctions, **8b:** 198–200
Coordination, **8b:** 198–200
Coordinators
commas with, 199, **23a:** 298–299, **25:** 318–319
definition of, **8b:** 198–200
Council of Biology Editors (documentation style of). *See* CBE style
Count nouns, 184
couple of, (gl) 520
Course names (capitalizing), 347
credible/credulous/creditable, (gl) 520
Credit tags (for sources), 78. *See also* Documentation
commas with, 326
plagiarism and, 402
for quotations, 82–83, 325, 326
Cultural differences (in language use), (esl) **30:** 365–372
argument and, (esl) **30d:** 371–372
direct vs. roundabout approach, (esl) **30c:** 368–371
narration vs. storytelling, (esl) **30b:** 367–368
qualities valued, (esl) **30a:** 366–367

Dangling modifiers, **14b:** 245–246
Dashes, 309, **29b:** 321–322
data is/data are, (gl) 520
Dates, **24c:** 314, 346, 357
Deductive thinking, 123
Definite articles, 376–377, (esl) **31b.1:** 377
Definite pronouns, 185
Dependent clauses, 201
Determiners. *See* Noun markers
Dialects, 280. *See also* English as a second language
Dialogue (in drama), 139
Dictionaries, **6g:** 176–181. *See also* Reference books
different than/different from, (gl) 520
Direct quotations, 80, **27a.1:** 326–327, 435, 444, 445. *See also* Quotations
Discovery frames, **1d.3:** 17–18
disinterested/uninterested, (gl) 521
Dividing words, **29b.3:** 351–352
Documentation, **36:** 454–514
- AIP style, 514
- APA style, **36c:** 487–513. *See also* APA style; References list
- of books, 431, 464–468, 493–497, 498
- CBE style, 514
- *Chicago* style, 455–456, 514
- definition of, 400, 454
- of electronic sources, 430, 467–470, 497–498
- footnotes/endnotes, 455–456, 514
- MLA style, **36b:** 456–486. *See also* MLA style; Works Cited list
- overview of styles, **36a:** 454–456, 514
- parenthetic, 454–456, **36b.1:** 457–459, **36c.1:** 487–489
- of periodicals, 430–431, 462–464, 491–493
- recording details of, 430–431
- References list (APA style), 455, **36c.2:** 489–499. *See also* References list
- Works Cited list (MLA style), 455, **36b.2:** 460–471, 472. *See also* Works Cited list

Double comparatives/superlatives, (std) **21d:** 288
Double negatives, (std) **21c:** 287
Double pronouns, 169, 235, 236
Double subjects/objects, **13a:** 238–239
Doubled final letters (words with), **28b.2:** 341–342
Drama, **5a.3:** 138–140
due to as preposition, (gl) 521

each other/one another, (gl) 521
Edited written English, 159
Editing, **1i:** 43–46. *See also* First drafts; Revising; Rewriting
- checklist for, 44
- for formality, **6b.1:** 160–161
- for redundancy, **6c.2:** 166–167
- sample of, 46–47
- sentences, **17:** 256–261
- symbols used in, 45–46

Editing symbols, 45–46
Electronic sources, **3c:** 88–93. *See also* Internet; Online sources
- documenting, 430, 467–470, 497–498
- evaluating, **3c.2:** 90–91
- examples of, 88–89, 91–92
- nature of, **3c.4:** 93
- locating, **3c.1:** 89–90, **3c.3:** 91–92

Ellipses, 82, **27c:** 329–330
Encyclopedias, 408, **33f:** 426–429. *See also* Reference books
Endnotes/Footnotes, 455–456, 514
English as a second language (ESL), 363–364, (esl) **30:** 365–372, (esl) **31:** 373–396
- articles and nouns, (esl) **31b:** 376–380
- cultural differences, (esl) **30:** 365–372
- dialects, 280
- first language interference, 373
- idiomatic expressions, (esl) **31b.4:** 379, (esl) **31e:** 387–394
- plurals of nouns, (esl) **31a:** 374–376
- sentence structure, (esl) **31f:** 394–396

English as a second language (esl) *continued*
subjects of sentences, (esl) **31f.2–3:** 395
verbs and tenses, (esl) **31c–e.1:** 380–388, **31f.1–2:** 394–395
writing tips, 364
Entertainment/Art work (capitalizing titles of), **27e.2:** 332, 347, **29g.4:** 361, 499
enthused/enthuse, (gl) 521
etc., (gl) 521
Etymologies, 179
Euphemisms, **6b.5:** 164–165
Exact-wording quotes, 83
Examples, **2b.1–3:** 53–55, 275–276
Exclamation marks, **22a:** 294, 328
expect/reckon/calculate/guess, (gl) 519
Exploratory reading, 432–434

False analogies, 125–126
False dilemmas, 125
Feedback (on writing), **1f.1:** 27–29. *See also* Instructor feedback; Peer reviews
fewer/less, (gl) 522
Fiction, **5a.1:** 132–134
Final editing, **1i:** 43–46. *See also* Proofreading; Revising; Rewriting
First drafts
guidelines for writing, 446
of research papers, **35a–b:** 443–447
writing from outlines, **1e.3:** 21–25
First language interference, 373
First person reference, 254–255
flout/flaunt, (gl) 521
flunk, (gl) 521
Focused reading, **3b.2:** 77–78
Follow-up quotes, 83
Footnotes/Endnotes, 455–456, 514
Foreign terms, 331
Formal vs. informal research, 13
Formal outlines, **34d.3:** 440–442
Formality (of writing), **6b:** 158–165
Fragments. *See* Sentence fragments
Fused sentences, 198, **22d:** 297
Future perfect tense, 186
Future tense, 186, 381

Gender-balanced pronouns, **12e.1:** 235. *See also* Sexist language
Generalizations, **1g.4:** 32, 125
Generic pronouns, 235, 236
Genres (in drama), 139
Gerunds. *See* Verbal nouns
Greetings (of business letters), **38a.2:** 527–528
guess/calculate/reckon/expect, (gl) 519

had ought/hadn't ought to, (gl) 521
Hasty generalizations, 125
Helping verbs, 186–187, 224, 239, (esl) **31d:** 384–387. *See also* Auxiliary verbs; Linking verbs
Highlight paragraphs, 56
himself/myself, (gl) 523
Homonyms, **28a.2:** 335–337
hopefully, (gl) 522
Hyperlinks, 409
Hyphens, **29b:** 349–352

Idiomatic expressions
definition of, 387–388
nouns and articles, (esl) **31b.4:** 379
verbs and prepositions, (esl) **31e:** 387–394
ie/cei rule (for spelling), **28b.1:** 341
if-clauses, **9d.1:** 213
if/whether, (gl) 522
illusion/allusion, (gl) 517
Imagery (in poetry), 134
in/into, (gl) 522
in terms of, (gl) 522
Indefinite articles, 376–377, (esl) **31b.1:** 377
Indefinite pronouns
agreement with, **11e2:** 229
antecedents of, 236
definition of, 185
possessive forms of, **29c.3:** 354

Independent clauses, 197–198, 204
Indexes (to)
  books, **33d2:** 422–424
  periodicals, **33c:** 418–421
Indirect objects, 189–190
infer/imply, (gl) 522
Infinitives, 187, 212, 310, (gl) 524
Informal adverbs, 243
Informal outlines, **13.1:** 19
Informal pronouns, **12b:** 234
Initials, **29f.1:** 359
Institutions (capitalizing names of), 347, **29a.1:** 348
Instructor feedback
  marginal glosses, 44–45
  nature of, 27–28
  on research papers, **35c.2:** 448–453
  samples of, 40, 43, 70, 449–453
Internet, **33a:** 408–412. *See also* Electronic sources; Online sources
  cautions regarding materials found on, 411
  conversations via, 93
  hyperlinks, 409
  publishing on, 90, 93
  searching, **3c.1–3:** 89–92, **33a.3:** 410–412
  sources found on, 408, **33a.2:** 409–410
  websites, **33a.1:** 409
Interviews, **3d:** 94–97
Intransitive verbs, 189
Introductions (of papers)
  development of, 21
  in literature critiques, **5b.1:** 142–143
  rewriting, **1g.2:** 30–31
Irony (in poetry), 137–138
irregardless, (gl) 522
Irregular verbs, **10d:** 220, 221, (esl) **31c.2:** 383
is when sentences, **17c:** 258
ISBN numbers, 423
Italics (for), **29g:** 360–362
  emphasis, **27d:** 330–331, **29g.1–2:** 360–361
  names of ships/aircraft, **27e.3:** 333, **29g.5:** 362
  titles of art/entertainment, **27e.2:** 332, **29g.4:** 361
  titles of publications, **27e.1:** 332, **29g.3:** 361
It's/Its, **28a.5:** 340, 357

Jargon, **6b.4:** 162–163, 529
Journal (writing), 7, 67–68
Journals (professional), 414–416. *See also* Magazines; Periodicals
  documenting, 463–464, 492, 498
  refereed, 400

Key words, 89–90

Legal terms, 331
less/fewer, (gl) 522
Letters (business), **35:** 525–533
  application, **38b:** 530–531
  conclusions/notations of, **38a.3:** 528–529
  formats for, **38a:** 526–529
  guidelines for, 525–526
  inside addresses/greetings of, **38a.2:** 527–528
  postscripts of, 528
  return addresses of, **38a.1:** 526–527
  samples of, 527, 528, 529, 530–531
  signatures of, 528
  subject headings in, 527–528
  written style of, **38a.4:** 529
lie/lay, **10e:** 222
like/as, (gl) 522
Link words, 89–90, 418–419
Linking verbs, 190, 239, 244, 265. *See also* Auxiliary verbs; Helping verbs
literally, (gl) 523
Literature, **5:** 132–150
  drama, **5a.3:** 138–140
  fiction, **5a.1:** 132–134
  poetry, **5a.2:** 134–138
  writing about, **5b:** 142–150
Logical agreement, **11d:** 228

Logical fallacies, **4e.3:** 124–126
Loose agreement, **11e.6:** 231
Lurking, 93

Magazines, 408, 409–410, **33b:** 412–418
documenting, 462–463, 492
general interest, 413–414
online, 408, **33a.2:** 409–410
of opinion, 413
special audience, 414
weekly news, 413
Manuscript preparation, **29:** 346–362
abbreviations, **29f:** 359–360
APA style, **36c.3:** 499
apostrophes, **29c–d:** 352–357
capitalization, **29a:** 346–349
hyphenation, **29b:** 349–352
italics, **29g:** 360–362
MLA style, **36b.3:** 472
numbers, **39e:** 357–360
Marginal glosses, 44–45
may/can, (gl) 519
Measurements (expressions of), 314, 357, **29f.4:** 360
media is/media are, (gl) 523
Metaphors
effective vs. mixed, **6f.3:** 174–175
in poetry, 134–135
Meter and rhythm (in poetry), 136
Mismatched predicates, **17b:** 257–258
Misplaced modifiers, **14c:** 246–247
Mixed metaphors, **6f.3:** 174–175
MLA style, **36b:** 456–486
block quotations in, 458
endnotes/footnotes, 472
guides to, 456
manuscript preparation, **36b.3:** 472
parenthetic documentation, **36b.1:** 457–459, 472
running heads, 472
sample research paper, **36b.4:** 473–486
Works Cited list, 455, **36b.2:** 460–471, 472. *See also* Works Cited list
Modals/Modal auxiliaries, 186
Modern Language Association (documentation style of). *See* MLA style
Modifiers, **7c:** 192–196, **14:** 242–247
adjectives, **7c.1:** 192. *See also* Adjectives
adverbs, **7c.2:** 193, **14a:** 242–244. *See also* Adverbs
commas with, **24a:** 308–312
dangling, **14b:** 245–246
group, **29b.2:** 351
hyphenating, **29b.2:** 351
introductory, **24a:** 308–312
misplaced, **14c:** 246–247
nouns, **7c.4:** 194. *See also* Nouns
prepositional phrases, **7c.3:** 193. *See also* Prepositions/Prepositional phrases
verbals, **7c.5:** 194. *See also* Verbals
Movements (capitalizing names of), 347, **29a.1:** 348
myself/himself, (gl) 523

Names and personal titles, 346, 347
Narrative, (esl) **30b:** 367–368
Newspapers, 408, 409–410, **33b:** 412–418
documenting, 462, 469, 491
local, 412
online, 408, **33a.2:** 409–410
of record, 412–413
Nonprint sources, **33e:** 425–426, 470–471, 498–499
Nonrestrictive clauses, 201, **23b–c:** 399–303, **24:** 308–12, **25:** 318–319
Notes/Note-taking, **1c.2:** 13–14
focused reading and, 77
kinds of, 434–435
organizing, **34c:** 436–437
outlining from, 19. *See also* Outlines/Outlining

- recording system for, **34b:** 434–436
- for research papers, **34b–c:** 434–437
- samples of, 14, 19, 434–435, 436–437
- writing from, **35a:** 443–446, 481

Noun clauses, 199, **8f:** 206–208, **23e:** 306, 319

Noun markers, 184

Nouns, **7a.1:** 184–185
- articles with, (esl) **31b:** 376–380
- bulk, 378
- combined subjects/objects, 190–191
- count, 184
- ESL topics, (esl) **31a–b:** 374–380
- idiomatic, (esl) **31b.4:** 379
- as modifiers, **7c.4:** 194
- plural. *See* Plural nouns
- possessive, **29c:** 352–355, (gl) 524
- singular. *See* Singular nouns
- verbs vs., 187

Nominative case. *See* Subjects

number/amount, (gl) 518

number of, (gl) 523

Numbers, **29e:** 357–359
- with abbreviations, **29f.3:** 359
- for addresses, 357, **29f.4:** 360
- agreement with, **11e.3:** 229
- for dates, 357
- for measurements, 357, **29f.5:** 360
- round, 358
- for pages, 357
- for time, 357

Numerical key (of handbook), 45–46

Objective case. *See* Objects

Objects (direct)
- combined, 190–191
- double, **13a:** 238–239
- of prepositions, **13b:** 239
- pronouns as, **13a–b:** 238–239, **13d:** 240

Odd word pairs (spelling), **28a.4:** 338–339

off of, (gl) 523

Offensive language
- quotation marks with, 331
- racist, **6d.1:** 167
- sexist, **6d.2:** 168–169, **12e:** 235–237

Omitted final letters (words with), **28b.3:** 342

one/one's, (gl) 523

one another/each other, (gl) 521

One-of-a-kind words (spelling), **28a.5:** 340

Online sources, **33a:** 408–412
- cautions regarding, 411
- encyclopedias, 408, 427–428
- newspapers/magazines, 408, **33a.2:** 409–410
- search engines, **33a.3:** 410–412
- websites, 93, **33a.1:** 409

Open punctuation style, 211, 305, 310. *See also* Punctuation

Opinion quotes, 83

Organization (methods of), **4:** 98–131
- argument, **4d–e:** 114–129. *See also* Argument
- cause and effect, **4c:** 111–113
- classification, **4b:** 106–111
- comparison and contrast, **4a:** 100–106
- ESL topics, (esl) **30c–d:** 367–371
- literature critiques, **5b.3:** 143
- notes/note-taking, **34c:** 436–437
- paragraphs, 50–52
- preliminary steps in, **1e:** 18–22
- problem to solution, 438
- process, **4f:** 129–131, 438
- research papers, **34d:** 437–442, 481
- revising for, **1g.5:** 32–33
- streamlining, **1g.5:** 32–33
- then and now, 438
- use of examples, 98

Outlines/Outlining
- formal, **34d.3:** 440–442
- informal, **13.1:** 19
- from notes, 19
- samples of, 19, 22, 439, 440, 441, 442

Outlines/Outlining *continued*
scratch, 19
working, 19, 20, 21–22, **34d.1:** 438–439, 440
writing from, **1e.3:** 21–22

Page numbers, **24c:** 314, 357
Paired connectives, **15c:** 249–250
Pamphlets/Brochures, 467, 496
Paradox (in poetry), 137–138
Paragraphs, **2:** 49–65
bridge, 56
developing, **2b:** 53–57
focusing, **2a:** 50–53
highlight, 56
organization of, 50–52
purposes of, 49
revising, **2d:** 60–65
supporting details in. *See* Supporting details
topic sentences of, 50–53, 369
transitions in. *See* Transitions
Parallel order method (of comparison and contrast), 102
Parallel structure, **15:** 248–251, **18c.1:** 268–269, 276–277, 296
Paraphrases, 80, 444, 445
Parentheses, **26c:** 322–323
Parenthetic documentation, 454–456
APA style, **36c.1:** 387–389
MLA style, **36b.1:** 457–459, 472
Partial quotations, 80, 326, 445
Participles, 188, 212
Parties (capitalizing names of), 347, **29a.1:** 348
Parts of speech, 184. *See also specific parts of speech*
Passive vs. active voice, **18a:** 262–264
Passive verbs, 219, 220, (esl) **31d.2:** 386
Past participles, 188, 310
Past perfect tense, 186, 381
Past tense
definition of, 186, 381
ESL topics, (esl) **31c.2:** 383
nonstandard, (std) **21a.3:** 284
recent vs. distant past, **16a.2:** 253
regular vs. irregular verbs, **10b:** 218, (esl) **31c.2:** 383
shifting from, **16a.1:** 252–253
Peer reviews, **1f.2:** 28–29
checklist for, 448
questions for, 29
of research papers, **35c.1:** 447–448
samples of, 7–9, 37–38, 43, 69–70
Perfect tenses, 186, **10c:** 219, 220, 381
Periodicals, **33b:** 412–418
abstracts of, 420–421
computer listings of, 419–420
documenting, 430–431, 491–493
indexes to, **33c:** 418–421
journals. *See* Journals (professional)
magazines. *See* Magazines
newspapers. *See* Newspapers
online, 408, **33a.2:** 409–410
summaries of articles, 419
Periods
with abbreviations, **29f:** 359–360
with ellipses, **27c:** 329–330
at ends of quotations, **27b:** 328–329
at ends of sentences, 294, **22b:** 295–296
Personal experiences/connections
in literature critiques, **5b.5:** 144
in reading fiction, 134
as source materials, **3a:** 66–74
Personal pronouns, 185, 238
Personification (in poetry), 135
Places (capitalizing names of), 346, **29a.2:** 348
Plagiarism, **32b:** 401–402
Plot (in fiction), 133
Plural nouns. *See also* Nouns
ESL topics, (esl) **31a:** 374–376
forming by adding *-s,* 184, 224, 374–375
possessives of, **29c.1:** 353
regular vs. irregular, 184, 224, **11e4:** 230, 353, (esl) **31a:** 374–376
symbols, **29c.5:** 355
unmarked, 184

plus, (gl) 523
Poetry, **5a.2:** 134–138
Point by point method (of comparison and contrast), 101–102
Point of view (in fiction), 133
Pointing pronouns, 375
Possessive nouns, **29c:** 352–355, (gl) 524
Possessive pronouns, 184–185, 340, 354
Post hoc fallacies, 112
Postponed subjects, **11c:** 227
Predicates
  definition of, 191
  mismatched, **17b:** 257–258
  strong vs. weak, **18b:** 265–267
predominate, (gl) 524
Prefixes, 180, **29b.1:** 351
Premises (of arguments), 123–124
Prepositions/Prepositional phrases
  commas with, 308, 310
  definition of, **7c.3:** 193
  due to, (gl) 521
  ending sentences, (gl) 524
  ESL topics, (esl) **31e.2:** 388–389
  idiomatic, (esl) **31e.2:** 388–389
  missing, **17e.2:** 260
  objects of, **13b:** 239. *See also* Objects
  as sentence fragments, **9b.1:** 210–211
Present participles, 188, 310
Present tense, 186, **10a:** 217–218, 381
Prewriting techniques, **1d:** 14–18
  brainstorming, **1d.1:** 14–15
  clustering, **1d.2:** 16–17
  discovery frames, **1d.3:** 17–18
Primary vs. secondary sources, **33d.1:** 422
Process (method of organization), **4f:** 129–131
Progressive verbs, 187, 219, (esl) **31d.3:** 386–387
Pronouns, **12:** 233–237, **13:** 238–241
  agreement of, **12d:** 235
  antecedents of, **12:** 233–237
  case, **13:** 238–241
  definite, 185
  definition of, 185, 233
  double, 235, 236
  gender-balanced, **12e.1:** 235
  generic, 235, 236
  indefinite, 185, 236, **11e.2:** 229, **29c.3:** 354
  informal, **12b:** 234
  nonstandard, (std) **21b:** 286–287
  object forms of, **13a–b:** 238–239, **13d:** 240
  personal, 185, 238
  pointing, 375
  possessive, 184–185, 340, 354
  reflexive, 286
  relative, 199, **8e:** 205–206, **11e.5:** 230–231
  repeated, (std) **21b.3:** 287
  restrictive, 206
  -self, (std) **21b.1:** 286–287
  sexist vs. nonsexist, **6d.3:** 169, **12e:** 235–237
  subject forms of, **13a:** 238–239, **13c–d:** 239–240
Proofreading. *See also* Editing; Revising; Rewriting
  sentences, **17a:** 256–257
  for verb errors, (esl) **31c:** 380–384
Publishing (classroom), **1j:** 48
Punctuation. *See also specific punctuation marks*
  end punctuation, 291, **22:** 294–297
  inside punctuation, 292, **24:** 308–317
  linking punctuation, 292, **23:** 298–307
  open style of, 211, 305, 310
  reference chart, 293
Purposes (of writing), **1a:** 5–7

Question marks, **22a:** 294–295, 328
Quotation marks, 80, 82, **27:** 324–333
  apologetic, 331
  with block quotations, **27a.3:** 327–328
  commas with, 328

Quotation marks *continued*
direct/indirect quotations, **27a:** 325–328
distancing, 331
with end punctuation, **27b:** 328–329
with offensive language, 331
plagiarism and, 402
with quotations-within-quotations, **27a.2:** 327
single, **27a.2:** 327
with special terms, **27d:** 330–331
with titles, **27e.1:** 332
Quotations
block, 80–81, **27a.3:** 327–328, 444, 446, 458
booster, 84
clincher, 84
credit tags for, 82–83, 325, 326. *See also* Documentation
direct vs. indirect, 325, 435, 444, 445
exact-wording, 83
follow-up, 83
insertions/omissions in, 82, **27c:** 329–330
interrupted, 326
opinion, 83
partial, 80, 326, 445
of poetry, 328
punctuating, **27:** 324–333. *See also* Quotation marks
in research papers, 444, 445, 479
starter, 83
as supporting details, **2b.5:** 56
timeframe of, **16a.4:** 254
types of, **3b.4:** 80–84
weaving into text, 83–84
within quotations, 82, **27a.2:** 327
Quotations-within-quotations, 82, **27a.2:** 327

Racist language, **6d.1:** 167
Radio/Television programs, 471, 499
Rationalizations, 126
Reading, **3b:** 74–87
basic skills, 75–76
exploratory, 432–434
fiction, 134. *See also* Literature
focused, **3b.2:** 77–78
note-taking from. *See* Notes/Note-taking
writing from, **3b.3:** 78–80
reason is because, (gl) 524
Redundancy, **6c.2:** 166–167
Reference (shifts in), **16b:** 254–255
Reference books
dictionaries, 176–181
encyclopedias, 408, **33f:** 426–429
References lists (APA style), 455, **36c.2:** 489–499
art work, 499
books, 493–497, 498
correspondence, 498
electronic sources, 497–498
encyclopedias, 496
features of, 489
guide to sample entries, 490
journals, 492, 498
magazines, 492
newspapers, 491
nonprint sources, 498–499
pamphlets/brochures, 496
periodicals, 491–493
sample of, 513
speeches/lectures, 499
television/radio programs, 499
unpublished material, 496
Referents (of pronouns). *See* Antecedents
Reflexive pronouns, 286
Regions (capitalizing names of), 346, **29a.2:** 348
Relative clauses, 205–206, 213–214, **23c:** 302–303
Relative pronouns, 199, **8e:** 205–206, **11e.5:** 230–231
Repetition, **18c:** 268–269. *See also* Parallel structure
Research logs, 402–403
samples of, 411–412, 421, 425, 426
Research papers, **32:** 399–407, **33:** 408– 431, **34:** 432–442, **35:** 443–453
definition of, **31a:** 399–401
documenting. *See* Documentation

exploratory reading for, **34a:** 432–434, 475
first drafts of, **35a–c:** 443–453
instructor feedback on, **35c.2:** 448–453
length of, **32c.1–2:** 404–406
note-taking for, **34b–c:** 434–437. *See also* Notes/Note-taking
organizing, **34d:** 437–442, 481
peer reviews of, **35c.1:** 447–448
plagiarism, **32b:** 401–402
quotations in, 444, 445, 479
revising, **35c:** 447–453
samples of, 473–486, 500–513
source materials for. *See* Source materials
topic selections for, **32c:** 403–407
trial theses for, **34d.2:** 439–440
working outlines for, **34d.1:** 438–439, 440
writing, **35a–b:** 443–447
Restrictive clauses, 201, **23b–c:** 299–303, **24:** 308–312, **25:** 318–319
Restrictive pronouns, 206
Résumés, 4–5, **38c:** 532–533. *See also* Business communication
Return addresses (of business letters), **38a.1:** 526–527
Revising, **1f:** 26–29. *See also* Editing; Rewriting
common tasks in, 26
feedback used in, **1f.1–2:** 27–29
literature critiques, 145
paragraphs, **2d:** 60–65
research paper, **35c:** 447–453
Rewriting, **1g:** 30–36. *See also* Editing; Revising
conclusions, **1g.10:** 36
for generalizations, **1g.4:** 32
introductions, **1g.2:** 30–31
for organization, **1g.5:** 32–33
samples of, 39–40, 41–43
for style, **1g.9:** 36
for supporting details, **1g.6:** 33
thesis statements, **1g.3:** 31–32
titles, **1g.1:** 30
for transitions, **1g.7:** 34–35
for word choice, **1g.8:** 35
Rhetoric, 275
Root words, **6g.5:** 180, 338
Rhyme and pattern (in poetry), 137
Running commentary (as feedback), 27

Scapegoating, 112, 125
Scientific terms, 331
Scratch outlines, 19
Search engines, **33a.3:** 410–412
Second person reference, 254–255
-self pronouns, (std) **21b.1:** 286–287
Semicolons (with)
closely related sentences, **22c:** 296, **22d:** 297
connecting adverbs, 204, **23d:** 304–305
coordinators, 299
independent clauses, 197–198
quotations, 328
series, 296
Sentence fragments, **9:** 209–216. *See also* Sentences
acceptable, **9f:** 214
correcting, 294, **22b:** 295–296
diagnosing, **9a:** 209–210
definition of, 194
modifiers as, **9b:** 210–211
subordination and, 201, **9d:** 213
verbals as, **9c:** 212
who/which clauses and, **9e:** 213–214
Sentences, **7:** 182–196, **8:** 197–208
beginning with *and/but,* (gl) 518
clincher, 51
comma splices. *See* Comma splices
coordinating, **8b:** 198–200
editing, **17:** 256–261
ESL topics, (esl) **31f:** 394–396
emphatic vs. unemphatic, **19b:** 272–273, 278
end punctuation for, **22:** 294–297
fragments. *See* Sentence fragments
fused, 198, **22d:** 297
modifiers used in, **7c:** 192–196. *See also specific parts of speech*
parallel structure in, **15:** 248–251, **18c.1:** 268–269, 276–277

Sentences *continued*
parts of, **7a:** 183–188. *See also specific parts of speech*
patterns of, **7b:** 189–191
proofreading, **17a:** 256–257
punctuating, 197–198, 294, **22b:** 295–296
rhetoric of, **20:** 275–279
rhythms of, **19c:** 273–274
short vs. long, **19a:** 270–272
styles of, **19:** 270–274
subordinating, **8c:** 200–203
types of, **20:** 275–279
Series
parallelism in, **15b:** 249
punctuating, 296, **24b:** 312–313, 319
Setting (in fiction), 132
Sexist language, **6d.2:** 168–169, **12e:** 235–237
Shifts
to passive voice, **18a.3:** 263
in reference, **16b:** 254–255
in tense, **16a:** 252–254
Ships/Aircraft (capitalizing names of), **27e.3:** 333, **29g5:** 362
Short stories. *See* Fiction
Sic, 329
Silent letters (and spelling), **28a.3:** 337
Similes (in poetry), 135
Simple sentences. *See* Sentences, patterns of
Singular nouns, 184, 224, 352–353. *See also* Nouns; Plural nouns
Sit/Set, **10e:** 222
Situation (in drama), 138–139
Slang, **6b.2:** 161, 331
Slanting (in reasoning), 126
Slashes, **26d:** 323
Smokescreens, 126
Soliduses, **26d:** 323
Soundalike words (spelling), **28a.2:** 335–337
Source materials, **3:** 66–97, **33:** 408–431, **34:** 432–442
amount of information needed, 432
books, **33d:** 421–425
computer search for, **33a:** 408–412
correlating information from, 481
credit tags for, 78, 82–83, 325, 326, 401. *See also* Documentation
documenting. *See* Documentation
electronic, **3c:** 88–93. *See also* Internet; Online sources
encyclopedias, 408, **33f:** 426–429
exploratory reading for, **34a:** 432–434
indexes to books, **33d.2:** 422–424
indexes to periodicals, **33c:** 418–421
Internet, 408, **33a.2:** 409–410. *See also* Electronic sources; Online sources
interviews, **3d:** 94–97
journals (professional). *See* Journals (professional)
magazines. *See* Magazines
newspapers. *See* Newspapers
nonprint, **33e:** 425–426
note-taking from. *See* Notes/Note-taking
online, **33a:** 408–412. *See also* Electronic sources; Internet
overreliance on, 446
periodicals. *See* Periodicals
personal experiences, **3a:** 66–74
quotations from. *See* Quotations
range of, **1c.1:** 12–13
reading. *See* Reading
recording, **33g:** 430–431. *See also* Documentation
reference books, 176–181, 408, **33f:** 426–429
use in writing, **3b.3:** 78–80
writing process and, **1c:** 12–14
Speeches/Lectures, 471, 499
Spellcheck (computer), 334, 335
Spelling, **28:** 334–345
alternatives in, **28c:** 343–344
British vs. American, 344, 379
common errors in, **28a:** 334–340, 356

  computer check of, 334, 335
  contractions, 356
  doubled final letters, **28b.2:** 341–342
  homonyms, **28a.2:** 335–337
  ie/cei rule, **28b.1:** 341
  memory aids for, **28a.1:** 334
  odd word pairs, **28a.4:** 338–339
  omitted final letters, **28b.3:** 342
  one-of-a-kind words, **28a.5:** 340
  root words and, 338
  rules for, **28b:** 341–343
  silent letters, **28a.3:** 337
  soundalike words, **28a.2:** 335–337
  y/ie rule, **28b.4:** 343
Split infinitives, (gl) 524
Square brackets, 82, **27c:** 329–330
Standard English, (std) **21:** 280–290
  definition of, 280
  nonstandard verbs, (std) **21a:** 280–286
Starter quotes, 83
Statistics, **2b.4:** 55, 435
Style (of writing)
  in business, **38a.4:** 529
  in drama, 140
  rewriting for, **1g.9:** 36
Subject headings (of business letters), 527–528
Subject-verb agreement. *See* Agreement
Subjective case. *See* Subjects
Subjectless verbs, (esl) **31f.2:** 395
Subjects (of sentences)
  agreement with verbs. *See* Agreement
  combined, 190–191, **11b:** 226–227
  definition of, 183
  double, **13a:** 238–239
  ESL topics, (esl) **31f.2–3:** 395
  postponed, **11c:** 227
  pronouns as, **13a:** 238–239, **13c–d:** 239–240
Subjunctive case, 222
Subordinating conjunctions, 199
Subordination, **8c:** 200–203, **9d:** 213
Subordinators, 199, **23b:** 299–301
Suffixes, 180
Summary (note-taking), 434–435
Superlative/comparative forms (of adjectives), 192, (std) **21d:** 288, (gl) 524
Supporting details, **2b:** 53–57
  in literature critiques, **5b.4:** 144
  paragraph development and, 50–53
  quotations as, **2b.5:** 56
  rewriting for, **1g.6:** 33
  types of, 53–57
Syllogisms, 123–124
Symbolism (in)
  fiction, 133
  poetry, 134–136
Symbols (plurals of), **29c.5:** 355
Synonyms, **6a.2:** 154–155, **6g.2:** 178

Technical terms, 330
Television/Radio programs, 471, 499
Tenses (of verbs), 217, 381
  definitions of, 186, 217
  ESL topics, (esl) **31c:** 380–384
  future, 186, 381
  future perfect, 186
  past, 186, **10b:** 218, **16a.1–2:** 252–253, (std) **21a.3:** 284, 381, (esl) **31c.2:** 383
  past perfect, 186, 381
  perfect, 186, **10c:** 219, 220, 381
  present, 186, **10a:** 217–218, 381
  progressive, 187
  shifts in, **16a:** 252–254
that/who, (gl) 524
Themes (in fiction), 133
Thesis statements
  development of, **1e.1:** 20–21
  in literature critiques, **5b.2:** 143
  of research papers, **34d.2:** 439–440
  rewriting, **1g.3:** 31–32
  trial, 20, **34d.2:** 439–440
Third person reference, 254–255
Third person singular (forms of verbs), **10a:** 217–218, (std) **21a.2:** 282–283
  ESL topics, (esl) **31c.1:** 382–383

Thought links. *See* Transitions
Time (expressions of)
- abbreviations for, **29c.3:** 359
- apostrophes with, **29c.2:** 354
- numerals for, 357

Titles
- of art work/entertainment, 347
- capitalizing, 347, **29a.3–4:** 349
- personal/professional, **29f.2:** 359
- of publications, **29a.4:** 348–349
- of student papers, 21, **1g.1:** 30, **29a.4:** 348–349

Topic sentences, 50–53, 369
Topics (for research papers), **32c:** 403–407
Tragedy, 139
Transitions, **2c:** 57–60
- commas with, **24a.3:** 310–311
- examples of, 35, 58
- rewriting for, **1g.7:** 34–35
- sentence fragments and, **9b.4:** 211
- use in comparison and contrast, 103

Transitive verbs, 189
Trial thesis statements, 20, **34d.2:** 439–440. *See also* Thesis statements

Underlining
- to highlight words, **27d:** 330–331
- names of ships/aircraft, **27e.3:** 333
- titles of publications, **27e.1:** 332
- titles of art work/entertainment, **27e.2:** 332

uninterested/disinterested, (gl) 521
Unrepresentative samples, 125
URLs (uniform resource locators), 410
- in References lists, 497
- in Works Cited lists, 468–469

Usage labels (of words), **6g.3:** 178

Value (expressions of), **29c.2:** 354
Verbal nouns, 187, 190, **7c.5:** 194
Verbals
- commas with, 308, 310
- dangling modifiers and, 245
- ESL topics, (esl) **31e.2:** 388–389
- idiomatic, (esl) **31e.2:** 388–389
- possessive nouns with, (gl) 524
- as sentence fragments, **9c:** 212

Verbs, **7a.2:** 185–188
- active vs. passive, 219, 220, **18a:** 262–264, (esl) **31d.2:** 386
- agreement with nouns. *See* Agreement
- auxiliary, 186–187, 224, 239, 381. *See also* Helping verbs; Linking verbs
- conditional, 253
- *-d/-ed* ending for, **10b–c:** 218–219, (esl) **31d.2:** 386
- definition of, 183, 380
- ESL topics, (esl) **31c–e.1:** 380–388, (esl) **31f.1–2:** 394–395
- with *have/be,* **10c:** 219, (std) **21a.4:** 284–285
- helping, 186–187, 381, (esl) **31d:** 384–387. *See also* Auxiliary verbs; Linking verbs
- idiomatic, (esl) **31e1:** 387–388
- incomplete, **17e.1:** 260
- irregular, **10d:** 220, 221, (esl) **31c.2:** 383
- linking, 190. *See also* Auxiliary verbs; Helping verbs
- nonstandard, (std) **21a:** 280–286
- nouns vs., 187–188
- plain/unmarked, **10a:** 217–218
- progressive, 187, 219, (esl) **31d.3:** 386–387
- proofreading for, (esl) **31c:** 380–384
- regular, **10b:** 218
- *-s* ending for, **10a:** 217–218, 224, (std) **21a.2:** 282–283
- subjectless, (esl) **31f.2:** 395
- tenses of, 186, 187, 217, **10:** 217–223. *See also specific tenses*
- transitive vs. intransitive, 189

was when sentences, **17c:** 258
Websites, 93, **33a.1:** 409. *See also* Internet
when-clauses, **9d.1:** 213
where at, (gl) 524
whereas, **9d.2:** 213
whether/if, (gl) 522
which-clauses, **9e:** 213–214, **11e.5:** 230–231
who-clauses, **9e:** 213–214, **11e.5:** 230–231
who/that, (gl) 524
who/whom, 240–241
Word choice, **6:** 153–181
  clichés/buzzwords, **6e:** 170–171
  common errors in, (gl) **37:** 517–524
  connotations of, **6a.3:** 155–157
  dictionary use in, **6g:** 176–181
  effective, **6a:** 153–158, **6f:** 172–175
  euphemisms, **6b.5:** 164–165
  formality of, **6b:** 158–165
  highlighting, **27d:** 330–331
  jargon, **6b.4:** 162–163, 529
  responsible, **1g.8:** 35, **6d:** 167–170
  rewriting for, **1g.8:** 35
  slang, **6b.2:** 161, 331
Word division, **29b.3:** 351–352
Word histories, **6g.4:** 178–179
Wordiness, **6c:** 165–167, **18b.3:** 266–267
Working bibliographies, **33g:** 430–431
Working hypotheses, 439
Working outlines, 19, 20, 21–22, **34d.1:** 438–439, 440. *See also* Outlines/Outlining
Works Cited lists (MLA style), 455, **36b.2:** 460–471, 472
  books, 464–468
  correspondence, 467, 470
  electronic sources, 468–470
  encyclopedias, 467, 470
  features of, 460
  guide to sample entries, 461
  interviews, 470–471
  journals, 463–464
  magazines, 462–463
  newspapers, 462, 469
  nonprint sources, 470–471
  pamphlets/brochures, 467
  periodicals, 462–464
  sample of, 486
  speeches/lectures, 471
  television/radio programs, 471
Writing process, **1:** 3–48
  audience and, **1b:** 9–10
  checklist for, 3–4
  computer's effect on, 93
  editing, **1i:** 43–46. *See also* Editing
  first drafts, **1e.3:** 21–25. *See also* First drafts
  nature of, 3
  organizing information, **1e:** 18–22. *See also* Organization
  prewriting techniques, **1d:** 14–18
  publishing, **1j:** 48
  purpose and, **1a:** 5–7
  research papers. *See* Research papers
  revising, **1f:** 26–29. *See also* Revising
  rewriting, **1g:** 30–36. *See also* Rewriting
  sample of, **1h:** 36–43
  source materials and, **1c:** 12–14. *See also* Source materials
  thesis statement development, **1e.1:** 20–21. *See also* Thesis statements

y/ie rule (for spelling), **28b.4:** 343
yes-but style of argument, (esl) **30d:** 371–372

Text Credits

GUIDELINES AT A GLANCE

	SEE PAGE
WRITING ESSENTIALS: Author Standards	xxxviii
WRITING ESSENTIALS: A Checklist for Student Writers	3–4
WRITING ESSENTIALS: Common Revision Tasks	26
WRITING ESSENTIALS: Questions for Peer Review	29
WRITING ESSENTIALS: Transitions: The Missing Link	35
WRITING ESSENTIALS: An Editor's Checklist	44
PARAGRAPH ESSENTIALS: Paragraphs and the Reader	49
PARAGRAPH ESSENTIALS: Using Thought Links	58
READING GUIDELINES: Basic Reading Skills	75–76
QUOTE/UNQUOTE: Weaving Quotations into Your Text	83–84
INTERNET GUIDELINES: Evaluating Electronic Sources	91
GUIDELINES FOR WRITING AND REVISION: Tracing a Comparison	102–103
GUIDELINES FOR WRITING AND REVISION: Setting Up Categories	108
GUIDELINES FOR WRITING AND REVISION: Tracing Cause and Effect	112
GUIDELINES FOR WRITING AND REVISION: Weighing Alternatives	117
THINKING STRAIGHT: A Checklist of Logical Fallacies	125–126
GUIDE TO REVISION: Revising a Critical Paper	145
USING YOUR DICTIONARY: The Range of Meanings	177
PLURALS OF NOUNS: How Nouns Show Number	184
TENSES OF VERBS: How Verbs Show Time	186
SENTENCE ESSENTIALS: Kinds of Connectives	199
ENGLISH ESSENTIALS: A Checklist of Irregular Verbs	221
PUNCTUATION ESSENTIALS: Comma/No Comma with Subordinator	301
PUNCTUATION ESSENTIALS: Logical Links and the Semicolon	305
PUNCTUATION ESSENTIALS: Removing Unnecessary Commas	319
PUNCTUATION ESSENTIALS: Using the Colon	321
PUNCTUATION ESSENTIALS: Punctuating Quotations	324
SPELLING ESSENTIALS: Distinguishing Homonyms (Soundalikes)	335–336
SPELLING ESSENTIALS: Using Capitals	346–347
SPELLING ESSENTIALS: Where to Use Hyphens	350
EDITOR'S GUIDELINES: Using Numbers	357
TIPS FOR BILINGUAL WRITERS: Working on Your English	364
PRIORITIES FOR BILINGUAL WRITERS: How Verbs Show Time	381
EXTENDING THE RANGE: Generating English Verbs	384–385
TIPS FOR BILINGUAL WRITERS: Using Idiomatic Prepositions	389
RESEARCH ESSENTIALS: Insurance against Plagiarism	402
GOING TO THE SOURCES: Scholarly and Research Journals	416
PEER REVIEW: Research Paper Review Checklist	448
DOCUMENTATION ESSENTIALS: Works Cited—MLA Style	460
DOCUMENTATION ESSENTIALS: References—APA Style	489
BUSINESS COMMUNICATION ESSENTIALS: Basic Guidelines	525–526